Genealogies of New Testament Rhetorical Criticism

Genealogies of New Testament Rhetorical Criticism

Troy W. Martin, editor

Fortress Press
Minneapolis

GENEALOGIES OF NEW TESTAMENT RHETORICAL CRITICISM

Cover design: Alisha Lofgren

Library of Congress Cataloging-in-Publication Data is available

ISBN: 978-0-8006-9974-1

The paper used in this publication meets the minimum requirements of American National Standard for Information Sciences — Permanence of Paper for Printed Library Materials, ANSI Z329.48-1984.

Manufactured in the U.S.A.

This book was produced using PressBooks.com, and PDF rendering was done by PrinceXML.

Dedicated to

Hans Dieter Betz

Contents

Preface   ix

Introduction   1
Lillian I. Larsen

1. Hans Dieter Betz: Ur-ancestor of New   *13*
Testament Rhetorical Criticism
Troy W. Martin

2. Response to Troy W. Martin and Additional   *45*
Reflections
Hans Dieter Betz

3. Genealogies of Rhetorical Criticism: *51*
The Kennedy Family
C. Clifton Black

4. Response to C. Clifton Black and Further Insights   *79*
Duane F. Watson

5. The Contribution of Wilhelm Wuellner to New   *93*
Testament Rhetorical Criticism
James D. Hester and J. David Hester

6. Response to James D. Hester and J. David Hester: *127*
A Personal Reflection
Thomas H. Olbricht

7. Elisabeth Schüssler Fiorenza and the Rhetoric and   *133*
    Ethic of Inquiry
    John R. Lanci

8. Response to John R. Lanci: Transforming the   *165*
    Discipline—The Rhetoricity/Rhetoricality of
    New* Testament Studies
    Elisabeth Schüssler Fiorenza

9. The Pesky Threads of Robbins's Rhetorical   *201*
    Tapestry: Vernon K. Robbins's Genealogy of
    Rhetorical Criticism
    L. Gregory Bloomquist

10. Response to L. Gregory Bloomquist: From the   *225*
    Social Sciences to Rhetography
    Vernon K. Robbins

11. Of Mappings and Men (and Women): Reflections   *245*
    on Rhetorical Genealogies
    Todd Penner and Davina C. Lopez

    Bibliography   *271*

    Index   *323*

Preface

My purpose in this volume is to provide insights into the development of New Testament rhetorical criticism from those who actually participated in its development and those who were eyewitnesses to the origins of this method. The idea for this volume originated in 2010 with my being invited to join the Steering Committee of the Society of Biblical Literature Rhetoric and the New Testament Group. At our annual committee meeting on November 20, 2010, I proposed that we devote one of our sessions at the 2011 Society of Biblical Literature Meeting to a reflection on those scholars who shaped and developed the method of rhetorical criticism. I proposed that we name this session "Genealogies of New Testament Rhetorical Criticism" and assess the contributions of those whom we might designate as the early ancestors of this method. The committee was very enthusiastic about pursuing this idea.

After considering those scholars most often cited by subsequent rhetorical critics and identified as somehow foundational to this method, the committee decided to focus on Hans Dieter Betz, George A. Kennedy, Wilhelm Wuellner, Elisabeth Schüssler Fiorenza, and Vernon K. Robbins. We decided to structure this session around presentations on each of these rhetorical forefathers and foremother with a response from the respective ancestor. As a student of Betz, I volunteered to evaluate his contributions. After reflecting on students, colleagues, or close associates of the other ancestors, the committee invited C. Clifton Black to discuss Kennedy's contributions, James D. Hester to describe Wuellner's, John R. Lanci to assess Schüssler Fiorenza's, and L. Gregory Bloomquist to address Robbins'. The committee also invited Betz, Kennedy, Schüssler Fiorenza, and Robbins to respond to these presentations. Everyone except Kennedy enthusiatically accepted these invitations. Since Kennedy was unable to attend the session, the committee invited Duane F. Watson, one of Kennedy's former students, as a respondent in Kennedy's place. Since Wuellner had died, Thomas H. Olbricht, a close associate of Wuellner, was asked to stand in for him. Both Watson and Olbricht eagerly accepted, and our session was set after the committee invited Lillian I. Larsen to chair and Todd Penner to present some concluding thoughts. Both Larsen and Penner were members of the committee.

This session took place on Saturday, November 19, 2011, at the Annual Meeting of the Society of Biblical Literature in San Francisco, CA. It was well attended and received. Following this session, several commented to me that these presentations deserved to be published. I contacted the participants in the session, and all agreed to revise their presentations for publication. The five essays and the five responses in the present volume represent the essence of the presentations at this session but are greatly expanded and revised. All are written by the original participant although James D. Hester invited J. David Hester, his son, to join him in the preparation of his essay for publication, and Penner invited Davina C. Lopez to co-author the conclusion with him. As chair of the session, Larsen wrote an introduction to the essays to complete the present volume.

I would like to express my gratitude to Sheryl Martin for preparing the Index and to Fortress Press for accepting this manuscript for publication in the new Fortress Academic imprint. I must also thank Neil Elliott for his patience and expert assistance in bringing this volume to press. Its publication will allow subsequent generations of scholars to appreciate and benefit from the contributions of the five rhetorical ancestors discussed and celebrated here.

Troy W. Martin

Introduction

Lillian I. Larsen

In large scale, this volume maps a historical trajectory that spans past and contemporary generations. On a more intimate level, it presents sound bites of ongoing dialogue among five seminal scholars, and their progeny. The former are figures who forged paths where none existed; the latter are those who have walked these paths and refined their contours. Structured as a series of discrete exchanges, this volume's essays represent discussions that took place in the fall of 2011 at the San Francisco meeting of the Society of Biblical Literature.

At this meeting, a session devoted to the "Genealogies of New Testament Rhetorical Criticism" traced the stages of a comprehensive shift in the focus of twentieth-century biblical scholarship. The five seminal figures whose works are explored in this volume largely precipitated this shift and produced subsequent generations of scholars who continue to use and refine the methods of rhetorical criticism.

Antiphonally arranged, the discussions that structured the San Francisco exchanges are collected here in essay form. They are framed as five units consisting of a presentation of the contributions of one seminal figure, paired with a response by this figure or by a close associate. Each unit affords readers the opportunity and privilege to recognize and reflect on the contributions of these illustrious ancestors of New Testament rhetorical criticism. Each underscores the degree to which contemporary scholarship remains both grounded in and indelibly shaped by their influence.

Discourse commences with Troy W. Martin's eloquent encomium, designating Hans Dieter Betz the "Ur-ancestor" of New Testament rhetorical criticism. In his response, Betz balances Martin's structured *argumentio* with anecdotal recollection of emergent understandings. In successive exchanges, C. Clifton Black and Duane F. Watson explore the degree to which the foundational work of George A. Kennedy marks a transitional juncture in studies of both New Testament and classical rhetoric. James D. Hester and his son J. David Hester with a response by Thomas H. Olbricht examine Wilhelm Wuellner's commitment to elucidating the "something more" of rhetorical expression. Elisabeth Schüssler Fiorenza's nuanced introduction of the ethical dimensions of rhetorical criticism is the subject of John R. Lanci's extended accolade. Schüssler Fiorenza, in turn, offers a summative refraction of the social and scholarly confluences that have, at once, "enabled" and "shaped" her groundbreaking analyses. In a final exchange, L. Gregory Bloomquist traces the sociorhetorical emphases emblematic of Vernon K. Robbins's interpretive approach. Robbins then re-caps, refines, and extends its contemporary implications. Finally, Todd Penner and Davina C. Lopez reflect on these essays and the responses setting out a distinct agenda for the criticism of New Testament Rhetorical Criticism itself.

Hans Dieter Betz

In this volume's initial exchange, Troy W. Martin considers the rhetorical legacy of Hans Dieter Betz in an *encomiastic* argument for Betz' singular stature in the field. Advancing the *propositio* that Betz belongs at the very beginning of any genealogical list of New Testament rhetorical criticism, Martin claims for Betz the status of "Ur-ancestor." Framing his "case" in direct address of a hypothetical "audience," he adopts (and adapts) the conventions of *ratio*, an extensive *argumentio*—complete with three proofs—and a concluding *peroratio* to detail the seminal contributions Betz has advanced. As Martin affirms Betz's distinguished status as "progenitor," he just as effectively traces a broader, disciplinary history. Martin's stylized prose functions simultaneously to contextualize Betz's approach and to introduce the New Testament rhetorical critical methods articulated in the volume's successive "generations."

Hans Dieter Betz' succinct response offsets Martin's stylistic flourishes with personal anecdote and reflection. Likening his "discovery" of rhetorical analysis to "the unknown ancestor who 'invented' the wheel," Betz observes that "certainly the wheel was there as a possibility, but the 'inventor' discovered its usefulness for transportation." He names the lack of precision characterizing prevailing attempts to structure the content of New Testament documents as a catalyst for his own rhetorical investigations. The degree to which existing approaches appeared to be "mere guesswork," re-formulated and packaged as "theology," inspired his interpretive shift aimed at discovering "what the text itself had to say." Only gradually did it become apparent, Betz observes, that rhetorical criticism afforded "a new way to understand texts and their 'hermeneutics.'" While the potential impact was not immediately apparent, Betz notes that interpretive methodologies shifted as the text itself became the starting point. Countering the "application of external labels or the imposition of predetermined conceptual grids," Betz suggests that the "validity" of emergent interpretive approaches such as Rhetorical Criticism must instead be assessed by whether these approaches afford "better understanding of texts [and so] lead . . . to a better understanding of their significance."

George A. Kennedy

In a second exchange, C. Clifton Black and Duane F. Watson engage the foundational work of George A. Kennedy. Black introduces the contributions of Kennedy as, at once, a complement and counterpoint to Betz. Black's treatment simultaneously invites wider consideration of "the Kennedy Family's" significance in shaping the field. He observes that as the first non–New Testament specialist to apply the tools of rhetorical criticism to the New Testament, Kennedy synthesized and systematized the "implications of classical rhetoric for New Testament exegesis as a whole." Black notes that Kennedy provided an enduring bridge between classical scholarship and New Testament studies and that, even today, Kennedy's "six steps of analysis" remain standard to the field.

Over decades of development, Kennedy's approach has been "adopted, adapted, and extended," and the various threads of New Testament and classical rhetorical criticism have become so intertwined that disentangling them is difficult. As a result, his scholarship marked a transition that has left an indelible print on both classical rhetoric and New Testament studies. Black remarks that "Betz was the first to bring [the] dish [of New Testament rhetorical criticism] to the table, Kennedy add[ed] his own seasonings, and the kitchen has been bustling ever since."

Since Kennedy was able neither to attend the Society of Biblical Literature meeting in San Francisco nor to participate in this session honoring him, Duane F. Watson, his former student, responds to Black's assessment of Kennedy's work. Trading on Black's metaphors, Watson names Kennedy's seminal volume, *New Testament Interpretation through Rhetorical Criticism*, "a veritable feast of discovery." He likewise follows Black in offering a general survey that outlines the foundational significance of Kennedy's work. Watson assigns particular significance to the ways in which Kennedy's general consideration of New Testament literary genres introduced rhetorical criticism to new practitioners without training in Greco-Roman rhetoric. Simultaneously, he balances the breadth of Black's synthesis with closer analysis of Kennedy's impact on the various genres of source material included in the New Testament canon. Through exploring the ways in which Kennedy's foundational assessments continue to be refined, Watson deploys Kennedy's conversation partners—whether critical or complementary—to holistically (and usefully) situate Kennedy's work along a broader, more extensive scholarly trajectory.

Wilhelm Wuellner

This volume's third exchange addresses the scholarly legacy of Wilhelm Wuellner. As introduced by James D. Hester and J. David Hester, the degree to which Wuellner wanted to demonstrate the "something more" of the rhetorical enterprise, emerges as a point of particular emphasis. Tracing the formulation of a critical theory characterized by "explorations," "cul-de-sacs," and repeated "revision," Hester and Hester traverse a discursive arc that is, at once, chronological and topical. Their initial focus on "defining Wuellner's theories of rhetoric" and identifying "features of Wuellnerian rhetorical critical analysis" lead them to explore Wuellner's understanding of the "power of rhetoric as the power of the sublime."

These considerations conclude with the query "Where Could Wuellnerian Criticism Take Us?" Exploring this question, Hester and Hester call attention to the ways that Wuellner's work marked a fundamental change in the theoretical and philosophical foundations of rhetorical theory. This Wuellnerian shift introduced the dimensions of rhetoric not only "as utterance, arrangement and style, and elements of argumentation" but also as a method of communication that "intends not only to engage an audience but to persuade it to do something."

Wilhelm Wuellner's death on February 14, 2004, preceded this session honoring him, and so his friend and associate Thomas H. Olbricht offers a response to Hester and Hester. Olbricht addresses the hands-on role Wuellner played in creating a community of scholars that were willing to encounter rhetorical criticism as a "holistic discipline." He suggests that Wuellner's cognizance of the degree to which rhetoric impacts "not only the understanding but the very lives of human beings" spurred his contemporaries to "contemplate...words, worlds, and transcendence" in existential terms. Conceiving of verbal expression as a source of well-being and healing, Wuellner, in Olbricht's estimation, viewed rhetoric as a "rapprochement between 'heaven and earth'" that is able to influence and impact the mundane occurrences of daily life. In exploring a "chain of transcending dimensions" that extend into the beyond," Olbricht affirms the untapped richness of Wuellner's analytical approach. He observes, however, that just as Wuellner's assessments took years to unfold, it may take contemporary scholars decades to grasp and to develop the full potential of his rhetorical insights.

Elisabeth Schüssler Fiorenza

In this volume's fourth exchange, John R. Lanci and Elisabeth Schüssler Fiorenza consider Schüssler Fiorenza's seminal explorations of the ethical dimensions of rhetorical criticism. Lanci initiates discussion with the observation that while Schüssler Fiorenza is best known as a "feminist scholar," this terminology runs the risk of mis-categorizing and circumscribing her legacy. Although Schüssler Fiorenza's work rightfully retains singular status in emergent trajectories of rhetorical and theological discourse, Lanci suggests that she will be most remembered for introducing a paradigm shift rendering scholarship "accountable and relevant to the wider Christian community without sacrificing . . . rigor or legitimacy." Through expanding "the use of rhetorical criticism to include the scholarly inquiry itself as an object of study," Schüssler Fiorenza's work, he asserts, "challenges the trajectories of virtually all of the rhetorical criticism that has gone before."

As Lanci offers an overview of Schüssler Fiorenza's critical approaches to the Bible, he details a multi-stage journey of exploration and discovery. Emphasizing the singularity of her cognizance of "the potential of rhetorical criticism to decenter biblical studies," he simultaneously explores the effect of her application of "an ethic of inquiry" in moving biblical studies from the "exclusive purview of the academy to the wider community." By introducing alternate approaches to understanding biblical authority, Lanci argues, Schüssler Fiorenza has placed rhetorical criticism in the "service of . . . establish[ing] a just world for all."

Schüssler Fiorenza adds particular detail to the parameters of Lanci's synthetic overview of her work. She names her own project as one that has "sought to integrate and transform elements of the*logical, historical, and literary paradigms of biblical studies into a fourth paradigm of rhetorical-ethical inquiry." Noting that "the renaissance of rhetoric corresponds to the same five decades in which feminist biblical studies emerged and matured," she affirms the degree to which this confluence has, at once, enabled and shaped her work.

Recounting her experience as one of the earliest feminist scholars in biblical studies, she notes the degree to which feminist rhetorical analyses are uniquely equipped to leverage a critique of both language and ideology through probing "the structures of kyriarchical . . . domination that are controlling the production of knowledge in a given discipline."

Schüssler Fiorenza situates her own contributions along a trajectory comprised of four stages. The first stage was her initial inquiry to efforts aimed at conceptualizing and developing a "feminist standpoint and theoretical perspective." This first stage led her to the second of focusing anew on "the rhetoricality or rhetoricity of scholarship, knowledge, and science." The third stage was her emergent understanding of the inseparable character of "rhetoric and ethics" that brokered the fourth stage of her conceptualization of a radical democratic practice of conscientization engendered as an "*ekklesia* of wo/men" engaged in "the 'dance' of interpretation."

Schüssler Fiorenza maintains that the last of these stages most aptly captures the essence of a feminist approach. She suggests that because "dancing involves body and spirit . . . feelings and emotions," it carries the potential "to take us beyond our limits and create . . . community." Like dancing, "rhetorical moves and movements" can organically shift between "present" and "past," between "realism" and "imagination." Rather than providing "the transcript of a process," rhetorical approaches afford "basic steps [for] textual and contextual explorations that...must [be] execute[d] in order to keep dancing."

Vernon K. Robbins

The work of Vernon K. Robbins is the focus of this volume's fifth and final exchange. Highlighting the nature of "transformative performance" that runs through Robbins' scholarship, L. Gregory Bloomquist traces the development of Robbins's interpretive strategies, played out along six discrete trajectories. The first, a praxis of "critical rhetoric," moves toward "demystifying the conditions of domination . . . even as it promotes a realignment in the forces of power that construct social relations." The second is embodied in the "interactionist" character of Robbins's "interpretive analytic." Its aim is to bring alternate ways of interpreting a text "into energetic, interactive dialogue on an equal playing field." A third trajectory engages the "materiality of discourse" through "envisioning the landscape within the world of ancient texts." A fourth is expressed in the "doxastic nature" of rhetoric. Privileging face to face discussion over dogmatic assertion, it "deals not with knowledge but with beliefs and opinions that are critically tried out and navigated locally." Bloomquist identifies the fifth trajectory as an emphasis on "local rhetoric" that understands meaning "as an ongoing process [of] active reconstruction by people" in local settings. A sixth and final trajectory is linked to making audible the "absent voices" in a text, by attending not only to existing expressions and *topoi* but also to those that have potentially been effaced. Bloomquist ends his appraisal of Robbins's approach with a series of concluding queries that evocatively underscore the degree to which Robbins' "sociorhetorical interpretation" retains its potential to affect past, present and future understandings.

Robbins responds to Bloomquist's analyses by reflecting on four key developments that directed the trajectory of his emergent thought. Moving chronologically, he first emphasizes the degree to which concurrent strains in sociology and cultural anthropology as well as the need to move beyond form- and redaction-critical analyses shaped the "reintroduction of rhetoric to the study of the Bible." In a second development, he registers the ways in which the "blending of Judaism and Hellenism with help from the *Progymnasmata*" freed interpretation from the "horizons of courtroom, political assembly, and civil ceremony . . . [and] the oratorical rhetoric of the Greek city-state" to consider "the progymnastic modes rhetoricians used to elaborate sayings, short stories, fable-like parables, and other literary genres." Robbins notes that these two intersecting developments, in turn, invited a third development that conceived of the "real and imagined locations for emerging progymnastic Christian rhetoric [through] merging Social Science with Cognitive Science." The fourth development, in turn, involved the shift from rhetorology or rhetoric that produces argumentation to rhetography or rhetoric that evokes graphic images and pictures in the mind. As the shape of studies and commentaries shifted and became increasingly "informed by rhetography and rhetorical force," the importance of engaging the real and imagined *loci* from which Christian rhetoric emerged could no longer be ignored. Robbins concludes that considerable insight has been gained by linking literary-historical methods with socio-rhetorical strategies of analysis and interpretation, but it is essential for the next generation to embrace new strategies that likewise address "how texts participate in historical, social, cultural, ideological, and visual material culture."

Conclusions

Cumulatively, the essays included in this volume comprise something of a "handbook" for the producers of contemporary scholarship. Simultaneously, the volume's genealogical trajectories underscore the significance of both established and emergent contributions. The field has changed dramatically since these forefathers and foremother began reframing established questions and forging new configurations. Perhaps the most compelling aspect of their respective analyses, however, is the degree to which each still retains its import. For those of us who are the heirs of these scholars' seminal work, the voices captured in this volume serve as both historical record and contemporary resource. They deliver, at once, a lofty challenge and an invitation to produce scholarship just as enduring in its significance. As each of these ancestors of the method of rhetorical criticism underscores the degree to which biblical literacy remains essential, the patterns that link privilege with scriptural interpretation run a cyclical course. Although the questions have changed, the stakes have hardly grown less significant.

1

Hans Dieter Betz: Ur-ancestor of New Testament Rhetorical Criticism

Troy W. Martin

I am honored to write this chapter describing the rhetorical legacy of my *Doktorvater*, Prof. Hans Dieter Betz. I came to the University of Chicago in 1981 to study with him and discovered a New Testament scholar and teacher of the first order. As far as I could tell, he knew everything there was to know about the New Testament and its world. In class, he taught as if he had been there when the New Testament was being written and was personally acquainted with its authors, especially Paul. Prof. Betz inspired me and my fellow classmates to place ourselves in the New Testament world as much as possible and to read its text against the background of the first century. Postmodernism has of course deemed our quest impossible, and Peter Lampe therefore asks "why New Testament exegesis should still work on the basis of *ancient* rhetorical text theory at all."[1] He quickly responds, however, "From the *historical-critical* point of view, the answer is that it still makes sense to confront the then-speaking and then-writing people with the then-current theories of text and language—no matter how adequate or inadequate from today's philosophical perspective these ancient theories might have been."[2] I along with the majority of Betz's other students concur with Lampe. We learned so much that it is difficult for us to deem our quest to have been in vain. We gained new insights not only about the New Testament text but about ourselves as well, and all of us owe a great debt to Prof. Betz. I hope this chapter I write in his honor will in some small way be an installment on that debt.

Exordium

My impossible mission is to describe in a single chapter the influence of Prof. Betz on the method of rhetorical criticism. My mission would be daunting enough even if he had only written his landmark commentary on Galatians. However, he has also written a massive commentary on 2 Corinthians 8–9, and an even more massive commentary on the Sermon on the Mount.[3] All of these works plus his many articles and especially his seminal essay on Galatians significantly influenced the method of rhetorical criticism, and in the

---

1. Peter Lampe, "Rhetorical Analysis of Pauline Texts—Quo Vadit?" in *Paul and Rhetoric*, ed. J. Paul Sampley and Peter Lampe (New York: T&T Clark, 2010), 7.
2. Ibid.
3. Hans Dieter Betz, *Galatians: A Commentary on Paul's Letter to the Churches of Galatia* (Hermeneia; Philadelphia: Fortress, 1979); idem, *Second Corinthians 8 and 9: A Commentary on Two Administrative Letters of the Apostle Paul* (Hermeneia; Philadelphia: Fortress, 1985); idem, *The Sermon on the Mount: A Commentary on the Sermon on the Mount, including the Sermon on the Plain (Matthew 5:3–7:27 and Luke 6:20–49)* (Hermeneia; Minneapolis: Fortress, 1995). These commentaries have all been translated and published in German as well.

short space that I have, I cannot even begin to list his numerous and important contributions to this method.[4]

I cannot imagine that the other contributors to this volume on rhetorical genealogies do not also feel the daunting task of an impossible mission. After all, we each share a similar challenge to describe in a single volume the diverse contributions of the rhetorical ancestors who developed and shaped the method of rhetorical criticism.

Propositio

Given the theme of this volume and my need for a manageable mission, please consider with me a single issue, namely Betz's position in the genealogy of New Testament rhetorical criticism. Genealogies are usually represented by lists of ancestors and descendants. Ancestors include those progenitors who are responsible for the descendants who follow them. The earlier an ancestor occurs in a genealogical list, the greater number of descendants that ancestor usually has. In any genealogical list of New Testament rhetorical criticism, Betz belongs at or near the very beginning. In this chapter, let us consider the proposition that he belongs at the very beginning of the genealogical list of New Testament rhetorical criticism and that his position in this list is that of Ur-ancestor or progenitor.

To be sure, this proposition designating Betz as the Ur-ancestor of New Testament chetorical criticism has its opponents. The most vocal is of course Carl Joachim Classen, who raises the question, "As Betz stresses the novelty of his method, it seems obvious to ask: why was it not discovered and used before?"[5] In particular,

---

4. Hans Dieter Betz, "The Literary Composition and Function of Paul's Letter to the Galatians," *New Testament Studies* 21, no. 3 (1975): 353–79; repr. *The Galatians Debate: Contemporary Issues in Rhetorical and Historical Interpretation*, ed. Mark D. Nanos (Peabody: Hendrickson, 2002), 3–28. Citations are from the original publication.

Classen addresses "to what extent ancient rhetoric was made use of for the interpretation of the Bible before 1974," the year of Betz's seminal rhetorical-critical lecture and subsequent essay on Galatians.[6] Classen then cites a number of exegetes who use rhetoric for the interpretation of the Bible before Betz. Specifically, Classen describes Philip Melanchthon's use of rhetorical species, arrangement, and argumentation in his notes on Galatians.[7] Classen indeed makes a persuasive case that rhetoric was used in biblical interpretation before Betz, but Classen raises and argues a different proposition than the one we are considering in this chapter.

If the question is "was rhetoric used for biblical interpretation before Betz," then the answer must be a resounding "Yes." Even Betz himself recognizes many of his rhetorical predecessors who were rhetoricians and teachers of rhetoric as well as biblical interpreters.[8] Augustine, for example, initially rejects the Scriptures "on account of their unrefined style."[9] Reading the Scriptures again during his

---

5. Carl Joachim Classen, "St. Paul's Epistles and Ancient Greek and Roman Rhetoric," in Nanos, *The Galatians Debate*, 97. Classen's article appears in a number of his publications sometimes with only slight changes or in translation. See Carl Joachim Classen, "Paulus und die antike Rhetorik," *ZNW* 82, nos. 1–2 (1991): 15–27; idem, "St. Paul's Epistles and Ancient Greek and Roman Rhetoric," *Rhetorica* 10, no. 4 (1992): 319–44; and idem, "St. Paul's Epistles and Ancient Greek and Roman Rhetoric,"in *Rhetoric and the New Testament: Essays from the 1992 Heidelberg Conference*, ed. Stanley E. Porter and Thomas H. Olbricht (JSNTSup 180; Sheffield: Sheffield Academic, 1993), 265–91. See also the first chapter of his book *Rhetorical Criticism of the New Testament* (Tübingen: Mohr Siebeck, 2000), 1–28.

6. Classen, "St. Paul's Epistles," 98. Classen is referring to Betz, "Literary Composition," 352–79.

7. Classen, "St. Paul's Epistles," 101–3.

8. Hans Dieter Betz, *Galatians*, 14; idem, *Second Corinthians 8 and 9*, 129 n. 2; idem, "The Problem of Rhetoric and Theology According to the Apostle Paul," in *L'apôtre Paul: Personnalité, style et conception du ministère*, ed. A. Vanhoye (BETL 73; Leuven: Leuven University, 1986): 16–23. For the references, see Classen, "St. Paul's Epistles," 96 n. 6. Also see Troy W. Martin, "Invention and Arrangement in Recent Pauline Rhetorical Studies: A Survey of the Practices and the Problems," in Sampley and Lampe, *Paul and Rhetoric*, 50 n. 6; and Janet Fairweather, "The Epistle to the Galatians and Classical Rhetoric: Parts 1 & 2," *TynBul* 45 (1994): 2–22. There may even have been some rhetorical discussions prior to Betz in the Paul Seminar of the Society of Biblical Literature. See Wilhelm Wuellner, "Paul's Rhetoric of Argumentation in Romans: An Alternative to the Donfried–Karris Debate over Romans," in *The Romans Debate: Revised and Expanded Edition*, ed. Karl P. Donfried (Peabody: Hendrickson, 1995), 130–31.

spiritual crisis, however, Augustine changes his mind and concludes that Paul in particular was an "eloquent teacher because of his ability to apply all three [rhetorical] styles judiciously."[10] Examples of those who use rhetoric before Betz could be multiplied, but they only answer questions we are not considering in this chapter.

We are not asking Classen's question of whether or not Betz is the first to use rhetoric for biblical interpretation. We also are not asking if Betz is the first to apply rhetorical criticism to biblical studies in general. That honor arguably goes to James Muilenberg for his 1968 SBL Presidential Address.[11] At least, Muilenberg is credited with naming the method *rhetorical criticism*, and, according to David E. Aune, Old Testament scholars used rhetorical rriticism as a method of interpretation before New Testament scholars, including Prof. Betz, extend this method to the interpretation of the New Testament.[12] No, the question we are considering is this: Does Betz belong at the beginning of a genealogical list of *New Testament rhetorical criticism*? Our proposition is that he does belong at the head of this list as Ur-ancestor of this method and hence the present volume begins with him.

Ratio

Now there are many reasons we should accept our proposition, but we shall consider only three. First, Betz belongs at the very beginning of this genealogical list because numerous notable New Testament scholars in 1974 recognize his method as initiating a new approach

---

9. Augustine, *Confessionum libri xiii*, ed. L. Verheijen (CCSL 27; Turnholti: Brepols, 1981), 3.5.9. For this reference and an analysis, see Aaron Canty, "Saint Paul in Augustine," in *A Companion to St. Paul in the Middle Ages*, ed. Steven R. Cartwright (Leiden: Brill, 2013), 115–42.

10. Ibid.

11. James Muilenberg, "Form Criticism and Beyond," *JBL* 88(1969): 1–18.

12. Ibid, 8. See David E. Aune, *The Westminster Dictionary of New Testament and Early Christian Literature and Rhetoric* (Louisville, KY: Westminster John Knox, 2003), 416. Aune credits Muilenberg with introducing the name for the method.

to the interpretation of the New Testament. Second, Betz belongs at the head of this genealogical list because he develops this method in the 1970s as a way of moving beyond the impasses of epistolographic studies. Third, Betz deserves the designation of "progenitor" because his application of this method establishes distinct foci in the subsequent application of rhetorical criticism to the New Testament. These three reasons, among others, demonstrate our proposition that Betz deserves the designation of Ur-ancestor of New Testament rhetorical criticism.

Argumentatio

First Proof: Betz as the Initiator of New Testament Rhetorical Criticism

As Betz teaches us, let us begin with an ethos proof. Consider the numerous outstanding New Testament scholars who hail Betz's rhetorical-critical interpretation of Galatians as initiating a new era in New Testament scholarship. These notable and well-respected scholars include Jean-Noel Aletti, David E. Aune, Charles K. Barrett, W. D. Davies, Hans Hübner, Wayne A. Meeks, and Paul W. Meyer, to name just a few.[13] All these scholars know the field of New Testament studies inside and out, and yet in their reviews of Betz's Galatians commentary, they all see Betz's rhetorical method as initiating something new and different.

Aune's review of Betz's Galatians commentary is representative of the reviews of these other scholars. Aune comments:

---

13. Jean-Noel Aletti, "Review of H. D. Betz, *Galatians*," *RSR* 69 (1981): 601–2; Charles K. Barrett, "Review of H. D. Betz, *Galatians*," *Int* 34 (1980): 414–17; W. D. Davies, Paul W. Meyer, and David E. Aune, "Review of H. D. Betz, *Galatians: A Commentary on Paul's Letter to the Churches of Galatia*," *RelSRev* 7 (1981): 310–28; Hans Hübner, "Review of H. D. Betz, *Galatians*," *TLZ* 109 (1984): 341–50; Wayne A. Meeks, "Review of H. D. Betz, *Galatians*," *JBL* 100, no. 2 (1981): 304–7.

The single most innovative feature of this commentary is, I would judge, the author's proposed analysis of the surface structure of Paul's letter to the Galatians in terms of Greco-Roman rhetorical theory. ... In several respects this commentary of Galatians is a groundbreaking enterprise which sets the direction of future investigation.[14]

Aune further comments, "It is clear that this must be regarded as a groundbreaking commentary which will doubtless dominate the discussion of Galatians for the next generation."[15] Aune and these other scholars repeatedly use words such as *innovative* and *groundbreaking* to describe Betz's new rhetorical approach. They further realize that his commentary "sets the direction" for future investigations of Galatians by the use of rhetorical theory.

All of these prominent scholars thus realize that Betz's rhetorical-critical interpretation of Galatians initiates a new era in New Testament scholarship, and the method of this new era will be rhetorical criticism. Thirty years after the publication of Betz's seminal essay and commentary on Galatians, Peter Lampe observes:

What has been new in the last three decades is the attempt rhetorically to analyze a Pauline letter in its *entirety* and to understand the flow of thoughts and arguments within the framework of the entire structure of the letter. In 1975 (1974), Hans Dieter Betz discovered that the disposition of an ancient speech and the structure of the main part of Galatians are alike, thus laying the cornerstone for his groundbreaking commentary on Galatians.[16]

Lampe further notes that Betz's "method became popular" and initiated a new "school of research."[17]

Considering their reputations, what more trustworthy group of New Testament scholars could we assemble than these who all affirm

---

14. Aune, "Review of H. D. Betz, *Galatians*," 323–24.
15. Ibid., 328.
16. Lampe, "Rhetorical Analysis," 4.
17. Ibid., 4–5.

that New Testament rhetorical criticism begins with Betz? This ethos proof therefore establishes Betz as the initiator of New Testament rhetorical criticism and supports our claim that he is the Ur-ancestor of this method.

Second Proof: Betz as the Discoverer of New Testament Rhetorical Criticism

Again as Betz teaches us, let us next continue with a logos proof that he is the first to discover the method of New Testament rhetorical criticism in the 1970s. Now, necessity is indeed the mother of invention and discovery. What necessity prompts him to discover this method in the 1970s? Betz himself answers this question in his seminal lecture at the 29th General Meeting of the *Studiorum Novi Testamenti Societas* in Sigtuna, Sweden on August 13, 1974. Betz states, "In the process of my studies I also found that the letter of the Galatians can be analyzed according to Graeco-Roman rhetoric and epistolography."[18] The necessity facing Betz and indeed other New Testament exegetes in 1974 is the failure of epistolography to answer two key interpretive questions related to New Testament epistles.

The method of epistolography began early in the twentieth-century when scholars such as Ferdinandus Ziemann and Francis Xavier Exler turned their attention to letter formulae and conventions.[19] The method flourished, and by mid-century Heikki Koskenniemi produced his influential work on the idea and phraseology of the Greek letter.[20] This method is very productive

---

18. Betz, "Literary Composition," 353.
19. Ferdinandus Ziemann, *De Epistularum Graecarum Formulis Sollemnibus Quaestiones Selectae* (Berlin: Haas, 1912), passim; and Francis Xavier Exler, *The Form of the Ancient Greek Letter: A Study in Greek Epistolography* (Washington, D.C.: Catholic University of America, 1923), passim.
20. Heikki Koskenniemi, *Studien zur Idee und Phraseologie des griechischen Briefes bis 400 n. Chr.* (Helsinki: Akateeminen Kirjakauppa, 1956), passim.

and informs numerous studies that increase our understanding of epistolary salutations, thanksgiving and health-giving sections, greetings, and farewells. However, this method has its limitations.[21]

By the 1970s, two limitations become glaringly obvious as demonstrated by the works of John L. White and Abraham J. Malherbe. In 1972, White published a book entitled *The Form and Function of the Body of the Greek Letter*.[22] White's book provides scholars with the three analytical categories of body-opening, body-middle, and body-closing. Although these categories are somewhat helpful, they do not provide for an analysis of large sections of the letter body.[23] White's book thus demonstrates that the method of epistolography does not supply sufficient analytical categories for an analysis of the entire letter body. In 1974, two years after the publication of White's book, Hendrikus Boers commented, "The *formal* characteristics of the central section of the Pauline letter remain unclear."[24] In that very year, Betz "discovered" and developed rhetorical criticism as a way of moving beyond this impasse in the epistolary analysis of New Testament letters.

In contrast to the analysis of form, Malherbe's article entitled *Ancient Epistolary Theorists* addresses epistolary genres and translates some early epistolary handbooks that type and classify ancient letters.[25] From the beginning, epistolary theorists recognize the

---

21. For some of the extensive bibliography in epistolary studies, see Lampe, "Rhetorical Analysis," 12 n. 31.
22. John L. White, *The Form and Function of the Body of the Greek Letter: A Study of the Letter-Body in Non-Literary Papyri and in Paul the Apostle* (SBLDS 2; Missoula, MT: Society of Biblical Literature, 1972), passim. See also White's other works including idem, "Introductory Formulae in the Body of the Pauline Letter," *JBL* 90, no. 1 (1971): 91–97; idem, "Epistolary Formulas and Cliches in Greek Papyrus Letters," *Society of Biblical Literature 1978 Seminar Papers* 2 (1978): 289–319; and idem, *Light from Ancient Letters* (Philadelphia: Fortress, 1986), passim.
23. Troy W. Martin, *Metaphor and Composition in First Peter* (SBLDS 131; Atlanta: Scholars, 1992), 74–75.
24. Hendrikus Boers, "The Form Critical Study of Paul's Letters: 1 Thessalonians as a Case Study," *NTS* 22, no. 2 (1974): 145.

importance of identifying the genre of ancient letters. Of course, the designation *letter* is a genre itself with characteristic form and function.[26] The great diversity of letters, however, demonstrates that the letter genre is only a framing genre that presses other genres into its service.[27]

Exler distinguished familiar letters from business letters, petitions, and official letters.[28] Other epistolary theorists propose even more types of letters but need a taxonomy that avoids the criticisms that it is arbitrary, contrived, or imposed.[29] Malherbe's article appears to meet that need. It translates Pseudo-Demetrius's *Epistolary Types*, which describes and illustrates 21 types of letters, and Pseudo-Libanius's *Epistolary Styles*, which contains 41 styles of letters. These types and styles initially hold great promise for classifying New Testament letters.

Several scholars apply these types and styles to New Testament epistles but with mixed results. The New Testament epistles are just too long, and each contains material that can be classified as any number of genres or types. Aune comments, "Early Christian letters tend to resist rigid classification…in terms of the many categories listed by the epistolary theorists. Most early Christian letters are multifunctional and have a 'mixed' character, combining elements from two or more epistolary types."[30] Although initially viewed with great optimism, Malherbe's article clearly documents the difficulty

---

25. Abraham J. Malherbe, "Ancient Epistolary Theorists," *Ohio Journal of Religious Studies* 5 (1977): 3–77; repr. *Ancient Epistolary Theorists* (SBLSBS 19; Atlanta: Scholars, 1988).

26. Martin, *Metaphor and Composition*, 81.

27. Klaus Berger, "Hellenistische Gattungen im Neuen Testament," *ANRW* 25, no. 2 (1884): 1338.

28. Exler, *Form of the Ancient Greek Letter*, 24–60.

29. For example, see Stanley K. Stowers, *Letter Writing in Greco-Roman Antiquity* (Library of Early Christianity; Philadelphia: Westminster, 1986), 49–173.

30. David E. Aune, *The New Testament in Its Literary Environment* (Library of Early Christianity; Philadelphia: Westminster, 1987), 203.

encountered by epistolography in classifying the specific genre of New Testament letters.

By the 1970s, therefore, epistolography leaves Betz and other New Testament scholars without an adequate method for analyzing the letter-body or for identifying the specific genre of New Testament letters. Betz's important discovery in 1974 that Galatians can "be analyzed according to Graeco-Roman rhetoric and epistolography" thus provides a new and different method for addressing the two key interpretive questions left open by epistolography. Betz's method enables him to analyze Galatians according to the parts of a speech that are explained in the rhetorical handbooks and to identify the genre of Galatians as judicial or forensic rhetoric, which is one of the three species of rhetoric along with deliberative and epideictic. This "new and different" method comes to be known as rhetorical criticism, and Betz is the first to discover this method as a way for moving beyond the limitations of epistolography.

In his 1974 seminal paper, Betz notes, "At the outset I would like to acknowledge my great indebtedness to the members of the S.B.L. Seminar on 'The Form and Function of the Pauline Letters.'"[31] He then explains, "Although in the present paper I take a somewhat different approach, I would never have been able to do so without their continuous stimulation and gracious sharing of ideas."[32] Thus, Betz admits his dependence on epistolary studies but then takes a "somewhat different approach" by using rhetorical criticism to address the deficiencies of epistolary studies in regard to the analysis and genre of New Testament letters. As a method, therefore, New Testament rhetorical criticism originates in the 1970s from epistolography but moves beyond it by providing for analysis of the

---

31. Betz, "Literary Composition," 354 n. 4.
32. Ibid.

letter-body and for identification of the genre of New Testament letters.

During the decade of the 70s, the only scholar we can identify as the *discoverer* of this method is Betz. Although others before him may have used rhetoric for interpreting the Bible, they were not utilizing the method of rhetorical criticism as we designate it since this method only arose in the 1970s as a response to the limitations of epistolography. Still others, such as Amos N. Wilder, Wilhelm Wuellner, and George A. Kennedy, were working with rhetoric before Betz; but their approach to rhetoric either falls outside the method of rhetorical criticism, as is the case with Wilder, or is applied to the New Testament after Betz, as is the case with Kennedy and Wuellner.[33] Hence, our argument from logos demonstrates that Betz belongs at the very beginning of the genealogical list of New Testament rhetorical criticism because he "discovered" this method as a way of moving beyond the interpretive limitations of epistolography.

Third Proof: Betz as First Practitioner of New Testament Rhetorical Criticism

As Betz further teaches us, let us consider yet another logos proof. As initiator and discoverer, Betz becomes the first practitioner of New Testament rhetorical criticism and thus anticipates and shapes

---

33. Amos N. Wilder, *Early Christian Rhetoric: The Language of the Gospel* (New York: Harper & Row, 1964), passim. Wuellner's first article applying rhetorical criticism to a New Testament text postdates Betz by two years. See Wilhelm Wuellner, "Paul's Rhetoric of Argumentation in Romans," *CBQ* 38, no. 2 (1976): 330–51. He published an earlier form critical article that does not employ the method of rhetorical criticism. See idem, "Haggadic Homily Genre in 1 Cor. 1–3," *JBL* 89, no. 2 (1970): 199–204. For Kennedy's extensive work in classical rhetoric before Betz, see the chapter on Kennedy in this volume. However, Kennedy's specific application of classical rhetoric to the New Testament postdates Betz. See George A. Kennedy, *Classical Rhetoric and Its Christian and Secular Tradition from Ancient to Modern Times* (Chapel Hill: University of North Carolina Press, 1980), passim; and idem, *New Testament Interpretation through Rhetorical Criticism* (Chapel Hill: University of North Carolina Press, 1984), passim.

the subsequent application of this method in New Testament interpretation. Since the 1980s, three distinct foci have characterized New Testament rhetorical criticism. First is the focus on rhetorical species as numerous scholars attempt to identify the genre of New Testament letters to be one of the three species of ancient rhetoric. Second is the focus on rhetorical arrangement as several more scholars try to analyze the structure of New Testament letters according to the rhetorical arrangement of an ancient speech. Third is the focus on rhetorical invention as even more scholars investigate the arguments of New Testament letters according to ancient rhetorical recommendations for discovering and inventing arguments. Each of these three foci are clearly represented in Betz's pioneering work, and he is indeed the first practitioner who has brought all three of these foci together to provide answers to interpretive questions not answered by epistolographic studies.

Focus on Rhetorical Species

In his seminal 1974 lecture, Betz states, "It is my thesis that Paul's letter to the Galatians is an example of the 'apologetic letter' genre."[34] He explains, "The 'apologetic letter' presupposes the real or fictitious situation of the court of law, with the jury, the accuser and the defendant."[35] In this legal context according to Betz, the addresses are the jury, Paul is the defendant, and his opponents are the accusers. Since Paul cannot appear in person, his letter carries his "defense speech to the jury."[36] Betz further explains, "The 'apologetic letter' is

---

34. Betz, "Literary Composition," 354. See also idem, "In Defense of the Spirit: Paul's Letter to the Galatians as a Document of Early Christian Apologetics," in *Aspects of Religious Propaganda in Judaism and Early Christianity*, ed. Elisabeth Schüssler Fiorenza (Notre Dame: University of Notre Dame Press, 1976), 99–114. See also idem, *Der Apostel Paulus und die sokratische Trdition* (Beiträge zur historischen Theologie; Tübingen: Mohr Siebeck, 1972), passim.
35. Betz, "Literary Composition," 377.
36. Ibid.

by definition a part of rhetoric and, for that reason, limits its writer to the devices of the 'art of persuasion.'"[37] Betz states, "The 'art of persuasion' has its proper place in the courts of law," and he thus classifies Galatians as an example of forensic or judicial rhetoric.[38]

Betz's classification of Galatians as judicial or forensic rhetoric initiates an intense interest in classifying all New Testament letters as one of the three species of rhetoric.[39] In 1987, Robert G. Hall writes:

> Ancient rhetoricians, following Aristotle, divided speeches into three species: judicial, epideictic, and deliberative. Since these species differed in time reference, goal, mode of argument, and form, any analysis of a document by the categories of ancient rhetoric must begin by determining the species of rhetoric to be applied.[40]

Hall credits Betz as the first to apply the judicial designation to Galatians, and New Testament scholars quickly realized that assigning any of the New Testament letters to one of the species of rhetoric informs the social location as well as the argumentative strategy and form of that letter.

Duane F. Watson writes, "Species or genre classification is one more important tool for interpretation. It is a window on the social situation of Paul and his addressees."[41] Watson then quotes Karl Paul Donfried, who states, "To recognize…which of the three types (*genera*) of rhetoric—deliberative, judicial or epideictic—a document is employing already gives important clues to its social situation as well as its intention."[42] These advantages offered by the species of rhetoric

---

37. Ibid.
38. Ibid., 378.
39. For an overview, see Duane F. Watson, "The Three Species of Rhetoric and the Study of the Pauline Epistles," in Sampley and Lampe, *Paul and Rhetoric*, 25–47.
40. Robert G. Hall, "The Rhetorical Outline for Galatians: A Reconsideration," *JBL* 106, no. 2 (1987): 277; repr. Nanos, *The Galatians Debate*, 29.
41. Watson, "The Three Species of Rhetoric," 27.
42. Karl Paul Donfried, "The Theology of 1 Thessalonians," in *The Theology of the Shorter Pauline Letters*, ed. idem and I. Howard Marshall (NTT; Cambridge: Cambridge University Press, 1993), 3–4. Quoted in Watson, "The Three Species of Rhetoric," 27.

to move beyond the genre impasse of epistolographic studies have elevated the scholarly interest in rhetorical criticism.

A number of scholars including Hall would eventually disagree with Betz's designation of Galatians as forensic, and they designate the letter as deliberative or epideictic. Nevertheless, they clearly take their point of departure from Betz. Hall explicitly contrasts his own identification of Galatians as deliberative rhetoric with Betz's forensic designation.[43] Likewise, Joop Smit begins his study of Galatians as epideictic rhetoric by writing, "This study's point of departure is the important article of H. D. Betz, 'The Literary Composition and Function of Paul's Letter to the Galatians.'"[44] These and other scholars therefore recognize Betz as the first to use rhetorical criticism to identify the rhetorical species of a New Testament letter, and he is thus the first practitioner of the rhetorical-critical focus on rhetorical species.

This interest in rhetorical species eventually extends beyond Galatians to each of the New Testament letters as representative of one or the other of the three species of rhetoric. Just as with Galatians, various scholars would eventually assign each of the letters to all three of the species. This diversity of opinion leads Watson to comment, "Trying to assign one of Paul's epistles rigidly to a particular rhetorical species is a venture fraught with pitfalls.... Paul's epistles are typically not a single rhetorical species, but rather a mix of species."[45] In spite of the difficulties, however, Watson concludes, "Determination of the rhetorical species of portions of a Pauline epistle and an epistle as a whole is an important enterprise."[46] Watson cites Betz as the pioneer who initiated this enterprise. We therefore

---

43. Hall, The Rhetorical Outline," 277; repr. Nanos, *The Galatians Debate*, 29.
44. Joop Smit, "The Letter of Paul to the Galatians: A Deliberative Speech," New Testament Studies 35, no. 1 (1989): 1; repr. Nanos, *The Galatians Debate*, 39.
45. Watson, "The Three Species of Rhetoric," 42.
46. Ibid., 46.

appropriately designate Betz as the first practitioner who inspires subsequent studies designating the rhetorical species of New Testament letters. His influence as the first practitioner, however, extends beyond rhetorical species and also includes rhetorical arrangement.[47]

Focus on Rhetorical Arrangement

Again in his seminal 1974 lecture, Betz states, "In the process of my studies I also found that the letter of the Galatians can be analysed (analyzed) according to Graeco-Roman rhetoric and epistolography."[48] Betz then uses epistolary analysis to identify the epistolary prescript as Gal 1:1–5 and the epistolary postscript as 6:11–18. He describes these epistolary conventions as "a kind of external bracket for the body of the letter."[49] Betz next uses rhetorical analytical categories to identify the *exordium* (Gal 1:6–11), *narratio* (1:12–2:14), *propositio* (2:15–21), *probatio* (3:1–4:31), *exhortatio* (5:1–6:10), and *peroratio* (6:11–18). Betz's initial blending of epistolary and rhetorical categories has dominated the subsequent application of New Testament rhetorical criticism as scholars have attempted to specify the relationship between the parts of speech and letter conventions, the criteria used to identify the parts of a speech, and the place of paraenesis in rhetorical arrangement.

Parts of Speech and Letter Conventions

Betz's blending of epistolary and rhetorical analytical categories does not specify the precise relationship between these two types of analysis.[50] In his explanation of the epistolary postscript and *peroratio* of Galatians, for example, Betz writes:

47. Ibid., 36.
48. Betz, "Literary Composition," 353.
49. Ibid., 355.

In vi.11–18 Paul adds a postscript in his own handwriting. This conforms to the epistolary convention of the time. . . . The postscript must be examined not only as an epistolographic convention but also as a rhetorical feature. As a rhetorical feature, the postscript of the letter to the Galatians serves as the *peroratio* or *conclusio*, that is, the end and conclusion of the apologetic speech forming the body of the letter. ... When we look at Paul's postscript (vi.11–18) as a *peroratio*, some very interesting structures emerge, all confirming that we do, in fact, have this part of a speech before us.[51]

Commenting on Betz's work, Hans Hübner states, "What scholarship must further investigate is the relationship of rhetoric and epistolography in reference to the Pauline letters."[52] In this further investigation, many scholars agree with Betz that the parts of a letter "must be examined" as both epistolographic conventions and rhetorical features. Others, however, do not.[53] Watson and Hauser explain this polarity:

Interpreters find themselves either embracing one of the following positions, or standing between them: 1) the New Testament epistles are just that—epistles—and rhetoric has only a secondary influence. Rhetorical influence is mostly limited to matters of style and some invention, and 2) the epistles of the New Testament are speeches in epistolary form and can be analyzed using Greco-Roman rhetorical theory in its three main parts: invention, arrangement, and style.[54]

---

50. Classen complains that Betz does "not pay attention sufficiently" to the precise relationship between rhetoric and epistolography. See Classen, "St. Paul's Epistles," in Nanos, *The Galatians Debate*, 98; idem, "St Paul's Epistles," in Porter and Olbricht, *Rhetoric and the New Testament*, 269.

51. Betz, "Literary Composition," 357.

52. Hans Hübner, "Der Galaterbrief und das Verhältnis von antiker Rhetorik und Epistolographie," *TLZ* 109 (1984): 249 (translation mine).

53. For summaries of the various proposals, see Porter, "Paul of Tarsus and His Letters," in *Handbook of Classical Rhetoric in the Hellenistic Period, 330 bc–ad 400*, ed. idem (Leiden: Brill, 1997), 541–567; and Jerome Murphy-O'Connor, *Paul the Letter-Writer: His World, His Options, His Skills* (Collegeville, MN: Liturgical, 1995), 77–79.

54. Duane F. Watson and Alan J. Hauser, *Rhetorical Criticism of the Bible: A Comprehensive Bibliography with Notes on History and Method* (Biblical Interpretation Series 4; Leiden: E. J. Brill, 1994), 120–21.

In this further investigation relating epistolary conventions and rhetorical arrangement, Betz is the first practitioner of New Testament rhetorical criticism and clearly provides the catalyst.

Those who disagree with Betz argue that a letter is not a speech and should not be analyzed as such.[55] Jeffrey T. Reed explains, "In part, the reason epistolary theorists do not prescribe rhetorical arrangements to epistolary structures is due to the formulaic traditions long established in letter writing.... There is no necessary connection between the basic theory of epistolary structure and the technical teachings about rhetorical arrangement."[56] Reed and a few others thus deny the "must" in Betz's use of rhetorical arrangement to analyze New Testament letters.

Many others, however, accept Betz's "must" and proceed to analyze all of the epistles in the New Testament according to the parts of an ancient speech.[57] In 1992, Stanley E. Porter noted that Betz "has been so influential that one of the newest sub-genres of commentary

---

55. Representatives of those who disagree with Betz include Classen, "St. Paul's Epistles," 106, 109; Philip H. Kern, "Rhetoric, Scholarship and Galatians: Assessing an Approach to Paul's Epistle," *TynBul* 46 (1995): 202; idem, *Rhetoric and Galatians: Assessing an Approach to Paul's Epistle* (SNTSMS 101; Cambridge: Cambridge University Press, 1998), 119; Stanley E. Porter, "Paul as Epistolographer and Rhetorician?" in *The Rhetorical Interpretation of Scripture: Essays from the 1996 Malibu Conference*, ed. idem and Dennis L. Stamps (JSNTSup 180; Sheffield: Sheffield Academic, 1999), 232, and idem, "The Theoretical Justification," in idem and Olbricht, *Rhetoric and the New Testament*, 115–16; and Jeffrey T. Reed, "Using Ancient Rhetorical Categories to Interpret Paul's Letters: A Question of Genre," in Porter and Olbricht, *Rhetoric and the New Testament*, 304, 308.

56. Ibid., 304, 308.

57. Representatives include Raymond F. Collins, *First Corinthians* (Sacra Pagina Series 7; Collegeville, MN: Liturgical Press, 1999), 17–20; Frank W. Hughes, "The Rhetoric of Letters," in *The Thessalonians Debate: Methodological Discord or Methodological Synthesis?*, ed. Karl P. Donfried and Johannes Beutler (Grand Rapids: Eerdmans, 2000), 236; Robert Jewett, *The Thessalonian Correspondence: Pauline Rhetoric and Millenarian Piety* (Philadelphia: Fortress, 1986), 72–76; idem, *Romans: A Commentary* (Hermeneia; Minneapolis: Fortress, 2007), vii–x, 29–30; Fredrick J. Long, *Ancient Rhetoric and Paul's Apology: The Compositional Unity of 2 Corinthians* (SNTSMS 131; Cambridge: Cambridge University Press, 2004), passim; Gerd Lüdemann, *Paul Apostle to the Gentiles: Studies in Chronology* (Philadelphia: Fortress, 1984), 48; and Charles A. Wanamaker, *Commentary on 1 & 2 Thessalonians* (NIGTC; Grand Rapids: Eerdmans, 1990), 48–52.

writing is the rhetorical analysis of a Pauline epistle."[58] Even though these scholars do not always agree with Betz on the number or even the names of the parts of an ancient speech, they nevertheless name Betz as the first to practice this type of arrangement in New Testament letters, and the influence of Betz's initial practice of New Testament Rhetorical Criticism is clearly seen in the work of these scholars.

Analyzing Gal 6:11–18, Betz states that the epistolary postscript "serves as" the *peroratio* and that it "in fact" is the *peroratio*.[59] In the subsequent practice of New Testament rhetorical criticism, some understand that epistolographic conventions only "serve as" or functionally resemble the parts of a speech while others hold that they "in fact" are these parts.[60] A consensus about whether letter conventions "are," in Betz's terminology, formally parts of a speech or only to some degree functionally "serve as" parts of a speech is never reached by New Testament rhetorical critics. Regardless of how they understand the relationship between epistolary conventions and the parts of a speech, however, these critics nevertheless take their cue from Betz's initial practice of New Testament rhetorical criticism. The necessity of relating epistolary and rhetorical analysis therefore definitely points to Betz as the first practitioner and hence the Urancestor of New Testament rhetorical criticism.

Identifying Parts of a Speech

Betz's influence as the first practitioner is further seen in the criteria subsequent rhetorical critics use to identify the parts of speech. Kieran O'Mahony observes, "Betz presents no theory of rhetorical methodology in regard to *dispositio* [arrangement]. However, it

---

58. Porter, "The Theoretical Justification," 102.
59. Betz, "Literary Composition," 357.
60. For representatives of both sides of this issue, see Martin, "Invention and Arrangement," 52–62.

would be unfair to say that he simply asserts this outline."[61] Indeed, Betz establishes in his seminal 1974 lecture three essential criteria drawn from the rhetorical handbooks for identifying the parts of speech in Galatians. Identifying the *propositio* of Galatians, Betz comments, "Gal. ii. 15–21 conforms to the form, function, and requirements of the *propositio*."[62] Earlier Betz states that a requirement of the *propositio* is its position between the *narratio* and the *probatio*. Position, form, and function are thus three essential criteria upon which Betz bases his rhetorical arrangement of Galatians.

Frequently, Betz appeals to position as substantiation for his identification of a part of speech. Identifying the *exordium*, Betz comments, "Generally speaking this first part of the body of the Galatian letter [1:6–11] conforms to the customary *exordium*, which is otherwise known as the *prooemium* or *principium*."[63] He makes a similar comment about the epistolary postscript's (6:11–18) serving as the *peroratio* or *conclusio* of the speech.[64] According to Betz, the beginning and ending of the letter correspond to the beginning and ending of a speech. Betz argues similarly on the basis of position for identifying the *narratio* (1:12–2:14), *propositio* (2:15–21), and *probatio* (3:1–4:31) of Galatians. Thus, position is an essential criterion Betz introduces for identifying the parts of speech.

No less frequently, however, Betz appeals to form and function. After identifying *enumeratio* (*recapitulatio*), *indignatio*, and *conquestio* as the three conventional parts of the *peroratio*, Betz states, "When

---

61. Kieran J. O'Mahony, *Pauline Persuasion: A Sounding in 2 Corinthians 8–9* (JSNTSup 199; Sheffield: Sheffield Academic, 2000) 64. Of course, O'Mahony's observation pertains to Betz's rhetorical analysis of 2 Corinthians 8–9 rather than of Galatians, but Betz uses similar criteria in both analyses. On pp. 64–69, O'Mahony presents an epitome of Betz's rationale. The unfairness O'Mahony mentions may refer to Classen's assessment that Betz applied labels without providing supporting argumentation. See Classen, "St. Paul's Epistles," 109–110.

62. Betz, "Literary Composition," 368.

63. Ibid., 359.

64. Ibid., 368.

we look at Paul's postscript (vi. 11–18) as a *peroratio*, some very interesting structures emerge, all confirming that we do, in fact, have this part of a speech before us."[65] Betz concludes, "The final section of Galatians conforms to the *enumeratio* [vi. 12-17], *indignatio* [vi. 12-13], and *conquestio* [vi. 17]."[66] Betz explains that this tripartite form performs the twofold function of the *peroratio* to remind the listeners of the case and to make a strong emotional appeal upon them. Betz concludes that Gal 6:11–18 is the *peroratio* because it conforms to the form and performs the function of a *peroratio*. In addition to position, therefore, form and function are essential criteria Betz introduces to identify the parts of speech in Galatians.

Rhetorical critics after Betz have continued utilizing these same three criteria in their identifications of the parts of speech. Regarding position, for example, Hughes notes, "What is important is that the section of a letter designated as an *exordium* be at the beginning of the letter."[67] Similarly, Watson and Hauser explain, "The body opening, middle, and closing roughly parallel *exordium, narratio-confirmatio*, and *peroratio* respectively."[68] Thus, rhetorical critics rely heavily on Betz's criterion of position as determined by the arrangement of a speech as an essential indicator of where to find a particular part of speech in Paul's letters.

The rhetorical critics that follow Betz use his criteria of position as well as form but eventually come to rely more heavily on his criterion of function to identify the parts of speech.[69] In his rhetorical arrangement of 1 Cor 12:1–3, for example, Johan S. Vos explains,

---

65. Ibid., 357.
66. Ibid., 357 n. 7.
67. Hughes, "The Rhetoric of Letters," 198.
68. Watson and Hauser, *Rhetorical Criticism and the Bible*, 122.
69. See for example Hermann Probst, *Paulus und der Brief: Die Rhetorik des antiken Briefes als Form der paulinischen Korintherkorrespondenz (1 Kor 8–10)* (WUNT 2.45; Tübingen: Mohr Siebeck, 1991), 99–107.

"Verse 1 should be designated as a *praefatio*. In a speech that treats more than a single subject, there can be according to Quintilian several introductory beginnings, which often only have a transitional function. Verse 2 has the function of a short *narratio*. . . . Verse 3 has the function of a *propositio*."[70] Vos clearly relies on function to determine these parts of speech.

Another example is Church's identification of the *exordium* in Philemon. He states, "Three things appropriate to the exordium in deliberative rhetoric are accomplished here by Paul. . . . If, as Quintilian writes, 'the sole purpose of the exordium is to prepare our audience in such a way that they will be disposed to lend a ready ear to the rest of our speech,' Paul accomplishes this with economy and tact."[71] An additional example is Robert Jewett's defense of his rhetorical analysis of 1 Thessalonians by a sustained appeal to the function of the parts of speech.[72]

Similar examples could be multiplied, but these are sufficient to demonstrate rhetorical critics' heavy reliance upon Betz's criterion of function for identification of the parts of speech.[73] Thus, these three criteria of position, form, and function that are used by subsequent rhetorical critics to determine the parts of a speech also point to Betz as the first practitioner of New Testament Rhetorical Criticism, and his position as the progenitor of this method is further demonstrated by his inclusion of paraenesis in rhetorical arrangement.

---

70. Johan S. Vos, "Das Rätsel von 1 Kor 12:1–3," *NovT* 35 (1993): 268 (translation mine).
71. F. Forrester Church, "Rhetorical Structure and Design in Paul's Letter to Philemon," *HTR* 71 (1978): 22.
72. Jewett, *Thessalonian Correspondence*, 76–78.
73. For other examples, see ibid.; and David A. DeSilva, "Meeting the Exigency of a Complex Rhetorical Situation: Paul's Strategy in 2 Corinthians 1 through 7," *AUSS* 34 (1996): 16.

Paraenesis in Rhetorical Arrangement

In his 1974 seminal lecture, Betz himself recognizes the difficulty of including paraenesis in the rhetorical arrangement by saying, "It is rather puzzling to see that *paraenesis* plays only a marginal role in the ancient rhetorical handbooks, if not in rhetoric itself. Consequently, modern studies of ancient rhetoric also do not pay much attention to it."[74] He designates Gal 5:1–6:10 by the Latin term *exhortatio*, which is consistent with the other Latin labels of arrangement that he uses, but this Latin term does not resolve the difficulty.[75]

Aletti writes, "A ticklish question, that of the pertinence of exhortations to a rhetorical model, is not addressed…. The difficulty arises therefore from the long sections of exhortations in Romans 12–15 and Galatians 5–6, for if one relies on the rhetorical manuals, these sections do not appear to pertain to the *dispositio* of ancient discourse."[76] Smit describes the issue similarly: "Gal 5:1–6:10 is considered by Betz as the paraenesis. This part creates, as he himself remarks, a serious problem for his rhetorical analysis. In classical rhetoric an exhortative passage such as this is completely unknown as a separate part of a normal speech."[77]

Subsequent rhetorical critics propose numerous solutions to resolve this difficulty. Betz himself appeals to the philosophical letters that end with a paraenetic section.[78] Several, however, consider such parallels as inconclusive proof that the rhetorical categories are applicable to paraenesis, and some propose excluding paraenesis from

---

74. Betz, "Literary Composition," 375–76.
75. See Hübner, "Der Galaterbrief," 244; and François Vouga, "Zur rhetorischen Gattung des Galaterbriefes," *ZNW* 79, no. 4 (1988): 291.
76. Jean-Noël Aletti, "La Dispositio Rhétorique dans les Épitres Pauliniennes," *NTS* 38, no. 3 (1992): 400 (translation mine).
77. Joop Smit, "The Letter of Paul to the Galatians: A Deliberative Speech," repr. Nanos, *The Galatians Debate*, 42.
78. Betz, "Literary Composition," 376.

rhetorical arrangement altogether.[79] Aletti further writes, "The discourse models of ancient rhetoric did not have long exhortations like those of Galatians and Romans. In other words, one should not see in these exhortations elements belonging to the *dispositio* of the speech, but they should rather be seen as *epistolary* components, surely inherited from the *typos nouthetètikos*."[80] Smit even suggests that the paraenetical section could be a later addition to the letter.[81] Hughes excludes paraenesis from the parts of speech but nevertheless thinks it is compatible with the function of deliberative discourses.[82]

Others also perceive a functional connection between paraenesis and deliberative speeches that attempt to persuade and dissuade regarding some proposed course of action.[83] Neil Elliott explains, "Attention is thus shifted from formal characteristics of text segments, treated in isolation, to the rhetorical function of argumentative parts…within a purposeful whole. This new perspective on rhetorical and social aspects of paraenesis alerts us to the importance of the social world in which the paraenetic activity makes cognitive and affective sense."[84] Attempting to specify the "cognitive and affective sense" that paraenesis makes, Aune sees the paraenetic section of Romans

79. Wolfgang Harnisch, "Einübung des neuen Seins: Paulinische Paränese am Beispiel des Galaterbriefs," *ZTK* 84 (1987): 286. Harnisch comments, "If one follows the rudiments of the rhetorical form of Galatians, the paraenetic part appears strange. As Betz must also take into account, the Pauline *exhortatio* has no fitting equivalent in the structure of a forensic speech and his reference to known analogies in the ancient tradition of philosophical letters is scarcely able to compensate for that deficit" (translation mine). See also Porter, "Paul of Tarsus," in idem, *Handbook of Classical Rhetoric*, 562–563, and idem, "Rhetorical Categories," in idem and Olbricht, *Rhetoric and the New Testament*, 104.

80. Jean-Noël Aletti, "Rhetoric of Romans 5–8," in *The Rhetorical Analysis of Scripture: Essays from the 1995 London Conference*, ed. Stanley E. Porter and Thomas H. Olbricht (JSNTSup 146; Sheffield: Sheffield Academic, 1997), 295.

81. Joop Smit, "Redactie in de brief aan de Galaten: Retorische analyze van Gal. 4,12–6,18," *TvT* 26 (1986): 113–114. For a summary, see Smit, "The Letter of Paul to the Galatians," repr. Nanos, *The Galatians Debate*, 45.

82. Hughes, "The Rhetoric of Letters," in Donfried and Beutler, 237, and idem, "Rhetoric of 1 Thessalonians," in *The Thessalonian Correspondence*, ed. Raymond F. Collins (BETL 87; Leuven: Leuven University Press, 1990), 106.

83. Harnisch, "Einübung des neuen Seins," 286.

as a fitting conclusion to a *logos protreptikos*, and Hellholm integrates paraenesis into rhetorical arrangement as a practical-nonlogical argument related to *ethos*.[85] Betz himself considers but rejects the possibility of solving the difficulty of paraenesis by an appeal to deliberative speeches, which in his opinion have "no apparent connection to paraenesis."[86] Several agree with Betz and assign paraenesis to epideictic rhetoric.[87]

In spite of the numerous suggested solutions, integrating paraenesis into rhetorical arrangement remains a ticklish question, and this difficulty once again emphasizes Betz's foundational role. His initial introduction of this difficulty in his 1974 seminal lecture presents a problem that subsequent rhetorical critics must address. This problem of the place of paraenesis in rhetorical arrangement as well as his focus on rhetorical arrangement in general thus demonstrates that Betz is the first practitioner of New Testament rhetorical criticism.

---

84. Neil Elliott, *The Rhetoric of Romans* (JSNTSup 45; Sheffield: Sheffield Academic, 1990), 101. Elliott (p. 66) comments, "These parts of the epistolary 'frame', we will argue, correspond functionally to the rhetorical *exordium* and *peroratio*." See also Probst, *Paulus und der Brief*, 99–107; Wiard Popkes, "Paraenesis in the New Testament: An Exercise in Conceptuality," in *Early Christian Paraenesis in Context*, ed. James Starr and Troels Engberg-Pedersen (BZNW 125; Berlin: Walter de Gruyter, 2005), 13–46; Troels Engberg-Pedersen, "The Concept of Paraenesis," in Starr and Engberg-Pedersen, *Early Christian Paraenesis*, 47–72; and especially James Starr, "Was Paraenesis for Beginners?" in Starr and Engberg-Pedersen, *Early Christian Paraenesis*, 73–111.

85. David E. Aune, "Romans as a Logos Protreptikos in the Context of Ancient Religious and Philosophical Propaganda," in *Paulus und das antike Judentum: Tübingen-Durham-Symposium im Gedenken an den 50. Todestag Adolf Schlatters (†19.Mai 1938)*, ed. Martin Hengel and Ulrich Heckel (WUNT 58; Tübingen: Mohr Siebeck, 1991), 119; David Hellholm, "Enthymemic Argumentation in Paul: The Case of Romans 6," in *Paul and His Hellenistic Context*, ed. Troels Engberg-Pedersen (Minneapolis: Fortress, 1995), 135–138, and idem, "Amplificatio," in Porter and Olbricht, *Rhetoric and the New Testament*, 141.

86. Betz, " Literary Composition," 375 n. 9.

87. Lauri Thurén, "Motivation as the Core of Paraenesis: Remarks on Peter and Paul as Persuaders," in Starr and Engberg-Pedersen, *Early Christian Paraenesis*, 354–356.

Focus on Invention

New Testament Rhetorical Critics eventually turn their attention from arrangement to invention. In 1996, Anders Eriksson observes, "This interest in the text's power to persuade is distinctive for the present-day phase of rhetorical criticism. Interest in the *dispositio* of the text has given way to an interest in the *inventio* that is, the rhetorical situation, the rhetorical strategy and the argumentation in the text."[88] Once again, these critics rely on Betz's pioneering efforts, and this third focus on invention points to him as the first practitioner of New Testament rhetorical criticism.[89]

In his lecture, Betz states that invention or the selection and marshaling of proofs is "the most decisive part of the speech."[90] He further states that Paul's letter to the Galatians has a coherent flow of thought that responds persuasively to the *causa* of the case. Betz then explores the means of argumentation as outlined in the rhetorical handbooks that respond to the *causa*. Although he concentrates on the logical means of argument, he also mentions ethical and pathetic as well as topical argumentation. Subsequent rhetorical critics explore all of these aspects of invention. Thus, the "new" *inventio* phase of

88. Anders Eriksson, "Special Topics in 1 Corinthians 8–10," in *The Rhetorical Interpretation of Scripture: Essays from the 1996 Malibu Conference*, ed. Stanley E. Porter and Dennis L. Stamps (JSNTSup 180; Sheffield: Sheffield Academic, 1999), 272–273. On p. 277, Eriksson explains this new development: "During the era of form-critical investigation of the pre-Pauline traditions in the Pauline text, attention was focused on the pre-history of the text. . . . In the new *inventio* phase of rhetorical criticism, attention is focused upon how these traditions function as rhetorical proofs in Paul's argumentation." See also idem, *Traditions as Rhetorical Proof: Pauline Argumentation in 1 Corinthians* (ConBNT 29; Stockholm: Amqvist & Wiksell International, 1998), 10. For examples of this shift of emphasis, see Anthony C. Thiselton, *The First Epistle to the Corinthians: A Commentary on the Greek Text* (NIGTC; Grand Rapids: Eerdmans, 2000), 41–52; Dieter Sänger, "'Vergeblich bemüht' (Gal 4.11)?: Zur paulinischen Argumentationsstrategie im Galaterbrief," *NTS* 48, no. 3 (2002): 377–399; and Hans-Josef Klauck, *Ancient Letters and the New Testament: A Guide to Context and Exegesis* (Waco: Baylor University, 2006), 225.

89. For a survey of the numerous studies on rhetorical invention since Betz, see Martin, "Invention and Arrangement," 75–117.

90. Betz, "Literary Composition," 368.

Pauline rhetorical studies takes its direction from Betz as the first practitioner of this focus in New Testament rhetorical criticism.

Determining the *Causa*

In his lecture, Betz comments on Gal 1:6, "This statement of the *causa* of the case, the reason why the letter was written, contains the 'facts' that occasioned the letter." Apart from this brief comment, Betz proposes no method for identifying the *causa* even though such identification is crucial for understanding the argumentation.[91] Subsequent rhetorical critics are therefore left to devise their own means. Some find the *causa* in the parts of speech and especially in the *partitio* or the *propositio*.[92] Others find the *causa* in the stasis or issue addressed in a speech.[93] Due to the influence of Kennedy's programmatic book, however, the majority find the *causa* in the rhetorical situation.[94] Regardless of where they find the *causa*, subsequent rhetorical critics nevertheless follow Betz's lead as the first practitioner to recognize the importance of the *causa* for understanding argumentation in New Testament documents.

---

91. Hellholm, "Enthymemic Argumentation," 139. Hellholm explains, "In argumentation analyses one must first establish the thesis of the proponent. Only then is it meaningful to relate the pro- and counter-arguments of the disputing parties to each other."

92. Watson, "Contributions and Limitations of Greco-Roman Rhetorical Theory," in Porter and Stamps, *The Rhetorical Interpretation of Scripture*, 144; Margaret M. Mitchell, *Paul and the Rhetoric of Reconciliation: An Exegetical Investigation of the Language and Composition of 1 Corinthians* (Louisville: Westminister John Knox, 1993), 65-66; and Hellholm, "Enthymemic Argumentation," 139. For additional examples, see Martin, "Invention and Arrangement," 78–79.

93. For a description of stasis theory, see Troy W. Martin, "Apostasy to Paganism: The Rhetorical Stasis of the Galatian Controversy," in Nanos, *The Galatians Debate*, 74–75. For a discussion and examples of those who use stasis theory to find the *causa*, see Martin, "Invention and Arrangement," 87–92.

94. Kennedy, *New Testament Interpretation*, 34–35. For a discussion of the rhetorical situation and examples of those who use it to find the *causa*, see Martin, "Invention and Arrangement," 79–87.

Means of Argumentation

In his 1974 lecture, Betz uses the Aristotelian categories of *logos*, *ethos*, *pathos*, and *topos* as well as the theories of other ancient rhetoricians to describe the means of argumentation in Paul's letter to the Galatians. Following Betz's lead, subsequent rhetorical critics principally rely on these four categories. Again, following Betz's lead, these critics initially concentrate on the logical means of argumentation by exploring the enthymeme and the paradigm. In his keynote address to the 1995 London Conference on Rhetorical Criticism, Vernon Robbins outlines an agenda for rhetorical critics and states, "The first place I see us working together is with assertions and rationales—the components of the rhetorical enthymeme."[95] Both the enthymeme and the paradigm become important tools to analyze New Testament logical argumentation, but this concentration on logical argumentation begins with Betz.

Betz's lesser emphasis on the other means of argumentation probably contributes to the delay of investigating them as a means of argumentation in New Testament texts. Regarding *ethos*, John Marshall observes, "Though ethos is almost universally praised as an extremely powerful means of persuasion, it has received only cursory treatment in both ancient and modern theories and applications of rhetoric, and what treatment it has received is confused and confusing."[96] Watson's survey of rhetorical studies from 1975 to 1995 cites Marshall's article on Philippians as "one of the few discussions of ethos in biblical argumentation."[97]

---

95. Vernon K. Robbins, "The Present and Future of Rhetorical Analysis," in Porter and Olbricht, *The Rhetorical Analysis of Scripture*, 33.

96. John W. Marshall, "Paul's Ethical Appeal in Philippians," in Porter and Olbricht, *Rhetoric and the New Testament*, 358.

97. Duane F. Watson, "Rhetorical Criticism of the Pauline Epistles since 1975," *CurBS* 3 (1995): 235. See also David E. Aune, "Ethos," in idem, *The Westminster Dictionary of New Testament and Early Christian Literature and Rhetoric* (Louisville, KY: Westminster John Knox, 2003), 169–73.

Regarding *pathos*, Thomas Olbricht comments in his 2001 volume entitled *Paul and Pathos*, "This volume undertakes to address a neglected aspect of the rhetorical analysis of the Scriptures, that is, emotional appeal, or as designated by the Greek rhetoricians *pathos*."[98] Although slow to investigate *ethos* and *pathos*, rhetorical critics would eventually explore these means of argumentation far beyond what Betz did in his 1974 lecture.[99] Even here, however, Betz's influence as the first practitioner is evident.[100]

Wilhelm Wuellner certainly recognizes Betz as the first practitioner of topical argumentation in New Testament studies. In his classic article addressing topical argumentation, Wuellner writes:

> What H. D. Betz introduced at the S.N.T.S. Meeting in Sigtuna, Sweden in 1974 in regard to the method of exegeting Galatians in general and of interpreting the Pauline view of the law in particular shall here be expanded and in part corrected. The correction refers to what was said there about rhetorical topos in particular and about rhetoric in general.[101]

In this article, Wuellner neither explicitly engages Betz nor specifically states his criticisms of Betz's analysis of the topical

Aune only mentions Mario M. DiCicco as a Pauline rhetorical critic that has investigated ethos in a Pauline letter. See Mario M. DiCicco, *Paul's Use of Ethos, Pathos, and Logos in 2 Corinthians 10–13* (MBP Series 31; Lewiston: Mellen, 1995), passim. However, Aune overlooks George Lyons, *Pauline Autobiography: Toward a New Understanding* (SBLDS 73; Atlanta: Scholars, 1985), 191–201. Lyons is one of the first to examine ethos as a proof in 1 Thessalonians.

98. Thomas H. Olbricht, "Introduction," in *Paul and Pathos*, ed. idem and Jerry L. Sumney (SBLSymS 16; Atlanta: Society of Biblical Literature, 2001), 1. For a summary of pathos in early Christian literature, see Aune, "Ethos," 339–42.

99. For a survey of these studies, see Martin, "Invention and Arrangement," 103–13.

100. For examples of this influence, see Troy W. Martin, "Veiled Exhortations Regarding the Veil: Ethos as the Controlling Proof in Moral Persuasion (1 Cor 11:2–16)," in *Rhetoric, Ethic, and Moral Persuasion in Biblical Discourse: Essays from the 2002 Heidelberg Conference*, ed. Thomas H. Olbricht and Anders Eriksson (ESEC 11; New York: T. & T. Clark, 2005), 255–273; and idem, "The Voice of Emotion: Paul's Pathetic Persuasion (Gal 4:12–20)," in Olbricht and Sumney, *Paul and Pathos*, 189–201.

101. Wilhelm H. Wuellner, "Toposforschung und Torahinterpretation bei Paulus und Jesus," *NTS* 24, no. 4 (1978): 463 (translation mine).

argumentation in Galatians. Instead, he simply presents his own topical analysis and leaves the reader of his article to supply the necessary corrections to Betz's analysis. Although he disagrees with Betz, Wuellner nevertheless recognizes him as the one who introduces topical argumentation into New Testament rhetorical criticism.

In this "new *inventio* phase," therefore, rhetorical critics follow Betz's lead and investigate the New Testament according to classical invention, which includes the logical, ethical, pathetic, and topical means of arguing the *causa* or rhetorical argumentative issue. Betz is thus the first practitioner of this third rhetorical-critical focus on *inventio* just as much as he is the initial practitioner of the first focus on rhetorical species and of the second on rhetorical arrangement. As the first practitioner of these three foci, Betz is therefore the Ur-ancestor or progenitor of the method of New Testament rhetorical criticism, as prominent New Testament scholars recognized as early as the 1970s.

Peroratio

Although our mission in this chapter appeared impossible, the demonstration of our proposition was not. Betz indeed belongs at the very beginning of the genealogical list of New Testament rhetorical criticism. He is the Ur-ancestor and progenitor because he initiates, discovers, and first practices this method in the 1970s before anyone else. The massive number of rhetorical-critical studies produced from that time until now only confirms our proposition.

By calling Betz the "Ur-ancestor" or "progenitor" as the initiator, discoverer, and first practitioner of this method, we are not claiming that the method of rhetorical criticism has not developed beyond him, for indeed it has. His seminal rhetorical insights give rise to a rich diversity in the application and use of rhetorical criticism for interpreting and understanding the New Testament. In the chapters that follow, the other contributors to this volume will describe some of the other early important mothers and fathers who also belong in the genealogical list of New Testament rhetorical criticism. These other rhetorical ancestors contribute significantly to the new and diverse directions taken by this method first introduced, discovered, and practiced in 1974 by Betz as the Ur-ancestor of New Testament rhetorical criticism.

2

Response to Troy W. Martin and Additional Reflections

Hans Dieter Betz

It is an honor and pleasure to respond briefly to Troy Martin's appreciative chapter he has so enthusiastically written. After expressing my thanks to him, I will make every effort to avoid Plutarch's caveats in his essay "On Inoffensive Self-Praise (Periautologia)," on which I once wrote a paper myself.[1] Then, I shall comment on some of Troy Martin's assertions. The question raised by Carl Joachim Classen is serious and deserves a thoughtful answer. Why was rhetorical criticism not discovered before my 1974 lecture, since in some forms it was already there? If I discovered that

1. Hans Dieter Betz, "De laude ipsius (Plut. *Mor.* 539A–547F)," in *Plutarch's Ethical Writings and Early Christian Literature*, ed. idem (SCHNT 4; Leiden: Brill, 1978), 367–93.

rhetorical analysis was applicable to the Pauline letters, I mean by the term *invent* (*inventio*) to have "discovered" something in a way similar to the unknown ancestor who "invented" the wheel. Certainly, the wheel was there as a possibility, but the "inventor" discovered its usefulness for transportation.

In 1974, I did not at first understand the impact of my first attempt to analyze Galatians according to Greco-Roman rhetoric. My experience was similar to Ernst Käsemann's when he gave his famous lecture on the "Historical Jesus" in 1953.[2] I myself was present at his lecture, but I did not understand it. When I confessed this to Käsemann many years later, he said that he himself also did not understand at that time what kind of storm of research he had unleashed.

When I gave my own lecture on the rhetorical analysis of Galatians about 20 years later in 1974, there was at first an almost total rejection of my approach by the *Studiorum Novi Testamenti Societas* membership. Only half a dozen members expressed their approval. Afterwards, approval came slowly but increasingly. Slow approval is typical, especially in the practical sciences where acceptance of a hypothesis occurs only after tests and experience with a new product.

My discovery of rhetorical criticism began long before 1974. After all, I had read Georg Heinrici's commentaries, Rudolf Bultmann's dissertation of 1910, and the works and debates on *Formgeschichte* and *Redaktionsgeschichte*, not to mention scores of texts in Greek and Latin. Lucian of Samosata, the subject of my doctoral dissertation, offers plenty of examples of all sorts of rhetoric.

---

2. Ernst Käsemann, "Das Problem des historischen Jesus," *ZTK* 51, no. 1 (1954), 125–53. Käsemann gave this lecture at a reunion of the "Old Marburgers" on 20 October 1953. It was later translated and published as "The Problem of the Historical Jesus," in idem, *Essays on New Testament Themes* (SBT 41; London: SCM, 1964), 15–47.

What left me puzzled, however, was a specific oddity. When I consulted New Testament commentaries, I noticed that they used concepts such as "Aufbau" or "Inhaltsverzeichnis" to establish an outline for New Testament documents without explaining what these terms mean and how one would go about substantiating these outlines. These commentaries provided no rationale beyond what their authors "guessed" the outline and contents to be. These outlines were thus mere "guesswork," and much of the learned debates about the content of these New Testament documents was therefore also "guesswork," often declared to be "theology."

Simply joining these kinds of debates did not make sense to me, and I did not think it worthwhile to write another such commentary on Galatians that was based on guesswork. Otherwise, understanding the text of Galatians would simply come down to agreeing or disagreeing with doctrinal presuppositions. My goal had to be to "discover" what the text itself had to say not only in its own time but also in our own time as well. As I worked out the Galatians commentary, only gradually did it dawn on me that rhetorical criticism opens up a new way to understand texts and their "hermeneutics."

Years later when I met with some colleagues in Geneva (thanks to an invitation from François Bovon), Jean Zumstein said his French-educated parishioners told him that with this rhetorical method they could now understand what Paul was talking about. Why? They could understand because part of their school training was determined by their French "rational" education based on ancient Latin rhetoric.

Why was rhetorical criticism not discovered earlier? Well, as many have now found out, there was rhetorical criticism of sorts at work in some patristic authors, especially St. Augustine, Erasmus, and of course Melanchthon. Even Luther's principle of "dem Volke auf das

Maul schauen" was rhetorical. However, subsequent trends in the sixteenth to nineteenth centuries emphasized theological doctrines as affirmed by "Scripture," and, consequently, rhetoric was denigrated as pretentious jargon or superficial babble. This period of Scripture interpretation largely ended with the twentieth century, but lingered on into the twentieth century under the banners of Barthianism, Heideggerism, or other "-isms."

The significance of "rhetorical criticism" is missed if it simply becomes a new faddish jargon, replacing older jargons. In my understanding, "rhetorical criticism" is a scientific approach to expressions of language in literary as well as non-literary traditions. The objects are therefore the "texts" at hand and not ideological overlays. First, these texts must be established by the methods of "textual criticism." Then, their category and transmission must be determined by "form-, redaction- and literary criticism." These methods must also be informed by their general literary, historical, social, cultural and religious environments, and their specific contexts. The combination of these methods constitutes the so-called "historical-critical" methodology to be applied to the specific texts at hand. The results can then be applied to our own "contexts" in present situations through the multifaceted process of "hermeneutics."

In my view, every text at hand, Christian or non-Christian, is a specific linguistic entity requiring a fresh "invention" regarding its various rhetorical forms. Rather than the application of external labels or the imposition of predetermined conceptual grids, the text must always be the starting point. Consequently, my own initial efforts to analyze Galatians rhetorically led to quite different applications of rhetoric in my works on the "administrative letters" of 2 Corinthians 8–9, the "catechetical epitomes" of the "Sermon on the Mount (Matt

5–7)" and the "Sermon on the Plain (Luke 6:20–49)," and the "'Mithras' Liturgy."[3]

As far as my own work as a "Neutestamentler" is concerned, I can only say that my gradual understanding of rhetorical criticism has profoundly changed my perception of the New Testament and other ancient and even modern texts. For me, the test of validity of any method and especially rhetorical criticism is a better understanding of texts that leads to a better understanding of their significance.

3. Hans Dieter Betz, *Galatians: A Commentary on Paul's Letter to the Churches of Galatia* (Hermeneia; Philadelphia: Fortress, 1979); idem, *Second Corinthians 8 and 9: A Commentary on Two Administrative Letters of the Apostle Paul* (Hermeneia; Philadelphia: Fortress, 1985); idem, *The Sermon on the Mount: A Commentary on the Sermon on the Mount, including the Sermon on the Plain (Matthew 5:3–7:27 and Luke 6:20–49)* (Hermeneia; Minneapolis: Fortress, 1995); and idem, *The "Mithras Liturgy:" Text, Translation and Commentary* (Studien und Texte zu Antike und Christentum 18; Tübingen: Mohr Siebeck, 2003).

3

———

Genealogies of Rhetorical Criticism: The Kennedy Family

C. Clifton Black

Gauging the impact of George A. Kennedy (b. 1928) on biblical studies is not easy.[1] Like the work of other exponents of rhetorical investigation considered in this volume, Kennedy's approach has been adopted, adapted, and extended to such a degree that assessing its full measure is practically impossible. After decades of development, the various threads of rhetorical criticism have by now become so intertwined that disentangling them is difficult.

1. I am grateful to Baylor University Press for permission to include material from my chapter "Kennedy and the Gospels: An Ambiguous Legacy, A Promising Bequest," in *Words Well Spoken: George Kennedy's Rhetoric of the New Testament*, ed. C. Clifton Black and Duane F. Watson (SRR 8; Waco, TX: Baylor University Press, 2008), 63–80.

Of all the interpreters recognized in this book, Kennedy is the only non-New Testament specialist. Let us pause to ponder that achievement. Few scholars in any field produce works that establish critical points of reference for their colleagues. Far fewer generate scholarship with which those standing beyond their tightly hedged perimeters are expected to become conversant. Kennedy belongs among that rare breed. In three substantial tomes plus numerous one-volume histories and handbooks, his scholarship has set a standard for depth and breadth unlikely to be bettered in our generation.[2] Beyond that, Kennedy is the most hospitable of critics and is happy to push himself beyond an expert's comfortable boundaries to maintain conversation with those in other academic sectors.

While offering biblical interpreters an important study that reframes conventional approaches to the Gospels' source criticism, Kennedy is best known for his book *New Testament Interpretation through Rhetorical Criticism*, now a standard entry in exegetes' footnotes and bibliographies.[3] When published in 1984, a foundation

2. George A. Kennedy's magisterial "History of Rhetoric" comprises *The Art of Persuasion in Greece* (Princeton: Princeton University Press, 1963); idem, *The Art of Rhetoric in the Roman World 300 B.C.–A.D. 300* (Princeton: Princeton University Press, 1972), and idem, *Greek Rhetoric under Christian Emperors* (Princeton: Princeton University Press, 1983). Kennedy's single-volume histories and handbooks include idem, *Quintilian* (TWAS; New York: Twayne, 1969); idem, *Classical Rhetoric and Its Christian and Secular Tradition from Ancient to Modern Times* (Chapel Hill: University of North Carolina Press, 1980); Aristotle, *On Rhetoric: A Theory of Civic Discourse*, trans. George A. Kennedy (New York: Oxford University Press, 1991); George A. Kennedy, *A New History of Classical Rhetoric* (Princeton: Princeton University Press, 1994).

3. George A. Kennedy, *New Testament Interpretation through Rhetorical Criticism* (Chapel Hill: University of North Carolina Press, 1984). For his important study on source criticism, see George A. Kennedy, "Classical and Christian Source Criticism," in *The Relationship among the Gospels: An Interdisciplinary Dialogue*, ed. William O. Walker Jr. (TUMSR 5; San Antonio: Trinity University Press, 1978), 125–55. Wisely sidestepping the controversies swirling around Q, Griesbach, and hypotheses two-source and two-Gospel, Kennedy posits an intervening use of notes (*hypomnēmata*) that were privately recorded at the time of a discourse or soon thereafter. These notes were "the raw material from which more formal publications [could] be created" (ibid., 136). Such publications could take the form of memoirs (*apomnēmoneumata*), and Justin Martyr uses this very term to characterize the Gospels (*1 Apol.* 66.3; 67.3). Thus, some of the earliest witnesses of Jesus' ministry may have made and later returned to such notes,

for this handbook's reception had already been laid. In the 1950s and 1960s, James Muilenburg and Amos Wilder had drawn attention to the inherently literary properties of biblical discourse.[4] During the following decade, Hans Dieter Betz's seminal article on Galatians offered a preview of his Hermeneia commentary, both of which drew from classical models of discourse.[5] Drawing from his vast knowledge of the history of oratory, Kennedy's distinctive contribution was to synthesize and systematize the implications of classical rhetoric for New Testament exegesis as a whole.

Revisiting Kennedy's Rhetorical Criticism

The practice of oratory is as old as Homer (ninth or eighth century BCE), whose epics are punctuated with heroic speeches that are

as did Plutarch, Suetonius, and other ancient historiographers. See Kennedy, "Classical and Christian Source Criticism," 147–52, and compare the comments of Papias of Hierapolis cited in Eusebius, *Hist. eccl.* 3.39.15–16. Kennedy intended to rein in a reflexive skepticism toward patristic commentators: "ancient writers sometimes meant what they said and occasionally even knew what they were talking about" (p. 126). For critical appreciations of this postulate, see Wayne A. Meeks, "*Hypomnēmata* from an Untamed Sceptic: A Response to George Kennedy," in Walker, *The Relationship Among the Gospels*, 157–72; W. D. Davies and Dale C. Allison, Jr., *A Critical and Exegetical Commentary on the Gospel according to Saint Matthew* (ICC; Edinburgh: T&T Clark, 1988), 1:12–17; and C. Clifton Black, *Mark: Images of an Apostolic Interpreter* (SPNT; Minneapolis: Fortress and T&T Clark, 2001), 92–94.

4. James Muillenburg, "The Book of Isaiah, Chapters 40–66: Introduction and Exegesis," in *The Interpreter's Bible, Volume 5: Ecclesiastes, Song of Songs, Isaiah, Jeremiah*, ed. George A. Buttrick (Nashville: Abingdon, 1956), 381–773; idem, "Form Criticism and Beyond," *JBL* 88, no. 1 (1969): 1–18; Amos N. Wilder, "Scholars, Theologians and Ancient Rhetoric," *JBL* 75, no. 1 (1956): 1–11; idem, *Early Christian Rhetoric: The Language of the Gospel* (Cambridge, MA: Harvard University Press, 1964).

5. Hans Dieter Betz, "The Literary Composition and Function of Paul's Letter to the Galatians," *NTS* 21 (1975): 353–79; idem, *Galatians: A Commentary on Paul's Letter to the Churches in Galatia* (Philadelphia: Fortress, 1979). Even before Betz, interpreters used rhetoric to interpret scripture. See the Venerable Bede (c. 672–735), "Concerning Figures and Tropes," available in *Readings in Medieval Rhetoric*, ed. Joseph M. Miller, Michael H. Proser, and Thomas W. Benson (Bloomington: Indiana University Press, 1973), 96–122; Judah Messer Leon (c. 1420–1498), *The Book of the Honeycomb's Flow* (Ithaca: Cornell University Press, 1982); Eduard Norden, *Die antike Kunstprosa vom VI. Jahrhunderts vor Christus in die Zeit der Renaissance* (Leipzig: Teubner, 1909); idem, *Agnostos Theos: Untersuchungen zur Formgeschichte religiöser Rede* (Leipzig: Teubner, 1913).

exquisite testimonies of the bard's own oratorical craft.[6] By the fifth century BCE, the Sicilian teacher Corax (Tisias) compiles technical handbooks on rhetoric for use by Greek citizens in political assemblies and courts of law.[7] Gorgias (c. 480–375 BCE) and Isocrates (c. 436–338 BCE) refine the sophistic approach to rhetoric that includes the orator's skillful deployment of rhyme and rhythmic embellishments to move or to entertain an audience. A backlash against the morally vacuous exploitation of sophistic rhetoric appears in some of Plato's dialogues (c. 429–347 BCE; esp. *Gorgias* and *Phaedrus*). Yet, Plato's own pupil Aristotle (384–322 BCE) systematizes the theoretical substructure of classical rhetoric and relates its practice to the arts, sciences, and dialectical logic in particular.[8]

With the Hellenization of the Mediterranean world, first by Alexander the Great (356–323 BCE) and later by imperial Rome (27 BCE–476 CE), rhetoric becomes essential in secondary education for preparing Roman citizens to advance in public life.[9] Although it is impossible and perhaps needless to demonstrate that Jesus, the earliest apostles, or the Gospel writers were formally trained in rhetoric, indisputably they live in a culture whose everyday modes of discourse are saturated with a rhetorical tradition that is mediated by such practitioners and theoreticians as Caecilius (a Sicilian Jew of the late first century BCE), Cicero (106–43 BCE), and Quintilian (c. 40–95 CE).

---

6. Peter Toohey, "Epic and Rhetoric" in *Persuasion: Greek Rhetoric in Action*, ed. Ian Worthington (London; Routledge, 1994), 153–73. Toohey articulates the structure and elaboration in Nestor's four speeches of the *Iliad* (1.254–84; 7.124–60; 11.656–803; 23.626–50)—an unexpected level of development, since Homeric epic antedates the disciplined formulation of rhetoric by centuries. The following summary draws heavily on C. Clifton Black, *The Rhetoric of the Gospel: Theological Artistry in the Gospels and Acts* (2nd ed.; Louisville: Westminster John Knox, 2013), 2–19.

7. See Edward M. Harris, "Law and Oratory," in Worthington, *Persuasion,* 130–40.

8. Consult Amélie Oksenberg Rorty, ed., *Essays on Aristotle's Rhetoric* (Berkeley: University of California Press, 1996).

9. A standard history of the subject is Stanley F. Bonner, *Education in Ancient Rome: From the Elder Cato to the Younger Pliny* (Berkeley: University of California Press, 1977).

Throughout the patristic period, the influence of technical and sophistic rhetoric on Christian preaching, teaching, and apologetics is conspicuous in the Greek sermons of John Chrysostom (c. 347–407 CE) and the three great Cappadocians: Gregory of Nazianzus (c. 329–389 CE), Basil of Caesarea (c. 330-379 CE), and Gregory of Nyssa (c. 330-395 CE).[10] Of the eight most notable Latin fathers of the church, three are schooled in rhetoric: Hilary of Poitiers (c. 315–367 CE), Ambrose (c. 337–397 CE), and Jerome (c. 342–420 CE). The rest had been professional rhetoricians before their conversion to Christianity. These include Tertullian (c. 160–225 CE), Cyprian (d. c. 258 CE), Arnobius (d. c. 330 CE), Lactantius (c. 240–320 CE), and Augustine (354-430 CE). In *De doctrina christiana*, Augustine is the first to tease out implications of rhetorical theory for Christian belief and practice as well as for hermeneutics and homiletics.[11]

Not only does rhetorical study pervade the Christian patrology; it also enriches the medieval, Renaissance, and Enlightenment academic legacy of which modern students are legatees. As barbarism descends on Italy, Cassiodorus Senator (c. 490–585 CE) keeps aflame the study of rhetoric and the other six liberal arts (grammar, dialectic, geometry, arithmetic, astronomy, and music) from his monastery at Vivarium.[12] During the European Renaissance and Reformation, the renewal of biblical criticism and the recovery of Ciceronian rhetoric fits hand-in-glove in the humanistic scholarship of Lorenzo Valla (c. 1406–1457 CE), Desiderius Erasmus (1469–1536 CE), Philipp

---

10. See Jaroslav Pelikan, *Divine Rhetoric: The Sermon on the Mount as Message and as Model in Augustine, Chrysostom, and Luther* (Crestwood: St. Vladimir's Seminary Press, 2001), and Margaret M. Mitchell, *The Heavenly Trumpet: John Chrysostom and the Art of Pauline Interpretation* (Louisville: Westminster John Knox, 2002).

11. Augustine, *De Doctrina Christiana*, trans. R. P. H. Green (Oxford: Clarendon, 1995). Green's is the standard critical edition. On Augustine's approach to rhetoric, see Black, *The Rhetoric of the Gospel*, 142–46.

12. Cassiodorus Senator, *An Introduction to Divine and Human Readings*, trans. Leslie Webber Jones (New York: Norton, 1969).

Melanchthon (1497–1560 CE), and John Calvin (1509–1564 CE). Buoyed by the neoclassical revival of the arts in Europe and North America during the eighteenth and nineteenth centuries, rhetorical modes of New Testament analysis ripple into the early twentieth century, as illustrated by the dissertation of the young Rudolf Bultmann (1884–1976 CE)[13] and the still standard grammar of New Testament Greek by Friedrich Wilhelm Blass (1843–1907 CE).[14] All told, the exercise and conceptualization of classical rhetoric constitute one of the oldest approaches to New Testament interpretation.

Enter Kennedy, for whom rhetoric refers to the disciplined art of persuasion practiced and theorized by Greeks and Romans of the classical and Hellenistic periods. Kennedy explains, "What we need to do is to try to hear [early Christian authors'] words as a Greek-speaking audience would have heard them, and that involves some understanding of classical rhetoric."[15] In particular, Kennedy advocates an understanding of the norms of discourse conceptualized in classical handbooks.[16]

To amplify our audition, Kennedy's method of rhetorical criticism unfolds in six steps.[17]

1. Determine the rhetorical unit to be analyzed. As form critics identify discrete pericopae, so also rhetorical critics such as Kennedy search for evidence of *inclusio*, opening and closure, in a unit of discourse with some magnitude.

---

13. Rudolf Bultmann, *Der Stil der paulinischen Predigt und die kynisch-stoische Diatribe*, FRLANT 13 (Göttingen: Vandenhoeck & Ruprecht, 1910).
14. Friedrich Wilhelm Blass and Albert Debrunner, *A Greek Grammar of the New Testament*, ed. and trans. Robert W. Funk (Chicago: University of Chicago Press, 1961; 1st German ed. 1896).
15. Kennedy, *New Testament Interpretation,* 10.
16. Principally, Aristotle's *Ars rhetorica*, Cicero's *De inventione, Rhetorica ad Herennium* (of disputed authorship), and Quintilian's *Institutio oratoria*. All are available, with English translation, in the LCL. See also Hermogenes, *On Types of Style*, trans. Cecil W. Wooten (Chapel Hill: University of North Carolina Press, 1987).
17. For Kennedy's discussion of these six steps, see his *New Testament Interpretation*, 33–8.

2. Define the rhetorical situation. What complex of persons, events, and relations generates pressure for a verbal response? With this move, one might compare the form critic's discovery of a genre's *Sitz im Leben* or setting in life.

3. Identify the primary problem addressed by the discourse. Kennedy suggests two classical frameworks within which such identification can be made. One may pinpoint the *stasis* or specific question at issue.[18] Alternatively, the critic can ascertain the kind of judgment an audience is asked to render. Is it a *judicial* assessment of past circumstances such as the character of Paul's prior ministry in Corinth, to which much of 2 Corinthians refers? Is it a *deliberative* reckoning of actions expedient or beneficial for the listeners' future performance, such as Jesus' exhortations in the Sermon on the Mount in Matthew 5–7? Or is it the *epideictic* instillation and enhancement of beliefs or values in the present as, for instance, Jesus' farewell address to his disciples in John 14–17?[19]

4. Consider the arrangement (*taxis*) of the parts into a unified discourse. Compared with the structure of deliberative and

---

18. Stasis theory differentiates legal questions at issue. Whether or not Jesus healed on the sabbath (John 5:19, 16; 9:14) is a question of fact. One may admit a fact but debate its definition by asking whether the healer was a sinner (John 9:24–25). Facts and definitions may be granted, though their circumstances are controversial (Mark 2:23–27; 3:2–4) or an agent's jurisdiction is disputable (Mark 2:7, 10, 28). Hermogenes of Tarsus (2nd century CE) refined older theories of stasis; see Raymond E. Nadeau, ed. and trans., "*On Stases*: A Translation with an Introduction and Notes," *SM* 31 (1964): 361–424.

19. Examples of all these genres are found in W. Robert Connor, ed., *Greek Orations, 4th Century B.C.: Lysias, Isocrates, Demosthenes, Aeschines, Hyperides, and Letter of Philip* (Prospect Heights: Waveland, 1987). Great speeches in modern history also conform to these basic types. Lincoln's Gettysburg Address (19 November 1863) is an unforgettable instance of epideictic "that government of the people, by the people, for the people, shall not perish from the earth." Zola's demand that Dreyfus be exonerated of treason (22 February 1898) lodges a judicial plea: "[Dreyfus] is innocent: I swear it; I stake my life on it—my honor!" Churchill's appeal to Parliament for approval of Britain's war against Germany (13 May 1940) is essentially deliberative and memorable for his alliterative offer of "nothing … but blood, toil, tears, and sweat."

epideictic address, judicial oratory displays the most elaborate arrangement. It includes an introductory *proem*, followed by a *narration* of background information, the *proposition* to be proved, the *proof* itself, *refutation* of contrary views, and a concluding *epilogue*.

5. Analyze the discourse's invention (*heuresis*) and style (*lexis*). Invention is the crafting of arguments based on proofs. These proofs include *ēthos*, the persuasive power of the speaker's authoritative character (see Mark 1:22); *pathos*, the emotional responses generated among listeners (thus, Acts 2:37); and *logos*, the deductive or inductive arguments of the discourse itself (e.g., Heb. 1:1–2:14). Style refers to the text's choice of words and their formulation in "figures" of speech and of thought.

6. Finally, assess the unit's rhetorical effectiveness in light of the entire analysis.

These six steps constitute Kennedy's method of rhetorical criticism, and many rhetorical critics consider them standard procedure for rhetorical analysis.

Critical Receptions of Kennedy's Approach

Commenting on *New Testament Interpretation through Rhetorical Criticism*, Wayne Meeks proves perceptive and prescient when he writes that "up until now there has been no general introduction to this kind of analysis.... Kennedy's book is therefore sure to find an eager audience, especially because of his acknowledged stature as one of the leading authorities of classical rhetoric."[20] Embedded in that accolade are three reasons why Kennedy's work made an impression.

---

20. Meeks's endorsement appears on the dust jacket of Kennedy, *New Testament Interpretation*.

First, Kennedy's approach is a "general introduction." Except for the Catholic Epistles and Revelation, Kennedy surveys New Testament discourse as a whole while Betz offers total immersion only in Galatians.[21] Kennedy invites us aboard a Chris-Craft to zip across Gospels, the speeches in Acts, and Paul's epistles.[22]

Second, Kennedy offers a "kind of analysis" and not merely an interpretive attitude but an articulated method of study that attempts to bridge the gap between the oral and aural environment assumed by form critics and the redactional properties of written documents. Instead of typing paradigms and tales and legends, now we can grade genres for their deliberative, epideictic, and forensic intent. Kennedy gives us tools to distinguish pertinent stases, and we can itemize invention, arrangement, style, and, hypothetically, memory and delivery as well.[23] An overlooked quality of Kennedy's own style is the clarity of his prose. Had his own rhetoric been turbid, I doubt his path would have encouraged many followers, notwithstanding a masochism that thrives like kudzu in the groves of academe.

Third, Meeks recognizes Kennedy's "stature as one of the leading authorities of classical rhetoric." That acknowledgement is no fulsome praise but a statement of fact. Nevertheless, the present volume would not devote chapters to Kennedy's scholarship had he not pushed beyond his guild's bounds and actually conversed with biblical scholars. That conversation is evident during the 1980s in his

---

21. One of the book's briefest, most biting reviews is by Hans Dieter Betz, "Review: George A. Kennedy, *New Testament Interpretation through Rhetorical Criticism* (Chapel Hill: University of North Carolina Press, 1984)," *JTS* 37 [1986]: 166–67. Betz criticizes the book's "almost total disregard for current scholarship" and analyses lacking any "independent and informed research." Betz further upbraids Kennedy for consigning much New Testament rhetoric to the "'sacred language' of revelation…exist[ing] still in modern existentialism and fundamentalism" and impervious to criticism. Betz's criticism, in my judgment, misreads much of Kennedy's argument and especially his book's conclusion (127–60).

22. Kennedy, *New Testament Interpretation*, 97–113, 114–40, and 141–56 (focused on Thessalonians, Galatians, and Romans).

23. Classical handbooks regard these five elements as rhetorically indispensable: *De Inv.* 1.7.9; *De or.* 1.31.142; *Rhet. ad Her.* 1.2.3; *Inst.* 3.3.1.

seminars at UNC Chapel Hill, where he welcomed many graduate students in New Testament from Duke. Among them was Duane F. Watson, who, more than any scholar I know, has developed Kennedy's approach to New Testament study.[24]

New Testament Epistles

To paraphrase Wilhelm Wuellner, where has Kennedy's rhetorical criticism taken us?[25] The New Testament's letters, Pauline and otherwise, have received the lion's share of attention. Within that ambit, much research to date has been concentrated on formal concerns such as a letter's pattern of argument and the degree to which that structure conforms with, or deviates from, classical canons for oratorical arrangement. In recent scholarship, Betz is among the first to bring this dish to the table, Kennedy adds his own seasonings, and the kitchen has been bustling ever since.[26]

After years of educing exordia, narrations, refutations, and perorations from the Pauline, Deutero-Pauline, and Catholic epistles, we have now arrived at a highly contentious point—namely, whether ancient writers of letters intended to adopt rhetorical canons and, therefore, whether we should be reading epistles as though they

24. Representative among Watson's many books and essays are *Invention, Arrangement, and Style: Rhetorical Criticism of Jude and 2 Peter* (SBLDS 104; Atlanta: Scholars, 1988); "Paul's Speech to the Ephesian Elders (Acts 20.17–38): Epideictic Rhetoric of Farewell," in *Persuasive Artistry: Studies in New Testament Rhetoric in Honor of George A. Kennedy*, ed. Duane F. Watson (JSNTSup 50; Sheffield: JSOT, 1991), 184–208; and "James 2 in Light of Greco-Roman Schemes of Argumentation," *NTS* 39 (1993): 94–121.

25. Wilhelm Wuellner, "Where Is Rhetorical Criticism Taking Us?" *CBQ* 49, no. 3 (1987): 448–63.

26. For surveys of ancient rhetoric and the Pauline corpus, see Carl Joachim Classen, "Paulus und die antike Rhetorik," *ZNW* 82 (1991): 1–32; Frank W. Hughes, "George Kennedy's Contribution to Rhetorical Criticism of the Pauline Letters," in Black and Watson, *Words Well Spoken*, 125–37; James D. Hester, "Kennedy and the Reading of Paul: The Energy of Communication," in Black and Watson, *Words Well Spoken*, 139–61; and Troy W. Martin, "Invention and Arrangement in Recent Pauline Rhetorical Studies: A Survey of the Practices and the Problems," in *Paul and Rhetoric*, ed. J. Paul Sampley and Peter Lampe (New York: T&T Clark, 2010), 48–118.

did. Among others, Stanley E. Porter, R. Dean Anderson, Jr., and Philip Kern have issued blistering critiques of what they consider an overwrought appeal to rhetorical handbooks in reading Paul's letters.[27] Jeffrey T. Reed sums up a fundamental concern: "*Functional* similarities between Paul's argumentative style and the rhetorical handbooks do not prove a *formal* relationship between them."[28] Such demurrals have activated a healthy recalibration by such scholars as Thomas Tobin, Michael F. Bird, and Carl Joachim Classen.[29] These scholars are loath to press the Pauline epistles into a Ciceronian cookie-cutter yet refuse to dismiss the apostle's apparent affinity with aspects of classical rhetoric that Eduard Norden noted as far back as 1898.[30] Doubtless that debate will continue.

Meanwhile, stimulating research in Kennedy's mode continues along other tracks. Peter Lampe's exploration of "Affects and Emotions in the Rhetoric of Paul's Letter to Philemon" augments F. Forrester Church's more *logos*-driven examination of the same letter's structure and design.[31] Classicist Carol Poster makes an elegant case for reading the Epistle of James as "philosophical protreptic," which attempts to turn souls to God and neighbor by good speech.[32] Janet

27. Stanley E. Porter, "The Theoretical Justification for Application of Rhetorical Categories to Pauline Epistolary Literature," in *Rhetoric and the New Testament: Essays from the 1992 Heidelberg Conference*, ed. Stanley E. Porter and Thomas H. Olbricht (JSNTSup 90; Sheffield: JSOT, 1993), 100–22; R. Dean Anderson Jr., *Ancient Rhetorical Theory and Paul* (rev. ed.; Leuven: Peeters, 1999); and Philip Kern, *Rhetoric and Galatians: Assessing an Approach to Paul's Epistles* (SNTSMS 101; Cambridge: Cambridge University Press, 1998).

28. Jeffrey T. Reed, "Using Ancient Rhetorical Categories to Interpret Paul's Letters: A Question of Genre," in Porter and Olbricht, *Rhetoric and the New Testament*, 293–324 (quotation, 322).

29. Thomas Tobin, *Paul's Rhetoric in Its Contexts: The Arguments of Romans* (Peabody: Hendrickson, 2004); Michael F. Bird, "Reassessing a Rhetorical Approach to Paul's Letters," *ExpTim* 119 (2008): 374–79; Carl Joachim Classen, "Kann die rhetorische Theorie helfen, das Neue Testament, vor allem die Briefe des Paulus, besser zu verstehen?" *ZNW* 100 (2009): 145–72.

30. Norden, *Die antike Kunstprosa*, passim.

31. Peter Lampe, "Affects and Emotions in the Rhetoric of Paul's Letter to Philemon: A Rhetorical-Psychological Interpretation," in *Philemon in Perspective: Interpreting a Pauline Letter*, ed. D. François Tolmie (Berlin: de Gruyter, 2005), 61–77; F. Forrester Church, "Rhetorical Structure and Design in Paul's Letter to Philemon," *HTR* 61 (1978): 17–33.

Fairweather and J. S. Vos find in Galatians evidence of Paul's practice of sophistic rhetoric.[33] Kennedy notes that this type of rhetoric "is not necessarily depraved, decadent, or in poor taste [but] is that natural aspect of rhetoric which emphasizes the role of the speaker...where allowance is made for genius and inspiration."[34] In these and other ways, researchers employ Kennedy's mode of rhetorical criticism in the study of NT letters.

The Acts of the Apostles and Revelation

In the light of Martin Dibelius's groundbreaking studies of the speeches in Acts six decades ago, Kennedy's influence on reading Luke's second volume has been, to date, surprisingly soft.[35] However, one aspect of ancient rhetoric—the curriculum of *progymnasmata*, exercises in oral and written expression that inculcated Greco-Roman values—has stimulated some interesting explorations of Acts. Explicitly grounded in Kennedy's method and emphasizing Theon's *Progymnasmata* (first century BCE/first century CE), Blake Shipp argues that Luke uses multiple accounts of the Damascus Road episode (Acts 9; 22; 26) to construct a *Paulusbild* that demonstrates an oscillating pattern of resistance to God's will (eventuating in God's restraint) and obedience to God's will (whose consequence is empowerment).[36] Beginning with Theon but moving in a different direction, Kenneth

---

32. Carol Poster, "Words and Works: Philosophical Protreptic and the Epistle of James," in *Rhetorics in the New Millennium: Promise and Fulfillment*, ed. James D. Hester and J. David Hester (SAC; New York: T&T Clark, 2010), 235–53.

33. Janet Fairweather, "The Epistle to the Galatians and Classical Rhetoric," *TynBul* 45 (1994): 1–38, 213–43; Johan S. Vos, "Paul and Sophistic Rhetoric: A Perspective on His Argumentation in the Letter to the Galatians," in *Exploring New Rhetorical Approaches to Galatians: Papers Presented at an International Conference*, ed. D. François Tolmie (AcTSup 9; Bloemfontein: University of the Free State, 2007), 29–52.

34. Kennedy, *Classical Rhetoric and Its Christian and Secular Tradition*, 39–40.

35. Martin Dibelius, *Studies in the Acts of the Apostles*, trans. Heinrich Greeven (New York: Scribner's, 1956; German orig. Göttingen: Vandenhoeck & Ruprecht, 1951).

36. Blake Shipp, *Paul the Reluctant Witness: Power and Weakness in Luke's Portrayal* (Eugene: Wipf & Stock, 2005).

Bass examines a rhetorical aspect of Luke's use of *dei*, the language of divine necessity.[37] Todd Penner argues that pedagogy by *progymnasmata* provided historians such as Luke not only argumentative resources but also a cultural world of thought essentially configured by rhetoric.[38]

Daniel Lynwood Smith opens an avenue of rhetorical investigation that Kennedy barely recognizes by exploring Luke's peculiar technique of interrupting speeches to highlight Lukan Christology and salvation to the Gentiles.[39] Meanwhile, rhetorical exegesis of the Johannine Apocalypse seems still in its infancy, though Greg Carey and Robyn Whitaker are setting us on fresh paths with their complementary considerations of *pathos* in Revelation.[40]

The Gospels

What of the Gospels? Three of the eight chapters in Kennedy's handbook are devoted to them. One chapter is an analysis of Matthew's Sermon on the Mount and Luke's Sermon on the Plain, another focuses on John's Farewell Discourse, and a third summarizes conclusions on the Gospels' rhetoric.[41] Among the canonical Evangelists, Kennedy finds in Matthew the ablest deployment of rhetorical technique. Matthew's Sermon on the Mount displays unity of thought, diversity of tone, and maintenance of audience contact

37. Kenneth Bass, "The Narrative and Rhetorical Use of Divine Necessity in Luke–Acts," *JBPR* 1 (2009): 48–68.
38. Todd Penner, "Reconfiguring the Rhetorical Study of Acts: Reflections on the Method in and Learning of a Progymnastic Poetics," *PRS* 30 (2003): 425–39.
39. Daniel Lynwood Smith, *The Rhetoric of Interruption: Speech-Making, Turn-Taking, and Rule-Breaking in Luke–Acts and Ancient Greek Narrative* (BZNW 193; Berlin: de Gruyter, 2012).
40. Greg Carey, *Elusive Apocalypse: Reading Authority in the Revelation to John* (SABH 15; Macon, GA: Mercer University Press, 1999); idem, "Moving an Audience: One Aspect of Pathos in the Book of Revelation," in Black and Watson, *Words Well Spoken*, 163–78; Robyn Whitaker, "Rhetoric of Fear: Ekphrasis, Emotion, and Persuasion in Revelation 1:9–20," paper presented at the NT Colloquium, Princeton Theological Seminary, Princeton, NJ, 21 October 2011.
41. Kennedy, *New Testament Interpretation*, 39–72, 73–85, 97–113.

through topics and stylistic devices, an authoritative *ēthos*, and the form of logical argument.[42] Surprisingly for those who cut their teeth on Cadbury,[43] Luke's Sermon on the Plain (6:17–49) pales by comparison. Kennedy judges it "not a very good speech," because it is too concise, leaves too much unexplained, and relies almost entirely on Jesus' authority.[44]

John 14–17 exhibits a complex amplification of several repetitive topics that ultimately resolve themselves into "a kind of transcendent logic…constructed with the help of the authoritative ethos of Jesus."[45] Like John, Mark exemplifies what Kennedy calls "radical Christian rhetoric." Kennedy describes this type of oratory as "a form of 'sacred language' characterized by assertion and absolute claims of authoritative truth without evidence or logical argument." In this kind of rhetoric, Kennedy explains, "The truth is immediate and intuitively apprehended because it is true. Some see it, others do not, but there is no point in trying to persuade the latter.… [Yet] John makes far more demands than Mark on his readers in approaching the truth they are to perceive. He uses the forms of logical argument not so much as proof, as does Matthew, but as ways of turning and reiterating the topics which are at the core of his message."[46]

When one positions Kennedy's research on the canvas of Gospel scholarship, two things stand out. First, not since Wilder do we encounter a more intense appreciation of the Gospels' power as rhetorical products than we find here. Wilder's works make not a single reference to classical theorists of rhetoric.[47] In contrast,

---

42. Ibid., 63, 101–4.
43. Henry Joel Cadbury, *The Style and Literary Method of Luke*, Vol. 1: *The Diction of Luke and Acts* (Cambridge, MA: Harvard University Press, 1920).
44. Kennedy, *New Testament Interpretation*, 63–67 (quotation, 67).
45. Ibid., 85.
46. Ibid., 104–5, 113.
47. Wilder, "Scholars, Theologians and Ancient Rhetoric," 1–11, and idem, *Early Christian Rhetoric*, passim.

Kennedy unfolds his analysis in perpetual conversation with a dazzling array of such thinkers as Aristotle, Cicero, Pseudo-Demetrius (c. 2nd century CE), and Menander Rhetor (c. 4th century CE).

A second item worth underlining is that in the thirty years since publication of *New Testament Interpretation through Rhetorical Criticism*, few interpreters of the Gospels have followed the markers Kennedy laid down. In Watson and Hauser's comprehensive bibliography (1994),[48] published a decade after Kennedy's handbook, I count 183 articles, essays, and monographs on the Gospels. Of that number, 102 (56 percent) are published after 1985. Among that majority of entries, I reckon that not more than thirty (29 percent) operate within Kennedy's framework.

In the remaining seventy-two rhetorical analyses of the Gospels from 1985 to 1994 (71 percent), Kennedy's method appears little used. Between 1994 and 2011, another dozen essays bear traces of Kennedy's influence.[49] During the three decades since publication of *New Testament Interpretation through Rhetorical Criticism*, therefore, fewer than fifty articles, essays, and monographs on the Gospels engage Kennedy's approach. That number is probably greater than can be documented for Acts and Revelation, though considerably smaller than for the epistles and especially the Paulines.

As with history, so too with biblical scholarship: the wheels grind slowly. Has enough time elapsed for Kennedy's influence to have

---

48. Duane F. Watson and Alan J. Hauser, *Rhetorical Criticism of the Bible: A Comprehensive Bibliography with Notes on History and Method* (BIS 4; Leiden: Brill, 1994).

49. Representative are Evelyn R. Thibeaux, "'Known to Be a Sinner': The Narrative Rhetoric of Luke 7:36–50," *BTB* 23 (1993): 151–60, and Harold W. Attridge, "Argumentation in John 5," in *Rhetorical Argumentation in Biblical Texts: Essays from the Lund 2000 Conference*, ed. Anders Eriksson, Thomas H. Olbricht, and Walter Übelacker (Harrisburg: Trinity, 2002), 188–99; and Carl Joachim Classen, *Rhetorical Criticism of the New Testament* (WUNT 128; Tübingen: Mohr Siebeck, 2000), passim. Classen offers a striking contrast. In that book's 177 pages, Kennedy's work is mentioned only thrice yet never in conjunction with the Gospels (see esp. 69–98).

registered? Some comparisons are illuminative. On the rhetorical side, the works of Wilhelm Wuellner and Vernon Robbins have spawned, within the same period, a body of scholarship that considers the Gospels' rhetoric from a hermeneutical or socio-cultural point of view.[50] Not so with Kennedy. In the broader range of literary criticism, R. Alan Culpepper's *Anatomy of the Fourth Gospel*, published a year before Kennedy's book, has exerted on the Gospels' interpretation an impact beyond all capacity to footnote.[51] Can the same be said of Kennedy? I think not. Why not?

A Ruminative Interlude

A bit like "the curious incident of the dog in the night-time," the bark of Kennedy's analysis of the Gospels has been strangely muzzled.[52] To account for this muting, I have considered various possibilities that are arranged here in degrees of ascending plausibility and satisfaction.

1. *Kennedy's assessments of the Gospels are more conservative than the biblical research that many scholars practice.* This assertion is rubbish. As far as I can see, Kennedy's method is ideologically neutral, apart from its unapologetically historical bias. It can be, and has been, practiced by scholars both conservative and liberal in their orientations toward the Gospels and the rest of the New Testament.

2. *Kennedy concentrates on elements of the Gospels that once were compelling but may now seem passé.* Here, one thinks of Kennedy's

50. An exemplary specimen is James D. Hester and J. David Hester (Amador), eds., *Rhetorics and Hermeneutics: Wilhelm Wuellner and His Influence* (ESEC 9; New York: T&T Clark International, 2004). On Wuellner, see the chapters addressing his work in the present volume. For a socio-cultural point of view, see Vernon K. Robbins, *The Tapestry of Early Christian Discourse: Rhetoric, Society, and Ideology* (London: Routledge, 1996), and also the chapters on Robbins's work in the present volume.

51. R. Alan Culpepper, *Anatomy of the Fourth Gospel: A Study in Literary Design* (Philadelphia: Fortress, 1983).

52. Arthur Conan Doyle, "Silver Blaze" (1892), in idem, *The New Annotated Sherlock Holmes*, vol. 1, ed. Leslie S. Klinger (New York: Norton, 2005). Colonel Ross: "The dog did nothing in the night-time." "'That was the curious incident,' remarked Sherlock Holmes" (411).

recent translation of ancient textbooks of *progymnasmata*, whose contents resonate with earlier, form-critical studies of Dibelius and Bultmann.[53] Is the Society of Biblical Literature still interested in such things? Well, some must be, if the Society's own Press deemed Kennedy's version of these texts worth publishing in a series of Writings from the Greco-Roman World.[54] Furthermore, Kennedy's approach is too expansive and inclusive of many more elements of ancient discourse to be so easily dismissed.

3. *Kennedy's proposal is formalist and concentrates on such matters as rhetorical invention, arrangement, and style, whereas many critics are now more interested in socio-cultural and hermeneutical questions, both ancient and modern.* This statement is a twist on the preceding suggestion that Kennedy's approach is out of synch with current fashions, which wax and wane. There may be truth in that suggestion, but it cannot be the whole truth. Even more formalist in approach than Kennedy's *New Testament Interpretation* is Culpepper's *Anatomy*, though its forms are more congruent with modern narrative theory. Formalism as such has hardly stemmed the tide of recent literary criticism of the Gospels.

4. *Kennedy is a classicist; most New Testament scholars have not been as capable as he in reaching across disciplinary boundaries.* In this claim, too, is a grain of truth, given the multiformity of New Testament studies and historical accidents attending the ways in which a new generation of biblical scholars is trained. On the other hand, we have

---

53. George A. Kennedy, trans., *Progymnasamata: Greek Textbooks of Prose Composition and Rhetoric* (WGRW 10; Atlanta: SBL, 2003); Martin Dibelius, *From Tradition to Gospel*, trans. Bertram Lee Woolf (New York: Scribner's, 1965; German orig. Tübingen: Mohr, 1919); Rudolf Bultmann, *History of the Synoptic Tradition*, trans. John Marsh (New York: Harper & Row, 1963; German orig. Göttingen: Vandenhoeck & Ruprecht, 1921).

54. See also Ronald F. Hock and Edward N. O'Neil, eds., *The Chreia and Ancient Rhetoric: Classroom Exercises* (WGRW 2; Atlanta: SBL, 2002); and George A. Kennedy, ed., *Invention and Method: Two Rhetorical Treatises from the Hermogenic Corpus* (WGRW 15; Atlanta: SBL, 2005). At present, Kennedy's deepest impression on Gospel scholarship appears *umweltlich,* by encouraging translations of ancient classical texts whose subject matter intersects with some of the Gospels' subgenres.

detected no evidence that interpretation of the New Testament's epistles by Kennedy's canons has suffered such blinkered vision.

5. *The Gospels are complex amalgams of many different genres*—bioi, *ancient history, novella, drama, aphorisms, apocalyptic, and speeches*—*that resist uniform analysis.* Although this statement is surely accurate, it is inadequate to account for the meager analysis, to date, of constitutive materials that accord with Kennedy's principles. For instance, interpreters such as J. Louis Martyn and Andrew Lincoln have encouraged us to take seriously the heavily juridical tenor of the Fourth Gospel.[55] Forensic rhetoric, as Kennedy reminds us, is the social location for a vast body of theory and practice of rhetoric among the ancients. Why have Johannine critics so little availed themselves of its resources?[56]

6. *Kennedy's program is too idiosyncratic, or too recondite, to be easily appropriated.* This proposition is tricky. As we have seen, the study of New Testament rhetoric is hardly eccentric; its heritage in the modern era reaches back as far as C. G. Wilke.[57] Moreover, Kennedy's presentation is crystalline. If Gospel critics can swallow Derrida, Kennedy is a slice of coconut angel-food.

To practice Kennedy's species of rhetorical criticism, on the other hand, one must master a considerable body of ancient literature that speaks in terms distant from us in space and time. Kennedy is every bit as lucid as Culpepper. That the same may be said of Quintilian and Seymour Chatman, I am unsure. Kennedy's method lives in a world where such concepts as "ekphrasis" and "enthymemes" are common

---

55. J. Louis Martyn, *History and Theology in the Fourth Gospel* (3rd ed.; NTL; Louisville: Westminster John Knox, 2003); Andrew Lincoln, *Truth on Trial: The Lawsuit Motif in the Fourth Gospel* (Peabody: Hendrickson, 2000).

56. George L. Parsenios: *Rhetoric and Drama in the Johannine Lawsuit Motif* (WUNT 258; Tübingen: Mohr Siebeck, 2010). Owing much to Parsenios, that tide may be turning.

57. C. G. Wilke, *Die neutestamentliche Rhetorik: ein Seitenstück zur Grammatik des neutestamentlichen Sprachidioms* (Dresden: Arnold, 1843).

coins of its philosophical realm.[58] Chatman's *Story and Discourse* and Culpepper, following Chatman, breathe the atmosphere of plot, characterization, and implied audiences, all of which are more accessible for those whose literary sensibilities are now shaped by novels, movies, and television.[59]

7. *Kennedy's rhetorical criticism, based on ancient handbooks detailing the proper construction of* speeches*, is less well suited for exegesis of the Gospels because they are* narratives. Here, we may draw nearer to the problem's nub. Whether exegetes have been wise to interpret New Testament epistles as though they were speeches remains for me an open question. A document such as Hebrews, which amplifies a sustained argument, lends itself to Kennedy's method. "It was the intent of the evangelists," he claims, "to present speeches, and early Christian audiences, listening to the Gospels read, heard these chapters as speeches."[60] That assertion expresses an assumption, not a fact. In point of fact, the Gospels are *not* speeches, though all of them *contain* speeches.[61] This fact is especially true of the Fourth Gospel, whose Jesus delivers a series of extended, stylized discourses. Even in John, however, those speeches are embedded in an indelibly narrative structure, which may not be amenable to Kennedy's method. Kennedy's form of rhetorical criticism requires of the Gospels' interpreters an oblique angle and intellectual suppleness.

8. *Kennedy's approach subliminally awards pride of place to* logos *or logical argument whereas the Gospels tend towards* ēthos, *the power of Jesus' authority.* This point is debatable, but worth debating. Kennedy

---

58. Ekphrasis is vivid description intending to excite the listeners' emotions (*Rhet. ad Her.* 4.38.51) An enthymeme is a rhetorical syllogism or statement with a supporting reason that may or may not be formally valid (Aristotle, *Rhet.* 1.2.8–22; 2.22–25).

59. Seymour Chatman, *Story and Discourse: Narrative Structure in Fiction and Film* (Ithaca: Cornell University Press, 1980); Culpepper, *Anatomy of the Fourth Gospel*, esp. 3–49, 101–9, 205–11.

60. Kennedy, *New Testament Interpretation*, 39.

61. See Black, *The Rhetoric of the Gospel*, esp. 43–66, 83–99, and 118–33.

esteems the rhetoric of the Sermon on the Mount over that of the Sermon on the Plain on the grounds of logical force. He states, "The Beatitudes [in Matthew] take enthymematic, and thus syllogistic form, and are *formally* valid."[62] He further emphasizes, "[Matthew's Sermon] repeatedly utilizes the form of logical argument with premises based on nature and experiences well known to the audience."[63] By contrast, Kennedy explains, "What persuasive power Luke's speech has inheres almost solely in the ethos, or authority of Jesus. In Matthew too ethos is primary, *but more attempt is made to couch statements in logical form*, and greater pathos is achieved."[64]

Kennedy approves the divine messenger who appears to Joseph in Matthew's infancy narrative as "a *logical* angel who wants Joseph to understand and is not content simply to make authoritative announcements."[65] Kennedy says nothing of Gabriel's logic in Luke 1. The real question, however, is whether logic is as important to any of the Evangelists as Kennedy's comments might lead one to expect. As I read them, all of the Gospels lay greater stress on Jesus' inspired authority, not on his logic. In that regard, they seem more exemplary of sophistic rhetoric than of its technical or philosophical versions. In Matthew, disciples should obey what Jesus says, not because it is logical—often it seems to flout logic (e.g., 5:3–12, 21-48)—but because Jesus is Immanuel, God-With-Us (1:23).

9. *Kennedy assumes that the Evangelists intend to persuade. Is that a valid, or adequate, assumption?* Kennedy himself evinces ambivalence at this point. On the one hand, he states, "[The Gospels] are rhetorical works in the sense that their intention is to persuade the readers that the Christian message is true or to deepen their understanding of

---

62. Kennedy, *New Testament Interpretation*, 49.
63. Ibid., 63.
64. Ibid., 67 (emphasis added).
65. Ibid., 103 (emphasis added).

this message."[66] Luke 1:1–4 and John 20:30–31 confirm this estimate. On the other hand, Kennedy also argues, "Christian preaching is thus not persuasion but proclamation, and is based on authority and grace, not on proof." Accordingly, Kennedy holds that "the basis of Jesus' [rhetoric] did not lie in rational proof and his rhetoric is much like that . . . found in the Old Testament," namely "truth known from revelation."[67] If we accept Willi Marxsen's dictum that the Gospels function as sermons ("Christian preaching"), then their rhetoric across the board—not only in Mark—may be more radical than Kennedy's method is designed to measure and evaluate.[68]

Consider the parables. Contrary to Kennedy's assessment that they "could have been useful to Jesus in avoiding confrontation with the Pharisees," in all the Synoptics they solidify resistance to Jesus among those so predisposed.[69] Mark's famous hardening theory (4:10–12) is only the most blatant expression of their effect and intent throughout. Granting that the Gospels intend to fortify the faith of Jesus' disciples, would their rhetoric persuade anyone to whom God had not already revealed his Son's identity and authority? In John, it's just the reverse. Jesus' deeds and words convict when they do not convince, and they expose both those who live in darkness and those who live in light (3:17–21; 9:38–41). Essentially, the same is true also of the Synoptics.

Nevertheless, Kennedy's technique may be gathering steam in the Gospels' interpretation, notably with John, whose distinctive discourse catches even the ear of a smart novice. Jerome Neyrey makes a good case that the Fourth Evangelist deploys the rhetoric of praise for Jesus' disciples and blame for his adversaries by means of ancient techniques of *encomia*.[70] Tom Thatcher boldly proposes

---

66. Idem, "Classical and Christian Source Criticism," 137.
67. Idem, *Classical Rhetoric and Its Christian and Secular Tradition*, 121, 127.
68. Willi Marxsen, *Mark The Evangelist: Studies on the Redaction History of the Gospel* (trans. James Boyce et al.; New York: Abingdon, 1969; Germal orig. 1956).
69. Kennedy, *New Testament Interpretation*, 71.

that John composed "stories about Jesus through a process of interior visualization," reminiscent of ancient mnemonic techniques.[71] John Carlson Stube has given us a discerning study of the argument in John's Farewell Discourse.[72] All these studies open windows of perception that only a classical approach such as Kennedy's can afford. Comparable research in the Synoptics on Matthew's five great discourses (5:1–7:27; 10:5–11:1; 13:1–52; 18:1–35; 24:1–25:46) or on the brilliant oratorios in Luke's infancy narrative (1:14–17, 32–35, 46–55, 67–79; 2:14, 29–35) could do the same. In time, I expect they shall.

To summarize: the surprising neglect of Kennedy's rhetorical criticism in the Gospels' interpretation may be explained in different ways. Some of those explanations are more convincing than others. Built into Kennedy's approach are assumptions that, in my judgment, the Gospels themselves resist for literary, theological, and other reasons. In any event, the promise of his rhetorical criticism, articulated in 1984, has not yet been fulfilled for the Gospels, even in those areas—like Matthew's five great discourses, the *oratorios* in Luke's infancy narrative, the forensic cut-and-thrust of the Johannine Jesus—where the fields look ripe for the harvest.

New Horizons: Comparative Rhetoric

This is not the story's end. Kennedy's lifetime of scholarship is marked not only by mastery of a field but also by a relentless inquisitiveness. As Margaret D. Zulick reminds us, Kennedy has put rhetorical study on the map of both classicists and theorists in

70. Jerome Neyrey, "Encomium versus Vituperation: Contrasting Portraits of Jesus in the Fourth Gospel," *JBL* 126, no. 4 (2007): 529–52.
71. Tom Thatcher, "John's Memory Theater: The Fourth Gospel and Ancient Mnemo-Rhetoric," *CBQ* 69, no. 3 (2007): 487–505.
72. John Carlson Stube, *A Graeco-Roman Rhetorical Reading of the Farewell Discourse* (LNTS 309; London: T&T Clark, 2006).

speech communication at a time when many regarded the subject as recherché at best.[73] His later forays in New Testament studies arise from an intelligent curiosity that spurs him to proceed from his own academically safe quarters into an area of inquiry in which his own learning and that of his readers might be extended with profit and delight.

That pioneering spirit is obvious in Kennedy's most recent monograph to date, *Comparative Rhetoric* (1998).[74] Greek and Roman rhetoricians claim that the phenomena they describe and categorize are universal. Kennedy's latest work tests that proposition's validity across an extraordinary range of civilization. He surveys not only the ancient literate societies of Mesopotamia, Egypt, China, and India, but also such non-literate cultures as aboriginal Australians, the Ethiopian Mursi, Philippine Ilongots, and North American Indians.

Most fascinating is the book's first chapter in which Kennedy explores rhetoric among nonhuman, social animals including quadrupeds such as deer and elk as well as birds and primates. Kennedy is too wise and too generous a scholar to fall into the trap of imposing Western, anthropomorphic biases. He states, "[M]y objective is rather the opposite: to modify Western notions by comparison with other traditions in the interests of coming to an understanding of rhetoric as a more general phenomenon of human [and animal] life."[75]

In the hands of an inept dilettante, the outcome of such an exercise could be pure bosh. For Kennedy, who has done his homework in such disciplines as biogenetics, zoology, and comparative anthropology, the result is altogether educational and provocative.

73. Margaret D. Zulick, "The Recollection of Rhetoric: A Brief History," in Black and Watson, *Words Well Spoken*, 7–19.
74. George A. Kennedy, *Comparative Rhetoric: An Historical and Cross-Cultural Introduction* (New York: Oxford University Press, 1998).
75. Kennedy, *Comparative Rhetoric*, 217.

Experts in those fields must speak to the cogency of those aspects of his investigation. For my part, I can underline a few dimensions of Kennedy's *Comparative Rhetoric* that might send readers back to biblical texts with clarified vision.

1. Kennedy's study of traditional Australian "Dreamtime" as a font from which tropes, metaphors, and poetry have sprung offers a fresh approach to the biblical rhetoric of dreams and visions.[76] Traditionally, the interpretation of passages like Joseph's dreams in Matthew (1:18–25; 2:13–15, 19–23) has been somewhat constrained by the (doubtless correct) notation of parallels with another Joseph, who is the son of Jacob (himself a dreamer; Gen. 28:10–17; 31:11–16) and a dreamer (Gen. 37:5–11) and interpreter of others' dreams (Gen. 40:1–19; 41:14–36). Comparable to such dreams in the New Testament (note Acts 2:17, following Joel 2:28) are the angelic visions of Zechariah (Luke 1:8–23), Mary (Luke 1:26–38), Simon Peter (Acts 10:1–16), and Paul (2 Cor. 12:1–10).

2. Adopting Kennedy's earlier rhetorical technique, modern interpreters could analyze such texts' invention, arrangement, and style, though few have done so. Considering "kaleidoscopic visualization in the ancient 'Dreamtime,'" however, Kennedy now invites us to venture beyond strictly logical analysis to the "proto-metaphorical" power of dreams and visions as *expressions of rhetoric in their own right.*[77] It is at once ironic and fitting that Kennedy, who more than anyone else has encouraged New Testament exegetes to consult rhetorical handbooks for interpretive strategies, is encouraging us to reach beyond them—more accurately, backwards from them—to re-envision biblical rhetoric more comprehensively.

3. Following Jane Atkinson's lead, Kennedy observes among the Indonesian Wana the phenomenon of conventional *kyori,* "wrapped

76. Ibid., 58–59.
77. Ibid., 60.

words," which (as Atkinson puts it) "encapsulate a state of affairs in a fitting image, express opinions or sentiments, pose questions, or propose a course of action."[78] In such discourse, Kennedy notes, "speakers disguise their meaning, however, and say something indirectly"—often with a millenialist bent—"in an elegant way to one who understands."[79] Such rhetoric can be documented among Native Americans, especially as they were forced to respond to European occupation of their territories.[80] One cannot help but be reminded of Jesus' parables of God's kingdom that are eschatological in tenor, indirect in referent, and implicitly subversive of many first-century political and religious mores. Kennedy's recent research opens yet another entrée into Jesus' characteristic discourse that issues from an ancient, largely nonliterate environment.

4. Finally, we should note that Kennedy's latest excursion has prompted him, upon return to his "native land," to reconsider some of its working assumptions. "Classical rhetorical theory," he concludes, "turns out to have some universal features, some features unique to Greek and Roman culture—especially its focus on judicial oratory—and a number of central concepts, including epideictic and ethos, that require some redefinition if they are to describe rhetoric in general."[81] That deduction requires modification of one's definition of rhetoric itself, and in *Comparative Rhetoric*, Kennedy tenders that modification. Rhetoric may be better conceived as something more than the art of persuasive speech or writing. Viewed through a lens wider than that polished by Greek and Roman theorists, "Rhetoric is apparently a form of energy that drives and is imparted to

---

78. Jane M. Atkinson, "'Wrapped Words': Poetry and Politics among the Wana of Central Sulawesi, Indonesia," in *Dangerous Words: Language and Politics in the Pacific*, ed. Donald Brennis and Fred R. Meyers (Prospect Heights: Waveland, 1984), 40.
79. Kennedy, *Comparative Rhetoric*, 71.
80. Ibid., 89–108.
81. Ibid., 230.

communication," and as a natural phenomenon, "rhetoric is prior logically and historically to human speech."[82]

Grant that proposition, and bright light may be thrown on a text such as the prologue of John's Gospel, which creatively extends the Priestly creation account in Genesis 1:1–2:3:

> In the beginning was the word [*logos*], and the word was alongside God, and what God was the word was. This one was in the beginning beside God. Everything came to be through him, and apart from him there was nothing. What came to be in him was life, and the life was the light of mortals. . . . And the word came to be flesh and dwelled among us; and we beheld his glory, glory as the only begotten of the Father, full of grace and truth (John 1:1-4, 14 [AT]).

Regarding this pericope, the student of comparative religions is better positioned to recognize the truth in Kennedy's comment, "Exclusively oral societies [like those among P's audience, and many in the Fourth Evangelist's] usually think in specific terms and feel little need to erect systems of abstract thought. Their religion too is primarily mythological, not philosophical."[83] The historian of Hellenistic-Jewish religions, including early Christianity, can see in John's prelude a development beyond Genesis that is molded by the OT's sapiential tradition (Prov. 8:22–31; Sir. 1:4; 24:1–12) and such thinkers as Philo (*Opif.* 20; *Somn.* 1.229–30), in which a myth of origins has been enriched by reflection on the activity of personified σοφία (*sophia*) or λόγος.

Thanks to Kennedy, the biblical theologian may recognize in this passage something else at work: the Evangelist's stunning assertion that the "energy" at work before creation, prior to all human speech or animal communication of any kind, not only exerted its power in creation but also became one with it in a particularized human

---

82. Ibid., 215, 216.
83. Ibid., 218.

form "that dwelled among us." To divert Kennedy's reconsidered definition of rhetoric onto a theological avenue he has not traveled, we may assert that God is—among other things—an inherently *rhetorical* power, whose creation by speech and whose renewal of that creation by λόγος, manifests the Creator's desire to communicate with creation and to remain in eternal companionship with it. When, probably building on the Fourth Gospel, the author of 1 John identifies God as love (1 John 4:16b), that ἀγάπη is more than a sentiment or affection. It is the character of God's rhetorical power, which fans out among creatures begotten of and dependent on that God's energizing love (1 John 3:16; 4:7–12).

The language of "Dreamtime," the power of "wrapped words," rhetoric as a form of energy: these are among the new horizons to which Kennedy's eyes are turned. If we follow his gaze, we may become more sensitive to the New Testament's complexity and wonder.

An Open-Ended Conclusion

For as long as George Kennedy continues to open the frontiers of rhetorical study, it will remain impossible to take full measure of his scholarship's impact on New Testament study. This chapter serves only as an interim report, one surveyor's attempt to chart the terrain's peaks and valleys. Kennedy's spacious erudition strains for a progressively deeper understanding of human beings as communicative creatures seeking to understand and to be understood by how they speak and what they write. We are now of the second generation of Kennedyesque rhetorical criticism and its promise of scholarly maturity. One hopes that his many-faceted lens will in time be applied to larger, more creative questions in New Testament interpretation of the sort I have sought to acknowledge here.

That expanded vision, in fact, is my hope for the many rhetorical approaches represented in this book. Biblical literature is too vast to be comprehended by a single method or collectivity of methods. None of us can be expert in everything. Across a lifetime few of us become truly expert in anything. The blind spots of youth eventually yield to the cataracts of age. The complementary visions arrayed in these chapters correct our myopia and, at their best, help us see the New Testament more clearly.

4

———

Response to C. Clifton Black and Further Insights

Duane F. Watson

George Kennedy's volume *New Testament Interpretation through Rhetorical Criticism* is a tantalizing appetizer for a veritable feast of discovery.[1] I worked through a draft or two of this volume as a PhD student at Duke University while I was taking courses with Professor Kennedy at the University of North Carolina at Chapel Hill. As I did so, my mind reveled in all the possibilities I was seeing for analyzing and better understanding the New Testament. I decided to explore these possibilities in my dissertation on Jude and 2 Peter at Duke

---

1. George A. Kennedy, *New Testament Interpretation through Rhetorical Criticism* (Chapel Hill: University of North Carolina Press, 1984).

and invited Professor Kennedy to join my dissertation committee. He graciously accepted and his contribution to my research was more than considerable.[2]

Kennedy's influence on rhetorical criticism in the New Testament field as a whole is due in large measure to his volume's being a general introduction to the rhetoric of three of the four major genres of the New Testament. It provides a simple and workable methodology undergirded by his ethos as a prominent classical scholar with a specialty in rhetoric.[3] The methodology outlined in the book opens up the discussion of the Gospels, the Acts of the Apostles, and Pauline Epistles. The method is simple and consists of five basic components: determine the rhetorical unit; analyze the rhetorical situation; determine the species of rhetoric, the question, and the stasis; analyze invention, arrangement, and style; and evaluate the rhetorical effectiveness of the rhetoric.

Having written five influential books and many articles on the subject of Greek and Roman rhetoric prior to this volume, Kennedy's authority in this arena helps carry his approach to the New Testament into this field where practitioners are not typically trained in Greco-Roman rhetoric.[4] He also is reviving the once thriving and respected art of rhetorical analysis of the New Testament that had been all but forgotten since the early twentieth century. This longstanding

2. The resulting dissertation was published as Duane F. Watson, *Invention, Arrangement, and Style: Rhetorical Criticism of Jude and 2 Peter* (SBLDS 104; Atlanta: Scholars, 1988).

3. For more discussion of the influence of Kennedy upon New Testament studies, see C. Clifton Black and Duane F. Watson, eds., *Words Well Spoken: George Kennedy's Rhetoric of the New Testament* (SRR 8; Waco: Baylor University Press, 2008).

4. George A. Kennedy, *The Art of Persuasion in Greece* (Princeton: Princeton University Press, 1963); idem, *Quintilian* (TWAS 66; New York: Twayne, 1969); idem, *The Art of Rhetoric in the Roman World: 300 B.C.–A.D. 300* (Princeton: Princeton University Press, 1972); idem, *Greek Rhetoric under Christian Emperors* (Princeton: Princeton University Press, 1983); idem, *Classical Rhetoric and Its Christian and Secular Tradition from Ancient to Modern Times* (Chapel Hill: University of North Carolina Press, 1980, 1999). For further bibliography, see Black and Watson, *Words Well Spoken*, 196–203.

approach to biblical studies also contributes to Kennedy's success in reintroducing this art to this field of study.[5]

The Broader Study of the New Testament

Kennedy understands rhetorical criticism of the New Testament as an historical investigation of literature created within a highly rhetorical Hellenistic culture. This literature and its settings are illumined by the study of its rhetorical strategies. Kennedy's work thus appeals to the social and cultural analysis of the New Testament that is budding in the 1980s, for it helps considerably in placing the New Testament within the broader literary culture of the Mediterranean world. For just one example, similar interest can be seen in two works by David Aune from this period that describe the major literary genres and forms used in Jewish and Greek literature and then compares how these genres and forms are used in the New Testament.[6]

As an historical investigation using Greco-Roman rhetoric, Kennedy's work inadvertently helps fuel a debate about the role of modern rhetoric in the analysis of the New Testament. Many argue that using only Greco-Roman rhetoric in this analysis is too limiting. Since modern rhetoric is more highly conceptualized, it should be utilized as well to see what help it can bring to interpretation.[7] One transition to the use of modern rhetoric that emerges early in the debate is the use of the New Rhetoric, a reconceptualization of Greco-Roman rhetoric with a focus on the historical and social

---

5. For a brief history of this earlier period, see Duane F. Watson and Alan J. Hauser, *Rhetorical Criticism of the Bible: A Comprehensive Bibliography with Notes on History and Method* (BIS 4; Leiden: Brill, 1994), 101–109.
6. David E. Aune, *The New Testament in Its Literary Environment* (LEC 8; Philadelphia: Westminster, 1987); idem, *Greco-Roman Literature and the New Testament* (SBLSBS 21; Atlanta: Scholars, 1988).
7. Wilhelm Wuellner, "Where is Rhetorical Criticism Taking Us?" *CBQ* 49 (1987): 448–63.

aspects of speech.[8] The New Rhetoric offers enough familiarity to those trained in Greco-Roman rhetoric to lead them to venture further into the arena of more modern rhetoric.

The Rhetoric of the Gospels

In regard to the Gospels, Kennedy gives a brief overview of their rhetorical features. However, he gives more specific analysis of the Sermon on the Mount (Matthew 5–7) and of the Sermon on the Plain (Luke 6:17–49) as examples of deliberative rhetoric, and the Farewell Discourse (John 13–17) as an example of epideictic rhetoric.[9] Even though it is quite enlightening on these three sermons, Kennedy's analysis of the Gospels does not capture the attention of Gospel studies.

This inattention is partly due to at least two factors. First, ancient rhetoric does not have a theory of narrative, and the Gospels are primarily narrative.[10] Second, conventions of invention, arrangement, and style as discussed in the rhetorical handbooks pertain primarily to judicial, political, and ceremonial speeches. In the Gospels, these conventions are only involved in description and speeches in smaller units of narrative. While intended to persuade, the Gospel narratives are primarily structured by juxtaposing units to develop topics, to compare and contrast words and deeds, and to create a forward and climactic movement. Even in the Gospel of John, which contains many speeches of Jesus, the speeches are embedded in larger narrative frameworks.

---

8. Chaim Perelman and Lucie Olbrechts-Tyteca, *The New Rhetoric: A Treatise on Argumentation*, trans. John Wilkinson and Purcell Weaver (Notre Dame: University of Notre Dame Press, 1969).

9. Kennedy, *New Testament Interpretation*, 39–85; 97–113.

10. Burton L. Mack, *Rhetoric and the New Testament* (GBSNTS; Minneapolis: Fortress, 1990), 79–80.

Kennedy's work is also sidetracked by the contemporaneous analysis of the Gospels according to the exercises of the *progymnasmata*. This analysis shows that the Gospel writers use elaboration of theses and *chreiai* to structure many of the exchanges and discourses of Jesus. Based on the pioneering work of Burton Mack and Vernon Robbins, we now see how the Gospel writers elaborated theses and the *chreiai* of Jesus to suit their own literary, theological, and polemical concerns.[11] This elaboration is seen most clearly in the pronouncement stories.[12] The chreia elaboration includes recitation, inflection, commentary, objection, antithesis, expansion, condensation, and refutation and/or confirmation of the sayings and actions of Jesus.

While Kennedy briefly mentions the forms of the *progymnasmata* exercises and notes that the *chreiai* are the basis for some rhetorical units of the New Testament,[13] he does not illustrate their use by the Gospel writers. In fact, he states of these forms in the Bible that "they are rarely developed there in accord with the specific suggestions of the Greek and Roman schools."[14] Unfortunately this assessment is overstated, and he does not pursue the more studied use of these forms in the New Testament as do Robbins and Mack. However, Kennedy now provides us with a new edition of the *progymnasmata* that makes these texts available for such analysis of the Gospels.[15]

---

11. Burton L. Mack and Vernon K. Robbins, *Patterns of Persuasion in the Gospels* (FFLF; Sonoma, CA: Polebridge, 1989).
12. Vernon K. Robbins, ed., *The Rhetoric of Pronouncement* (Semeia 64; Atlanta: Scholars, 1994).
13. Kennedy, *New Testament Interpretation*, 22–23.
14. Ibid., 22.
15. George A. Kennedy, trans., *Progymnasmata: Greek Textbooks of Prose Composition and Rhetoric* (WGRW 10; Atlanta: SBL, 2003). For more on Kennedy's influence on the rhetorical analysis of the Gospels, see C. Clifton Black, "Kennedy and the Gospels: An Ambiguous Legacy, a Promising Bequest," in Black and Watson, *Words Well Spoken*, 63–80.

The Rhetoric of the Acts of the Apostles

Speeches are a key element of Greek historiography. They are created to suit the speaker, audience, and occasion that are described in the narrative, and they have teaching, moral, and political concerns. The speeches of key participants in the events narrated in such history often interpret the significance of the events in general and for the audience in specific.[16] The rhetoric of the law court, political arena, and public encomium is summarized in the rhetorical handbooks. This rhetoric is appropriate to the analysis of the speeches of Greek historiography, for these speeches are portrayed as deriving from these three public spheres.

The Acts of the Apostles is a product of Greek historiography, and the speeches in Acts readily lend themselves to rhetorical analysis. Kennedy analyzes these speeches and concludes that they utilize rhetoric, especially *prosopopoeia* or speech in character. They are creations of Luke as would be expected within the confines of Hellenistic historiography.[17] Currently, many rhetorical features of ancient rhetoric including the *progymnasmata*, declamation, and *imitatio* are being investigated in Acts for which Kennedy's work is very helpful.[18]

However, Kennedy's work has had a minimal influence on the interpretation of the Acts of the Apostles because he does not analyze the broader narrative framework of Acts of which the speeches are an integral part. Analysis of historical prose is complicated by the fact that such history is written with many different approaches, with complexity of construction, and by people from a variety of

---

16. See Stefan Rebenich, "Historical Prose," in *Handbook of Classical Rhetoric in the Hellenistic Period 330 B.C. to A.D. 400*, ed. Stanley E. Porter (Leiden: Brill, 2001), 265–337.
17. Kennedy, *New Testament Interpretation*, 115–40.
18. For recent works, see Duane F. Watson, *The Rhetoric of the New Testament: A Bibliographic Survey* (TfBS 8; Blandford Forum: Deo, 2006), 111–16.

life stations without the luxury of any formal curriculum in history writing.[19] These complexities of historiography contribute to the resistance to Kennedy's approach to rhetorical analysis in the interpretation of Acts.[20]

The Rhetoric of the Epistles

Regarding the epistles of the New Testament, Kennedy assumes that if Paul's epistles are to be read in the churches, they are written to be read as speeches and constructed with public reading in mind. These and the other letters of the New Testament are written to be read to an audience to address exigencies that demand important decisions be made and to persuade an audience to make them. Kennedy assumes that these letters lend themselves to rhetorical analysis by rhetorical conventions as found in the rhetorical handbooks, especially as consolidated by Quintilian, a contemporary of Paul.

Kennedy analyzes Romans, 2 Corinthians, Galatians, and 1 Thessalonians. He identifies 2 Corinthians as judicial rhetoric, 1 Thessalonians and Galatians as deliberative rhetoric, and Romans as epideictic rhetoric.[21] He demonstrates that these letters are examples of judicial, deliberative, and epideictic rhetoric. He further shows that they contain invention of standard arguments chosen to address identified stases, careful arrangement of these invented arguments, and stylistic devices and amplification of these arguments to enhance their persuasive effect.

---

19. Rebenich, "Historical Prose," 287–89.
20. For further analysis of speeches and narrative in Acts, see Todd Penner and Caroline Vander Stichele, *Contextualizing Acts: Lukan Narrative and Greco-Roman Discourse* (SBLSymS 20; Atlanta: Society of Biblical Literature, 2003). For further assessment of the influence of Kennedy on the rhetorical analysis of Acts, see Blake Shipp, "George Kennedy's Influence on Rhetorical Interpretation of the Acts of the Apostles," in Black and Watson, *Words Well Spoken*, 107–23.
21. Kennedy, *New Testament Interpretation*, 86–96, 142–56.

Of special note, Kennedy's analysis of Galatians is an important catalyst in a debate about its rhetorical species and how the letter is best interpreted. This analysis is partly a response to the important commentary on Galatians by Hans Dieter Betz, who classifies Galatians as an apologetic letter employing judicial rhetoric in which Paul defends himself against accusations. Betz identifies the narration in the first two chapters as a statement of the facts common to judicial rhetoric and part of Paul's defense against accusations. However, Betz is puzzled as to how to account for the exhortation in the last two chapters since exhortation is foreign to judicial rhetoric.[22]

In contrast, Kennedy identifies Galatians as using deliberative rhetoric meant to persuade an audience to take a certain course of action. The narration in the first two chapters establishes the ethos of Paul and his proclamation, while the exhortation in the last two chapters outlines the course of action that Paul is aiming to persuade the Galatians to take in light of that proclamation. Kennedy's response to Betz's analysis set the opinions of two titans in their own fields against each other. This creates a vigorous debate in which not only the rhetorical nature of Galatians but also the use of rhetoric in analyzing Pauline letters in general is scrutinized.[23]

Kennedy's influence on rhetorical analysis of all of the epistles of the New Testament has also been substantial, with many works published on the subject that utilize his methods and insights.[24]

---

22. Hans Dieter Betz, *Galatians: A Commentary on Paul's Letter to the Churches in Galatia* (Hermeneia; Philadelphia: Fortress, 1979), esp. 14–25.
23. Many of the key works in this debate are collected in Mark D. Nanos, ed., *The Galatians Debate* (Peabody: Hendrickson, 2002). See also Troy W. Martin, "Invention and Arrangement in Recent Pauline Rhetorical Studies: A Survey of the Practices and the Problems," in *Paul and Rhetoric*, ed. J. Paul Sampley and Peter Lampe (New York: T&T Clark, 2010), 48–118; and idem, "Investigating the Pauline Letter Body: Issues, Methods, and Approaches," in *Paul and the Ancient Letter Form*, ed. Stanley E. Porter and Sean A. Adams (Leiden: Brill, 2010), 197–212.
24. For an overview, see Frank W. Hughes, "George Kennedy's Contribution to Rhetorical Criticism of the Pauline Letters," in Black and Watson, *Words Well Spoken*, 125–37. For bibliography, see Watson, *The Rhetoric of the New Testament*, 120–80.

Interpreters are quick to classify letters as either judicial, deliberative, or epideictic in nature. In the epistles of the New Testament, they identify many elements of rhetorical invention, arrangement, and style as found in speeches. They catalogue various types of argumentation in the epistles, outline portions of epistles or entire epistles according to the elements of arrangement, and identify stylistic devices that enhance the persuasive effect of these epistles. Romans, 1 and 2 Corinthians, Galatians, Philippians, 1 and 2 Thessalonians, Philemon, 2 Peter, and Jude are all analyzed according to the conventions of Greco-Roman rhetoric with varying degrees of persuasion.

Perhaps the best example of this use of rhetoric in the Pauline letters is 2 Corinthians 10–13, which indicates that Paul is highly trained in rhetoric and skillfully used rhetorical conventions. These chapters utilize virtually all the methods that Plutarch suggests could be used to boast without offending. They also utilize an irony and value reversal that demonstrates to the Corinthians that Paul can pull out all the rhetorical stops when he wants.[25]

Rhetorical analysis of New Testament epistles that uses Greco-Roman rhetorical conventions is quickly challenged by other interpreters.[26] The challenge arises in part because rhetorical and epistolary theories are not explicitly integrated in antiquity. Rhetorical handbooks contain little discussion of the rhetoric of epistles except regarding style, and, in turn, epistolary handbooks contain little about the role of rhetoric in letters beyond the style

---

25. Duane F. Watson, "Paul's Boasting in 2 Corinthians 10–13 as Defense of His Honor: A Socio-Rhetorical Analysis," in *Rhetorical Argumentation in Biblical Texts: Essays from the Lund 2000 Conference*, ed. Anders Eriksson, Thomas H. Olbricht, and Walter Überlacker (ESEC 8; Harrisburg: Trinity, 2002), 260–75; idem, "Paul and Boasting," in *Paul in the Greco-Roman World*, ed. J. Paul Sampley (Harrisburg: Trinity, 2003), 77–100.

26. See Martin, "Invention and Arrangement," in Sampley and Lampe, *Paul and Rhetoric*, 48–118; and idem, "Investigating the Pauline Letter Body," in Porter and Adams, *Paul and the Ancient Letter Form*, 197–212.

appropriate to each type of letter.[27] This fact raises concerns about looking for rhetorical sophistication in epistles, especially to the point of classifying epistles according to the three species of rhetoric, delineating argumentative strategies, and identifying the key elements of arrangement within them.[28]

Kennedy's methodology assumes that epistles can be classified according to the three species of rhetoric: judicial, deliberative, and epideictic. As many point out, however, there are several reasons why this classification of epistles only partially works. The fact that there are a variety of types of letters addressing audiences with purposeful communication just like speeches naturally creates functional parallels with all three species of rhetoric. However, David Aune summarizes, "Early Christian letters tend to resist rigid classification, either in terms of the three main types of oratory or in terms of the many categories listed by the epistolary theorists."[29]

There is also some question about finding in epistles the elements of invention, arrangement, and style used in speeches. In epistolary theory, topics of invention are selected according to the needs of the type of epistle used in a particular social context, not by the needs of formal argumentation.[30] Epistolary theory does not discuss rhetorical arrangement of epistles because traditional formulas and their order of presentation provide the arrangement. There are only similarities of function shared by the arrangement of epistles and speeches. The epistolary body opening, middle, and closing roughly parallel the

---

27. For discussion of the relationship between rhetorical and epistolary theory, see Abraham J. Malherbe, *Ancient Epistolary Theorists* (SBLSBS 19; Atlanta: Scholars, 1988), 3–6; Stanley K. Stowers, *Letter Writing in Greco-Roman Antiquity* (LEC 5; Philadelphia: Westminster, 1986), 51–52; Georg Strecker, *Literaturgeschichte des Neuen Testaments* (Göttingen: Vandenhoeck & Ruprecht, 1992), 86–95.

28. R. Dean Anderson, Jr. *Ancient Rhetorical Theory and Paul* (rev. ed.; Leuven: Peeters, 1999); Carl Joachim Classen, "St. Paul's Epistles and Ancient Greek and Roman Rhetoric," *Rhetorica* 10 (1992): 319–44.

29. Aune, *The New Testament in its Literary Environment*, 203.

30. Stowers, *Letter Writing*, 53–56 .

exordium, narratio-probatio, and *peroratio* of speeches respectively. Both rhetorical and epistolary theories discuss style, but epistolary theory differentiates between the style appropriate to epistles and that appropriate to speeches (Quintilian, *Institutio Oratoria* 9.4.19–22).

It might be concluded that since rhetorical and epistolary theory are found to be marginally integrated in the rhetorical and epistolary handbooks of the Greco-Roman era, finding development of invention, arrangement, and style in epistles is somewhat pointless. However, it is clear from existent letters that by the first century BCE, epistolary composition is guided by rhetorical practice to become "sophisticated instruments of persuasion and media for displaying literary skill."[31] Also, epistolary theory is part of the rhetorical tradition.[32] Rhetorical handbooks are mainly concerned with the rhetoric of the oral speeches of the law court and thus do not emphasize written epistles addressed to virtually every other context of life, but this concern does not rule out the influence of rhetoric on the composition of epistles. More rhetorical analysis of extant literary epistles needs to be performed to substantiate this discussion.

Since Paul is the main writer of the epistles of the New Testament, there is a natural focus upon him and his letters. Kennedy helps reignite the debate with this comment: "Rhetorical schools were common in the Hellenized cities of the East when Paul was a boy, and he could have attended one; certainly he was familiar with the rhetorical conventions of speeches in Roman lawcourts, the oral teachings of Greek philosophers, and the conventions of Greek letter-writing."[33] Kennedy thus raises the question of whether Paul had a rhetorical education and, if so, how formal and how extensive

---

31. Aune, *The New Testament in its Literary Environment*, 160.
32. Hermann Peter, *Der Brief in der römischen Literatur: Literargeschichtliche Untersuchungen und Zusammenfassungen* (Abh Leip 20.3; Leipzig: Teubner, 1901; repr. Hildesheim: Georg Olms, 1965), 14, 19.
33. Kennedy, *Classical Rhetoric*, 130; cf. Kennedy, *New Testament Interpretation*, 9–10.

it was. Some argue that the rhetorical conventions found in Paul's epistles are due to his unconscious borrowing from the practice of rhetoric that he had experienced, especially from the rhetoric of the Old Testament.[34] Others claim that these conventions are due to formal study of rhetoric.[35] This question will undoubtedly continue to be debated.

The Rhetoric of Revelation

For reasons unknown, Kennedy does not provide an initial analysis of the Book of Revelation. Analysis of Revelation by Greco-Roman rhetoric does not readily suggest itself. Revelation is an extensive vision report by a Jewish-Christian prophet. Its invention is not by rational argumentation using enthymemes or examples, and its arrangement is not structured by *exordium* through *peroratio*. Rather, its invention relies heavily upon divine ethos and the ethos of the prophet, and the pathos generated by the imagery. Its arrangement is by numbers sacred to Judaism (especially 3, 7, and 12) and interlocking series. Consequently, Kennedy's work has not readily influenced works on Revelation.[36] What is perhaps the most extensive analysis of the rhetoric of Revelation to date only contains scattered references to Kennedy.[37]

Conclusion

Kennedy helps reinvigorate the study of the rhetoric of the New Testament, a study that had languished at the beginning of the

---

34. Carl Joachim Classen, "St. Paul's Epistles and Ancient Greek and Roman Rhetoric," in *Rhetorical Criticism of the New Testament*, ed. idem (WUNT 128; Tübingen: Mohr Siebeck, 2000), 1–28.
35. Ronald F. Hock, "Paul and Greco-Roman Education," in *Paul in the Greco-Roman World: A Handbook*, ed. J. Paul Sampley (Harrisburg: Trinity, 2003), 198–227.
36. For rhetorical works on Revelation, see Watson, *Rhetoric of the New Testament*, 180–82.
37. For an extensive analysis of the rhetoric of Revelation, see David A. deSilva, *Seeing Things John's Way: The Rhetoric of the Book of Revelation* (Louisville: Westminster John Knox, 2009).

twentieth century. He gives the discussion some initial guidelines, terminology, methodology, and resources that have clearly spurred advancement in our understanding of how the documents of the New Testament were constructed, how they were intended to function, and how the cultures and subcultures produced them. In addition, his own ethos as a noted classicist gives New Testament interpreters confidence to pursue rhetorical analysis against considerable initial skepticism and even opposition to rhetorical analysis in the 1980s, when his book emerged. While the rhetorical anomalies and complexities of the genres of gospel, history, epistle, and apocalypse that comprise the New Testament have posed challenges to his initial foray into the rhetoric of the New Testament, Kennedy has had a strong and positive influence in reintroducing rhetorical criticism to New Testament studies.

5

The Contribution of Wilhelm Wuellner to New Testament Rhetorical Criticism

James D. Hester and J. David Hester

During the course of his career, Wilhelm Wuellner came to be recognized as one of the major contributors to the late–twentieth-century rebirth of New Testament rhetorical criticism. His work on rhetorical criticism began a little more than a decade after the publication of Amos Wilder's study of the rhetoric of the early church and followed James Muilenberg's challenge to biblical scholars to move beyond form criticism in the analysis of the literature of the Bible.[1] Wuellner began to publish a series of articles that explored

---

1. Amos Wilder, *Early Christian Rhetoric: The Language of the Gospel* (Cambridge: Harvard University Press, 1964). James Muilenberg, "Form Criticism and Beyond," *JBL* 88, no. 1 (1969): 1–18.

and then re-explored the shape and goal of the argumentation he found in the literature of the New Testament and some other types of literature that had not before been understood as making an argument. His legacy includes his work for twenty years as editor of *The Protocols of the Colloquies of the Center for Hermeneutical Studies* as well as more than twenty articles he published in numerous and prestigious international journals and Festschriften. No less important were the numerous lectures he gave to rhetorical and biblical scholars in the United States, Europe, and South Africa. Throughout it all, Wuellner wanted to show that there was something "more" to be discovered by the rhetorical-critical enterprise and that texts had and have the power to be relevant and persuasive to audiences both in and through time.

At the end of his life, Wuellner published what may be the most important piece of his career. The article was entitled "Reconceiving a Rhetoric of Religion: A Rhetorics of Power and the Power of the Sublime."[2] In typical Wuellnerian fashion, the article outlines a philosophical foundation for a fundamental change to rhetorical theory, a change that is revolutionary. At its core, this article demonstrates that Wuellner had finally discerned the fundamental underlying and elusive issue that dogged his efforts to articulate a rhetoric of religion throughout his career. This issue unconsciously shaped all his works and their effort to advocate for something *more*, something *else* and *other than* the ubiquitous "rhetoric restrained" he saw happening all about him. With the publication of this article, we can finally begin to understand the direction and culmination toward which his previous works were building.

---

2. Wilhelm Wuellner, "Reconceiving a Rhetoric of Religion: A Rhetorics of Power and the Power of the Sublime," in *Rhetorics and Hermeneutics: Wilhelm Wuellner and His Influence*, ed. James D. Hester and J. David Hester (Amador) (New York: T&T Clark, 2004), 23–77. Wuellner died in February 2004, shortly before this essay appeared. As far as the authors know, it was the last thing he wrote for publication.

More importantly, however, this article also allows us to understand the unique contribution Wuellner wished to make to rhetorical theory, particularly as practiced by rhetorical critics of the Bible. It provides a theoretical reconfiguration of critical practices that has the potential to transform rhetorical approaches not only to the Bible but also in other disciplines and interdisciplinary arenas as well. As such, it helps give definition to what it means to bring a Wuellnerian approach to rhetorical theory and criticism and offers fertile new territories of exploration for those wishing to take up his call.

In what follows, we begin by defining both his general and his special theories of rhetoric. No definition can avoid the explorations, the cul-de-sacs, and the revisions in his work that represent early efforts to formulate his rhetorical-critical theory. We need, therefore, to trace some of the significant lines of thought and development exhibited in his analytical works and show how these constitute a programmatic effort to describe the argumentative power of rhetoric in its various contexts. In this way, we shall explore the path Wuellner took that led him to his final insight.

Next, we shall outline and lay out a little more fully his reinvention of rhetoric through the return of the sublime. In this section, we shall uncover the new ground and direction that his theory of power as a theory of the sublime can take and how this theory shapes new ideas of and in rhetorical criticism. We shall see ramifications of rhetoric not only upon analytics and criticism but also upon ethics and its integration into rhetorical practices.

From there, we outline how Wuellner's rhetoric of power as a rhetoric of the sublime enables biblical rhetorical critics to make a significant contribution to discussions taking place outside of biblical criticism. Very promising are the discussions on the introduction of ethics into the heart of rhetorical analytics, theory, and practice.

Building upon this ethical foundation, the interdisciplinary steps that Wuellnerian critics can and must take as diagnosticians and therapists of power become important. These steps serve as examples of what an exploration of the reintroduction of the sublime in rhetorical criticism will offer biblical critics and their colleagues in rhetoric.[3]

Defining Wuellner's Theories of Rhetoric

Perhaps the most important contribution Wuellner makes to rhetorical criticism is his insistence that there is more to rhetorical criticism than was or is being practiced by many New Testament rhetorical critics. He exhorts critics to throw off the restraints of analyses that deal primarily with issues identified by form and literary criticism and to move to practical criticism that studies literary devices as argumentation and investigates their effects on the reader or hearer. He argues that rhetoric should be "re-conceptualized as theory of argumentation, or as theory of practical reasoning."[4] Therefore, the analysis of the "art" of rhetoric lies not in the description of the stylish use of the constructs of topics, tropes, and trajectories of argumentation, although such descriptions have a place in criticism.[5] Rather, the analysis of the "art" of rhetoric lies in the description of those elements as argumentation seeking to persuade

---

3. Thomas Olbricht, "Wilhelm Wuellner and the Promise of Rhetoric," in Hester and Hester, *Rhetorics and Hermeneutics*, 78–104; and Vernon Robbins, "Where is Wuellner's Anti-Hermeneutical Hermeneutic Taking Us?," in Hester and Hester, *Rhetorics and Hermeneutics*, 105–25, http://www.religion.emory.edu/faculty/robbins/Pdfs/WuellnerRhetHerm.pdf. Olbricht and Robbins have written significant and insightful analyses of Wuellner's work that elaborate some features of his thought that we cannot elaborate here. See also J. David Hester, "The Wuellnerian Sublime: Rhetorics, Power and the Ethics of Commun(icat)ion," in Hester and Hester, *Rhetorics and Hermeneutics*, 3–22; and J. David Hester Amador, *Academic Constraints in Rhetorical Criticism of the New Testament: An Introduction to a Rhetoric of Power* (JSNTSup 174; Sheffield: Sheffield Academic, 1999), 87–112.

4. Wilhelm Wuellner, "Reading Romans in Context," in *Celebrating Romans: Template for Pauline Theology*, ed. Sheila McGinn (Grand Rapids: Eerdmans, 2004), 109. In an "editor's note" on p. 106, McGinn says that "this essay is perhaps [Wuellner's] last contribution to New Testament scholarship." In fact, the essay was first presented as a paper to a seminar at the annual meeting of the Society for New Testament Studies in Göttingen in August 1987.

and convince the members of the audience, real and implied, to take action based on insights derived from their encounter with the rhetorical artifact.[6] The "more" to be done by criticism involves not just an appreciation for and description of the aesthetics of an argument but also an awareness and description of the dynamism of power at work in the outcomes of argumentation. In his view, the New Testament rhetorical critic should move from analysis of the mundane to critical commentary on the "sublime." Wuellner's agenda broadens and deepens our understanding of rhetorical criticism and recasts our understanding of rhetoric as communication to that of argumentation that leads to action. His rhetoric of power is thus a rhetoric informed by the power of the sublime.

Wuellner takes a broad approach to rhetorical theory. Grounded in classical rhetorical-critical theory, Wuellner's awareness not just of the history of rhetoric but also the *historicity* of rhetoric leads him to explore a range of communication theories that cohere around a core principle of rhetoric as *activity*. In his writing, he makes frequent reference to traditional and classical rhetoric but expands

---

5. See Wilhelm Wuellner, "Putting Life Back into the Lazarus Story and Its Reading: The Narrative Rhetoric of John 11 as the Narration of Faith," in *Postculturalism as Exegesis*, ed. David Jobling and Stephen D. Moore (Semeia 54; Atlanta: Scholars, 1991), 114, 121–23.

6. In several places, Wuellner describes what he terms "rhetoric restrained," i.e., rhetoric that was reduced to stylistics and then further to tropes and figures. For example, see idem, "Where is Rhetorical Criticism Taking Us?" *CBQ* 49, no. 3 (1987): 451. He also identifies restraints on rhetorical criticism as including such things as "reduc[ing] it to social description or to historical reconstruction." See idem, "Rhetorical Criticism," in *The Postmodern Bible: The Bible and Culture Collective*, ed. Elizabeth A. Castelli et al. (New Haven: Yale University Press, 1995), 161. In other places, he describes the history and decries the development of the tendency to view rhetoric as a closed system based on western and patriarchal ideologies that narrowed its focus to that of style as represented, e.g., in the reforms of Peter Ramus. See idem, "Biblical Exegesis in the Light of the History and Historicity of Rhetoric and the Nature of the Rhetoric of Religion," in *Rhetoric and the New Testament*, ed. Thomas Olbricht and Stanley Porter (JSNTSup 90; Sheffield: Sheffield Academic, 1993), 495–506; and idem, "Hermeneutics and Rhetorics: From 'Truth and Method' to 'Truth and Power,'" *Scriptura* Special Issue S3 (1989): 2–13; and idem, "Death and Rebirth of Rhetoric in Late Twentieth Century Biblical Exegesis," in *Texts and Contexts: Biblical Texts in Their Textual and Situational Contexts*, ed. David Hellholm and Tord Fonberg (Oslo: Scandanivian University Press, 1995), 917–30.

the disciplinary boundaries usually associated with classical rhetoric. He introduces theories of the New Rhetoric, literary criticism, socio-rhetorical criticism, philosophical hermeneutics, philosophy of language, and comparative rhetorics. Wuellner draws from the works of George Kennedy, Chaim Perelman, William Brandt, Harold Bloom, Walter Ong, David Jaspers, Mikhail Bakhtin, Wayne Booth, Steve Mailloux, Jonathan Culler, J. Hillis Miller, Hans-Georg Gadamer, Kenneth Burke, John Searle, and Terry Eagleton.[7] He cites works in non-Western rhetorics, feminist rhetorics, ideological criticism, modern theories of author and reader, meaning and interpretation, semiotics, structuralism, and the materiality of communication.[8] Overwhelming as this range of interests is, at its core lies a commitment to the exploration of the *continuing* power of a rhetorical utterance to influence and persuade and an investigation of how that power changes over time and between cultures and audiences.

Wuellner's use of insights from his study of modern theoretical material shapes his approach to classical rhetorical theory. He comes to understand ancient rhetorical theory and its modern critics and analyses as a "special theory" of rhetoric.[9] That is, classical theory reflects rhetorical practices used by a particular community within a given time frame and because it participates in a common culture or

---

7. A quick perusal of footnotes in any of Wuellner's writings reveals an astonishing breadth of disciplines in which he read. For example, see the notes in his article "Reconceiving a Rhetoric of Religion," where he cites publications dealing with everything from theosophy to the semantics of electronic forms of communication, to varieties of literary criticism, to philosophical hermeneutics, and to pragmatism and the New Historicism.

8. Olbricht expressed appreciation for Wuellner's wide reading in secondary literature but argues that he did not engage deeply enough in "fundamental research" that might have provided bases for theorizing. See Olbricht, "Wuellner and the Promise of Rhetoric," 104. Given his agenda, it is unlikely Wuellner shared Olbricht's concept of what might constitute "fundamental" research.

9. The distinction between "special" and "general" theories of rhetoric was proposed by Ernest Bormann, *The Force of Fantasy: Restoring the American Dream* (Carbondale: Southern Illinois University Press, 1985), 4–5. Wuellner never explicitly uses the distinction.

paideia and provides guidelines on how effectively to communicate within that community. Examples of these culturally conditioned rhetorical practices are, quite obviously, found in the so-called "handbooks" written for students in the Hellenistic and Roman schools. However, they are also included in studies of classical rhetoric such as that of Heinrich Lausberg, which Wuellner references.[10]

Wuellner never totally abandons the "special theory" of classical rhetoric, but develops over time elements of what can be called a "general theory" of rhetoric. His "general theory" describes what he believes to be features of "human communication events that cannot be ignored or rescinded by the participants" in those events.[11] For example, while it might be both possible and desirable to change the coding of a message to enhance understanding among recipients, it is self-evident that some form of utterance is necessary for communication, regardless of the code used. General theories can account for the use of a form of utterance in a particular social setting, and Wuellner embraces general rhetorical theories not only to inform and critique, and to expand and elaborate, but also to help categorize and make distinctive the practices of special rhetorical theories.

To put it differently, typical rhetorical *analysis* uses special theory to describe authorial intention evident in a rhetorical artifact associated with a particular time and community.[12] This analysis

---

10. Heinrich Lausberg, *Handbuch der Literarischen Rhetorik* (2 vols.; München: Max Hueber, 1960); idem, *Handbook of Literary Rhetoric: A Foundation for Literary Study*, ed. and trans. D. E. Orton and R. D. Anderson (Leiden: Brill, 1998). See also idem, *Elemente der Literarischen Rhetorik* (München: Max Hueber, 1963).

11. Bormann, *The Force of Fantasy*, 4.

12. Coming from both literary critics and philosophers of language, a huge body of literature discusses the concept of authorial intention. The debate derives from claims made by the so-called "new critics," who argue that the author's intention in writing a poem or narrative is irrelevant to the task of interpretation and can be ignored. Wuellner's notion of intention is influenced in part by his understanding of reader-response criticism and the role of the reader in interpreting a text. Uncovering the author's intent and the reader's response to the argument are, for him, part of rhetorical analysis.

should be familiar to most biblical rhetorical critics, whose disciplinary foundational explorations were inspired by George Kennedy and profoundly shaped by the dominant model published by Hans Dieter Betz.[13] In contradistinction to this typical analytic approach, Wuellner understands rhetorical *criticism* as the effort to describe how and why that artifact continues to exert power to influence the actions of communities and individuals not related to the original exigence of the artifact.

Wuellner's understanding of the nature of rhetorical criticism is formulated over time as he seeks to discover what "more" the critic can do. In some early studies, he outlines what he calls "features of modern theories and practices of rhetorical criticism."[14] He says that modern theories turn from consideration of a text as a repository of social description(s) or an object of analysis that seeks to describe elements of its literary nature. Instead, modern theories regard a text as a form of argumentation and are interested in the pragmatic nature of argument. Argumentative technique is understood as a means to an end, not as an ornament to be described. Thus, the critic can show that a narrative can both describe the world of the author *and* make an argument for a value represented in the world that the author wishes to advocate.

Later, Wuellner makes a new theoretical claim. In describing what he calls the three levels of rhetorical reading, he claims that the second level "is concerned with what readers (whether as the original readers...or *all subsequent readers*, past, present, future) *experience* in the ever changing, never static reading of John's narrative rhetoric."[15]

---

13. See, e.g., Hans Dieter Betz, "The Literary Composition and Function of Paul's Letter to the Galatians," *NTS* 21 (1975): 353–79; and idem, *Galatians: A Commentary on Paul's Letter to the Churches in Galatia* (Hermenia; Philadelphia: Fortress, 1979).
14. Wilhelm Wuellner, "Rhetorical Criticism and Its Theory in Cultural Critical Perspective: The Narrative Rhetoric of John 11," in *Text and Interpretation: New Approaches in the Criticism of the New Testament*, ed. P. J. Hartin and J. H. Petzer (NTTS 15; Leiden: Brill, 1991), 167–81.

In other words, the text is rhetorically always subject to the context of any reader, and the act of reading is an "ongoing," primarily corporate process of "performance." As such, multiple readings and interpretations enable the power of the rhetoric of the text.[16] The clear implication of this claim, which Wuellner elaborates in several other places in his writings, is that the reader is actively engaged in creating the meaning of the text.

This engagement is enabled by a dynamic perspective that Wuellner introduces to the concept of the "rhetorical situation."[17] As first described by Lloyd Bitzer, the rhetorical situation is an exigence to which a rhetorical utterance is directed to change "reality through mediation of thought and action." Bitzer claims that rhetoric is situational, even to the point of being "the very ground of rhetorical activity."[18] The exigence is some issue that confronts an individual or group that the speaker believes can be resolved by argumentation. It is the "organizing principle," because it designates both the audience and what change the speaker hopes to affect in that audience. In this context, the audience consists of those whom the speaker identifies as capable of being influenced by discourse and who are the "mediators of change." In responding to the exigence and attempting to persuade the audience, the speaker is confronted by constraints such as

15. Wilhelm Wuellner, "Putting Life Back into the Lazarus Story," 114 (emphasis in original). On p. 113, Wuellner describes the three levels of rhetorical reading as "(a) author and produced text; (b) reader interacting with the text, thereby bringing the text to life…and (c) the scholarly critic."

16. Wuellner maintains a distinction between the rhetoric *in* the text—the tropes, topics, forms, formulas, and conventions of argumentation used by the author—and the rhetoric *of* the text—the persuasive impact the text has on the hearer or reader, whether the real or intended audience or subsequent readers and audiences. See Wuellner, "Rhetorical Criticism and Its Theory," 176.

17. This concept is first described by Lloyd F. Bitzer in "The Rhetorical Situation," *Ph&Rh* 1 (1968): 1–14. Curiously enough, Wuellner never cites this article but instead seems to derive his understanding of the concept from other authors and critics. Bitzer provided further explanation of his theory in "Rhetoric and Public Knowledge," in *Rhetoric, Philosophy, and Literature*, ed. D. Burks (Lafayette: Purdue University Press, 1978), 67–93.

18. Bitzer, "The Rhetorical Situation," 4–5.

"persons, events, objects, and relations" that the speaker has to identify and address.[19]

Any rhetorical situation shares some general characteristics. Perhaps the most obvious is that the situation generates discourse. No one writes for exigences that never exist. Even if the writing evidences the tropes, topics, and styles of an argument, it is not rhetorical in the absence of exigence and situation. Furthermore, not just any response will do. The question the critic must explore is whether or not the response is "fitting." It is possible for any given response to continue to be fitting if elements of a rhetorical situation persist and the original discourse is regarded as continually able to engage those elements. Sacred texts, for example, would seem to have that utility.

Wuellner takes this concept of the rhetorical situation and marries it to the concept of the "argumentative situation," which he adapts from Chaim Perelman.[20] The argumentative situation is a construct of a trajectory of the arguments used in a given rhetorical situation. It includes "both the goal the speaker has set himself and the arguments he may encounter."[21] As the effects of an argument unfold and the argument is adapted to the audience, the argumentative situation evolves so that it presents the speaker with opportunities to consider new strategies for making her argument. Furthermore, it is possible that developments in the argumentative situation might result in the emergence of a new exigence and thus create a new rhetorical situation.[22]

19. Ibid., 8–15.
20. Chaim Perelman and Lucie Olbrechts-Tyteca, *The New Rhetoric: A Treatise on Argumentation*, trans. JohnWilkinson and Purcell Weaver (Notre Dame: University of Notre Dame Press, 1969;), 96, 412, 452, 490–91. Without wanting to diminish the contribution of the co-author, it has become conventional to refer to Perelman alone when referencing the book.
21. Ibid., 96.
22. This dynamic can be demonstrated readily in the argumentative trajectories in the letters of Paul. For example, see James D. Hester, "Kennedy and the Reading of Paul: The Energy of

Wuellner's contribution to rhetorical criticism lies in his insight that an audience, any audience, may produce a new exigence that is not necessarily related to the original one, *each and every time a rhetorical artifact is encountered in time and place.* New participants and new constraints in the situation can be involved and thereby generate the need for further discourse. The only constraint on the elaboration of any given argument is its appropriateness to address an exigence currently being experienced by an audience or, in Wuellner's terms, a reader.

Rhetorical critics are also "readers" and bring to the act of reading and analysis social locations and issues that involve a context and constraints. Although they engage a text that was generated by an earlier exigence for another audience, they themselves are responding to an exigence and have in mind an audience they want to influence. For Wuellner, therefore, hermeneutics is a rhetorical activity, although most rhetorical critics fail to acknowledge Wuellner's insight.[23]

In identifying the medium containing rhetorical discourse, Wuellner speaks primarily of "texts."[24] It is the written word as well as the evolution of the technology of its production that interests Wuellner. However, he understands texts as products not only of authors but also of individual readers and the communities of which they are a part as they deal with texts in acts of reading.[25] Texts are

---

Communication," in *Words Well Spoken: George Kennedy's Rhetoric of the New Testament,* ed. C. Clifton Black and Duane F. Watson (Waco: Baylor University Press, 2008), 139–61.

23. In order more fully to appreciate Wuellner's point, the interested reader should carefully work through Robbins, "Where is Wuellner's Anti-Hermeneutical Hermeneutic Taking Us?" While a theory of hermeneutics is an important element in Wuellner's work, it is too complex to summarize here, and it likewise is unnecessary, since Robbins already has analyzed it.

24. As noted above, the oral nature of rhetoric does not seem to interest him. He mentions the importance of studies such as those of Whitney Shiner, *Proclaiming the Gospel: First Century Performance of Mark* (Harrisburg: Trinity, 2003); and Walter Ong, *Orality and Literacy: The Technologizing of the Word* (New York: Methuen, 1982). Wuellner's focus, however, is on materiality, not orality.

25. Wuellner, "Rhetorical Criticism," 163–64.

products of the context of both author and reader, and "[t]ext and context are complementary."[26] Texts provide content, while context shapes argumentation and practical reasoning in and of a text. Thus, "textuality" derives from both the intention of the author and the interpretation of the audience, and readers are always dynamically involved with the text.[27]

Wuellner's concept of "context" is an important element in his critical theory. He defines "context" as the "attitudinizing conventions, precepts that condition (both the writer's and the reader's) stance towards experience, knowledge, tradition, language, and other people."[28] Later, he elaborates this definition and defines "context" as "the overall argumentative and persuasive strategy that is designed to move the audience or reader to agree with the speaker or writer."[29] He goes on to say that "context" for him comes close to what Kenneth Burke meant by ideology *of* or *in* literature.[30] For Wuellner, limiting "context" only to that provided by Hellenistic and/or Roman rhetoric and their *paideia* by definition excludes consideration of *other* contexts provided by the rhetoric of religious, social, political, economic, cultural, or gender-identified communities throughout history. Wuellner frequently argues that "context" has to be understood as including a force for change that is motivated by the intention of the author and the reaction of any

26. Wuellner cites John Lyons in support of this claim. For this citation, see idem, "Reading Romans in Context," 109. See John Lyons, *Language, Meaning and Context* (Bungay: Suffolk-Chaucer, 1981), 200.

27. For a fuller theoretical discussion of this aspect of Wuellner's theory, see Hester Amador, *Academic Constraints*, 99–101.

28. Thomas O. Sloan, "Rhetoric: Rhetoric in Literature," in *The New Encyclopædia Britannica*, ed. Philip W. Goetz, Robert McHenry, and Dale Hoiberg (15th ed.; 32 vols.; Chicago: Encyclopædia Brittanica, 1985–2010), 26:758–62. For Wuellner's quotation of Sloan, see Wuellner, "Where is Rhetorical Criticism Taking Us?," 450.

29. Idem, "Rhetorical Criticism," 164.

30. Idem, "Biblical Exegesis in the Light of History and Historicity of Rhetoric and the Nature of the Rhetoric of Religion," in *Rhetoric and the New Testament*, ed. Stanley Porter and Thomas Olbricht (Sheffield: JSOT, 1993), 502.

audience.[31] Therefore, "context" has to be understood *synchronically* and *diachronically*, as well as argumentatively. To say it differently using Vernon Robbins's marvelous metaphor, "context" is a "tapestry" woven by argumentation both *in* time and *through* time. This more "global" or "universal" understanding of "context" is an important feature of Wuellner's general theory of rhetoric.

One example of its importance is the way in which Wuellner adapts Kennedy's analytical method, in particular the identification of a rhetorical unit. While Kennedy wishes to describe context with reference to traditional rhetorical units, Wuellner rejects this limitation and elaborates the concept of rhetorical unit ultimately to include the whole of the canon. Even though context can be buried in other contexts, the larger context is always that which is derived from the *paideia* of a particular author and audience through time and in time.

Wuellner and Kennedy understand that the audience plays a role in completing the argument, but Wuellner also understands that the audience provides yet another context the rhetorical critic should consider in her analysis of how a rhetorical unit functions in the trajectory of argumentation.[32] Moreover, as we shall discuss below, the critic must recognize the role his own context plays in his critical analysis and interpretive activity.

Leaving aside other elements of Wuellner's general rhetorical theory, a word needs to be said about Wuellner's concept of "intentionality."[33] For Wuellner, "intention" includes such things as

---

31. For a fuller description of "context" in Wuellner's theory, see Hester Amador, *Academic Constraints*, 95–101.
32. Using John Lyons, Wuellner describes "context" as including the "surrounding co-text" and "features of the situation of the utterance." See Wuellner, "Reading Romans in Context," 109. He goes on to say that, "The rhetorician will speak here of the rhetorical situation(s)." It seems more accurate to identify these situations with the "argumentative situation."
33. Other elements of Wuellner's general theory include modalities and indices. Deriving his definition from Perelman, Wuellner describes modalities as those parts of speech that express

the intent of the author to write or to do something that influences what is written. It also includes the desired outcomes of argumentation. Thus, Wuellner can describe "intentionality" as "the whole range of mental states . . . [such] as the beliefs and convictions relating to the cognition [of author and reader], and the desires relating to volition [of author and reader]."[34] Clearly, Wuellner has elaborated a conventional understanding of "authorial intention" by relating intentionality to "context" and rhetorical situation.[35]

An examination of the components of Wuellner's general theory makes it clear that his theory bears little relation to classical rhetorical theory, for the underlying premise of Wuellner's theory is that rhetoric should be understood as both a theory of argumentation and a literary theory.[36] His theory regards literature as social discourse and texts as generated by *both* the act of writing *and* of reading.[37] Furthermore, theory accounts for both the rhetoric *in* the text and the rhetoric *of* the text as that text is performed, that is, read, in any given social location or context. In considering both the rhetoric *in* and *of* the text, Wuellner can describe the power of rhetoric to affect change in the audience and create new realities for the hearers/readers of the text. The boundary conditions of traditional rhetorical approaches are giving way to the *living word* and the argumentative power of the text each and every time it is read. His critical theory is giving shape to the eventual exploration into how the power of the

mood and focus meaning; they influence meaning. They are part of the potential of the text not only to express the intention of the author but also to influence the reader's "mood." "Indexicality" includes personal *deixis* such as names, personal pronouns, modifiers that focus the immediate nature of the utterance or text. It also includes spatial and temporal *deixes* that focus the social and cultural contexts of the utterance. For a more thorough discussion of these concepts, see Hester Amador, *Academic Constraints*, 101–7. On pp. 107–11, Hester Amador provides an overview of Wuellner's concept of intentionality.

34. Wuellner, "Reading Romans in Context," 123.
35. See note 12 above.
36. Wuellner, *Hermeneutics and Rhetorics*, 33.
37. Wuellner, "Where is Rhetorical Criticism Taking Us?," 462–63.

text to transform is experienced with every encounter with the text. It is now possible to see how rhetorical theory as a theory of power might eventually transform into a theory of power as the power of the sublime. However, we are not there yet.

Features of Wuellnerian Rhetorical-Critical Analysis

There is no easy answer to the question of how Wuellnerian critical analysis, based on the theory outlined above, functions. Wuellner's methodology and theory evolves over time, and he never writes a definitive description of "Wuellnerian criticism."[38] Despite the dense and multidisciplinary nature of much of what he wrote, there are places in his earlier interpretation of discrete passages in the NT where he seems to rely primarily on a model of analysis adapted from and informed by his reading of George Kennedy and Chaim Perelman.[39] At other times, he approaches a text from the perspective of postmodern criticism.[40] Later in his life, his focus on the power of the sublime hints at critical tasks that, as far as we can tell, are being undertaken by no one else in the field.[41] It is characteristic of Wuellner that his analytical work lacks clear methodological

38. For our purposes, "rhetorical analysis" is a description of how an argument is constructed, whether that construct is based on, for example, classical rhetorical theory or on narrative structures. In contrast, "rhetorical criticism" is a description of why a rhetorical artifact has the power to create new realities and knowledge for those who interpret the artifact. For an elaboration of this distinction, see James D. Hester, "Rhetoric in and for the New Millennium," in *Rhetorics in the New Millennium*, ed. James D. Hester and J. David Hester (SAC; London: T&T Clark, 2010), 6–12.

39. George A. Kennedy, *New Testament Interpretation through Rhetorical Criticism* (Chapel Hill: University of North Carolina Press, 1984). Wuellner relies especially on Perelman and Olbrechts-Tyteca, *The New Rhetoric*, and their understanding of argumentation as that which acts effectively on the minds of an audience to secure adherence to the values advocated in the argument and causes the audience to do something in response. Wuellner also adopted their emphases on the role of audiences in argumentation and their claim that almost all forms of communication function argumentatively.

40. See Wuellner, "Rhetorical Criticism," 166–68, 179–83. Although *The Postmodern Bible* is self-described as a collaborative effort, the chapter on "Rhetorical Criticism" bears the distinctive imprint of Wuellner's thought and analysis. A postmodern point of view can also be seen in Wuellner, "Reconceiving a Rhetoric of Religion."

constraints since, through the act of analysis, criticism uncovers more boundaries to traverse and directions to explore. The directions, however, are not without purpose, and, as we shall see, they show a consistent principle inexorably leading to his final ethical theoretical formulation.

A careful analysis of his work on Luke, John, 1 Thessalonians, 1 Corinthians, and Romans reveals important pieces of his method.[42] In his earlier work, Wuellner uses Heinrich Lausberg's detailed description of the components of classical Greco-Roman rhetoric, and Wuellner adopts and adapts George Kennedy's method for analyzing a text.[43] He thus appears to stay, in large part, within the conventional rhetorical-critical method. Later, he elaborates those conventional models by placing them within a rhetorical theory that views the text as a "synchronic whole" and "readers" as including not only the "real" and "implied" readers but also the rhetorical critic herself.[44] His work on 1 Corinthians, for example, uses both

41. Wuellner's understanding of the sublime comes in part from Longinus, *On the Sublime*, trans. W. Hamilton Fyfe (LCL 199; Cambridge, MA: Harvard University Press, 1982). However, Wuellner elaborates it considerably, as we shall discuss below.

42. Wilhelm Wuellner, "The Rhetorical Structure of Luke 12 in Its Wider Context," *Neotestamentica* 22 (1989): 283–310; idem, "Putting Life Back into the Lazarus Story", 113–132; idem, "Rhetorical Criticism and Its Theory," 176–177; idem, "The Argumentative Structure of 1 Thessalonians as Paradoxical Encomium," in *The Thessalonian Correspondence*, ed. Raymond F. Collins (BETL 87; Leuven: Leuven University Press, 1990), 117–136; idem, "Paul as Pastor: The Function of Rhetorical Questions in First Corinthians," in *L'Apôtre Paul: Personalité, Style et Conception du Ministère*, ed. A. Vanhoye (BETL 73; Leuven University Press, 1986), 49–77; idem, "Paul's Rhetoric of Argumentation in Romans: An Alternative to the Donfried-Karris Debate Over Romans," *CBQ* 38 (1976): 330–351, repr. in *The Romans Debate: Revised and Expanded Edition*, ed.Karl Donfried (Peabody: Hendrikson,1995), 128–46; idem, "Reading Romans in Context." See also Castelli, *The Postmodern Bible*, 150–156, 178–183, where Wuellner provides two different analyses of 1 Cor. 9:1–10:13, one based on George Kennedy's model in *New Testament Interpretation* and another based on Wuellner's "postmodern" reading.

43. See note 10 and Kennedy, *New Testament Interpretation*, 33–38.

44. Wuellner, "Where is Rhetorical Criticism Taking Us," 458, 460; idem, "Reading Romans in Context," in McGinn, *Celebrating Romans*, 118, 121, 127; idem, "Rhetorical Criticism, in Castelli, *The Postmodern Bible*, 183–184; idem, "Reconceiving a Rhetoric of Religion," 35 and passim.

conventional critical analysis and various forms of elaboration he creates as he re-visits that text within new analytical contexts.

In 1970, Wuellner looks at the first three chapters of 1 Corinthians, takes the concept of homily genres proposed by Peder Borgen, and argues that homily patterns are found in 1 Cor 1:19–25, 26–21, 2:6–16, and 3:1–23.[45] From Wuellner's perspective, however, the entire homily encompasses 1:19–3:21 and exhibits features of a haggadic midrash. He acknowledges that the homily genre has parallels in the Hellenistic Cynic-Stoic diatribe, but use of midrashic models affords a better analysis of the argument in the opening chapters of the letter than Hellenistic models. In making this argument, he introduces a theme that he will elaborate later. He perceives that when seeking to understand argumentation in texts in the NT, the rhetoric of the synagogue and Jewish teaching needs to be explored in addition to the rhetorical traditions of Greece and Rome.[46] Apart from this insight, however, his analysis is conventional.

In 1986, he takes up the question of the function of the rhetorical questions found in 1 Corinthians 9.[47] He challenges the notions that the questions are simply figures associated with a genre such as the diatribe, or that they function stylistically to heighten emotion, or that they are polemical. For Wuellner, they function within the context of Paul's argumentation as a tool for instruction in Paul's efforts to change "the multiplicity of different social and ethnic/cultural value systems into a unity."[48] They thus function to produce a more mature, stable church. It is this rhetorical strategy that accounts

---

45. Idem, "Haggadic Homily Genre in I Corinthians 1–3," *JBL* 89, no. 2 (1970): 199–204.
46. For example, see idem, "Topos Forschung und Torahinterpretation bei Paulus and Jesus," *NTS* 24, no. 4 (1978): 463–83.
47. Idem, "Paul as Pastor."
48. Ibid., 73.

for what appear to be contradictions in Paul's teaching on social values, particularly in chapters 11 and 14.

As suggestive as Wuellner's observations on Paul's rhetorical construction of social mores and norms are, his use of Perelman's theories of audiences or readers in the analysis of chapter 9 are more instructive for understanding his later work.[49] He identifies two types of readers implied in the text: empirical, that is, a "real" reader to whom an author/speaker has to adapt; and an implied reader, whom Wuellner, following Perelman, describes as a "construct" of the author and whom the speaker wants to influence. This category of reader is part of what Perelman calls the "universal audience," that is, a collection of individuals that the speaker wants to influence and considers competent and reasonable to judge the argument being made. To be a convincing argument, the premises must be acceptable to this audience. It then follows that if the universal audience is convinced, any reasonable individual should also be convinced.[50]

According to Wuellner, it is the "universal audience" that Paul addresses with the rhetorical questions in 1 Corinthians. When the "real" reader is confronted with the values implied in these questions, she is challenged to make a decision about those values based on

49. While alerting the critic to the complexity of the concept of "reader" or "audience," Wuellner concentrates primarily on the materiality of a "text" that is read or heard. While he does acknowledge the "performance" of texts and the role of readers, he pays less attention to the performative aspects of texts that occur when reading aloud to others and what role that subsequent level of reading might play in making an argument persuasive. See Wuellner, "Reconceiving a Rhetoric of Religion," 47–50. Consider the possible role of Phoebe in carrying Paul's letter to the house churches of Rome (Rom. 16:1–2). It is possible that she was commissioned to read the letter to them or that she had in her retinue someone who could. Alternatively, there may have been people in the churches who were educated enough to read it. Whatever Paul's intentions, the fate of the argument when the letter was read lay in part not only in the regard with which the reader was held by the group but also in the competence of the speaker as orator and in the effectiveness of delivery. Orality in the form of elocution adds yet another layer of complexity to those identified by Wuellner, and yet may lie beyond the ability of the critic to assess unless the critic examines issues of style and performance. For a theory-based elaboration of this issue, see Hester Amador, *Academic Constraints*, 119–124.

50. See Chaim Perelman, *Realm of Rhetoric*, trans. William Kluback (London: University of Notre Dame Press, 1982), 17–18.

implied membership in the larger audience. Acceptance of the values held by the universal audience leads to praise while rejection leads to blame. Thus, social location is rhetorically constructed.[51] This insight allows Wuellner, for example, to explain Paul's teaching about the behavior of women in the church, what Wuellner calls Paul's "pastoral strategy."[52]

Wuellner argues that social location explains this strategy. Instructions concerning relations between a believing spouse and an unbelieving partner have to do with the "private" location of a home versus the "public" location of the church. Questions need to be worked out in private. If the spouse becomes a believer, then his or her status changes from outsider to insider, the domestic role is redefined as being in Christ, and the patronage system can change to a friendship system. A spouse can now speak publicly from the status of a partnership.[53] For Wuellner, looking at the issue of the behavior of women in church is not an exercise in social description as such. It is an effort to understand how social codes can be used in argumentation to change the behavior of the reader or hearer.[54]

In his contribution to *The Postmodern Bible*, he uses more unconventional analytical techniques than he used in his earlier work on 1 Corinthians. In the chapter entitled "Rhetorical Criticism," he juxtaposes an analysis of 1 Corinthians 9 that uses Kennedy's model with what Wuellner labels "a postmodern rhetorical reading of 1 Cor. 9:1—10:13" that is based on results of his critical examination of "new biblical rhetorical criticism."[55] It is the postmodern analysis that is of interest for our purposes.

---

51. Wuellner, "Paul as Pastor," 58–63. This observation also applies to other Pauline literature. See Hester, "Kennedy and the Reading of Paul," 160 n. 63.
52. Wuellner, "Paul as Pastor," 74.
53. Ibid., 74–75.
54. Ibid., 65.
55. Kennedy, *New Testament Interpretation,* 33–37; Wuellner, "Rhetorical Criticism," 150.

Wuellner begins by noting that he will use Antoinette Clark Wire's work on the women prophets in 1 Corinthians as an example of rhetorical criticism moving beyond the conventional.[56] Specifically, he is interested in Wire's explicit attempt to provide a feminist reading of the letter to show "traces of a voice which that very argument [current biblical studies concerning the women prophets] is organized to suppress."[57] He describes Wire's attempt to show that the force of Paul's argument is not to convince the Corinthians that self-discipline on behalf of the whole community is a desirable social value. Rather, Paul is attempting to limit the spiritual freedom the women prophets found in Christ and establish himself as their leader whose own self-discipline should be imitated.

As he had done earlier, Wuellner deals with the concept of the rhetorical unit. However, he argues that the identity of a unit is not tied to a formal definition as such but is a function of the interpreter's perspective on the text. Therefore, different interpreters may delimit different units within the same text. Furthermore, the identity of a unit may also depend on context; that is, the identification of any given unit may be determined by the argumentative function of a larger unit, up to and including that of the entire text.

Moreover, there is another step to be made. "The persuasive power of a piece of Pauline literature . . . derives in large measure from its belonging to a collection of letters and finally to a canon of scripture."[58] In other words, the rhetorical critic must be self-aware by taking into account her own social location and value systems much as Wire did in making the self-conscious connection between feminist readings and her understanding of the women prophets in the Corinthian church. The critic must also recognize that the

---

56. Antoinette Clark Wire, *The Corinthian Women Prophets: A Reconstruction through Paul's Rhetoric* (Minneapolis: Fortress, 1990).
57. Wuellner, "Rhetorical Criticism," 178.
58. Ibid., 178.

argumentative power of tropes functions situationally (or contextually), so that describing their role solely in an author's argument is inadequate to understand how they function in new rhetorical and/or argumentative situations, whether those situations are created by the reader's response or by the interpreter's analysis.

To elaborate what he means, Wuellner turns to Perelman's concept of dissociative argumentation. In dissociation, the rhetor tries to construct the value of something by showing that what seems apparent is not what is "real."[59] In the case of the Corinthian church, Paul has to persuade the "spiritual" Christians that their behavior under the guise of "freedom" is in reality a danger to the church. Their freedom is not true freedom if it impacts negatively on other members of the community. In other words, it might become a form of tyranny or an affront to God (cf. 10:8–19).

In the course of Paul's argument, moreover, another dissociation unfolds. The apparent topos of the "enslaved leader" who is to be imitated is in reality the topos of a patron or benefactor who is to be heard and obeyed. This dissociation becomes even clearer when set into the larger context of the evaluation of Paul's teaching by the later church. Wuellner notes, "Whether or not [Paul] won the immediate contest, he has been successful in the eyes of history."[60]

Finally, Wuellner introduces the distinction Perelman makes between convincing and persuasive argumentation. Perelman says, "Discourse addressed to a specific audience aims to persuade, while discourse addressed to the universal audience aims to convince. ... A convincing discourse is one whose premises are . . . acceptable in principle to all members of a universal audience."[61] As Wuellner

---

59. The analogy often cited is Perelman's reference to the apparent break in an oar put into water when the feel of the oar makes it apparent that the oar is whole. See Perelman, *Realm of Rhetoric*, 126–127.
60. Wuellner, "Rhetorical Criticism," 181.
61. Perelman, *Realm of Rhetoric*, 18.

points out, it appears in 1 Corinthians as though Paul is interested in convincing his audience but, in point of fact, he apparently only succeeds in persuading a particular group, that is, those who were ready to be persuaded. Over the trajectory of both verbal and written communicative exchanges, Paul clearly continues to encounter opposition to his teaching.

The concept of the argumentative situation plays an important role in Wuellner's analysis of Romans. When framing the methodological issues typically addressed by interpreters of Romans, he attributes to Karl Donfried an interest in describing the "concrete issues" facing the Romans and thus a focus on aspects of "social and political history" or "sociological issues." In contrast, he attributes to Robert Karris an interest in "theological issues."[62] Wuellner labels both "false alternative[s]" and argues instead that Romans has to be seen as an argument in which an appeal to values is laid out in the exordium (1:1–15), elaborated in the body of the letter, and restated in the peroration (15:14–16:23). Paul is not defending himself or asking the Romans to deliberate over some issue. Instead, he is advocating a system of values. According to Wuellner, therefore, Romans generically is epideictic.[63]

In describing the argumentative situation for Romans, Wuellner appeals to classical stasis theory and structuralism as sources for identifying the underlying issue of the letter. He also appeals to matters related to the situation in Corinth and Paul's upcoming trip to Jerusalem, both of which would have provided Paul with "argumentative possibilities."[64] Although this early approach of Wuellner leans heavily on traditional rhetorical categories, he introduces new dimensions and aspects of rhetorical dynamics arising

---

62. Wuellner, "Paul's Rhetoric of Argumentation in Romans."

63. Ibid., 139–141.

64. Ibid., 131. As always, Wuellner's argument is far more nuanced and deserves closer reading by those interested.

from a Perelmanian view of the argumentative situation. Of particular interest is how he brings together *both* theology *and* sociology as argumentative expressions, and this fusion of the religious and the profane informs his analysis. Eventually, they will give shape to a concept of the argumentative situation encountered *each* and *every* time the text is taken up and read.

The body of Wuellner's work on New Testament texts is far more complex and nuanced than can be represented here. However, Wuellner clearly uses forms of analysis that evolve and develop from historical and form criticism into a "post-modern" new rhetorical criticism. Interest in incorporating first-century Jewish and synagogue rhetorical practices evolves into claims for the need to acknowledge the social and ideological locations of the critic. Warnings against formal and taxonomic approaches to the text develop into a call for rhetorical critics to become subversive and transformational.[65] To understand what he means by a postmodern rhetorical criticism, we must look at the most challenging element of his rhetorical theory, namely, his understanding of the power of the sublime.

Power of Rhetoric as the Power of the Sublime

Kennedy makes an important and interesting observation that provides the foundation for Wuellner's focus on the sublime. Kennedy observes, "All religious systems are rhetorical: they are attempts to communicate perceived religious truth."[66] Kennedy proceeds to argue that rhetorical criticism of the Bible explains the power of the text or, as he elaborates in his later writings, the ability of the text to transfer the energy of the speaker to the audience and convince them to do something.[67] During the course of his career,

---

65. Wuellner, "Rhetorical Criticism," 184–185.
66. Kennedy, *New Testament Interpretation*, 158.

however, Wuellner sees something more in Kennedy's dictum and reverses the terms of Kennedy's statement. Wuellner claims that all rhetorical systems are religious.[68]

In other words, for Wuellner the goal of rhetorical criticism is not the description of the aesthetics of a text but a description of its pragmatic and ethical implications, which he finally understands as something "more" than is conventionally the case. The exigence that creates the rhetorical situation can now be analyzed not simply from an historical or sociological point of view. The argumentative situation is no longer an object of literary analysis. Both situations are viewed as components of human experience *in* and *through* time. They are reflected in the affairs of a variety of communities as those communities act towards resolution and action. In his article "Reconceiving a Rhetoric of Religion," he finally elaborates how rhetorical systems are *religious.*[69]

Wuellner often refers to "a rhetoric of power," but he never provides a precise definition for that concept.[70] In general, rhetoric is understood as utterance, arrangement and style, and elements of argumentation and intends not only to engage an audience but also to persuade it to *do* something, namely to confront and effect a change upon an exigence. Because the intentions of both speaker and audience are at play in the processes of persuasion, rhetoric functions contextually by recognizing that values are derived from truth claims legitimized by context. A rhetoric of power views this dynamic

---

67. See especially George A. Kennedy, "A Hoot in the Dark: The Evolution of General Rhetoric," *Ph&Rh* 25, no. 1 (1992): 1–21. See also idem., *Comparative Rhetoric: An Historical and Cross-Cultural Introduction* (New York: Oxford University Press, 1998).

68. Wuellner, "Reconceiving a Rhetoric of Religion," 34.

69. Wuellner has a particular meaning for the term "rhetorics" that is used in the subtitle of the essay. In *Hermeneutics and Rhetorics*, 1, he distinguishes between rhetoric as argumentative practice and rhetorics as critical theory.

70. For one definition, see Hester Amador, *Academic Constraints*, 119–24.

exchange as expression of interests and of interstices of power and the systems that support them, in time and through time.

A rhetoric of power makes use of special theories of rhetoric to change and expose the worldview of an audience. In so doing, it develops variations of, or even creates new, special theories to explain, defend, or exhort adherence to the values that the audience has (re-) discovered by virtue of an engagement with an act of persuasion. A rhetorics of power exposes, explores, and produces new meaning for the audience.[71]

A rhetorics of power becomes part of a general theory of rhetoric when it is brought under the rubric of a rhetoric of religion and understood as expressing the power of the sublime.[72] When that happens, the phrase "a rhetorics of power *and* the power of the sublime" becomes "the rhetorics of power *as* the power of the sublime." Wuellner comes to understand that there is a symbiotic relationship between rhetoric and the sublime. The essence of rhetoric is not communication but rather the creation of *communion* (the Perelmanian "meeting of the minds"), the pursuit of (Burkean) "perfection," and the aim of "identification through transformation."[73]

The traditional canons of Aristotle's rhetoric—invention, arrangement, style, memory, and delivery—are part of an organic whole that includes three levels of language (exoteric, emotional, and esoteric) and three components of language (thinking, feeling, and acting). Speaking is not the only expression of language, and Wuellner elaborates the connections between utterance and bodily expressions of argument. The "materiality" of rhetoric includes far

---

71. New meaning may even arise for the critic or interpreter. See Wuellner, "Rhetorical Criticism," 167–68.
72. What follows is a very superficial overview of a far more dense and nuanced elaboration of Wuellner's general theory. See Wuellner, "Reconceiving a Rhetoric of Religion."
73. Wuellner, "Death and Rebirth of Rhetoric," 923.

more than texts; it is everything from the material expression of an argument to the context of the interpreter of the text. Rationality is the product of the interaction and integration of the cognitive, emotive, and volitional. Thus, Wuellner speaks of the "grandeur" of nature and "goadings of mystery" that are expressed by rhetoric as it takes on the function of the power of the sublime.

In part, Wuellner derives his concept of the power of rhetoric as the power of the sublime from the late-first-century(?) teacher of rhetoric and author Pseudo-Longinus.[74] In his tractate entitled "On the Sublime," Longinus says that he intends to discuss not the importance of the sublime, which he describes as "consummate excellence and distinction of language" that is not intended to persuade an audience but "to transport them out of themselves."[75] Rather, he intends to discuss how one attains it. He argues, "Invariably what inspires wonder casts a spell upon us and is always superior to what is merely convincing and pleasing."[76] For Longinus "a well-timed flash of sublimity" is not simply a matter of invention or style or the product of the application of the techniques of rhetoric but rather an event, like a bolt of lightning that illuminates everything. For Longinus, the goal of persuasion is not conviction conventionally understood but ecstasy or enthusiasm.[77] Setting aside any discussion of the caveats spelled out by Longinus regarding the identification and use of the sublime, two claims made by this author should be highlighted.[78]

74. The name of the author is unknown, but it is conventional to use "Pseudo-Longinus" to refer to the author. It is also conventional to shorten that to "Longinus."
75. Longinus, *On the Sublime*, 125. Rather than chapter or section numbers, page numbers in the LCL edition are used throughout to identify locations of references.
76. Ibid., 125.
77. W. Robert Connor, "Pygmies in the Cage," in *Literary Study, Measurement, and the Sublime: Disciplinary Assessment*, ed. D. Heiland and L. J. Rosenthal (New York: Teagle Foundation, 2011), 97–114.
78. Wuellner himself provides a commentary on these in "Reconceiving a Rhetoric of Religion," 70–72.

The first claim that Longinus makes is that the "true sublime … elevates us: uplifted with a sense of joyful pride, *as if we ourselves produced the very thing we heard.*" He argues that an educated man recognizes the sublime when it provides him with "more food for thought than the mere words at first suggest." The sublime "gives abundant food for thought." Thus, that which is "truly beautiful and sublime . . . pleases all people at all times."[79]

The second claim Longinus makes is that the "meaning" of the text in a state of sublimity is taken from the author. Susan Guerlac states, "The sublime enunciation appears to be 'wrung from the orator,' to overwhelm the speaker or speak through him. . . . The speaker vanishes into his text." Because of the power of language, the audience is "transported" to some other state of being and achieves "a fictive identity with the speaker," and its members must now interpret how to act and what to do. The intention of the author is changed in some way by its relocation in the audience and by what Gurlac describes as the "force of enunciation" that is carried into the audience.[80] At that point, the text is taken over by the audience and an understanding of it is made possible by the reader.[81] To borrow a concept from symbolic convergence theory, moreover, the audience then "chains out" or elaborates the power of the sublime through re-enunciation of the rhetoric of the speaker in new locations not within the purview of the speaker.[82]

The power of the sublime is enhanced by the power of "delivery." While Longinus places emphasis on what might be classified as elements of invention and arrangement such as "weight, grandeur,

---

79. Longinus, *On the Sublime*, 139 (emphasis added).
80. Suzanne Guerlac, "Longinus and the Subject of the Sublime," *New Literary History* 16 (1985): 275–76.
81. Frances Ferguson, "A Commentary on Susan Guerlac's 'Longinus and the Subject of the Sublime,'" *New Literary History* 16, no. 2 (1985): 293–95.
82. For a discussion of the theory see Bormann, *The Force of Fantasy*, 4–16.

and energy in writing," the forcefulness of delivery is of even greater importance to him.[83] Longinus explains, "What then is the use of imagination in rhetoric? It may be said generally to introduce a great deal of vigour and emotion into one's speeches, but when combined with argumentative treatment it not only convinces the audience, it positively masters them."[84] Longinus asserts that the power of the sublime lies in part with the ability of the speaker to give himself over to the text and let its power impact the hearer.[85]

Reading Wuellner as implying that rhetorical criticism should be primarily concerned with the condition of sublimity would be to mis-read him. His general theory of rhetoric attempts to change the focus of the rhetorical critic from a "reconstructionist paradigm of historical criticism" that tends to ignore any interest in the effects of the text to a "focus on the text as a form of power."[86] Like Longinus, Wuellner sees this power affecting the entire person—whether speaker or hearer—so that the argument resonates beyond the immediate experience of the reader or hearer and provides sustenance for future consideration. The trajectory of rhetoric is therefore linear and evolving, generating performance in new contexts. The critic must be aware of and take into account this power of the sublime to be recontextualized and generative.

Wuellner's move to the sublime is critical for integrating the various pieces of his theory.[87] The key lies precisely in Wuellner's

---

83. Longinus, *On the Sublime*, 141.

84. Ibid., 147.

85. Suggesting that Homer was carried away by his own text, Longinus writes, "Here indeed Homer is swept away by the whirlwind of battle and so affected that he stormily raves . . . fringed are his lips with foam-froth" (151). Furthermore, he writes, "For emotion is always more telling when it seems not to be premeditated by the speaker but to be born of the moment" (189). In speaking about the use of a figure of speech, he says, "The result is that his words do not seem premeditated but rather wrung from him" (195).

86. J. David Hester (Amador), "The Wuellnerian Sublime: Rhetorics, Power, the Ethics of Commun(icat)ion," in *Rhetoric, Ethic, and Moral Persuasion in Biblical Discourse: Essays from the 2002 Heidelberg Conference*, ed. Thomas H. Olbricht and Anders Eriksson (ESEC 11; New York: T&T Clark, 2005), 5, 11.

claim that transforms Kennedy's assertion that all religions are rhetorical. Wuellner agrees, but for him rhetoric is also religious in that to be fully human contains an element of the spiritual, and that element is the key to the fundamental nature of communication: the communion of minds, the argumentative starting point that *requires* people come together for reasoning and communication to begin. All rhetoric begins at that holy moment, as when YHWH calls to Isaiah, "Come, let us argue it out" (Isaiah 1:18, NRSV).

For Wuellner, however, this dialog is not mere words but a whole-body encounter. As Wuellner points out, the materiality of communication is more than text but *also* bodily language such as gestures, appearance, and the rhythm of enunciation, and, we might add, analogical references to the body in phrases such as "the body of Christ." On the emotional level, physical activity can express the response to utterance, as in Longinus's reference to the sublime's producing pleasure or activity as described, for example, by nineteenth-century American observers of reactions to revivalist preaching.[88] On the spiritual level, Wuellner refers to communication as dealing with the ineffable, the "mystery of the gospel."[89] Paul's description of being caught up into heaven (2 Cor. 12:1–4), for example, fits that category. It is the sublime that incorporates these elements of communication into an organic wholeness.

However, Wuellner pushes the function of the sublime beyond the integration of levels of language and communication. Describing the rhetoric of the letter of James, he points to an "ethics of speaking" found in the third chapter in which the goal of such speaking is the expression of "wisdom from above," which is "first pure, then peaceable, gentle, willing to yield, full of mercy and good fruits,

---

87. Ibid., 12–13.
88. For example, see Sidney Ahlstrom, *A Religious History of the American People* (New Haven: Yale University Press, 1972), 432–35.
89. Wuellner, "Reconceiving a Rhetoric of Religion," 35–36.

without a trace of partiality or hypocrisy" (3:17). With this reference and others from the New Testament, Wuellner illustrates the transformational power of the sublime, and then he quotes Kenneth Burke:

> "[P]erfection," as byproduct of the unending process of transformation, is one of "the primary motives of all rhetoric." In that sense, all rhetorical systems are religious. Perfection is, of course, an important biblical category. . . . And in our use of speech and sharing in the creative Word in this hoped for, assured state of perfection, in this our "inheritance" as "sons and daughters of God," we will become more and more fully aware of, and empowered to being co-creators with, God, Christ, and the Spirit.[90]

David Hester notes that understanding the rhetoric of power as the power of the sublime makes ethics foundational to rhetoric and moves away from a rhetoric restrained or constrained by conventional practice to a focus on the goal of rhetoric as creating communion.[91] Longinus may have been implying something of the same thing when he said that the sublime, "grandeur," comes from "full-blooded ideas," emotion, figures of thought and speech expressed in "nobility of phrase." The general effect of the whole is "dignity and elevation."[92] He argues later that imagination coupled with "argumentative treatment . . . masters" an audience. Recall that he has already made the point that "the effect of genius is not to persuade the audience but to transport them out of themselves." Whatever the means of argumentation, the goal is to inspire wonder and "cast a spell" on the hearer or reader. This spell is evidence of the truly sublime, which "pleases all people at all times."[93]

90. Ibid., 61.
91. Hester, "The Wuellnerian Sublime," 20.
92. Longinus, *On the Sublime*, 141. See particularly note b.
93. Ibid., 125. The Greek verb translated here as "pleases" can also mean "to conciliate" or "to make good" on something. The implication in Longinus's thought is that reconciliation is a result of sublimity.

Where Could Wuellnerian Criticism Take Us?

If we understand the goal of rhetoric to motivate the audience to do something, to seek resolution of an exigence, to take action of some kind, or to increase adherence to the values of a community, then rhetoric causes sublimity when it directs the energy of the hearer from the self to the other, when it transports the hearer from self into community or from self-interested community behavior into general communion. To elaborate Wuellner's point, rhetorical criticism must move from analysis of the features of special theories of rhetoric—such as description of the techniques of argumentation mutually acknowledged by participants and characteristic of a particular time and place—to the description of the power of the argument to induce the sublime in the audience. It must describe elements of the sublime revealed by the function of the argumentative strategies employed in the text that might be both effective and affective in any rhetorical situation. That description would entail the use of special theories of rhetoric guided by the general theory of a rhetorics of power. In other words, a rhetorics of power could be used for analyzing and describing argumentation based on special theories of rhetoric operative in the context(s) of racial, ethnic, feminist, gender-identified and LGBT, post-colonial, and non-Western discourse.[94]

More directly related to New Testament rhetorical criticism, use of Wuellner's special theory of rhetoric might help critics develop a more robust understanding and definition of what Thomas Olbricht calls "Christian" or "church" rhetoric found in the literature of the early church.[95] Moreover, Wuellner's understanding of "context" and the participation of an audience in effecting change in their

---

94. Wuellner advocates something similar in "Rhetorical Criticism," passim. A more detailed model of such an enterprise is elaborated by George Kennedy in *Comparative Rhetoric*, passim. What this means for us is that a rhetorics of power should not be considered "Eurocentric."

situation(s) might be coupled with elements of socio-rhetorical criticism to help shed light on the development of early Christian culture. Consider, for example, social and cultural shifts evident between the letters of the "radical" Paul and those of the "conservative" Paul, that is, the undisputed and Deutero-Pauline letters.[96] Problematization and argumentation can account for the differences. A full-blown theory of narrative rhetoric informed by a rhetorics of power could also be used to analyze the gospels by demonstrating the argumentative power of stories, sayings, and parables, as well as the overall argumentative arc of the plot of each.

On the whole, however, these suggestions represent rather conventional, mundane studies that only hint at the potential of Wuellner's vision. The exhortation that Wuellner left behind in his final article was that biblical rhetorical critics be both diagnosticians and therapists, and that we do more than just analyze for analysis' sake.[97] In every instance and in every reading, Wuellner compels us to diagnose the rhetoric *in* and *of* the text to ascertain its "intentionality." Does the text heal? Does it harm? Is the ethical imperative of communion (the meeting of the minds) met within the text, or is the text's intention to usurp and destroy that communion? Has the sublime encounter been used to transport the audience to "perfection," or is it cancerous? These questions must be addressed not only with respect to the specific text under consideration, but also in our *own* encounter and explication of that text as rhetoricians of the sublime. Here, the ethical dimensions as integral to rhetoric that were

95. Thomas H. Olbricht, "An Aristotelian Rhetorical Analysis of 1 Thessalonians," in *Greeks, Romans, and Christians: Essays in Honor of Abraham J. Malherbe*, ed. David L. Balch, Everett Ferguson, and Wayne A. Meeks (Minneapolis: Fortress, 1990), 216–36.

96. Marcus Borg and John Dominic Crossan, *The First Paul: Reclaiming the Radical Visionary Behind the Church's Conservative Icon* (New York: HarperOne, 2009).

97. Wuellner, "Reconceiving a Rhetoric of Religion," 74–75. In these and the following pages, the reader will find the vocabulary we use in the rest of this paragraph.

explored by The Heidelberg Conference can be mined for fruitful exploration and discovery.[98]

Nevertheless, there is more. As therapists of the sublime, we rhetorical critics are "committed to restoring health, and, as stewards, to maintaining and enhancing health in the 'institutional' or instrumental, 'material,' i.e, earthen vessels-forms of the power of the sublime."[99] Our task is not limited to the generation of analyses and critical theories but must take up the task of the creation and sustenance of systems and institutions wherein such analyses and theories are allowed to thrive. As rhetoricians of the sublime, we are not satisfied with rhetoric in its most limited, disciplinary, and restrained form but seek out intersections and cross-cultural disciplinary spaces wherein the symphonic, symbiotic, and museful inventions of communication bear the fruit of the unexpected through encounters across disciplines and even beyond academics into other arenas.

Examples of such an enterprise can be found in the series of meetings held at the University of Redlands under the title "International Interdisciplinary Conferences on Rhetoric and the Humanities." In these meetings, fruitful discussions were held on topics that drew from an extraordinary variety of disciplines including economics, cultural history, religious history, culture criticism, philosophy and ethics, comparative literature, queer theory, and intercultural education, to name a few.[100] The revolutionary

---

98. Olbricht and Eriksson, *Rhetoric, Ethic, and Moral Persuasion*, passim. See in particular the ramifications of Wuellner's sublime on the relationship of ethics and rhetorics in Hester (Amador), "The Wuellnerian Sublime: Rhetorics, Power, the Ethics of Commun(icat)ion," 103–17.

99. Wuellner, "Reconceiving a Rhetoric of Religion," 74.

100. The conferences were held under the auspices of the Rhetorical New Testament Project of the Institute for Antiquity and Christianity in Claremont, CA, of which the authors were codirectors. At the time of this publication, both the Project and the Institute are closed, but some of the work of the Project continues to be available at two websites: www.rhetjournal.net and www.ars-rhetorica.net. Long term access is not guaranteed, however.

online publication *Queen: A Journal of Rhetoric and Power* also became a place where rhetoricians and biblical critics could contribute to topical explorations of contemporary interests such as issues of sex, power, postcolonialization, beauty, medicine, and place.

The meetings at the University of Redlands have been discontinued, and the journal *Queen* is no longer published. A new generation of biblical rhetorical scholars must take up the mantle left by Wuellner's generation and find new areas of interest and new intersections of power and sublimity to explore and create. Wuellner did not leave behind an analytic programmatics, but something larger: a call for future scholars and scholarship to "face up to the task of cultivating and maintaining a network of committed rhetorical critics . . . as 21st century stewards of the mysteries of compassionate humanness."[101]

Who will answer the call?

---

101. Wuellner, "Reconceiving a Rhetoric of Religion," 77.

6

Response to James D. Hester and J. David Hester: A Personal Reflection

Thomas H. Olbricht

I appreciate very much Jim and David Hester's careful comments regarding Wilhelm Wuellner's contribution to rhetorical criticism. Wilhelm first came to my attention in the Paul Seminar at the 1976 annual meeting of the Society of Biblical Literature in St. Louis, Missouri. I taught rhetoric at Penn State in the 1960s, but I had up to that date not encountered anyone in biblical studies with some expertise in rhetoric, except for my Harvard Divinity School professor Amos Wilder. When I heard Wilhelm make a few remarks in the seminar, I was amazed because here was someone who not only mentioned rhetoric but also had a competent grasp of what it was all about.

Wilhelm had already probed rhetoric through his contacts with the speech rhetoricians at the University of California, Berkeley. In 1970, he became chairperson of the Center for Hermeneutical Studies in Classical and Modern Culture, sponsored by the University of California, Berkeley, and the Graduate Theological Union. He had organized and edited nine of the Protocols by 1976 with such central figures as Hans Dieter Betz, Thomas Conley, Paul Ricoeur, and George Kustas. During this period, Wilhelm also engaged Stanley Fish and John Searle in literary criticism.[1] I was impressed that he had become friends with William Brandt, the chair of the Speech Rhetoric Department at Berkeley. In my judgment, Brandt had published the best college textbook on argumentation at that time.[2]

Whatever Wilhelm's own original contribution to our guild, he had laid by the 1980s and 90s a solid bibliographic foundation for those interested in rhetorical analysis of the Scriptures. He had also constructed a network of scholars. He was an early key person in the founding of the seven international Pepperdine conferences on rhetoric that convened at Heidelberg, Pretoria, London, Malibu, Florence, Lund, and Heidelberg II.[3]

Wilhelm and I started talking about the need for international conferences in 1990. William B. Phillips, my academic Vice President, announced the availability of an estate chateau in France that also offered support funds for the holding of academic

1. In my essay, I include a long statement Wilhelm sent me about his work in rhetoric. See Thomas H. Olbricht, "The Flowering of Rhetorical Criticism in America," in *The Rhetorical Analysis of Scripture: Essays from the 1995 London Conference*, ed. Stanley E. Porter and Thomas H. Olbricht (JSNTSup 146; Sheffield: Sheffield Academic, 1997), 79–102. For a complete list of Wilhelm's publications see *Rhetorics and Hermeneutics: Wilhelm Wuellner and His Influence at the Close of the Century*, ed. James D. Hester and J. David Hester (ESEC 9; Harrisburg: Trinity, 2004), 241–47.
2. William J. Brandt, *The Rhetoric of Argumentation* (Indianapolis: Bobbs-Merrill, 1970).
3. For a perceptive analysis of these conferences, see Vernon K. Robbins, "From Heidelberg to Heidelberg: Rhetorical Interpretation of the Bible at the Seven 'Pepperdine' Conferences from 1992 to 2002," in *Rhetoric, Ethic, and Moral Persuasion in Biblical Discourse*, ed. Thomas H. Olbricht and Anders Eriksson (ESEC 11; New York: T&T Clark, 2005), 335–77.

conferences. Wilhelm and I put together and submitted a proposal. My Vice President wasn't particularly supportive because he perceived the funds to be mostly for people in the sciences. Our proposal was rejected by the owner of the chateau, but this experience gave us a foot in the door in another way.

I proposed that we hold the conference at the Pepperdine University facilities in Heidelberg, Germany. Phillips did not seem overly supportive of a Heidelberg conference either, but he gave me permission to see if I could work it out. The persons who ran the Pepperdine International programs approved, and so I went around finding University and private money to support the conference. We were able to provide housing and food for all who made presentations at the conference.

Wilhelm's role was crucial. He had a better sense than I, especially when it came to the protocol of inviting European scholars to present at the conference. We were able to attract as presenters several European and South African scholars, and later Asian professors because of Wilhelm's prior contact with them. Wilhelm kept major files on all the scholars he could find who were interested in rhetorical analysis of the Scriptures. He even corresponded with many of them.

In another way, I think Wilhelm made a unique contribution to our work by probing the history of hermeneutics and rhetoric. He was focused upon the interlacing of hermeneutics and rhetoric and the cultural settings that impacted their development. Not much attention had been given to rhetoric as it related to biblical studies and hermeneutics. Wilhelm made several perceptive observations, especially, I think, in regard to the differences between classical, Jewish, and Christian discourse. His observations are worth investigating in depth. I think that whoever follows up on his suggestions will need to probe more into what was going on in the actual discourses of the time than did Wilhelm. Nevertheless, he has blazed a trail that can be improved and developed.[4]

I agree with Jim and David Hester that one will not find in Wilhelm's corpus a programmatic schema for rhetorical criticism. Neither can one identify an ongoing Wuellnerian school of rhetoric so as to determine where his rhetoric is taking us. On a more rudimentary level, however, I am impressed with the manner in which Wilhelm laid out the arguments in his essay on Romans.[5] I think this essay provides a fine example for anyone seeking to discern and set forth the arguments of a biblical document. I am also impressed with Wilhelm's essay on 1 Thessalonians that seeks to discover the paradoxical expressions of "tribulation" and "waiting" that give this text their rhetorical power.[6]

The chief theoretical merit of Wilhelm's rhetorical vision lies in what he attempts to convey in his final essay on the sublime.[7] I think whatever he means must somehow be perceived from his earlier interest in rhetoric as being a holistic discipline and drawing upon studies of all kinds. Somehow, he envisions words as impacting not only the understanding but also the very lives of human beings. I think his grandiose, unpolished and somewhat esoteric essay entitled "Reconceiving a Rhetoric of Religion: A Rhetoric of Power and the Power of the Sublime" was impacted by Wilhelm's battle over a ten-year period with prostate cancer, which finally brought about his

---

4. I have developed the items in the rest of this presentation in more detail in: Thomas H. Olbricht, "Wilhelm Wuellner and the Promise of Rhetoric," in Hester and Hester, *Rhetorics and Hermeneutics*, 78–104.

5. WilhelmWuellner, "Paul's Rhetoric of Argumentation in Romans: An Alternative to the Donfried-Karris Debate over Romans," *CBQ* 38 (1976): 330–351; repr. in *The Romans Debate: Revised and Expanded Edition*, ed. Karl Donfried (Peabody: Hendrickson,1995), 128–46.

6. Wilhelm Wuellner, "The Argumentative Structure of 1 Thessalonians as Paradoxical Encomium," in *The Thessalonian Correspondence*, ed. Raymond F. Collins (BETL 87; Leuven: Leuven University Press, 1990), 117–36.

7. Wilhelm Wuellner, "Reconceiving a Rhetoric of Religion: A Rhetorics of Power and the Power of the Sublime," in Hester and Hester, *Rhetorics and Hermeneutics*, 23–77.

death in 2004. During those years, he contemplated words, worlds, and transcendence with persons facing a similar end.

According to Wilhelm, sublime communication occurs in a moment of *ecstasis*, that is, at a moment of standing beyond. At this moment, reconciliation and healing occur. Wilhelm envisioned an existential, ontological significance to rhetoric. Sublime words have to do with wholeness and health. They contribute to well-being and healing and impact mundane regular occurrences in life. In a chain of transcending dimensions, however, they extend into the beyond. Wilhelm had in mind a rapprochement between "heaven and earth," for which words are somehow a means.

How he envisioned a flow of holistic transforming power through words and rhetoric is difficult to set out. I do not think he ended up with Heidegger nor concluded that words are the reality. Anyway for Wilhelm, rhetoric and being interact, even if they are not interchangeable. I am not sure at this stage that any of us are prepared or perhaps even capable of transforming Wilhelm's vision systematically into a major tome on rhetorical criticism. Should anyone nevertheless have that courage, Wilhelm's final document is worth in-depth scrutiny. Wilhelm Wuellner has left the guild with a major challenge that may be decades in reaching its full potential.

7

Elisabeth Schüssler Fiorenza and the Rhetoric and Ethic of Inquiry

John R. Lanci

In their introduction to an issue of the *Journal of Feminist Studies in Religion*, editors Nami Kim and Deborah Whitehead celebrate the occasion of Elisabeth Schüssler Fiorenza's seventieth birthday and generate a comprehensive list of the subjects upon which she has written. In addition to "feminist biblical hermeneutics" and "feminist New Testament scholarship," they list the following subjects:

> theology, feminist theory, hermeneutical theory, critical theory, ekklesia of wo/men as a radical democratic space, Christology, sophialogy, kyriarchy, inclusive G*d talk, interlocked structures of oppression, violence against wo/men, spirituality, American nationalism, theological

education, pedagogy, ecclesiastical hierarchy and the malestream academy, and solidarity with wo/men in/from the global South.[1]

This list is a fair one and the articles that follow in this journal attempt critically to engage some of these facets of her work and in the process to celebrate her prodigious scholarly output. Her bibliography, found at the end of the volume but now incomplete and out of date, spans nineteen pages, beginning with her first book that was published in Germany in 1964 and ending with citations from the five *Festschriften* published in her honor.[2]

I begin with Kim and Whitehead's summary of Schüssler Fiorenza's lifework for two reasons. First, I want to highlight and endorse their observation that while Schüssler Fiorenza is known primarily as a "feminist scholar," her work is not that easily categorized or circumscribed.[3] Yes, she would describe herself as a "feminist," but she asserts that her idea of what this means is best captured by a bumper-sticker that reads: "Feminism is the radical notion that women are people."[4]

When Schüssler Fiorenza quotes her car-fendered source, she actually modifies it by changing *women* to the neologism *wo/men*. The shift in wording carries with it a deep significance for understanding Schüssler Fiorenza's work. As she frequently notes, she wants to avoid an essentialist depiction of *woman* as a one-size-fits-all category.[5] Moreover, her work is not done in service of only

---

1. Nami Kim and Deborah Whitehead, "Editors' Introduction," *JFSR* 25, no. 1 (2009): 2.
2. Anonymous, "Published Works of Elisabeth Schüssler Fiorenza," *JFSR* 25, no. 1 (2009): 221–240.
3. It is regrettable that so many scholars never engage Schüssler Fiorenza's thought beyond what they find in her admittedly groundbreaking and foundational, but in many aspects only preliminary, book *In Memory of Her: A Feminist Theological Reconstruction of Christian Origins* (10th anniversary ed.; New York: Crossroad, 1994).
4. Idem, *Wisdom Ways: Introducing Feminist Biblical Interpretation* (Maryknoll: Orbis, 2001), 56.
5. The term *wo/man* acknowledges the instability and shifts of meaning with respect to *woman*, and that what the traditional term means depends more on the contextualization of individuals than it does on gender or sex.

gendered females. Instead, the term *wo/man* "is not only defined by gender but also by race, class, and colonial structures of domination." She uses the term in an inclusive way: "*Wo/man* denotes not one simple reality, and *wo/men* is often equivalent to *people*."[6]

For Schüssler Fiorenza, feminism is best understood "as a theoretical perspective and historical movement for changing sociocultural and communal-religious structures of domination and exploitation."[7] Her commitment to feminism is uncompromising, but as Kim and Whitehead point out, her life-project must be understood as "an inclusive social-political-religious movement and theoretical framework oriented toward justice for all marginalized persons."[8]

This observation brings me to the second reason for beginning this essay with reference to the work of Kim and Whitehead. Absent from their list of topics addressed by Schüssler Fiorenza over the years is any reference to her contribution to the genealogy of rhetorical criticism in biblical studies. Although it may be huddling silently under the subject of critical theory, I find the absence of an explicit reference to rhetorical analysis striking, for I believe that her work on rhetoric and texts—and the ethics of texts—is at the foundation of all of her other accomplishments.

Schüssler Fiorenza begins with the simple though still unfortunately radical notion that wo/men are indeed people, and her notion includes gendered females, the rural Appalachian poor of any gender, those held in social and economic submission in both the developed and developing world, gay men, lesbians, transgenders, and all those who have been marginalized by those in power. Then,

---

6. Idem, *Rhetoric and Ethic: The Politics of Biblical Studies* (Minneapolis: Fortress, 1999), ix. Other neologisms that appear in her work will be defined as they appear in this essay.
7. Schüssler Fiorenza, *Wisdom Ways*, 56.
8. Kim and Whitehead, "Editors' Introduction," 4.

she endeavors to move the work of biblical criticism further down the road.

Early on, she grounded her work in rhetorical analysis because, quite simply, constitutive to rhetoric is argument and argument implies two sides of a conversation or confrontation. This conversation makes it possible for ancient wo/men, so often left out of the discourse, to have a voice and find a place in the history of the early Christian movement and its texts. Over many years, Schüssler Fiorenza has laid a foundation for the use of rhetorical criticism that develops that discourse not only in new directions, as many prominent scholars have done, but also into whole new worlds and disciplines of inquiry, a claim that few scholars can make.

In this essay, I begin with an overview of rhetorical-critical approaches to the Bible as Schüssler Fiorenza configures them. I then describe the origins of the rhetoric of inquiry, a movement begun by historians, economists, and political scientists who applied rhetorical analysis to the way they and their peers do scholarship in their disciplines. I spend some time on the history of the "Iowa School" because at the same time that they were developing their ideas, Schüssler Fiorenza was working independently toward many of the same ends. Well before her SBL presidential address in 1987, she was exploring the potential of rhetorical criticism to decenter biblical studies and move it from the exclusive purview of the academy to the wider community, where the texts that the experts study were empowering—or oppressing—modern Christians.

Perhaps, Schüssler Fiorenza's most significant achievement with respect to rhetorical criticism of Christian texts involves both the introduction of the rhetoric of inquiry into biblical scholarly discourse and her consistent emphasis on the need to incorporate an ethic of inquiry into our work. She insists that this work—the work of the academy—must situate itself within, and connect itself to, the wider community that she terms the ekklesia, although, as we shall see, she has a particular understanding of what that venerable Greek term means. In other words, she focuses on the place—for her, the *ethos*—where biblical criticism is, and so we must examine the *ethos* of inquiry that she conceives as a "republic of many voices" where "all who can think" are welcome to join in the discussion and help to create the meanings—and the just world—that the biblical texts can support and nurture.[9]

J. David Hester Amador captures in a sentence the significance of Schüssler Fiorenza's thought to the genealogies of New Testament rhetorical criticism. Her work, he says, constitutes a "shift from a hermeneutical paradigm of meaning to a rhetorical one of pragmatic intentions and effects."[10] In the future, Schüssler Fiorenza may be remembered more for this paradigm shift than for any other part of her work and thought. By insisting that our scholarship can be accountable and relevant to the wider Christian community without sacrificing its rigor or legitimacy, she expands the use of rhetorical criticism to include the scholarly inquiry itself as an object of study, but always in service of the pragmatic goal to establish a just world for all. In doing so, she challenges the trajectories of virtually all of the rhetorical criticism that has gone before, and this challenge, I suggest, earns her a prominent place in any exploration of the genealogies of New Testament rhetorical criticism.

Rhetorical-Critical Approaches to the New Testament

The work of many New Testament scholars changed considerably in the late 20th century as they began to take seriously the rhetorical

9. Schüssler Fiorenza has developed these ideas in numerous articles, lectures, and books, from which I shall quote liberally. These numerous quotations provide a reader unfamiliar with her thought some guideposts for further exploration of her thought.
10. J. David Hester Amador, *Academic Constraints in Rhetorical Criticism of the New Testament* (JSNTSup 174; Sheffield: Sheffield Academic, 1999), 261.

theories espoused by critics in other disciplines. Even those who worked in other areas of biblical scholarship became familiar with the powerful ways that rhetorical analysis could open new possibilities for interpreting the ancient texts. Schüssler Fiorenza notes that two approaches dominated early rhetorical study of the New Testament, and Kathleen Welch refers to them as the "Heritage" and "Dialectical" Schools of rhetorical criticism.[11]

Those working out of the Heritage School ground rhetorical criticism within classical theories of analysis.[12] They reread Aristotle, the handbooks of Quintilian, and other ancient sources, and attempt to discern how the biblical writers they study use rhetorical theory to convince their readers of the correctness of their positions.[13] Those working in Pauline studies in the late 1980s, for instance, speculate about whether the author of the genuine letters might have been educated in classical theories of rhetoric and might have employed classical rhetorical theory. The judicious use of ancient rhetorical theory—one thinks here, for instance, of Margaret M. Mitchell's widely praised and cited study of 1 Corinthians—has added much to our understanding of how Paul employs argument and persuasion in his letters.[14]

For some scholars in the Heritage School, however, ancient practices of rhetoric provide an almost scientific method to approach biblical sources. For these scholars, the works of the ancient Greeks are "a series of objective writings that exist in a more or less objective

11. Kathleen E. Welch, *The Contemporary Reception of Classical Rhetoric: Appropriations of Ancient Discourse* (Hillsdale: Erlbaum, 1990). Cf. Elisabeth Schüssler Fiorenza, "The Rhetoric of Inquiry," in *Rhetorics in the New Millennium: Promise and Fulfillment*, ed. James D. Hester and J. David Hester (New York: T&T Clark, 2010), 25–28.

12. Welch, *Contemporary Reception*, 8–24.

13. For instance, see George A. Kennedy, *New Testament Interpretation through Rhetorical Criticism* (Chapel Hill: University of North Carolina Press, 1984), 4–12.

14. Margaret M. Mitchell, *Paul and the Rhetoric of Reconciliation* (Louisville: Westminster/John Knox, 1991). However, Schüssler Fiorenza critiques Mitchell's "antiquarian approach and technological method." See Schüssler Fiorenza, *Rhetoric and Ethic*, 86.

world of artifacts, knowledge, and retrievable reality."[15] In this school of thought, ancient rhetorical theory offers a new set of technological exegetical tools that, properly applied, can uncover the one true meaning of the ancient textual material. This meaning, in turn, provides a window into the actual reality behind the text, what "really happened" in the world that generated the texts that survived.[16] Not surprisingly, scholars employing traditional methods of historical-critical biblical study often find this approach to rhetoric attractive.

As Schüssler Fiorenza repeatedly notes, however, the use of rhetorical theory in this way is fraught with methodological problems. It sifts and blends the ideas of different ancient authors into a homogenous set of rhetorical principles much less complex than the various theories that define classical rhetoric and "replaces them with formulas, rules, lists, and simple categories."[17] By not taking into account the difficulties inherent in studying texts from cultures very different from the modern West, the approach of the Heritage School decontextualizes classical rhetorical texts and ignores the concrete purposes that the texts might originally have been created to address, and it ignores, too, their elite, androcentric nature.[18] Perhaps most importantly, those who use rhetoric as a tool for textual analysis in this way fail to take account of the rhetoricity of their own work but assume that what they are doing is empirical, scientific, and value-neutral, as though everyone using the agreed upon tools of rhetorical analysis in the agreed upon method would arrive at the same objective results.

---

15. Schüssler Fiorenza, "The Rhetoric of Inquiry," 25.
16. For example, George Kennedy suggests that an understanding of classical rhetorical principles make it possible for us to "try to hear [Paul's] words as a Greek-speaking audience would have heard them" (*New Testament Interpretation*, 10).
17. Schüssler Fiorenza, "The Rhetoric of Inquiry," 26.
18. Schüssler Fiorenza, *Rhetoric and Ethic*, 86–87. As she points out (p. 89), Plato and Aristotle have been used for millennia to legitimate relations of dominance and oppression.

Biblical scholars working in literary criticism gravitate toward Welch's second understanding of rhetorical analysis, namely the Dialectical School, which avoids many of the shortcomings of the Heritage School.[19] This approach to the rhetoric of a text is often referred to as the *New Rhetoric*, which does not pretend to be able to discover information about the objective reality inhabited by those who composed or received the text. It rejects decontextualized readings and acknowledges that all discourse, even scientific discourse, is inherently rhetorical and that "scholars have no choice but to rely on rhetorical appeals and arguments, selective evidence, value-laden propositions, and ideological frameworks."[20] The approach of the Dialectical School focuses on the production of rhetorical discourse and holds issues of translation as well as the methods and presuppositions of the interpreters to be important factors in the study of ancient material. The focus is on the production of rhetorical discourse, both ancient and modern, not just the analysis of archaic texts.

For those practicing in the Dialectical School, then, "rhetoric is contextual and context is rhetorical."[21] Nonetheless, Schüssler Fiorenza finds this approach inadequate. With the Dialectical School, scholars move away from understanding rhetoric as a tool in the positivistic quest to uncover immutable Truth, but even with this contextual nuancing, she finds the New Rhetoric to be only a "half-turn," a revival of "the technology of ancient rhetoric" that is often unable to resist the modern scholar's quest to recover "facts" about the ancient Mediterranean world.[22]

---

19. Welch, *Contemporary Reception*, 25–33.
20. Schüssler Fiorenza, "The Rhetoric of Inquiry," 27. For an example of this approach to rhetorical analysis, see Antoinette Clark Wire, *The Corinthian Women Prophets: A Reconstruction through Paul's Rhetoric* (Minneapolis: Fortress, 1990).
21. Schüssler Fiorenza, "The Rhetoric of Inquiry," 27.
22. Schüssler Fiorenza, *Rhetoric and Ethic*, 99. The image of the "half-turn" calls to mind the observation that Richard Rorty made when discussing movements made by scholars in the

Moreover, this school of rhetorical analysis takes place, as does the work of the Heritage School, in an academic situation radically removed from the rest of the world. For Schüssler Fiorenza, critical scholarly work must be reconceptualized and the radical detachment of academic work questioned.[23] What we see depends on where we stand. Therefore, we must attend more carefully to what we as readers bring to the texts we analyze.[24] The words we read do not themselves stand in place, immutable; nor do they stand alone. Language is not a closed system, and words create symbolic universes that, while powerful signifiers of what people understand as "real," are anything but universal.

"How meaning is constructed," she writes, "depends not only on how one reads the social, cultural, and religious markers inscribed in the text but also on the kinds of 'intertexts,' preconstructed 'frames of meaning,' common sense understandings, 'aha-experiences,' or reading paradigms one uses when interpreting kyriocentric linguistic markers and textualized symbols."[25] In short, the Heritage and Dialectical schools of rhetorical criticism create in their use of rhetoric a tool for textual analysis, but they do not sufficiently reflect upon their methods, their perspectives, or the social location of their work.

---

human sciences as they articulated their methods of inquiry. He observed, "First the 'linguistic turn,' then the 'interpretive turn,' and now the 'rhetorical turn.'" See Herbert W. Simons, *The Rhetorical Turn: Invention and Persuasion in the Conduct of Inquiry* (Chicago: University of Chicago Press, 1990), vii. Schüssler Fiorenza often strongly critiques her peers quite incisively and part of her critique of the work of Vernon Robbins, a colleague whom she very much respects for his use of rhetorical analysis, involves his assumption that there is some factual "ancient Mediterranean world" out there to rediscover, rather than recognizing that what scholars are dealing with are cultural reconstructions. See Schüssler Fiorenza, *Rhetoric and Ethic*, 86–87.

23. Elisabeth Schüssler Fiorenza, *Rhetoric and Ethic*, 24; idem, *Democratizing Biblical Studies: Toward an Emancipatory Educational Space* (Louisville: Westminster John Knox, 2009), 106.

24. Elisabeth Schüssler Fiorenza, *Jesus and the Politics of Interpretation* (New York: Continuum, 2000), 79.

25. Schüssler Fiorenza, *The Power of the Word: Scripture and the Rhetoric of Empire* (Minneapolis: Fortress Press, 2007), 21–22.

For Schüssler Fiorenza, rhetorical analysis involves more than the study of a text in and of itself. The rhetorical "half-turn" must be completed, and so she turns to a third school, the Rhetoric of Inquiry.

The Rhetoric of Inquiry

In the early 1980s, a group from several academic departments at the University of Iowa came together to discuss common concerns about the claims colleagues in their disciplines were making about the research they were doing. Led by Donald McCloskey (economics), Allan Megill (history), and John Nelson (political science), they began meeting in a biweekly colloquium. McCloskey, an economic historian, had encountered literary criticism at Iowa, specifically rhetorical criticism, and came to believe that to do academic work in the social sciences is actually to employ rhetoric, though no one in the discipline of economics appeared to understand what they did in this way.[26]

In 1984, the university hosted the Iowa Symposium on the Rhetoric of the Human Sciences. This symposium was sponsored by the National Endowment for the Humanities, and was attended by a number of prominent philosophers and scientists, including Richard Rorty, Gustav Bergmann, and Thomas Kuhn. By this time, the "Iowa School" was well on the way to developing what Nelson had dubbed the "rhetoric of inquiry."[27]

The group began to challenge scholars in economics and the social sciences to acknowledge the rhetorical nature of their work. Scholars

26. Deirdre N. McCloskey, *The Rhetoric of Economics* (2nd ed.; Madison: University of Wisconsin Press, 1998), xi–xiv. Donald N. McCloskey became Deirdre N. McCloskey in the mid-1990s and wrote a best-selling account of the change under that name *Crossing: A Memoir* (Chicago: University of Chicago Press, 2000).

27. For an account of the highlights of the discussion, see John Lyne, "Rhetorics of Inquiry," *Quarterly Journal of Speech* 71, no. 1 (1985): 65–73. The group went on to found the Project on the Rhetoric of Inquiry, which still functions within the Department of Rhetoric at the University of Iowa. See their website: http://poroi.grad.uiowa.edu.

"wearing masks of scientific methodology first donned in the seventeenth century," Nelson, Megill, and McCloskey claimed, "have forgotten about the rhetorical faces underneath."[28] The rhetoric of inquiry was to be a movement designed, in the broadest terms, to examine the role played by rhetoric in the production and dissemination of knowledge.[29] Following Nietzsche, Wittgenstein, and others, the advocates of this approach noted that "facts can never talk for themselves."[30] Context—not just the context of the sources studied, but also the context of those doing the studying—must be examined and evaluated.

The rhetoric of inquiry posits that scholarly argument is more unified than commonly thought.[31] "Broadly speaking," Herbert Simons suggests that "virtually all scholarly discourse is rhetorical in the sense that issues need to be named and framed, facts interpreted and conclusions justified; furthermore, in adapting arguments to ends, audiences and circumstances, the writer (or speaker) must adopt a persona [and] choose a style" of argument. In other words, "there is no escape from rhetoric."[32] Academic inquiry, then, is unified in that scholars in every field of the arts and humanities rely on tools of rhetoric, "on metaphors, invocations of authority, and appeals to audiences."[33]

The rhetorical arguments employed in different fields are not all the same, however. Rather, every academic field is "defined by its

---

28. John S. Nelson, Allan Megill, and Donald N. McCloskey, "Rhetoric of Inquiry," in *The Rhetoric of the Human Sciences*, ed. idem (Madison: University of Wisconsin Press, 1987), 3.

29. Lyne, "Rhetorics of Inquiry," 66.

30. John S. Nelson and Allan Megill, "Rhetoric of Inquiry: Projects and Prospects," *Quarterly Journal of Speech* 72 (1986): 24. For a more detailed exposition than can be included here of the philosophical antecedents to their project, see this article as well as Nelson, Megill, and McCloskey, "Rhetoric of Inquiry," 3–18.

31. Ibid., 4.

32. Herbert W. Simons, "The Rhetoric of Inquiry as an Intellectual Movement," in idem, *The Rhetorical Turn*, 9.

33. Nelson, Megill, and McCloskey, "Rhetoric of Inquiry," 4.

own special devices and patterns of rhetoric—by existing theorems, arguments from invisible hands, and appeals to textual probabilities or archives."[34] Thus, practitioners of the rhetoric of inquiry from the beginning promoted their work as interdisciplinary. Nelson, Megill, and McCloskey note, "Philosophers who practice it are startled to find, for instance, that it is arising in economics also; students of communication are surprised to see it in psychology; nonmathematicicans are amazed that mathematicians do it at all. Their varied practices are a part of a single project."[35]

The rhetoric of inquiry movement does not seek to develop an abstract model of argumentation applicable in all situations for all disciplines. That position belongs to those whom they are opposing, i.e., the idea that a single methodology (usually identified as "scientific") could be developed and accepted as legitimate for all fields of study. Those fields that could not accommodate such a method are not scientific and thus are less respectable or valuable to the scholarly enterprise.[36] In a rhetoric of inquiry, the goal is to discover "suggestive starting points for contextual and comparative studies of inquiry within a wide variety of academic and other practices."[37]

The focus is on the nature of academic inquiry itself and the insistence that scholarship is shaped not by objective fact but by what the scholar does with the facts, that is, by the values and meaning placed on the material studied by the one doing the study. This focus will sound familiar to those exploring a number of other recent developments in the interpretation of texts and other data. From the

---

34. Ibid.,4–5.
35. Ibid., 5.
36. Nelson and Megill point out that their resistance to these ideas had been anticipated by Perelman and Olbrechts-Tyteca, Kuhn, and Toulmin, who rejected clear distinctions between what is scientific and what is not. See Nelson and Megill, "Rhetoric of Inquiry: Projects and Prospects," 30.
37. Ibid.

beginning, the Iowa School understood there to be many rhetorics of inquiry, not just one. Its proponents noted similarities between their ideas and a number of other analytical approaches, most of which fall under the broad umbrella of postmodernism including "Kuhnian post-positivism, social constructionism, various ethnomethodological approaches to analyses of scientific texts, symbolic anthropology, the critical legal studies movement, critical pluralism, deconstructionism, and a good deal of feminist, neo-Marxian and neo-Freudian criticism."[38]

In summary, the originators of the rhetoric of inquiry understood themselves to be building upon the insights of earlier thinkers who moved scholarly discussion away from notions of objectivity found in modernism and into the realm of postmodernism. However, some important parts of the original Iowans' proposals concerning the rhetoric of inquiry are not shared with all of the movements listed above. Not all of these interpretive models are concerned about cooperation and communication between academic disciplines, and yet the interdisciplinary nature of the scholarly enterprise is critical for the rhetoric of inquiry. As a field of study, the rhetoric of inquiry "must remain interdisciplinary," Nelson and Megill assert. They explain, "To show how the sciences and professions rely not less but only differently on rhetoric than do the humanities can encourage scholars to rethink radically their relationships with one another."[39]

As one reads the early discussions that gave birth to the rhetoric of inquiry, one cannot help but recognize an urgency of purpose. The concern for communication among the disciplines, for instance, is not presented merely as an intellectual advance designed to improve the overall quality of academic scholarship. Something more is afoot, and this something more also separates the rhetoric of inquiry from

---

38. Simons, "The Rhetoric of Inquiry as an Intellectual Movement," 7.
39. Nelson and Megill, "Rhetoric of Inquiry: Projects and Prospects," 35.

many other postmodern developments. The rhetoric of inquiry does not settle for deconstructing previous approaches to knowledge acquisition; it is reconstructive rather than merely deconstructive, and the concern with construction is at the center of the enterprise.[40]

Clifford Geertz famously asserts that all knowledge is local and that providing "thick description" of the contexts and aspects of specific cultures is required if we are profitably to study, in his case, the lives of people in different cultures.[41] The rhetoric of inquiry builds on this insight, as well as on the work of philosophers such as Dewey and Wittgenstein, to bind the work of the scholar to "practical forms of life."[42] This practicality is foundational to the rhetoric of inquiry, which situates research in, and connects it to, actual human communities. The whole point of rhetoric, after all, is to interact with and persuade a specific audience. To this end, our pursuit of scholarship, if it is inherently rhetorical, "requires that we study concrete communities of inquiry instead of abstract logics."[43] "Rhetoric is contextual," then, "and context is rhetorical."[44]

However, a number of the rhetoricians of inquiry go a step further in their quest to promote interaction between the work of scholarship and the life of particular communities by questioning the conventional split that academics make between inquiry and advocacy. Once again honoring the basic essence of rhetoric in the West, they reject the idea that the only proper place for inquiry is in the quiet of the individual's study or a classroom isolated from the world outside of the proverbial "ivory tower."[45] Again, there is

40. Ibid., 28.
41. Clifford Geertz, "Thick Description: Toward an Interpretive Theory of Culture," in idem, *The Interpretation of Cultures* (New York: Basic, 1973), 3–30. Also, see the essays in his *Local Knowledge: Further Essays in Interpretive Anthropology* (New York: Basic, 1983).
42. Nelson and Megill, "Rhetoric of Inquiry: Projects and Prospects," 25.
43. Nelson, Megill, and McCloskey, "Rhetoric of Inquiry," in idem, *The Rhetoric of the Human Sciences*, 15.
44. Nelson and Megill, "Rhetoric of Inquiry: Projects and Prospects," 33.

no rhetoric without context and no context without rhetoric, and if scholarship is rhetorical, its proper place is within public discourse. "Our world is a creature and a texture of rhetorics," Nelson and Megill assert. With a bit of old-style rhetorical flourish, they perceive the rhetorics "of founding stories and sales talks, anecdotes and statistics, images and rhythms; of tales told in the nursery, pledges of allegiance or revenge, symbols of success and failure, archetypes of action and character." They state, "Ours is a world of persuasive definitions, expressive explanations, and institutional narratives. It is replete with figures of truth, models of reality, tropes of argument, and metaphors of experience. *In our world, scholarship is rhetorical.*"[46]

It is not surprising that Schüssler Fiorenza embraces the rhetoric of inquiry and invites it into the discussion of New Testament rhetorical criticism. What is startling is the degree to which her thought aligns with the rhetoric of inquiry movement, even though her ideas not only developed independently from the work done in Iowa but also predated the Iowa School by several years. One can imagine her pleasure upon discovering the work of McCloskey and her colleagues, but Schüssler Fiorenza's encounter with the rhetoric of inquiry movement seems only to have confirmed the path she was already taking, rather than inducing her to change course in any significant way.

Schüssler Fiorenza and the Rhetoric and Ethic of Inquiry

Within a year of the publication of the Iowa School's work on the rhetoric of inquiry, Schüssler Fiorenza had read their work, understood its potential to support her insights, and aligned it with her own. Her presidential address to the Society of Biblical Literature in 1987 provided a cogent summary of her work over the previous

---

45. For a number of explanations of this move, see the essays in Simons, *The Rhetorical Turn*, passim.
46. Nelson and Megill, "Rhetoric of Inquiry: Projects and Prospects," 36 (emphasis added).

decade and functioned as a call to biblical scholars to ask the sorts of self-reflective questions of their work that the rhetoric of inquiry invites. For her, the "rhetoric of biblical scholarship" is less about the concerns of the Heritage or Dialectical Schools of rhetoric than it is a decision to reflect on what we do and why we do it. She observes that since 1947, no SBL presidential address had invited scholars to reflect on the public nature and accountability of their work. Concerns about world politics and crises, the Holocaust, civil rights or other movements for change found no mention, nor did they play much of a part in the work of most biblical scholars. She asserted that this lack of attention must change.[47]

In numerous works since then, Schüssler Fiorenza has explored the insights of the rhetoric of inquiry movement and introduced them to the field of biblical scholarship.[48] She repeatedly highlights the need for attention to the ethics of such work. Ethics, typically understood as a system of moral principles, provides "a theory and a vision of well-being of the 'good life,'" she writes, which "articulates the values and goals of human beings, or society on the whole, and of living nature."[49] She does not focus for long on the often-assumed priority of personal ethics, since morality is not constructed through private, interior rumination but through conversation and public discourse.

Too often in the past, that conversation has been controlled and circumscribed by "scientistic objectivism, subjectivism, liberalism, and nationalism, or the masculine rationalism and European colonialism of modernity." What has been missing and is needed now is an ethic of inquiry that subjects the methods and ways of framing

---

47. Elisabeth Schüssler Fiorenza, "The Ethics of Biblical Interpretation: Decentering Biblical Scholarship," *JBL* 107, no. 1 (1988): 3–17, reproduced in idem, *Rhetoric and Ethic*, 17–30.
48. For example, see the essays in Schüssler Fiorenza, *Rhetoric and Ethic*, as well as more recently idem, "Disciplinary Matters: A Critical Rhetoric and Ethic of Inquiry," in *Rhetoric, Ethic, and Moral Persuasion in Biblical Discourse*, ed. Thomas H. Olbricht and Anders Eriksson (New York: T&T Clark, 2005), 9–32. See also idem, "The Rhetoric of Inquiry," 23–48.
49. Schüssler Fiorenza, *Rhetoric and Ethic*, 66.

knowledge and making moral decisions to rhetorical-ethical analysis. The objective of the ethics of inquiry is not to forge new technical ways of making decisions but to develop critical ways to reflect and analyze texts, scholarship, and culture.[50]

What we see depends on where we stand, and this perspective, along with the reminder that there is no rhetoric without context, calls for a new critical rhetorical conceptualization that Schüssler Fiorenza calls a rhetoric *and ethic* of inquiry for biblical studies. Such a program consists of four investigative areas.[51]

First, there is the area of a rhetoric and ethic of biblical reading and interpretation that studies the rhetoric inscribed in the text. This area encompasses the traditional concerns of rhetorical criticism, examines the argumentation, values and norms discovered in the text, and describes the "theoretical assumptions, intellectual frameworks, historical perspectives, and symbolic world inscribed in the text."[52] Even at this level of textual analysis, Schüssler Fiorenza advocates a degree of self-reflection on the part of the exegete, who does not see the text as descriptive of reality, a window into the world, but rather understands the text as an attempt to persuade the reader concerning its worldview, goals, and imaginative vision.

The text presents the reader with a context that has been constructed rhetorically, and to study it is to study the strategies of selection of materials and the use of models, images, and tropes. When investigating the rhetoric of the text, the critic studies not just what is on the page but the history of interpretation as well. How has this text been interpreted in its "communities of reading?"[53] This question leads to the second area of investigation.

---

50. Ibid., 67–68.
51. Schüssler Fiorenza, "Disciplinary Matters," in Olbricht and Eriksson, *Rhetoric, Ethic, and Moral Persuasion,* 13; Schüssler Fiorenza, "The Rhetoric of Inquiry," 34–36.
52. Ibid., 34.
53. Ibid.

A rhetoric and ethic of interpretive practices or scientific production critically analyzes the way research on the text has been conducted. What research methods are used by the person doing the interpretation? What theoretical assumptions does the critic make on approaching the text? "What lenses of reading, patterns of interpretation, categories of analysis," models, or metaphors does the critic bring to the text?[54] The focus never strays from the work of previous interpretation. How is the discourse of interpretation created? Which authorities are invoked? What boundaries are imposed on the interpretation? Which "questions are not admitted, which arguments are silenced"?[55]

The third area of investigation is the rhetoric and ethic of the discipline, and it examines the wider academic context of interpretation by exploring the social location and *ethos* of scholarship.[56] What sort of received wisdom or common-sense assumptions are at work in textual interpretation? What kind of scholarship is recognized and supported by academic institutions, and what kind excluded? Who is considered an "expert" in the discipline? Who has the power to authorize "legitimate" interpretations?

The fourth area of investigation is the rhetoric and ethic of communicative practices, the study of how textual interpretation is communicated and used. What criteria are put in place to determine the kind of knowledge that is disseminated? To whom is it promulgated, to everyone or to special audiences of colleagues or "experts?" How is the interpretation presented, and how is one educated into the discipline? What is one taught to value within the discipline? Is one taught to value "'pure' value-detached reasoning or…critical

---

54. Ibid., 35.
55. Ibid.
56. For an extended discussion of this aspect of inquiry, see Schüssler Fiorenza, *Democratizing Biblical Studies*, passim.

reflexivity, democratic debate, intellectual responsibility, culturally multilingual and multidisciplinary competence?"[57] Schüssler Fiorenza develops this fourth area more fully than other practitioners of the rhetoric of inquiry, and she stresses it unremittingly.

The rhetoric and ethic of inquiry espoused by Schüssler Fiorenza, then, involves a simultaneous broadening and deepening of the work of the critic. While the focus remains on the rhetoric inscribed in a text, one studies not just the techniques used by the author but also the author's presuppositions, values, and social location. In other words, one attempts to learn all one can about the context of the text's production. Beyond the text, one must study the history of the interpretation of the text in communities of readers and how the discipline of the critic has legitimated some interpretations while discouraging others. At its broadest, one must also interrogate one's own work and the work of other "experts" and evaluate how the interpretation of the text is received by communities of readers, and to what end.[58]

Although I have not dwelt on it much in this essay so far, Schüssler Fiorenza's commitment to feminism has been at the core of her work from its beginning in Germany in the 1960s and cannot be separated from her development of a rhetoric and ethic of inquiry. It is important to note here that the rhetoric and ethic of inquiry that she espouses is a feminist one and focuses especially "on the ambiguity and instability of grammatically gendered language as rhetorical language and text." An explicitly feminist rhetoric and ethic of inquiry, she suggests, contributes four important insights for the rhetorical study of biblical texts.[59]

---

57. Schüssler Fiorenza, "The Rhetoric of Inquiry," 36.
58. For a detailed presentation of her critical rhetorical model of analysis, see Schüssler Fiorenza, *Rhetoric and Ethic*, 123–28.
59. For the purposes of this essay, I cannot explore these four insights in any detail. The following material is taken from Schüssler Fiorenza, *Rhetoric and Ethic*, 93–94.

First, "language is not reflective but performative." Grammatically androcentric language does not describe reality; rather, it "creates and shapes the symbolic worlds it professes to evoke and describe." The worlds created—the social structures and commonly accepted norms and values—have marginalized or eliminated wo/men (the oppressed) from cultural and religious discourses. Second, language is not just performative; it is political; and as such, it shapes and is shaped by those promoting the interests of kyriarchal institutions and structures.[60] "Language and texts are always dependent on their rhetorical situation and sociopolitical location." Third, as a result, critical analysis of the language and rhetoric of texts is insufficient. One must critically examine as well the sociopolitical and religious structures of culture that foster domination and exclusion. Fourth, language and knowledge are rhetorical; that is, "they are articulated in specific situations, by particular people, for a certain audience and with certain articulated or suppressed goals and interests in mind." That being the case, the product of language and of knowledge, as well as the "cultural mind-sets" that foster their development, can be changed.

Even a quick summary of aspects of Schüssler Fiorenza's approach to the rhetoric of inquiry makes clear the focus of her work. She writes, "It does not suffice to know the world as it is; what is crucial is to transform and change it."[61] Her thought encourages reflection on the place where textual interpretation is accomplished; indeed, it demands that biblical scholarship break out of the conventional boundaries of the academy. The pathway out is lit by the rhetorical

---

60. "Kyriarchy/kyriarchal:" "[D]erived form the Greek term for lord, this coinage underscores that domination is not simply a matter of patriarchal, gender-based dualism but of more comprehensive, interlocking, hierarchically ordered structures of domination, evident in a variety of oppressions such as racism, poverty, heterosexism, and colonialism. See Schüssler Fiorenza, *Rhetoric and Ethic*, ix.

61. Ibid., 93.

approach to biblical texts, and where it takes us is into a new realm of critical space.

An *Ethos* of Inquiry: Where, and With Whom, Do We Work?

Even at its most basic and by virtue of its definition, the realm of rhetoric as the art of persuasion cannot long remain private or individual. Someone else in addition to the speaker or writer must be engaged to be persuaded, and all forms of rhetorical criticism are developed and implemented through argument. At the core of Schüssler Fiorenza's understanding of the nature and function of the rhetoric and ethics of inquiry, however, is the assertion that the discourse of rhetoric is a public one. Where the rhetorical-critical project takes place, and by whom, must be acknowledged and analyzed. For Schüssler Fiorenza, a rhetoric of inquiry involves an *ethos* of inquiry.

While scholars usually associate the etymological meaning of *ethos* with the Greek word *ethos* (custom or habit), Schüssler Fiorenza follows Susan Jarratt and Nedra Reynolds, who suggest that the word may derive from *éthea*, an early version of the word-group that indicates "accustomed places" or the "haunts or abodes of animals." For Schüssler Fiorenza, *ethos* is a place where "customs and character are formed."[62] In the words of Linda Alcoff, *ethos* should be understood as a "place from which values are interpreted and constructed rather than as a locus of an already determined set of values."[63] In this context in which *ethos* designates positioning, it is important to be aware that "one always speaks from a particular place

---

62. Schüssler Fiorenza, "Disciplinary Matters," 15–16. She follows Susan C. Jarratt and Nedra Reynolds, "The Splitting Image: Contemporary Feminisms and the Ethics of *ethos*," in *Ethos: New Essays in Rhetorical and Critical Theory*, ed. James S. Baumlin and Tita French Baumlin (Dallas: Southern Methodist University Press, 1994), 37–64.
63. Linda Alcoff, "Cultural Feminism Versus Post-Structuralism," *Signs* 13 (1988): 434.

in a social structure."[64] *Ethos* becomes an ethical and political tool and "a way of claiming and taking responsibility for our positions in the world, for the ways we see, the places where we speak."[65]

Schüssler Fiorenza urges a reconceptualization of the disciplinary *ethos* of rhetorical- critical biblical studies. She critiques and breaks down the dualisms she sees in the discipline, "opposites such as rational and irrational, objective and subjective, hard and soft, male and female, Europeans and colonials, secular and religious." She questions the existence of "value-neutral, apolitical, universal, empirical and methodologically objective" scholarship and an "unbiased arena of knowledge" that developed in the past two centuries.[66] Citing Bonnie Smith, she rejects the idea that it is possible to create an *ethos* in which scholars (in Smith's case, historians) "eliminate all personal or subjective meaning from their work . . . a space inhabited by an invisible 'I,' one without politics, without an ego or persona, and certainly ungendered."[67]

Who inhabits the disciplinary *ethos*, the place where rhetorical discourse is experienced, is of critical importance. Schüssler Fiorenza proposes an *ethos* of disciplinary rhetorical discourse that is radically democratic. Quoting a biographer of Hannah Arendt, Schüssler Fiorenza notes that "[o]nly where we create a certain kind of place can a certain kind of person emerge."[68]

---

64. Jarratt and Reynolds, "The Splitting Image," 47.

65. Schüssler Fiorenza, "Disciplinary Matters," 17.

66. Ibid., 18–19. Here, she is referencing the work of Nancy L. Stepan and Sander L. Gilman, "Appropriating the Idioms of Science: The Rejection of Scientific Racism," in *The "Racial" Economy of Science: Toward a Democratic Future,* ed. Sandra Harding (Bloomington: Indiana University Press, 1993), 170–93.

67. Bonnie G. Smith, "Gender, Objectivity, and the Rise of Scientific History," in *Objectivity and Its Other,* ed. W. Natter et al. (New York: Guilford, 1995), 52; cited in Schüssler Fiorenza, "Disciplinary Matters," 20.

68. John McGowan, *Hannah Arendt: An Introduction* (Minneapolis: University of Minnesota Press, 1998), 167; cited in Schüssler Fiorenza, "Disciplinary Matters," 16.

Members of the discipline of biblical studies must analyze the "kyriarchal (gendered, raced, classed, and colonized) structures and circumstances" that keep those in the margins—wo/men and subaltern, low-status men—firmly away from power, authority, or any potential for authentic self-authorization. Looking at traditions, texts, and their interpreters, Schüssler Fiorenza asks whether our work has any power for emancipation, for the transformation of society. Or does our work perpetuate oppression, injustice, and the received "wisdom" of kyriarchal structures of class, race, and gender?

The rhetorical space of our interpretation is also literal space and includes the location where scholarship is done, as well as the community of people with whom one works. Traditionally, the scholar's workspace has been the academy, the classroom and perhaps on occasion the parish or local church. Traditionally, the "expert's" tool has been the lecture in which the professional offers wisdom and insight to "the laity," "the people in the pew," or "the poor."

A rhetorical emancipatory critical approach to inquiry involves a democratizing of biblical studies. Biblical interpretation must serve as an emancipatory force, and it must inhabit a democratizing *ethos* where the experience and reflection of all people, especially wo/men, who make up the vast majority of the oppressed, are taken seriously.

In this approach, the "place" where scholars work is within the community, presumably a community with some vested interest in the power of the biblical texts to foster either oppression or liberation. This place does not produce interpretations that are objective or value-free. Neither does it produce interpretations that are the product of invisible, genderless, classless, "educated" elites. Rather, this is a place where those who have been traditionally trained can join conversations that have been going on for a very long time without "experts"—on street corners, around campfires, among the rural homeless, at breakfast tables, in soup kitchens and daycare centers, on union picket lines, in churches on Wednesday nights when the pastor is off doing hospital rounds, and in college dormitories late at night when the professors are home in bed.

Schüssler Fiorenza calls for a completely open rhetorical space as the place where analysis is to be done. She asks professional practitioners of biblical criticism to take seriously their responsibility to examine how they, not only each individually but also all together, have propagated and supported kyriarchal structures, and how they can join the rest of the human community, which is inhabited not just by Christians, to investigate how religious texts and traditions create and shape the world.

This radically democratic approach to the *ethos* of biblical studies and, indeed, of all academic work decenters traditional sources of authority and power and clearly places Schüssler Fiorenza at odds with modernist thought with its claims to intellectual objectivity and absolute and permanent truth. However, she is also at odds with the *ethos* of some movements within postmodernism as well. While she appreciates the ways that postmodernism exposes and rejects the scientism, intellectual certitude, kyriocentric, and value-neutral objectivism of modernist thought, even her natural intellectual allies such as the postcolonialists and some academic forms of feminism find their home in literary departments and rarely venture forth beyond them. Privileging the act of reading over sociopolitical analysis, their goal often seems to be to change the thinking of those within the academy rather than addressing the deep problems of justice in the world.[69] Schüssler Fiorenza challenges these movements to expand beyond their zone of comfort. "Is the task of post-colonial biblical scholarship only to 'read' the power politics and material conditions embedded in our societies and religions?" she asks. "Or is it also to

---

69. Schüssler Fiorenza, *The Power of the Word*, 115–16.

engage in the struggles for justice for colonized people, and hence for changing societies and religions?"[70]

Her concern for action and collaboration with all people, particularly the oppressed and marginalized, rather than scholarly isolation is at the core of all of Schüssler Fiorenza's thought. Her proposed *ethos* of inquiry, which incorporates not just the "experts" but also "all who can think," is central to her rhetorical-critical approach to biblical studies. What she claims in her pedagogical work for a "feminist, emancipatory, radical democratic model of education" is applicable to her understanding of the *ethos* of inquiry. She writes, "Its basic assumption is that knowledge is publicly available to all who can think and that everyone has something to contribute to knowledge."[71] Interpretation and the production of knowledge begin with a hermeneutic of experience that examines how human activity, particularly that of wo/men and all marginalized people, is socially located and shaped by encounters and relationships that result in domination and submission.[72] Analysis of one's experience, then, is the place where a critical rhetoric and ethic of inquiry begins.

A Republic of Many Voices

When Schüssler Fiorenza began teaching in the United States over forty years ago, she was told by a senior colleague to remember that she had been hired as a critical exegete and historian, not a theologian. "Consequently," she was cautioned, "never allow your students to ask what is the religious or theological significance of biblical texts and interpretation for today. If you allow this question, scholarship will founder on the slippery slope of relevance."[73] This

---

70. Schüssler Fiorenza, *Democratizing Biblical Studies*, 106.
71. Ibid., 141.
72. Schüssler Fiorenza, *The Power of the Word,* 163–64.
73. Schüssler Fiorenza, *Jesus and the Politics of Interpretation*, 76.

warning came as something of a shock to someone who had been trained in Germany in a hermeneutical-theological tradition. It made no sense to Schüssler Fiorenza to think that biblical scholars could make a neat separation between their historical-critical work, the theology embodied in the texts they studied, and the people for whom those texts offered the power to oppress or emancipate.[74]

Since the 1960s, Schüssler Fiorenza has been pursuing a kind of "interdisciplinarity" within the discipline of biblical studies. She rejects the notion of an anti-theological scientific positivism as a more pure and more true form of scholarship than the hermeneutical theological reflection and research that is not afraid to engage in the practical concerns of the wider community comprised of the ekklesia, the radical democratic assembly.[75] After all, as she points out and as rudimentary logic would seem to confirm, since the goal of rhetoric is persuasion, "the ethical knowledge rhetoric strives to achieve is that of commitment."[76]

The rhetoric and ethic of inquiry that Schüssler Fiorenza proposes insists on a re-envisioning of the role and work of the scholar by rejecting the radical detachment of scholarship that came to characterize the "scientistic *ethos* of biblical studies" in the nineteenth and twentieth centuries as scholars freed their work from dogmatic ecclesiastical control.[77] As noted earlier, in the interpretive space that she lays out, scholars from many disciplines come together along with "anyone who can think," that is, the members of the community

---

74. Cf. Fernando F. Segovia, "Looking Back, Looking Around, Looking Ahead: An Interview with Elisabeth Schüssler Fiorenza," in *Toward a New Heaven and a New Earth*, ed. idem (Maryknoll: Orbis, 2003), 1–30, specifically 13–16.

75. The term *ekklesia* was originally a Greek word to describe the political assembly of the full citizens of a polis or city-state; the early Christians used the term to describe their gatherings as a community. For Schüssler Fiorenza, the word signifies "the radical equality that characterizes the 'already and not yet' of religious community and democratic society." See Schüssler Fiorenza, *Rhetoric and Ethic*, ix.

76. Ibid., 57.

77. Ibid., 24.

whose interests are served—or suppressed—by the interpretation of biblical texts. The goal of interpretation in this space shifts away from the search for the "truth" behind the text (what the text "really means" or what the world of the author was "really like" or what the author "really intended") and toward engagement in conversation with the living ekklesia today. It is through such discourse in which all, and not just those designated by the kyriarchal institutions as appropriately credentialed, have a legitimate part to play.

This community is what Schüssler Fiorenza calls "a republic of many equal voices," and she conceives this republic to be "a space for people to dialogue, debate, argue, and collaborate with each other, to seek not only to understand the diverse voices of biblical texts but also to explore, assess, and evaluate them in terms of their impact on contemporary politics and religious communities."[78] Within this context, members of the academy function as critical transformative intellectuals rather than independent professionals. They are people who "must reclaim the public space of the ekklesia as the arena of historical, theological, and cultural" biblical studies to engage in radical democratic discourse.[79]

What the voices talk about as they reflect on how biblical texts have been or might be interpreted are justice and emancipation for the marginalized, for the oppressed, and for wo/men. For Schüssler Fiorenza, a commitment to rhetoric leads invariably to a rhetoric of commitment. As she has noted on a number of occasions, all interpretation of texts is done either for or against the oppressed.[80] All interpretation, therefore, must be studied closely, since no one

---

78. Schüssler Fiorenza, *Democratizing Biblical Studies*, 83.
79. Schüssler Fiorenza, *Jesus and the Politics of Interpretation*, 74–75. She notes that Stanley Aronowitz and Henry Giroux proposed that critical pedagogies require "transformative intellectuals [who] can emerge from and work with a number of groups, other than and including the working class, that advance emancipatory traditions and culture within and without alternative public spheres." See Aronowitz and Giroux, *Education Under Siege* (South Hadley: Bergin & Garvey, 1985), 45.

"paradigm" of biblical interpretation contains within it the sum of all emancipatory insight.[81]

The right thing for someone like Schüssler Fiorenza to do, some argue, would be to leave behind the Bible altogether, and she has been criticized for her unwillingness to do so.[82] The texts, she argues, have often been used as tools to subordinate and marginalize wo/ men, but they also "have the power to evoke potent emotions and creative responses and thereby create a sense of community necessary to sustain contemporary visions and struggles for a different society, church, and world."[83] This point is important for Schüssler Fiorenza's position in a genealogy of rhetorical criticism. She writes that a critical reading of the Bible is the reason, after all, for a rhetoric of inquiry approach to the text and that this critical reading "understands biblical authority not as something that requires subordination and obedience, but as a resource for creativity, courage, and solidarity."[84] She further writes about this critical reading of the Bible:

> It understands truth not as something given once and for all, as hidden and buried, and ready to be unveiled and unearthed by a spiritual reading of biblical texts. It does not understand scripture as tablets

---

80. Schüssler Fiorenza, *Rhetoric and Ethic*, 47; idem, *The Power of the Word*, 46–47; and idem, *Democratizing Biblical Studies*, 120. Note, however, that Schüssler Fiorenza does not idealize the oppressed by assuming their "innocence and purity," just as she does not assume that they are "victims incapable of being agents for change." See Schüssler Fiorenza, *Wisdom Ways*, 89–90.

81. Schüssler Fiorenza has done a great deal of work describing the different paradigms currently in use in the study of the Bible. For details, see in particular Schüssler Fiorenza, *Rhetoric and Ethic*, 31–55; and, more recently, idem, *Democratizing Biblical Studies*, 51–125. Note that she indicates repeatedly—though somehow this is overlooked by some of her critics—that when she critiques the approaches of other readings of texts, "I do so not in order to prove the others wrong but in order to ferret out the hermeneutical implications of different ways to approach the problem" of biblical interpretation. See Schüssler Fiorenza, *The Power of the Word*, 28.

82. For her own critique of Hector Avalos, who argues that modern biblical scholarship has rendered the Bible irrelevant, see Schüssler Fiorenza, *Democratizing Biblical Studies*, 38–41. See Hector Avalos, *The End of Biblical Studies* (Amherst, NY: Prometheus, 2007), passim.

83. Schüssler Fiorenza, *The Power of the Word*, 192.

84. Ibid., 67.

of stone but rather as nourishing bread. It understands revelation as something ongoing, as fermenting yeast of the empowering presence of Divine Wisdom, which can be experienced and articulated only in and through the rejection of the violent power and ethos of empire. It does not understand the bible as an immutable archetype but as an historical prototype of Christian community and life, as nourishing bread of Divine Wisdom that enables us to struggle against the violence and exploitation in our daily lives.[85]

Schüssler Fiorenza calls for continued engagement with biblical texts, for they are supremely relevant to the work for justice, democratic equality, and the end of oppression in any age. We must be able "to understand biblical texts not only as the memory of the suffering and the victimization of all who have been considered nonpersons and noncitizens," she writes. A rhetorical, emancipatory approach to the texts will also uncover and preserve "the memory of those wo/men who in their struggles against patriarchal domination have shaped Christian history as religious interlocutors, agents of change, and survivors."[86]

The Bible is here to stay, and it contains within itself texts of great power for liberation. It is the job of biblical critics of all persuasions to do what they can to join as equals with other members of the ekklesia in discourse with these texts and with one another and to remember those who have gone before, what suffering they endured, and what glory they made manifest. It is also the job of biblical critics to resist those who would continue to subordinate and oppress others in the name of God and to envision new ways to be followers of Divine Wisdom, incarnated for Christians in the person of Jesus of Nazareth. Jesus is at the heart of Christian memory, and Divine Wisdom is at the heart of the rhetorical trajectory of Schüssler Fiorenza, for

85. Ibid. This citation is part of an argument concerning the "imperial functions of authoritative scriptural claims [in antiquity as well as today] that demand obedience and acceptance;" hence the references to "empire."
86. Schüssler Fiorenza, *Rhetoric and Ethic*, 96.

Wisdom/wisdom is at the heart of the ekklesia's presence in the world. "If the memory of Jesus' suffering and resurrection, understood as an instance of unjust human suffering and survival, is at the heart and center of Christian memory," she writes, "then the critical, ethical and theological line must be drawn between injustice and justice, between the world of domination and a world of freedom and well-being."[87]

Indeed, this world of freedom, of radical democracy, *is* the ekklesia in her thinking. "I want a new earth and I want it passionately," she exclaims at the end of an interview with Fernando Segovia. This new earth would be one in which everyone has enough to live a life grounded in dignity and freedom.[88] To attain this vision of a new earth, "critical scholarship has to be reconceptualized as a part of activism, a part of the struggle for justice."[89] Biblical texts must be critically investigated and become "sites of struggle and conscientization." The goal of this work is an alternative vision of the world but not one that then becomes a new universal truth. The method and the goal are discourse, not prescription, but a discourse open to all, for in the process of the "imaginative pragmatism" that she envisions, "one never arrives but always struggles on the way."[90]

Schüssler Fiorenza was initially attracted to rhetorical criticism because it engages in argument, and argument is a two-way street. As a result, rhetoric and especially the rhetoric of inquiry allow wo/men to become visible and heard in discourses about biblical texts. Schüssler Fiorenza's rhetoric and ethic of inquiry beckons all trained biblical professionals who would be effective members of the ekklesia to embrace a radical emancipatory democratic paradigm for our research and a concomitant radical democratic pedagogy for our

87. Schüssler Fiorenza, *Jesus and the Politics of Interpretation*, 75–76.
88. Segovia, "Looking Back," 26.
89. Schüssler Fiorenza, *Democratizing Biblical Studies*, 106.
90. Schüssler Fiorenza, *The Power of the Word*, 193.

classrooms. We are to be called away from an exclusive devotion to the solitude and radical detachment of the research cubicle and into the midst of a visionary, imaginative gathering of many voices in the public square.

8

Response to John R. Lanci: Transforming the Discipline—The Rhetoricity/ Rhetoricality of New* Testament Studies

Elisabeth Schüssler Fiorenza

First of all, I want to thank John R. Lanci for his excellent presentation and perceptive discussion of my rhetorical approach and interpretive work.[1] As John has eloquently elaborated, my work

---

1. I am grateful to Dr. John Lanci for his feedback and to Ms. Kelsi Morrison-Atkins for proofreading and polishing my text. The term *rhetoricality* is used in the title and throughout this essay. For a definition and discussion of this term, see John Bender and David E. Wellbery, eds., *The Ends of Rhetoric: History, Theory, Practice* (Stanford: Stanford University Press,1990), 25. They explain, "The classical rhetorical tradition rarified speech and fixed it within a gridwork of limitations: it was a rule governed domain whose procedures themselves were delimited by the institutions that organized interaction and domination in traditional European society. Rhetoricality by contrast is bound to no specific set of institutions. It manifests the

has sought to integrate and transform elements of the the*logical, historical, and literary paradigms of biblical studies into a fourth paradigm of rhetorical-ethical inquiry and has done so in the framework and interest of a critical feminist hermeneutics and rhetoric of liberation.[2] My ensuing elaborations are not to be read as corrections or additions to his work but as a rhetorical accounting in my own voice.

Feminist Standpoint and Theoretical Perspective

As John has so eloquently elaborated, I have conceptualized and developed my work on *Rhetoric and Ethic* in terms of my social-historical location as one of the first feminist scholars in biblical studies.[3] Hence, I have sought to change and develop the discipline of biblical studies in critical feminist terms. It is significant that the renaissance of rhetoric corresponds to the five decades in which

---

groundless infinitely ramifying character of discourse in the modern world. For this reason, it allows for no explanatory discourse that is not already itself rhetorical."

2. For this work, see Elisabeth Schüssler Fiorenza, *In Memory of Her: A Feminist Reconstruction of Christian Origins* (New York: Crossroad, 1983); idem, *But She Said: Feminist Practices of Biblical Interpretation* (Boston: Beacon, 1992); idem, *Jesus: Miriam's Child, Sophia's Prophet* (New York: Continuum, 1995); idem, *Rhetoric and Ethic: The Politics of Biblical Studies* (Minneapolis: Fortress, 1999); idem, *Jesus and the Politics of Interpretation* (New York: Continuum, 2000); idem, *Grenzen überschreiten: Der theoretische Anspruch feministischer Theologie* (Münster: Lit, 2004); idem, *Wisdom Ways: Introducing Feminist Biblical Interpretation* (Maryknoll: Orbis, 2005); idem, *The Power of the Word: Scripture and the Rhetoric of Empire* (Minneapolis: Fortress, 2007); idem, *Democratizing Biblical Studies: Toward an Emancipatory Educational Space* (Louisville: Westminster John Knox, 2009); idem, *Transforming Vision: Explorations in Feminist The*logy* (Minneapolis: Fortress, 2011); and idem, *Changing Horizons: Explorations in Feminist Interpretation* (Minneapolis: Fortress, 2013).

3. I understand "feminist/feminism" to refer to a social movement and critical theory that endeavors to make wo/men recognized as responsible citizens with a full set of rights in society and religion. The word *wo/men* includes marginalized men. For discussion of the various theories of feminism, see Anne C. Herrmann and Abigail J. Stewart, *Theorizing Feminism: Parallel Trends in the Humanities and Social Sciences* (2nd ed.; Boulder: Westview, 2001). Feminist studies are not only gender studies but also studies of pyramidal intersecting power structures such as gender, race, class, nation, religion, and culture.

feminist biblical studies emerged and matured. The confluence of both developments has enabled and shaped my work.

I understand feminist New* Testament/Early Christian studies as an important area of scholarly research that seeks to produce knowledge in the interest of wo/men who by law and custom have been excluded from philosophy, the*logy, and biblical interpretation for centuries.[4] Hence, a critical feminist approach must examine the structures of kyriarchal (i.e., lord-emperor, slave-master, father, husband, elite educated male) domination that are controlling the production of knowledge in a given discipline. This kyriarchal pyramid of domination is structured by the intersecting social systems of race, gender, sexuality, class, empire, age, and religion. Taken together, these systems can result in multiplicative effects of dehumanizing exploitation and subordination of the "other."

The study of *Woman in the Bible* was already flourishing when I began to study theology in the late 1950s. Virginia Woolf was

4. For example, see Janice Capel Anderson, "Mapping Feminist Biblical Criticism," *CRBR* 2 (1991): 21–44; Elizabeth Castelli, "Heteroglossia, Hermeneutics and History: A Review Essay of Recent Feminist Studies of Early Christianity," *JFSR* 10, no. 2 (1994): 73–78. For Jewish feminist interpretations, see the work of Esther Fuchs, Ilana Pardes, Adele Reinhartz, Tal Ilan, Amy-Jill Levine, Cynthia Baker, Alicia Suskin Ostriker, and many others. See also Esther Fuchs, "Points of Resonance," in *On the Cutting Edge: The Study of Women in Biblical Worlds*, ed. Jane Schaberg, Alice Bach, and Esther Fuchs (New York: Continuum, 2003), 1–20. For Muslim feminist hermeneutics, see for example Amina Wadud, *Qur'an and Woman: Rereading the Sacred Text from a Woman's Perspective* (Oxford: Oxford University Press, 1999); Barbara F. Stowasser, *Women in the Qur'an: Traditions and Interpretations* (New York: Oxford University Press, 1994); and Asma Barlas, *"Believing Women" in Islam: Unreading Patriarchal Interpretations of the Qur'an* (Austin: University of Texas Press, 2002). However, I do not understand feminist studies merely as the study of gender or woman but as the study of intersecting structures of power and domination. My way of writing *wo/men* seeks not only to underscore the ambiguous character of the terms *woman* and *women* but also to retain the expression *women* as a sociopolitical category. Since the traditional rendering is often read as referring to white wo/men only, my unorthodox writing of the word seeks to draw the attention of readers to those kyriarchal structures that determine wo/men's lives and status and also impact men of subordinated race, class, country, and religion, albeit in different ways. *Wo/men* is therefore to be understood as an inclusive rather than as an exclusive universalized gender term. For the problematic meaning of the terms *woman* and *women*, see Denise Riley, *"Am I That Name?" Feminism and the Category of Women in History* (Minneapolis: University of Minnesota Press, 1988); and Judith Butler, *Gender Trouble: Feminism and the Subversion of Identity* (New York: Routledge, 1990).

correct in saying that just as the library shelves were filled with books written by men about wo/men, so also did the religious libraries hold a great array of tracts about "women in the Bible."[5] These were either moralistic tales to inculcate the standards of Christian femininity with the help of biblical wo/men characters and saints, or they were written to legitimate wo/men's exclusion from or admission to ordination. Others were apologetic in tone and argued that Jesus and the Christian religion had liberated wo/men. Such portrayals of Jesus and his liberation of wo/men were often used for missionary purposes or to serve anti-feminist and anti-Jewish interests.

Similar to studies about wo/men in which wo/men are treated not just as objects but as subjects of interpretation, wo/men's biblical studies has a long history beginning in antiquity and continuing throughout the Middle Ages and modernity. In the nineteenth century, Sojourner Truth, Anna Maria Stewart, and the Grimké sisters, for instance, claim such authority of interpretation in the struggle for the abolition of slavery. Elizabeth Cady Stanton edits the *Woman's Bible*, and Antoinette Blackwell writes a scientific paper on 1 Corinthians.[6] According to Cady Stanton, however, the wo/men scholars of the time were not willing to collaborate on the *Woman's Bible* project.[7]

This reticence is still true for some wo/men scholars in the twentieth and twenty-first centuries, but no longer the case for all. Rather, many wo/men scholars have collaborated in the centennial

5. Virginia Woolf, *Three Guineas* (New York: Harcourt Brace Jovanovich, 1966).
6. See Elisabeth Schüssler Fiorenza, *Sharing Her Word: Feminist Biblical Interpretation in Context* (Boston: Beacon, 1998), 50–74; and Kathi Kern, *Mrs. Stanton's Bible* (Ithaca: Cornell University Press, 2001).
7. Although the first wo/man to join the Society of Biblical Literature was Anna Ely Rhoads in 1894, the Society did not elect its first wo/man president until 1987. In 1970, wo/men constituted only 3.5 percent of its total membership. See Ernest W. Saunders, *Searching the Scriptures: A History of the Society of Biblical Literature, 1880–1980* (Chico: Scholars, 1982), 103. Saunders is citing a study by Dorothy C. Bass.

celebration of Cady Stanton's *Woman's Bible* by contributing either to the *Women's Bible Commentary*, edited by Carol Newsom and Sharon Ringe, or to the two volumes of *Searching the Scriptures*, which I edited.

In the early 1970s, a publisher asked me to write a book on wo/men in the Bible, and I responded that I could not think of a more boring task since I had discussed all the relevant texts in my first book on ministries of wo/men in the church that was published in Germany in 1964. In it, I reviewed most of the research about wo/men in the New* Testament and in early Christianity and thought nothing new could be said about this topic. However, my attitude changed radically after the first works appeared on feminist historiography, theory, literary studies, and rhetoric.

The emerging field of feminist biblical interpretation was not restricted to believing or Christian feminists. As early as the nineteenth century, Elizabeth Cady Stanton urges feminists to concern themselves with the Bible and religion because many wo/men still believe in them. She also points out that one cannot reform one segment of patriarchal society without reforming the whole. Feminist biblical studies, therefore, encompasses both cultural and theological studies. To understand Western art, music, and literature, for example, one needs a certain amount of biblical literacy. Many cultural ideologies and media stereotypes are based on and derived from the Bible. Biblical texts and images still fund some of the cultural language of hate against wo/men, African Americans, GLBT persons, Jews, and pagans.

A challenge presented by the feminist hermeneutical debates of the 1970s and early '80s was to articulate more fully a hermeneutical framework and methodology of interpretation that was critical and liberationist without being apologetic and defensive. My books *In Memory of Her* (1983) and *Bread Not Stone* (1984) seek to develop such a feminist model of critical interpretation and historical reconstruction.[8] In Memory of Her maps the field of early Christian interpretation and historiography in feminist terms. My goal was not to write a history of wo/men in early Christianity. Rather, I wanted to see whether sufficient materials existed to write a feminist history of Christian beginnings. This project required tracing ongoing struggles between those who sought to realize a radical egalitarian movement and those who advocated patriarchal structures of domination and exclusion.

In the three introductory chapters of In Memory of Her, I tried to chart a new field of study that encompassed the hermeneutical-methodological issues faced by feminist studies of the Christian Testament. These chapters address hermeneutics in general and theological hermeneutics in particular (chapter 1); the literary and ideological constructions of androcentric language and texts (chapter 2); and sociological-historical methods and models that would allow for a feminist-historical reconstruction (chapter 3). I conclude with an epilogue on the ekklēsia of wo/men to spell out my feminist hermeneutical center and socioreligious location. Later, in Bread Not Stone, I distinguish feminist hermeneutics from malestream theological hermeneutics to situate the emerging field of feminist biblical interpretation vis-à-vis the overarching discourses of malestream biblical studies.

First of all, a critical feminist rhetorical model of interpretation, I have consistently argued, must place wo/men as citizen-subjects, as the ekklēsia of wo/men, into the hermeneutical center.[9] Studies about

8. See also Elisabeth Schüssler Fiorenza, "Method in Wo/men's Studies in Religion: A Critical Feminist Hermeneutics," in Methodology in Religious Studies: The Interface with Women's Studies, ed. Arvind Sharma (Albany: SUNY Press, 2002), 207–41.
9. I developed the qualification "rhetorical" in my critical hermeneutical model in concert with the emerging literature on the rhetoricality or rhetoricity of knowledge and the emerging literature on feminist rhetorics. For examples, see Richard H. Roberts and James M. M. Good, eds., The Recovery of Rhetoric: Persuasive Discourse and Disciplinarity in the Human Sciences

"women or gender in the Bible" are not properly feminist unless they recognize wo/men in religion as historical, cultural, theological, and scientific subjects and agents.

Second, feminist biblical scholarship is to be done in the interest of all wo/men and should espouse a radically democratic societal, cultural, religious, and personal transformation. Hence it has to be especially careful not to reinscribe the traditional paradigms of interpretation and rhetorical analysis, since these are based on Western male cultural values and experiences. Theologically, such an approach must assess whether a biblical text reveals G*d as a G*d of domination and oppression or as a G*d of liberation and well-being. Additionally, such an approach must consider the context in which the text receives its meaning. This approach understands "revelation" as what is put into scripture by G*d "for the sake of 'our'—that is wo/men's—salvation or wellbeing." Utilizing an ancient Jewish hermeneutical insight, it seeks the Divine in "the white spaces" between the letters and words of scripture.[10]

Third, this model presupposes wo/men to be producers of critical knowledge and thus requires a double paradigm shift in the ethos

(Bristol: Bristol Classical; Charlottesville: University Press of Virginia, 1993); Krista Ratcliffe, *Anglo-American Feminist Challenges to the Rhetorical Traditions* (Carbondale: Southern Illinois University Press, 1996); Jane Donawerth, *Rhetorical Theory by Women before 1900* (New York: Rowman & Littlefield, 2002); Roxanne Mountford, *The Gendered Pulpit* (Carbondale: Southern Illinois University Press, 2003); Jennifer Richards, *Rhetoric: The New Critical Idiom* (New York: Routledge, 2008); and Eileen E. Schell and K. J. Rawson, eds., *Rhetorica in Motion: Feminist Rhetorical Methods and Methodologies* (PSCLC; Pittsburgh: University of Pittsburgh Press, 2010). For a very perceptive contextualization of this feminist articulation, see Castelli, *"Ekklēsia,"* in Schaberg, Bach, and Fuchs, *On the Cutting Edge,* 36–52. See also Jannine Jobling, *Feminist Biblical Interpretation in Theological Context: Restless Readings* (Burlington: Ashgate, 2002), 32–59 and 142–62. Jobling discusses the concept of the *ekklēsia of wo/men* but chooses *ekklēsia* without the qualification of wo/men as her hermeneutical key concept to restrict the concept to the Christian feminist movement (143). In so doing, she reinscribes the division between the Christian and the so-called secular wo/men's movements that I sought to overcome with this radically democratic, counter-kyriarchal image.

10. For instance, see Naomi M. Hyman, *Biblical Wo/men in the Midrash: A Sourcebook* (Northvale: Aronson, 1997).

of biblical studies. It requires a shift away from a positivist, allegedly interest-free and value-neutral objectivist ethos of scholarship on the one hand, and from a kyriocentric linguistically-based cultural ethos on the other, to a feminist rhetorical paradigm of biblical studies.

Such a rhetorical model of biblical studies has to be transdisciplinary. It not only must integrate the insights of philology, classics, archaeology, sociology, anthropology, ethnography, epistemology, and historiography, but also must recognize the fundamental feminist criticism of these academic disciplines and their feminist reconceptualizations.[11] This reconceptualization also has to be interreligious. This last point has engendered discussions on anti-Judaism in Christian biblical scholarship. However, it is increasingly recognized that feminists of different religious persuasions can learn from each other, since their sacred texts are for the most part androcentric, or, better, kyriocentric.

Fourth, just as critical theory, so also a critical feminist rhetorical analysis concentrates especially on the corruption and ideologically alienating power of speech acts. Its fundamental methodological insight is constituted by its ability to recognize the kyriocentric function of language.[12] It documents the kyriocentric rhetoricity of language in the following ways.

1. Grammatically andro-kyriocentric language pretends to be generic-inclusive language. It mentions wo/men only when

---

11. For instance, see Nancy Sorkin Rabinowitz and Amy Richlin, eds., *Feminist Theory and the Classics* (New York: Routledge, 1993).

12. Schüssler Fiorenza, *In Memory of Her*, passim; Dennis Baron, *Grammar and Gender* (New Haven: Yale University Press, 1986); Robert H. Robins, *A Short History of Linguistics* (London: Longman, 1979); Casey Miller and Kate Swift, *Words and Women: New Language in New Times* (Garden City: Doubleday, 1977); and Gloria A. Marshall, "Racial Classifications: Popular and Scientific," in *The "Racial" Economy of Science*, ed. Sandra Harding (Bloomington: Indiana University Press, 1993) 116–27. For a comparison between sexist and racist language, see the essays in Mary Vetterling-Braggin, *Sexist Language: A Modern Philosophical Analysis* (Totowa: Rowman and Littlefield, 1981).

they create difficulties, when they represent the exception to the rule, or when they are occasionally referred to by name. At all other times wo/men are subsumed under grammatically masculine expressions such as Christian, German, American, slave, or disciple.[13]

2. Grammatically, andro-kyriocentric language thus does not describe and reflect reality but regulates and constructs it.[14] Andro-kyriocentric language is not reflective but active-performative. It simultaneously creates and shapes the symbolic worlds it pretends simply to represent.

3. Language is not only active-performative but always already political and normative. Andro-kyriocentric language shapes and is shaped by existing concepts of reality and relations of domination. Andro-kyriocentric language serves hegemonic interests, and, in turn, hegemonic interests determine the content of andro-kyriocentric language. Hence, an intra- and intertextual analysis of language and text is insufficient. It must be corrected by a critical, systematic analysis of religiopolitical structures of domination that perpetuate violence and exclusion.[15]

---

13. Compare Luise F. Pusch, *Das Deutsche als Männersprache* (Frankfurt: Suhrkamp, 1984), passim; Marielouise Janssen-Jurreit, *Sexism: The Male Monopoly on History and Thought*, trans. Verne Moberg (New York: Farrar Strauss & Giroux, 1982; German orig. Munich: Hanser, 1976), 291–92 (orig. 623–44).

14. This function of andro-kyriocentric language has far-reaching consequences for the writing of history. Not only are wo/men historically marginalized or entirely written out of historical sources by androcentric texts, but they are also doubly marginalized by andro-kyriocentric models of reconstruction and eliminated from history altogether. For example, Alföldy's social model of reconstruction is very frequently used in biblical scholarship but does not explicitly mention wo/men. This omission is correctly observed by Ekkehard W. Stegemann and Wolfgang Stegemann, *The Jesus Movement: A Social History of its First Century*, trans. O. C. Dean, Jr. (Minneapolis: Fortress, 1999; German orig. Stuttgart: Kohlhammer, 1995), 65–67 (orig. 69–70). However, this omission is not corrected by Stegemann and Stegemann's addition of a fourth section on "social roles and situations of women," but it is instead intensified, since the remainder of the book then speaks about the social history of early Christian communities without specifying that this history refers only to men.

15. Although such feminist models of social reconstruction exist, they often go unrecognized.

4. Kyriocentric language and knowledge of the kyriarchal world are thus rhetorical. That is, they have been articulated by particular people for a particular group of readers, and they work with particular articulated or suppressed interests and goals. If all the texts of the Bible and all knowledge of the world are both rhetorical and political, however, it is possible to change the cultural and religious frames of reference and constructs that are constantly reinscribed by such texts.

In light of this analysis, a critical feminist rhetorical model of interpretation therefore has to reject the linguistic immanentism of the New Criticism that emerges in biblical studies in the 1970s and the linguistic positivism of historical and theological criticism. Hence, in *Rhetoric and Ethic*, I develop a critical rhetorical model of interpretation in dialogue with the literary compass developed by Paul Hernadi.[16] Biblical criticism, I argue, has remained in the captivity of empiricist-positivist science for far too long. Rhetorical biblical criticism shares in this captivity insofar as it has spent much of its energy in applying and re-inscribing to New* Testament texts ancient rhetorical methods, disciplinary technology, terminological stylistics, and the scattered prescriptions of oratorical handbooks in antiquity.

More importantly, by reviving the technology of ancient rhetoric, rhetorical criticism in biblical studies has failed to make the full turn to a political rhetoric of inquiry insofar as it has not developed critical epistemological discourses and a hermeneutics of suspicion. Instead, it has sought to validate its disciplinary practices in and through the logos of positivist or empiricist science that occludes its own

---

For example, see Hannelore Schröder, "Feministische Gesellschaftstheorie," in *Feminismus, Inspektion der Herrenkultur: Ein Handbuch*, ed. Luise F. Pusch (Frankfurt: Suhrkamp, 1983), 449–76. See also my work on kyriarchy.

16. Paul Hernadi, "Literary Theory: A Compass for Critics," *CI* 3, no. 2 (1976): 369–86.

rhetoricity.[17] To make this full turn, I argue, rhetorical criticism needs to distinguish between at least three levels of communication: the historical argumentative situation, the implied or inscribed rhetorical situation, and the rhetorical situation of contemporary interpretations that again can be either actual or textualized.

A rhetorical critical analysis has to move through at least *four* stages. It begins by identifying the rhetorical interests, interpretive models, and social locations of contemporary interpretation. In a second step, it must delineate the rhetorical arrangement, interests, and modifications introduced by the author to elucidate them. Thirdly, it establishes the rhetorical situation of the letter. Finally, it seeks to reconstruct the common historical situation and symbolic universe of the writer/speaker and the recipients/audience.

True, such a rhetorical reconstruction of the socio-historical situation and symbolic universe of a text is still narrative-laden and can only be constituted as a "sub-text" to the biblical text. Yet, this "sub-text" is, for example, not simply the story of Paul. Rather, it is the story of the Corinthian *ekklēsia* to which Paul's rhetoric is to be understood as an active response.[18] Therefore, it becomes necessary to assess critically Paul's theological rhetoric in terms of its function for early Christian self-understanding and community. The nature of rhetoric as political discourse necessitates critical assessment and theological evaluation.

In *The Rhetoric of Fiction*, Wayne Booth distinguishes between the actual author/reader and the implied author/reader.[19] The implied

---

17. For the tension between "science" and "rhetoric" as two different modes of thinking, see Stanley Fish, "Rhetoric," in *Critical Terms for Literary Study*, ed. Frank Lentricchia and Thomas McLaughlin (Chicago: University of Chicago Press, 1990), 202–22.

18. Fredric R. Jameson, "The Symbolic Inference," in *Representing Kenneth Burke*, ed. Hayden White and Margaret Brose (Baltimore: Johns Hopkins University Press, 1982), 68–91.

19. Wayne C. Booth, "Freedom of Interpretation: Bakhtin and the Challenge of Feminist Criticism," *CI* 9 (1982): 45–76. Booth has called for a revived ethical and political criticism in literary criticism. Compare also Gayle Greene and Coppélia Kahn, eds., *Making a Difference:*

author is not the real author, but rather the image or picture that the reader will construct gradually in the process of reading the work. In other words, the interpreter in the process of reading a biblical text follows the directives of the inscribed author, who is not identical with the "real" author.

These directives instruct the interpreter as to how to understand the recipients' reaction to the writing. For instance, that interpreters follow the directives of the implied author to understand the Corinthian Christians as "others" of Paul or as his "opponents" becomes obvious in all those interpretations that characterize the Corinthians as foolish, immature, arrogant, divisive, individualistic, unrealistic illusionists, libertine enthusiasts, or boasting spiritualists who misunderstood the preaching of Paul in terms of "realized eschatology" or Gnosticism.

Since many things are presupposed, left out, or unexplained in a text, the audience must in the process of reading "supply" the missing information in line with the rhetorical directives of the speaker/ writer. Historical-critical scholars seek to "supply" such information generally in terms of the history of religions, including Judaism, while preachers and Bible-readers usually do so in terms of contemporary values, life, and psychology.

In short, feminist rhetorical analysis is best understood as an analysis and critique of both language and ideology. Relationships of dominance and power produce distorted forms of communication and result in the self-deception of scholars who are unaware of their own distorted interests, needs, and perceptions of the social and religious world. Ideological criticism thus understands language as a means of inscribing forms of power in contexts of meaning and

Feminist Literary Criticism (New York: Methuen, 1985), passim; Judith Newton and Deborah Rosenfelt, eds., *Feminist Criticism and Social Change* (New York: Methuen, 1985), passim; and especially Elizabeth A. Meese, *Crossing the Double-Cross: The Practice of Feminist Criticism* (Chapel Hill: University of North Carolina Press, 1986), 133–50.

significance. Studying ideologies therefore does not mean merely analyzing a particular type of discourse but also investigating methods of interpretation and bestowal of meaning that serve either to maintain kyriarchal relationships or to undermine them. Hence, the goal of critical feminist rhetorical biblical studies is to engender a paradigm shift that conceptualizes biblical studies as a rhetoric and ethics of inquiry intended to engender change and transformation. According to Thomas Kuhn, a new scientific paradigm can only rival the existing paradigms if it produces not only new knowledge but also new institutions.[20] If this critical feminist paradigm of rhetorical biblical studies should gain sufficient strength to change the discourses of the discipline, then we will need to pay attention to the overall change in the humanities from a positivist to a rhetorical understanding of language and history.

The Rhetoricality or Rhetoricity of Scholarship, Knowledge, and Science

In recent decades, a renaissance of rhetoric has taken place that has made it possible to focus anew on the rhetoricality or rhetoricity of science.[21] This renaissance has significant connections to current

20. Thomas Kuhn, *The Structure of Scientific Revolutions* (Chicago: University of Chicago Press, 1962), passim.
21. The literature on the rhetoric of scholarship is almost limitless. A few examples can document this observation. Kurt Bayertz, *Wissenschaft als historischer Prozess: Die antipositivistische Wende in der Wissenschaftstheorie* (Munich: Fink, 1980), passim; Hartmut Schröder, ed., *Fachtextpragmatik* (Tübingen: Narr, 1993), passim; Lorraine Code, *Rhetorical Spaces: Essays on Gendered Locations* (New York: Routledge, 1995), passim; John S. Nelson, Allan Megill, and Donald N. McCloskey, eds., *The Rhetoric of the Human Sciences: Language and Argument in Scholarship and Public Affairs* (Madison: University of Wisconsin Press, 1987), passim; Ulrike Felt, Helga Nowotny, and Klaus Taschwer, *Wissenschaftsforschung: Eine Einführung* (Frankfurt: Campus, 1995), passim; Ludwik Fleck, *Entstehung und Entwicklung einer wissenschaftlichen Tatsache: Einführung in die Lehre vom Denkstil und Denkkollektiv* (Frankfurt: Suhrkamp, 1980; 1st ed. 1933), passim; Roberts and Good, *The Recovery of Rhetoric*, 1–21; Sandra Harding, *Whose Science? Whose Knowledge? Thinking from Women's Lives* (Ithaca: Cornell University Press, 1991), passim; Bettina Heintz, "Wissenschaft im Kontext: Neuere Tendenzen der Wissenschaftssoziologie," *KZSS* 45 (1993): 528–52; Josef Kopperschmidt, ed., *Rhetorik als*

efforts in the theory of science and the sociology of knowledge.[22] This revitalization of rhetoric has made it possible to focus anew on the rhetoricity or rhetoricality of scholarship and thereby has opened the doors for critical feminist work to be taken seriously. This development is no accident but is closely connected to the development and spread of the new media of communication. In the global communication society, rhetoric—that is, concern with the forms of public argumentation and persuasion—has attained a new significance.

Rhetoric is practiced today in four forms. First, as academic communication studies, it teaches the art of public speaking and debate. Second, the study of ancient rhetoric is devoted to the recovery of the classical handbooks and theories. Third, critical literary rhetorical studies seek to understand the arguments and

Texttheorie (Darmstadt: Wissenschaftliche Buchgesellschaft, 1990), passim; Reinhard Kreissl, *Text und Kontext: Die soziale Konstruktion wissenschaftlicher Texte* (Munich: Profil, 1985), passim; Heinz L. Kretzenbacher, "Wie durchsichtig ist die Sprache der Wissenschaft?" in *Linguistik der Wissenschaftssprache*, ed. idem and Harald Weinrich (Berlin: de Gruyter, 1994), 15–39; Andrew Pickering, "From Science as Knowledge to Science as Practice," in *Science as Practice and Culture*, ed. idem (Chicago: University of Chicago Press, 1992), 1–26; Kathleen Welch, "Compositionality, Rhetoricity, and Electricity: A Partial History of Some Composition and Rhetoric Studies," *Enculturation* 5, no. 1 (2003), http://www.enculturation.net/5_1/welch.html.

22. For example compare Richard H. Brown, *Society as Text: Essays on Rhetoric, Reason and Reality* (Chicago: University of Chicago Press, 1987), passim; Peter Wagner, Björn Wittrock, and Richard Whitley, eds., *Discourses on Society: The Shaping of the Social Science Disciplines* (Dordrecht: Kluwer Academic Publishers, 1990), 195–218; Ricca Edmondson, *Rhetoric in Sociology* (London: Macmillan, 1984), passim; Helga Heiden-Sommer, "Soziologische Forschung und politische Interessen: Vorurteile und Frauen benachteiligende Begriffe in empirischen Studien zur Arbeitsteilung in den Familien," *ÖZS* 19 (1994): 58–75; Warren J. Samuels, *Economics as Discourse: An Analysis of the Language of Economists* (Boston: Kluwer Academic, 1990), 129–54; Julie Thompson Klein, "Text/Context: The Rhetoric of the Social Sciences," in *Writing the Social Text: Poetics and Politics in Social Science Discourse*, ed. Richard H. Brown (New York: de Gruyter, 1992), 9–27; Christoph Lau and Ulrich Beck, *Definitionsmacht und Grenzen angewandter Sozialwissenschaften: Eine Untersuchung am Beispiel der Bildungs- und Arbeitsmarktforschung* (Opladen: Westdeutscher, 1989); Jürg Niederhauser, "Metaphern in der Wissenschaftssprache als Thema der Linguistik," in *Metapher und Innovation: Die Rolle der Metapher im Wandel von Sprache und Wissenschaft*, ed. Lutz Danneberg, Andreas Graeser, and Klaus Petrus (Bern: Haupt, 1995), 290–98; Annett Treibel, "Die Sprache der Soziologie: Eine ganz normale Wissenschaftssprache?" *ÖZ S* 20 (1995): 20–45; Peter Wagner, *Soziologie der Moderne: Freiheit und Disziplin* (Frankfurt: Campus, 1995), passim.

persuasive power of texts in their contexts. Fourth, as the rhetoric of scholarship, it investigates the rhetoricity or rhetoricality of knowledge and its institutions. Insight into the constructedness of all knowledge, including scientific knowledge, shifts the question of the criteria of scientific evidence from epistemology to the intersubjective-ethical, social, and political realm. Contexts of communication and thus ultimately power relationships determine the validity of representation.

This renaissance of rhetoric and of the recognition of the rhetoricity of knowledge has received important impulses from the feminist theory and practice of rhetoric as well as from the debates on postmodernism.[23] Its roots have to do with the linguistic-analytical turn in philosophy and its consequences for the theory of scientific knowledge as well as with the rise of semiotics as the "logic of science." Most important are the insights and approaches of the sociology of science or the so-called "sciences of science" (Wissenschaftswissenschaften). In different, but generally complementary ways, the rhetorical character of scientific publication is both described and confirmed.[24]

In contrast to a positivist understanding of science and language, the rhetoric of scholarship elaborates a rhetorical view of language and scholarship. With this distinction between positivist interpretation and rhetorical interpretation, I am in line with the scientific revival of rhetoric that has taken place in the last thirty years

23. Hilary Rose, "Rhetoric, Feminism and Scientific Knowledge: Or From Either/Or to Both/ And," in Roberts and Good, *The Recovery of Rhetoric*, 203–23; Ratcliffe, *Anglo-American Feminist Challenges*, passim; Jaqueline Jones Royster, *Traces of a Stream: Literary and Social Change Among African American Women* (Pittsburgh: University of Pittsburgh Press, 2000), 251–85; Donawerth, *Rhetorical Theory*, passim; Mountford, *Gendered Pulpit*, passim; Richards, *Rhetoric*, passim; and Schell and Rawson, *Rhetorica in Motion*, passim.

24. Bettina Bräuninger, Andreas Lange, and Kurt Lüscher, "Familienwissenschaftliche Rhetorik: Eine explorative Analyse ausgewählter Texte" (Arbeitspapiere / Forschungsbereich Gesellschaft und Familie 20; 1996), http://kops.ub.uni-konstanz.de/bitstream/handle/urn:nbn:de:bsz:352-opus-3853/385_1.pdf (accessed 17 August 2014).

in biblical studies, but I am trying to avoid its positivistic-literalist-antiquarian character.[25]

A rhetorical analysis emphasizes that, in the process of interpretation, texts and symbols are not simply understood or their true meaning grasped (hermeneutics). Rather, language is always already a construct, an exercise of power, and an action that either continues the ideologies of domination or tries to interrupt them. Interpretation is not simply a one-way street as in the positivist discovery of a single meaning of the text. It is rather a multivocal discourse that seeks by means of arguments to persuade and to convince.

This rhetorical nature of science applies to its language, its methods of interpretation, its sociohistorical models, its communicative situation, and the sociopolitical positioning and interests of interpreters. Like all scholars, interpreters of the Bible are flesh-and-blood people with particular personal experiences, social locations, and culturally-shaped horizons. They not only pursue particular interests and goals but also bring unconscious assumptions and unconsidered presuppositions with them when they seek to understand biblical texts and their world. Interpretation is best understood not as re-production but as creative action, since the interpretation of a text is always a creative re-creation. A claim to objective, clear reproduction of an original meaning of the text or intention of the author abstracted from the person of the interpreter and her sociopolitical location is no longer scientifically possible.

A critical-rhetorical interpretive paradigm requires a scientific approach that articulates the scholar's social location, theoretical perspectives, and rhetorical situation as integral parts of the

---

25. See Amos N. Wilder, "Scholars, Theologians, and Ancient Rhetoric," *JBL* 75 (1956): 1–11; idem, *Early Christian Rhetoric: The Language of the Gospel* (Cambridge, MA: Harvard University Press, 1971), passim; Dale Patrick and Allen Scult, *Rhetoric and Biblical Interpretation* (Sheffield: Almond, 1990), passim.

interpretive process. That requirement does not mean, however, that any and every interpretation of a text is acceptable. The text does indeed contain countless possible meanings, but it is best understood as a multivocal spectrum of meanings, each limited by a particular context. This multifaceted spectrum is differently activated in every particular act of interpretation and depends on the the*ethical and sociopolitical standpoints not only of the interpreter but also of her addressees.

Nevertheless, academic and popular biblical interpretation continues to operate largely with a concept of scholarship that has long since been rendered outmoded. Many interpreters still make the claim that they can objectively find a single correct meaning and objectively work out the true meaning of a biblical text with scholarly-controlled methods, and thus discover its kernel of truth.[26] But such a timeless, objectively discoverable truth cannot be filtered out of the text once and for all. Rather, the text must be understood as a speech act motivated by particular interests in specific sociopolitical and historical contexts. What is true on the level of the text applies also to the levels of interpretation and historical reconstruction. Only in this way can the multiple meanings of the textual signs and linguistic symbols be limited and the possible or probable field of meaning of a text be demarcated.

As opposed to a historical-positivist analysis that tries to establish historical facts, and as opposed to a literary-critical interpretation that concentrates on the literary form and deep structure of a text, a rhetorical analysis of discourse emphasizes the significance of the speech context, the power relationships, and the sociohistorical origin of the text to understand and evaluate the persuasive power of its

---

26. For example, Gerd Theissen, "Methodenkonkurrenz und hermeneutischer Konflikt: Pluralismus in Exegese und Lektüre der Bibel," in *Pluralismus und Identität*, ed. Joachim Mehlhausen (Gütersloh: Kaiser, 1995), 127–40.

argumentation. It asks, "What does the text do to those who subject themselves to its worldview?" A critical scientific rhetoric-analytic investigates the persuasive power of a biblical text not only with regard to linguistic conventions, literary style, or the overall composition but also with regard to the interaction between author and addressees, or interpreters and reading public as well as with a view to the socioreligious location and interests of the persuasive process inscribed in a text.[27] Such a rhetorical biblical interpretation thus requires a the*ethical evaluation.

Rhetoric analyzes, for instance, the letter to the Galatians as a moment of cultural-religious communication and the*logical argumentation between Paul and his hearers as well as between interpreters of the letter to the Galatians and their readers. An effective argumentative communication aimed at persuasion is only possible between Paul and his hearers or between the interpreters of the letter to the Galatians and their readers, because each pair respectively lives in the same cultural-religious, sociopolitical, and linguistic-symbolic worlds. The rhetorical situation is thus of decisive significance for the success of convincing and persuasive communication.

In short, this view of rhetoric as a communicative praxis that articulates interests, values, and visions is not simply another form of literary analysis.[28] Rather, critical-rhetorical analysis is a means

27. Susan Shapiro, "Rhetoric as Ideology Critique: The Gadamer-Habermas Debate Reinvented," *JAAR* 62, no. 1 (1994): 123–50; Lorraine Code, *Rhetorical Spaces: Essays on Gendered Locations* (New York: Continuum, 1995), passim; John Bender and David E. Wellbery, "Rhetoricality: On the Modernist Return of Rhetoric," in idem eds., *The Ends of Rhetoric*, 3–42; Cheryl Glenn, *Rhetoric Retold: Regendering the Tradition from Antiquity through the Renaissance* (Carbondale: Southern Illinois University Press, 1997), passim.

28. Brown, *Society as Text*, 85. See also John S. Nelson, Allan Megill, and Donald McCloskey, eds., *The Rhetoric of the Human Sciences: Language and Argument in Scholarship and Public Affairs* (Madison: University of Wisconsin Press, 1987), passim; Hayden White, *Tropics of Discourse: Essays in Cultural Criticism* (Baltimore: Johns Hopkins University Press, 1978), passim; John. S. Nelson, "Political Theory as Political Rhetoric," in *What Should Political Theory Be Now?*, ed. idem (Albany: SUNY Press, 1983), 169–240.

of showing how biblical texts and their interpretations take part in creating and legitimating structures of oppression and dominance or in enacting the*ethical values, liberating visions, and sociopolitical acts of liberation. The reconceptualization of biblical scholarship as a critical rhetorical–ethical field of study and not simply as a positivist or hermeneutical praxis of interpretation makes available a framework for research that cultivates historical, archaeological, sociological, literary, the*logical and other methods of reading but insists on sociopolitical and the*ethical questions of power as constitutive for the process of interpretation.

Rhetorics and Ethics

If biblical scholarship would abandon its centuries-old prejudice that regards rhetoric as "mere" rhetoric, as a technical means, style, or eloquence, and adopt an understanding of rhetoric as "the power to persuade and convince through argumentation," it would be able to analyze the process of communication anew as a powerful process of action.[29] Such an analysis could direct its attention, for example, to how Paul constructs his arguments and consider who is speaking, who is addressed, and who is overlooked and silenced. When something is said, it could focus on who and what is central and why, on the power relationships in which a text attempts to intervene, and on the ways the interpretive discourse itself attempts to influence the social circumstances of which it is a part. A critical rhetorical analysis not only seeks to uncover the means by which authors and interpreters seek to convince and motivate their readers but also asks about the structures of domination inscribed in the text and their function in particular rhetorical situations and particular sociohistorical locations.

29. See John Louis Lucaites, Celeste Michelle Condit, and Sally Caudill, eds., *Contemporary Rhetorical Theory: A Reader* (New York: Guilford Press, 1999), passim.

With reader response criticism, I thus agree that none of the four text-immanent factors—author, addressee, rhetorical situation, and symbolic world—is identical with the actual, historically real author, addressee, rhetorical situation, or symbolic world of the text.[30] However, these factors inscribed in individual texts are not to be understood as purely fictional. Rather, they must have a relationship to the reality about which the text speaks if communication is to succeed and people are to be persuaded.

If someone presents a rhetorical discourse, according to classical rhetoric, s/he must not only decide what questions and themes s/he will address and what position s/he will take, but s/he must also establish the tenor and goal of her rhetorical intervention. This often requires a mixture of genres of discourse. According to classical rhetoric, the persuasive power of an argument is determined by its *ethos*, *pathos*, and *logos*. Ethos and pathos must be at work throughout the whole speech, but ethos is effective especially at the beginning of the discourse and pathos at the end.

Topics with which rhetoric concerns itself refer to social and political problems that are worthy of discussion. Decisive for formulating arguments that seek to appeal to conservative readers are a traditional point of view, cultural conventions, commonplaces, and established moral concepts—in short, the way the conservative mind views the world. Such "common sense" arguments are supported by appeals to generally held points of view and convictions. These arguments are called *pisteis* or "proofs." Questions of strategies, or how to shape an argument, and what material should be chosen are at stake in the discussion of such proofs.

Three kinds of examples, or *paradeigmata*, are generally regarded as necessary in ancient rhetoric. These *paradeigmata* include a well-

30. Schüssler Fiorenza, *Rhetoric and Ethic*, 105–28.

known example from history, an analogy from the world of everyday life, and finally the *mythos*, which creates an imaginary world. All three are applied as proofs and not simply as illustrations. These rules and categories of ancient rhetoric must not, however, be misunderstood as molds into whose existing forms texts are to be pressed as is often the case in the reception of ancient rhetoric by positivist-scientific exegesis. Instead, these rules and categories are a means of analysis with which to examine a text's power of argumentation and persuasion. They are not technical introductions, but they seek to illuminate substantial questions about inscribed power relations. Rhetoric as discourse is inseparable from the sociopolitical conditions of its production.

Debates in public democratic gatherings, arguments in legal proceedings, and hymnal compositions celebrating heroes and heroines as well as gods and goddesses are the originating locations of classical rhetoric and are shaped by the pragmatic situations in which they arise.[31] A critical rhetorical interpretation has to discern not only the rhetorical stylistic means but especially also the ideological practices and persuasive strategies of a text. In short, a rhetorical analytic technique sees the text as a discursive interaction among its sociopolitical-religious locations, authors, hearers, and rhetorical situations. A critical rhetorical interpretive analytics has its social location in communities of interpretation that critically investigate power relationships and seek to transform them.

A critical-rhetorical interpretation understands the text neither as a window into reality nor as a double mirror for self-reflection, but rather as a political discourse that both reveals its perspective and remains bound to its context, which fulfills ideological functions. Unlike a formalistic and positivist scientific reading of the Bible,

---

31. Compare Susan C. Jarratt, *Rereading the Sophists: Classical Rhetoric Refigured* (Carbondale: Southern Illinois University Press, 1991), passim.

a critical-emancipatory rhetoric joins the the*logies of liberation in insisting that the context is just as important as the text. What we see always depends on where we stand. The social location and context of the interpreter determine how she sees the world, perceives reality, or reads biblical texts. Therefore, the turn to ethics and ideological critique is of central importance for an emancipatory-rhetorical paradigm.[32]

Debates over the relationship between rhetoric and morality have taken place throughout the history of rhetoric. In the modern era, however, scholars tend to adopt individualistic and privatized models of interpretation instead of creating a public space for biblical rhetoric that articulates, applies, and enriches ethics and morality through public argument. Positivist scholarship cannot engage biblical rhetoric as public-political rhetoric because it represses its sociopolitical location and pursues the ideal of value-neutrality. A value-free ethos of scholarship is said to be necessary because only freedom from values guarantees an objective perception of reality "as it is." Values supposedly destroy the objectivity of the scientific process of acquiring knowledge.

Max Weber, to whom such a positivistic theory is often attributed, in fact sees the matter in a more complex fashion. He distinguishes between non-explicated value judgments and ideas of value that are constitutive for the process of acquiring knowledge. He rejects the former but accepts the latter. Value judgments are only impermissible if they are not made explicit, since in that case they cloud the argument. Sharply and precisely defined evaluations, in contrast, can

---

32. Richard Bernstein, "What is the Difference that Makes a Difference? Gadamer, Habermas, and Rorty," in *Hermeneutics and Modern Philosophy*, ed. Brice R. Wachterhauser (Albany: SUNY Press, 1986), 343–76; Victoria E. Bonnell and Lynn Hunt, eds., *Beyond the Cultural Turn: New Directions in the Study of Society and Culture* (Berkeley: University of California Press, 1999), passim.

be very helpful to scientific insight and knowledge. Volker Kruse explains,

> Max Weber's doctrine of values is not exhausted by the postulate of freedom from value judgments. Moreover, values are for him constitutive of the process of social-scientific acquisition of knowledge; as theoretically reflected value-relations, they determine the topic and conceptuality of any scientific work on reality. This view is found among other historical sociologists as well.[33]

A critical biblical interpretation that understands itself as a rhetorical-ethical, discursive praxis therefore has to replace objectivistic, positivistic, and apolitical methods of interpretation, as practiced by dominant biblical scholarship, with critical-rhetorical investigations. It is interested in articulating a critical, historical-cultural, and religiopolitical scientific consciousness.

Rhetorical analysis is thus best understood as an analysis and critique of language and ideology. Relationships of dominance and power produce distorted forms of communication and result in the self-deception of scholars who are unaware of their own distorted interests, needs, and perceptions of the social and religious world. Ideological criticism thus understands language as a means of inscribing forms of power in contexts of meaning and significance. Studying ideologies therefore does not mean merely analyzing a particular type of discourse, but also investigating methods of interpretation and bestowal of meaning that serve either to maintain kyriarchal relationships or to undermine them.

According to John B. Thompson, ideology works through three strategies or methods of operation.[34] The *first* strategy grounds the

---

33. Volker Kruse, *"Geschichts- und Sozialphilosophie" oder "Wirklichkeitswissenschaft"? Die deutsche historische Soziologie und die logischen Kategorien René Königs und Max Webers* (Frankfurt: Suhrkamp, 1999), passim.
34. John B. Thompson, *Studies in the Theory of Ideology* (Cambridge: Cambridge University Press, 1984), 254.

legitimacy of kyriarchy on the basis of tradition, as for example in the Vatican's argument that Jesus and the apostles did not ordain any wo/men, although it is known that Jesus did not ordain anyone. The *second* strategy conceals kyriarchal relationships and keeps them from being known, as for example in the models of femininity that are used to impress on wo/men that their natural way of being is that of selfless service. This strategy prevents the bases of society, religion, or scholarship from being critically analyzed and called into question. The *third* strategy in turn reifies and naturalizes processes and attitudes that are social. For instance, this third strategy emphasizes that maternity is natural and/or corresponds to the nature of woman. It depicts transitory, cultural, social, and historical conditions as if they were natural, given, permanent, timeless, or revealed.

Ideology creates the self-concept of oppressed people and intensifies it. It determines the consciousness of people who thereby internalize their subordinated position as either natural and inborn or willed by G*d. A rhetorical liberation analysis of andro/kyriocentric biblical texts therefore demands not only awareness and ideological critique but also a critical ethics of interpretation.[35]

Biblical scholarship that continues to prescribe a value-neutral theory of scholarship represents an apolitical conservative interpretation of texts and the writing of history, and it continues to inscribe kyriarchal relationships.[36] It also is incapable of taking responsibility for the structures of prejudice, such as those of anti-Judaism, that are projected and cemented by biblical texts and their

---

35. For example, Danna Nolan Fewell and Gary A. Philips, eds., *Bible and Ethics of Reading* (Semeia 77; Atlanta: Scholars Press, 1997), passim.

36. For a defense of social-scientific objective interpretation, see Bruce J. Malina, "Rhetorical Criticism and Social-Scientific Criticism: Why Won't Romanticism Leave Us Alone?" in *Rhetoric, Scripture and Theology: Essays from the 1994 Pretoria Conference*, ed. Stanley E. Porter and Thomas H. Olbricht (Sheffield: Sheffield Academic, 1996), 72–96.

interpretations. Only when biblical scholarship begins to reflect on its own social location and religiopolitical interests that are determined by race, gender, nation, and socioreligious class membership will scholars be capable of giving an accounting to their hearers/readers. Therefore, ethics must assume a central place in an emancipatory-political and liberation-the*logical paradigm of interpretation.[37]

An intersubjective, political, and public conceptualizing of ethics has rhetoric at its heart. Rhetoric as an intersubjective democratic process is ethical in a twofold sense.[38] On the one hand, it opens up the author's range of realities and the methods she chooses for describing that reality. On the other hand, it offers readers a choice in place of a total and necessary acceptance. Truth, when rhetorically established, presumes freedom of choice and the apprehension of alternative realities. An intersubjective democratic ethics understands "world, truth, and reality" as rhetorically-linguistically established and as the responsibility of those who act. Since the turn to ethics has made clear that morality, truth, vision, and the knowledge of a good life are rhetorically-linguistically constructed and conveyed, biblical scholarship must develop both an ethics of life and an ethics of interpretation.

An ethics of interpretation, which sees texts as rhetorical practices of communication, cannot confine itself to an exegesis of the text but must also be critically responsible, ethically, politically, and the*logically, for its own methods of interpretation, goals, and interests. Such an ethical-rhetorical paradigm of interpretation sees objectivity and method differently. In a scholarly-positivistic paradigm, methods are understood as techniques, rules, instructions,

---

37. Rey Chow, *Ethics after Idealism: Theory-Culture-Ethnicity-Reading* (Bloomington: Indiana University Press, 1998), passim.
38. Celeste Michelle Condit, "Democracy and Civil Rights: The Universalizing Influence of Public Argumentation," *CM* 54 (1987): 1–20; Frank Lentricchia, *Criticism and Social Change* (Chicago: University of Chicago Press, 1983), passim.

or prescriptions while an ethical-rhetorical paradigm of interpretation can see them as questions to be asked or perspectives to be clarified.

Since biblical scholarship is at home in the kyriarchal institutions of the university and church or temple, a feminist biblical interpretation cannot simply assume that biblical research produces knowledge that liberates and transforms and serves the "good life" of wo/men. Instead, it must critically examine all textual interpretations and claims of knowledge to see if they interrupt the interests of the dominant or further inscribe them. Therefore, an ethics of interpretation insists that all scientific methods, proposals, and results be subjected to an ethical-rhetorical analysis and be examined to see how and whether they serve to continue discrimination or open opportunities for liberation and a good life for all without exception.

In short, an emancipatory-rhetorical hermeneutics and ethics of interpretation are no less scientific than the dominant biblical scholarship. On the contrary, the rhetorical-ethical paradigm of interpretation opens up the possibility for and points the way toward a scientific interpretation that can take responsibility for the impact of the Bible on the well-being of the cosmopolis. Thus, ethics and political responsibility become integral components of textual interpretation and historical reconstruction. If biblical scholarship is understood as a rhetorical and communicative praxis, then its task is to analyze and demonstrate how biblical texts and their present-day interpretations are part of a political and religious discourse that is always involved in power structures and is thus ethical and political.

The *Ekklēsia of Wo/men* and The "Dance" of Interpretation

As rhetorical texts, biblical texts need not just to be understood but also to be adjudicated in a critical process of feminist interpretation. If such a critical process of interpretation is conceptualized as a radical democratic feminist practice of conscientization, it requires a rhetorical understanding of language and interpretation. To enable such a democratic process of ethical adjudication and to protect the understanding of scripture from being coopted by fundamentalist literalism or academic positivism, it is necessary to articulate a radical democratic hermeneutical space that engenders such biblical evaluations and adjudications.

In my work, I have suggested the image of the *ekklēsia of wo/men* as such a decolonizing space and as a feminist horizon from where to interpret and adjudicate Scripture texts and interpretations in general and the biblical inscriptions of kyriarchy in particular. However, this theoretical proposal has not been widely discussed, perhaps because of the qualifier "wo/men" or because it is assumed that *ekklēsia* means "church." Often those who are interested in church are not interested in wo/men, and those engaged in feminist critique are not interested in church.

The expression is also misunderstood if it is reduced to "Western" notions of democracy. I have sought to defend against such a misunderstanding by adding the qualifier "wo/men" because neither Greece, nor the United States, nor any other democracy has established the full citizenship, equality, and well-being of all wo/men without any exceptions. *Ekklēsia of wo/men* is historically and theoretically conceptualized as the alternative and not as the counter or anti-space to kyriarchy. *Ekklēsia* is constituted not by super- and subordination but by egalitarian relationships. It is not a reversal of kyriarchal domination and subordination but a space that is "already" and "not yet." Elizabeth Castelli has rightly likened the notion of the *ekklēsia of wo/men* to a utopian space of "texts, institutions and worldviews that critique the historical or contemporary situation and promote an alternative vision of social and individual existence—generally a vision committed to more egalitarian and just stances."[39]

For conceptualizing the oxymoron *ekklēsia of wo/men*, I have built on the discussions of radical democracy in feminist political theory and on critical legal studies that seek to reconceptualize legal discourses as a site of political struggles.[40] By introducing the radical democratic notion of the *ekklēsia of wo/men* as an alternative religious symbolic space to "exodus and paradise/home," I seek to reframe theoretically the feminist either/or binary toward religion and also attempt to name an alternative emancipatory radical democratic theoretical space where different progressive and feminist movements and theoretical directions can articulate alternatives to global empire/kyriarchy. Four aspects—the political, the semantic, the ekklēsial and the religious-the*logical—are important for understanding the *ekklēsia of wo/men* as such a critical hermeneutical "utopian" space.

The Greek word *ekklēsia* literally means "the democratic assembly" and is best translated as "democratic congress" of full decision-making citizens. Democratic equality, citizenship, and decision-making power are constitutive for the notion of *ekklēsia*. However, the Greek word *ekklēsia* is also determined by a Christian language context and is usually translated as "church." This translation robs the term of its political character. For that reason, I prefer not to translate *ekklēsia*, so that the Greek term functions as a signifier that must be actively decoded to know what it actually means.

---

39. Castelli, "*Ekklēsia*," 38.
40. On feminist political theory, see for instance Seyla Benhabib, ed., *Democracy and Difference: Contesting the Boundaries of the Political* (Princeton: Princeton University Press, 1996), passim; and Chantal Mouffe, ed., *Dimensions of Radical Democracy* (London: Verso, 1992), passim. On critical legal studies, see for instance Mary Frug, *Postmodern Legal Feminism* (New York: Routledge, 1992), passim; Martha Minow, *Equality and the Bill of Rights* (Ithaca: Cornell University Press, 1992), passim; and idem, *Identities* (New Haven: Yale University Press, 1991), passim. See also H. Markus, R. Shweder, and M. Minow, eds., *The Free Exercise of Culture* (New York: Russell Sage Foundation, 2001), passim.

The root meaning of *ekklēsia* derives from the classical Greek institution of democracy, which, in theory, promised freedom and equality to all its citizens. In practice, however, it granted such rights only to imperial, elite, propertied, educated male heads of household by restricting full citizenship to them. The kyriarchal notion of equality grounded in sameness and uniformity is often labeled "Western" and has its roots in this restriction of democratic citizenship. Hence, the *ekklēsia*, understood as the radical democratic congress of citizen-subjects, has never been fully realized in history because neither the Greek polis nor the French and the American democratic revolutions fought for disenfranchised wo/men to become fully empowered decision-making citizens.

The struggles of the disenfranchised for full citizenship and civil rights in the past three hundred years and more have sought to correct this failure of modernity and to realize the vision of radical democratic equality. In short, the expression *ekklēsia of wo/men* calls for full citizens to come together not only to investigate critically cultural-religious traditions and texts but also to adjudicate them and make decisions in the interest of the well-being of everyone in the cosmopolis.[41]

According to the Greek philosopher Aristotle, democracy is best understood as a community of equals in the interest of the common good or well-being, or as the independent, responsible rule of equal citizens who however are not wo/men. Such a manner of government and rule is articulated and takes place in the *ekklēsia*, the assembly of full citizens of the *polis* (the city-state), the term from which "politics" is derived. Hannah Arendt explains,

---

41. See the important book by Kwame Anthony Appiah, *Cosmopolitanism: Ethics in a World of Strangers* (New York: Norton, 2006), passim.

The political realm arises directly out of acting together, the sharing of "words and deeds."…The polis properly speaking is not the city-state in its physical location; it is the organization of people as it arises out of acting and speaking together, and its true space lies between people living together for this purpose, no matter where they happen to be. …[A]ction and speech create a space between the participants which can find its proper location almost any time and everywhere.[42]

With *ekklēsia of wo/men*, I have thus in mind a heuristic and hermeneutical space that is influenced by Hannah Arendt's notion of the polis as a space for "acting and speaking together." It has affinities to what Chandra Talpade Mohanti has called "the imagined community" of Third World oppositional struggles. Talpade Mohanti envisions it as the kind of space that provides

political rather than biological or cultural bases for alliance. Thus it is not color or sex which constructs the ground for these struggles. Rather it is the way we think about race, class, and gender—the political links we choose to make among and between struggles. Thus potentially, women of all colors (including white women) can align themselves and participate in these imagined communities.[43]

Since the sociohistorical location of ancient and present-day rhetoric is the public sphere of democracy in the *polis* and *ekklēsia*, the scientific study of rhetoric in short requires a change of scientific ethos.[44] It demands the rejection of a value-neutral understanding of scholarship in favor of an ethics of interpretation that can articulate

42. Hannah Arendt, *The Human Condition* (Chicago: University of Chicago Press, 1958), 198.
43. Chandra Talpade Mohanti, "Introduction: Cartographies of Struggle," in *Third World Women and the Politics of Feminism*, ed. idem, Ann Russo, and Lourdes Torres (Bloomington: Indiana University Press, 1991), 1–47.
44. Jennifer Tolbert Roberts, *Athens on Trial: The Antidemocratic Tradition in Western Thought* (Princeton: Princeton University Press, 1994), passim; Jane Sutton, "The Death of Rhetoric and Its Rebirth in Philosophy," *Rhetorica* 4 (1986): 203–26; idem, "The Taming of Polos/Polis: Rhetoric as an Achievement without Women," in Lucaites, Condit, and Caudill, *Contemporary Rhetorical Theory*, 101–27.

and critically investigate the political interests, moral norms, and ethical demands of texts and their interpretation.[45]

With Jürgen Habermas, a scientific-rhetorical program insists, in contrast to a scientific-positivist hermeneutical program, that the question of power is central to understanding language, tradition, and canon.[46] It is well known that Habermas distinguishes three fundamental forms of knowledge including the empiric-analytical, the hermeneutic-historical, and the critical-emancipatory forms of knowledge of the world. We seek knowledge to control social relationships and natural circumstances (empiric-analytical), to understand and interpret these realities by evaluating them (hermeneutic-historical), and to transform our individual and collective awareness of reality (critical-emancipatory). We seek this knowledge so that human potentials and opportunities for justice, freedom, and equality may be multiplied and maximized.[47]

It must not be forgotten, however, that the political discourses of *ekklēsia* and *politeia* are articulated and practiced, in antiquity and in modernity, under the conditions imposed by kyriarchy, which excluded wo/men from public discourse and decision-making powers. Biblical texts and their inscriptions of kyriarchy, I have argued, need not just to be understood but also to be adjudicated in a critical process of feminist rhetorical interpretation. If such a critical process of interpretation is conceptualized as a radical democratic

---

45. Lawrence J. Prelli, "The Rhetorical Construction of Scientific Ethos," in *Rhetoric in the Human Sciences*, ed. Herbert W. Simons (London: Sage, 1989), 48; Robert K. Merton, "The Normative Structure of Science," in idem, *The Sociology of Science: Theoretical and Empirical Investigations* (Chicago: University of Chicago Press, 1973), 267–78; Michael Mulkay, *Science and the Sociology of Knowledge* (London: Allen & Unwin, 1979), passim; Rayme McKerrow, "Critical Rhetoric: Theory and Practice," in Lucaites, Condit, and Caudill, *Contemporary Rhetorical Theory*, 441–63.

46. Jürgen Habermas, "Ideology," in *Modern Interpretations of Marx*, ed. Tom Bottomore (Oxford: Oxford University Press, 1981), 166.

47. Raymond A. Morrow and David D. Baron, *Critical Theory and Methodology* (Thousand Oaks: Sage, 1994), passim.

feminist practice of evaluation, it requires not only a different understanding of the power and authority of scripture but also a different rhetorical process of interpretation. In *Rhetoric and Ethic*, I develop such a critical rhetorical model of analysis, whereas in *Wisdom Ways*, I spell out its analytic operations in the "dance of interpretation."

Whereas hermeneutical theory seeks to understand and appreciate the meaning of texts, rhetorical interpretation and its the*ethical interrogation of texts and symbolic worlds pay close attention to the kinds of effects not only biblical discourses but also biblical readers produce, and how they produce them. Hence, only a complex model of a critical process of feminist evaluative interpretation for liberation can overcome the hermeneutical splits between sense and meaning, between explanation and understanding, between critique and consent, between distanciation and empathy, between reading the text "behind" and "in front of" the text, between the present and the past, between interpretation and application, and between realism and imagination.[48]

Such a critical feminist rhetorical approach engages in a complex and exhilarating process of evaluative interpretation. Feminists have used different rhetorical metaphors and comparisons for naming such an emancipatory process of interpretation. These metaphors include "making visible," "hearing into speech," and "finding one's voice." I myself have favored metaphors of movement such as turning, walking, way, dance, ocean waves, or struggle. Since Plato attacked rhetoric as "mere cookery," I sometimes have borrowed this metaphor and spoken of biblical rhetorical interpretation as baking

48. For the elaboration of this critical process of feminist evaluative interpretation for liberation with reference to a particular text, see especially Schüssler Fiorenza, *But She Said*, 51–76 and 195–218. For such a hermeneutical reading of behind and in front of the text, see Sandra Schneiders, *The Revelatory Text: Interpreting the New Testament as Sacred Scripture* (New York: HarperSanFrancisco, 1991), passim.

bread, as mixing and kneading milk, flour, yeast, and raisins into dough, or as cooking a stew that utilizes different herbs and spices to season the potatoes, meats, and carrots, which, stirred together, produce a new and different flavor.

The metaphor of the dance seems best to express the method of feminist biblical interpretation and rhetorical analysis. Dancing involves body and spirit, it involves feelings and emotions, and it takes us beyond our limits and creates community. Dancing confounds all hierarchical order because it moves in spirals and circles. It makes us feel alive and full of energy, power, and creativity. Moving in spirals and circles, critical feminist biblical interpretation is ongoing. It cannot be done once and for all but must be repeated differently in different situations and from different perspectives. It is exciting because in every new reading of biblical texts different meanings emerge and a different evaluation is called forth.

By deconstructing the kyriarchal rhetoric and politics of inequality and subordination inscribed in the Bible or other sacred scriptures, feminist interpreters are able to generate ever-fresh articulations of radical democratic religious visions and emancipatory practices. Most importantly, such interpretive rhetorical evaluative practices always have to be bifocal and keep in sight the contemporary situation and location of the interpreter and that of the text. Such analytic evaluative processes or rhetorical moves between interpreter and text are:

- analysis of experience and social-cultural-religious location

- critical analysis of domination (kyriarchy)

- suspicion of andro-kyriocentric texts and frameworks as to the obfuscating work they do

- assessment and evaluation in terms of a scale of feminist emancipative values
- creative imagination and vision
- historical memory[49]
- inspiring transformative action for change.

These interpretive evaluative practices are not to be construed simply as successive independent methodological steps of inquiry or as discrete methodological rules or rhetorical recipes. Rather they are best understood as rhetorical moves and movements, as means of consciousness-raising, and as strategies that interact with each other simultaneously in the process of "making meaning" out of a particular biblical or any other cultural text in the context of the globalization of inequality.

This analytic-evaluative "dance" has two focal points of interpretation. One is the rhetoric of the *biblical texts*, and the other is *contemporary meaning making and evaluations* in kyriarchal situations of exclusions and exploitation. Such a rhetorical exploration continually moves between the present and the past and between realism and imagination. It moves, spirals, turns, and dances in the places found in "the white spaces between the black letters" of Scripture, to use a metaphor of Jewish interpretation. Hence, it is very difficult to boil down such a dynamic process of interpretation and reduce it to a logical consecutive description. I hope readers will not see my attempt of the spelling out of such rhetorical moves of evaluation as the transcript of a process but see it more as basic steps in textual and

---

49. See Elisabeth Schüssler Fiorenza, "Re-Visioning Christian Origins: *In Memory of Her* Revisited," in *Christian Beginnings: Worship, Belief and Society*, ed. Kieran O'Mahony (London: Continuum, 2003), 225–50. See also my recent books: Elisabeth Schüssler Fiorenza, *Transforming Vision* (Minneapolis: Fortress, 2011), passim; and idem, *Changing Horizons*, passim.

contextual explorations that they must execute in their own rhetorical manner to keep dancing.

This feminist "dance of interpretation" with its seven steps of rhetorical analysis and evaluation has been developed in a Christian context of biblical interpretation. It has been practiced in groups, workshops, and seminars that have been intercultural and trans-confessional. However, it has not been tested with groups of different religious persuasions or in seminars with a transreligious approach. Such a testing out is necessary, however, if we take seriously that the *ekklēsia of wo/men* is not identical with church but with the imagined decision-making assembly of a radical democratic society. Recent studies in feminist rhetorics and their configurations of transnationality will be critical conversation partners in exploring such a rhetorical transreligious approach.[50]

50. See Wendy S. Hesford and Eileen E. Schell, "Configurations of Transnationality: Locating Feminist Rhetorics," *CE* 70 (2008): 461–528; Schell and Rawson, *Rhetorica in Motion*, passim; and Jaqueline Jones Royster and Gesa E. Kirsch, *Feminist Rhetorical Practices: New Horizons for Rhetoric, Composition and Literacy Studies* (Carbondale: Southern Illinois University Press, 2012), passim.

9

The Pesky Threads of Robbins's Rhetorical Tapestry: Vernon K. Robbins's Genealogy of Rhetorical Criticism

L. Gregory Bloomquist

There are many ways to approach a "genealogy" of the work of a scholar, and the work of Vernon K. Robbins and his contribution to rhetorical criticism are no exception. There have, of course, been those who have sought to accomplish a kind of overview of the origins and development of Robbins's work and the approach that he calls "sociorhetorical."[1] Along the way in the development of

---

1. See especially the work of David B. Gowler, "The Development of Socio-Rhetorical Criticism," *New Boundaries in Old Territory: Form and Social Rhetoric in Mark*, ed. idem (ESEC 3; New York: Lang, 1994), 1–35; idem, "The End of the Beginning: The Continuing Maturation of Socio-Rhetorical Analysis," in *Sea Voyages and Beyond: Emerging Strategies in Socio-Rhetorical*

sociorhetorical interpretation (henceforward SRI), Robbins himself has provided important benchmarks beginning with the first volume in which a "sociorhetorical" approach figures (1984) and up to and including his most recent work (2012).[2]

In this presentation of Robbins's work, however, I have taken the term "genealogy" in a somewhat different direction. This difference is not to correct others who have sought to provide an analysis of the trajectory in Robbins's work. It is only to suggest an alternative approach to understanding SRI and Robbins. It is an approach, I believe, that will get at some of the essential elements involved in SRI as a critical rhetoric and in Robbins himself as a critical rhetorician.

SRI as a Critical Rhetoric

In a programmatic essay presented in final form to speech rhetoricians in 1989, Raymie McKerrow establishes "a theoretical rationale for a critical rhetoric." By "critical rhetoric" McKerrow understands a rhetoric that both "examines the dimensions of domination and freedom as these are exercised in a relativized world" and one that fosters first of all a "critique of domination" and "a critique of freedom."[3] Such a rhetoric, he argues, is fundamentally different from an exclusively analytical rhetoric that analyzes present or historic speech forms in a merely empirically descriptive way. Such a rhetoric also differs from an analytical rhetoric that analyzes speech forms in a positivistic way and that purports to indicate how such forms match or do not match what is the case. A "critical rhetoric," says

---

Interpretation, ed. Vernon K. Robbins and David B. Gowler (ESEC 14; Blandford Forum: Deo, 2010), 1–45.

2. Vernon K. Robbins, Jesus the Teacher: A Socio-Rhetorical Interpretation of Mark (Philadelphia: Fortress, 1984), passim; Robbins and Gowler, Sea Voyages, passim.

3. Raymie E. McKerrow, "Critical Rhetoric: Theory and Praxis," CM 56 (June 1989): 91. The essay was published in 1989 but was developed and presented in various forms over the course of the 1980s.

McKerrow, is not interested in Platonizing notions of static truth—even historical ones. A critical rhetoric is interested in moving towards "demystifying the conditions of domination" and toward a "self-reflexive critique that turns back on itself even as it promotes a realignment in the forces of power that construct social relations."[4]

To help us imagine a "critical rhetoric," McKerrow provides interpretive principles that a critic takes "toward the object of study."[5] Kenneth Burke has called these principles an "orientation," and such an orientation sees "mediated communication . . . in its fragmented, unconnected, even contradictory or momentarily oppositional mode of presentation." McKerrow explains: "[T]he process one employs is . . . geared to uncovering the 'dense web', not by means of a simple speaker-audience interaction, but also by means of a 'pulling together' of disparate scraps of discourse which, when constructed as an argument, serve to illuminate otherwise hidden or taken for granted social practice."[6] McKerrow sets forth a series of "principles of praxis" derived from these goals.

First, a critical rhetoric is above all a *praxis* rather than a method, a performance of the critique in varied, local contexts. Second, a critical rhetoric is about language, which forms part of "material" reality. Third, a critical rhetoric is doxastic and polysemic rather than epistemic and monosemic. In other words, instead of a rhetorical practice in which interpretations are decided in an absolute form, beliefs and opinions are tried out with various interpretations possible.[7] Fourth, a critical rhetoric is oriented to plausible namings

---

4. McKerrow, "Critical Rhetoric," 91.
5. McKerrow, "Critical Rhetoric," 91, 100. For the critical rhetorician, "invention" is not something that is performed by others, or even as a final product, but rather as something that first of all concerns the critic her- or himself.
6. McKerrow, "Critical Rhetoric," 101. McKerrow is quoting V. Mosco, "Critical Research and the Role of Labor," *JC* 33 (1983): 239.
7. How that happens may be by the establishment of a definition that effectively decides the issue or by establishing simple, straightforward, causal connections where several possible interpretations exist.

in local contexts rather than to what is or must be universally true. Fifth, a critical rhetoric recognizes the importance of absence as well as of presence.

What is the connection of McKerrow's presentation to the work of Vernon K. Robbins? It starts with the fact of synchronicity, that is, the fact that Robbins is developing an approach that he calls "sociorhetorical" at the very time that McKerrow is enunciating his critical "orientation."[8] This synchronicity is an important clue as to what the connection is, for it suggests, if not a causal connection between the two, then at least some possible common goals and common principles of praxis. We see this synchronicity in the work of other prescient New Testament rhetoricians, such as Elisabeth Schüssler Fiorenza, with whom Robbins also is in dialogue in the early 80s.[9]

As we shall see, Robbins's critical rhetorical analytic called "sociorhetorical" interpretation fits well with McKerrow's understanding of "critical rhetoric" in part because both are astute observers of the various critical rhetorical notions that are "in the air" at the time. As such, Robbins's work lends itself well to a very distinctive understanding of "genealogy" that also is in the air among all of the different critical rhetorical currents at the time, namely, the notion of "genealogy" as found in the work of Michel Foucault and

8. Robbins was promoting such a unique critical rhetoric in Robbins, *Jesus the Teacher*, passim. He continued to work out the shape of SRI in a whole host of articles throughout the 90s, as well as in his important 1996 books *Exploring the Texture of Texts: A Guide to Socio-Rhetorical Interpretation* (Valley Forge: Trinity, 1996) and *The Tapestry of Early Christian Discourse: Rhetoric, Society and Ideology* (London: Routledge, 1996). His most recent expression of the shape of SRI can be found in *The Invention of Christian Discourse: Volume 1* (Rhetoric of Religious Antiquity 1; Blandford Forum: Deo, 2009).

9. See for example Elisabeth Schüssler Fiorenza, *In Memory of Her: A Feminist Reconstruction of Christian Origins* (New York: Crossroad, 1983). Much of the material in this volume was developed and written during the same period of formation of McKerrow's and Robbins's ideas.

in his reception of Nietzsche.[10] It is this notion of "genealogy" that I will be using for this essay.

SRI as "Interpretive Analytics"

SRI represents a break with most late-twentieth-century approaches to the study of New Testament texts, approaches that may easily be identified by "genealogies" in the more conventional way of understanding that word. Though Robbins was trained in classical studies and in historical-critical analysis for the study of New Testament texts, he argues that what is needed in New Testament studies is an "interpretive analytic" that would move "'across discursive and nondiscursive practices of the present' to bring our different kinds of specialized knowledge into dialogue and to create a context for generating new insights, new areas of research and new specialties."[11] True, there would always be a value in ever greater analytical precision achieved through historical-critical study and indeed rhetorical tools honed for historical-critical study. However, these tools, he argues, are regularly seen to fail at the hermeneutical level. Accordingly, he writes:

> One of the goals of socio-rhetorical criticism is to nurture a broad-based interpretive analytics rather than simply to introduce another specialty into New Testament interpretation. An interpretive analytics invites the development of specialties that will programmatically explore aspects of human reality that have heretofore been unexplored. Of special concern

10. It is this particular understanding of Robbins's place within rhetorical criticism over against other attempts to restore classical rhetoric, and over against attempts to rescue rhetoric, that I want to underscore. McKerrow speaks of various attempts to rescue rhetoric from a "subservient role" to which it classically had been relegated by Plato's heirs, by Enlightenment logicians, or even by well-intentioned contemporary saviors of rhetoric such as Habermas, Perelman, and Toulmin, who, as McKerrow notes, only succeeded in making rhetoric further subservient to reason. See McKerrow, "Critical Rhetoric," 91.
11. Robbins, *Tapestry*, 11. Robbins is quoting Rebecca S. Chopp, *The Power to Speak: Feminism, Language, God* (New York: Crossroad, 1989), 103.

during this era in our history is the relation of power, practice and self-perspective.[12]

In other words, what is needed is a broader approach to history. Such an approach would take into consideration the kinds of findings associated with the cultural anthropological approaches of the Context Group and its major contributors including Bruce Malina, John Elliott, Richard Rohrbaugh, and others.[13] Such an approach would, however, also be able to bridge the gap between history and the contemporary reader, not just with a view to enabling the reader to understand, but also with a view to transforming the reader and the process of reading itself.

This "interpretive analytics" is the key element of SRI understood as a critical rhetoric. An "interpretive analytics" such as the one proposed by Robbins enables the analysis to be what McKerrow describes as "interactionist," that is, to bring several ways of interpreting a text "into energetic, interactive dialogue on an equal playing field." An "interpretive analytics" is also, in McKerrow's words, "transformative," that is, it envisions "the rigorous establishment of the relations of power and practice" in texts

---

12. Robbins, *Tapestry*, 13. For this task, Robbins argued that "the interpreter must take up a pragmatic stance on the basis of some socially shared sense of how things are going . . . the investigator must produce a disciplined diagnosis of what has gone on and is going on in the social body to account for the shared sense of distress or well-being . . . the investigator owes the reader an account of why the practices he [or she] describes should produce the shared malaise or contentment which gave rise to the investigation" (12). Robbins is quoting Hubert L. Dreyfus and Paul Rabinow, *Michel Foucault: Beyond Structuralism and Hermeneutics* (Chicago: University of Chicago Press, 1983), 199–200.

13. The works of the Context Group are too numerous to list but include the following salient works, among others: Bruce J. Malina, *The New Testament World: Insights from Cultural Anthropology* (3rd rev and exp. ed; Louisville: Westminster John Knox, 2001); John H. Elliott, "Social-Scientific Criticism of the New Testament: More on Methods and Models," in *Social and Scientific Criticism of the New Testament and Its Social World*, ed. J. H. Elliott (Semeia 35; Decatur: Scholars, 1986), 1–33; Richard L. Rohrbaugh, ed., *The Social Sciences and New Testament Interpretation* (Peabody: Hendrickson, 1996).

understood as discourse *and* the "courageous writing of a story of the emergence of these relations."[14]

On both counts, Robbins has proposed strategies of analysis that make such an interpretive analytic possible. He sets forth possible venues, arenas, or strategies for interpretation and continues to invite other strategies to the table. He never excludes but always includes and never pushes contributors away even when his colleagues have asked what possible contribution such a contributor could make. As I note in more detail below, Robbins seeks to ensure that the resultant story tells the whole story and not simply the story authorized by power.[15] In this way, SRI clearly breaks with a merely historical critical study of the text and begins to focus uncomfortable attention on the historical critic.

The Materiality of Discourse in SRI

SRI is also a "critical rhetoric" in that it assumes the materiality of discourse. From its inception, SRI has been known for envisioning the landscape within the world of ancient texts including the textures of the texts within the tapestry of the text. As noted above, SRI is able to achieve this goal in part by taking seriously the social-scientific attempt to grasp something of the materiality of the world behind the text.

However, like Wuellner, Robbins asserts that rhetoric is not just about material worlds that shape discourse but about the materiality of discourse that reshapes the material worlds from which the texts

14. Vernon K. Robbins, "The Rhetorical Full-Turn in Biblical Interpretation: Reconfiguring Rhetorical-Political Analysis," in *Rhetorical Criticism and the Bible: Essays from the 1988 Florence Conference*, ed. Stanley E. Porter and Thomas H. Olbricht (JSNTSup 195; Sheffield: Sheffield Academic, 2002), 49, http://www.emory.edu/COLLEGE/RELIGION/faculty/robbins/Pdfs/FullTurnFlorPubPgs.pdf (accessed 17 August 2014).

15. A classic example of Robbins's work can now be found in the retelling of the Mary–Elisabeth encounter and the role of women in the Gospel accounts. See especially the section on "ideological texture" in Robbins, *Sea Voyages*, 315–20.

themselves arise.[16] For Robbins, rhetorical agents are not the mere results of material forces beyond their control. They are not "passive bystanders, simply absorbing the ideology and having no power to alter its force or its character." Rather, as understood in critical rhetoric, rhetorical agents "have the capacity to interact in that world to modify the discourse."[17] In other words, while it is true that texts exist as a result of material worlds that have shaped them, they also evidence a material deconstruction and reconstruction of those worlds through "rhetorical argument, social act and religious belief."[18] In this respect, SRI's critical analysis seeks to unveil both the powerful *socio*-material structure of reality *and* the *rhetorical-material* transformation of reality. April DeConick has recently taken up the same challenge in what she calls "network criticism,"[19] a clear development of and from SRI as envisioned by Robbins.

This focus on the material, transformative process evidenced in the rhetorical languages *of* the past and rhetorical presentations *about* the past has led Robbins to explore theories of language and image formation. As a result of Robbins's engagement with critical spatiality theory, for example, he considers the ways in which people think through the constraints of material existence.[20] In doing so, he explores how people think about and conceive of other ways of

16. Wilhelm H. Wuellner, "Reconceiving a Rhetoric of Religion: A Rhetorics of Power and the Power of the Sublime," in *Rhetorics and Hermeneutics: Essays in Honor of Wilhelm Wuellner*, ed. James Hester and J. David Hester (Amador) (ESEC 9; Harrisburg: Trinity, 2004), 23–77.

17. McKerrow, "Critical Rhetoric," 102. McKerrow is citing D. K. Mumby, "The Political Function of Narrative in Organizations," *CM* 54 (1987): 113–27.

18. Robbins, *Tapestry*, 14. According to Robbins, these "intertwine in [the texts] like threads and yarn in a richly textured tapestry."

19. By "network criticism," DeConick means "an EMBODIED HISTORICAL APPROACH" that "understands physical embodiment of human beings in culture, society and material bodies to be essential to the creation and interpretation of cultural PRODUCTIONS." See April D. DeConick, *Network Criticism: An Embodied Historical Approach*, http://aprildeconick.com/network-historicism/ (emphasis in original). DeConick is citing Edward Slingerland, *What Science Offers the Humanities: Integrating Body and Culture* (Cambridge: Cambridge University Press, 2008), 210–12.

existing, ways that require transformative approaches to thinking, speaking, and being. This interest in counterfactual thinking and its expression in language also leads Robbins to explore the discipline of cognitive science in the form of conceptual blending and metaphor construction.[21] The employment of metaphors in the counterfactual process, the new expression of cognitive structures that emerge from that process, and the material actions designed to implement them have become significant foci of Robbins's attention in both early Christian discourse and the critical reflection on that discourse.[22]

20. For critical spatiality theory, see, for example, Jon L. Berquist and Claudia V. Camp, eds., *Constructions of Space I: Theory, Geography, and Narrative* (LHB/OTS; New York: T&T Clark, 2007), passim.

21. On conceptual blending, see especially Gilles Fauconnier and Mark Turner, *The Way We Think: Conceptual Blending and the Mind's Hidden Complexities* (New York: Basic, 2003), passim; and Vernon K. Robbins, "Conceptual Blending and Early Christian Imagination," in *Explaining Christian Origins and Early Judaism: Contributions from Cognitive and Social Science*, ed. Petri Luomanen, Ilkka Pyysiäinen, and Risto Uro (BIS 89; Leiden: Brill, 2005), 161–95. On metaphor construction, see J. David Sapir and J. C. Crocker, eds., *The Social Use of Metaphor: Essays on the Anthropology of Rhetoric* (Philadelphia: University of Pennsylvania Press, 1977), passim; George Lakoff and Mark Johnson, *Metaphors We Live By* (Chicago: University of Chicago Press, 1981), passim; Joseph Grady, Todd Oakley, and Seana Coulson, "Blending and Metaphor," in *Metaphor and Cognitive Science*, ed. Gerard J. Steen and Raymond W. Gibbs, Jr. (Amsterdam and Philadelphia: John Benjamins, 1999), 101–24, http://www.cogsci.ucsd.edu/~coulson/joe1.html (accessed 17 August 2014); Raymond W. Gibbs, Jr., and Gerard J. Steen, eds., *Metaphor in Cognitive Linguistics: Selected Papers from the Fifth International Cognitive Linguistics Conference, Amsterdam, 1997* (CILT 175; Amsterdam and Philadelphia: John Benjamins, 1999), passim; Christopher Tilley, *Metaphor and Material Culture* (Social Archaeology Series; Oxford: Blackwell, 1999), passim; Zoltán Kövecses, *Metaphor in Culture: Universality and Variation* (Cambridge: Cambridge University Press, 2005), passim.

22. On this point, see Robbins, *Invention*, 8. This reflection has borne fruit in the Rhetoric of Religious Antiquity (RRA) commentary series and in the newly created Rhetoric of Religious Antiquity Group of the SBL. At its 2011 meetings, the Rhetoric of Religious Antiquity Group discussed emergent rhetorical structures in some Second Temple and early Christian texts and how SRI is itself an example of emergent rhetorical structures in new critical approaches to the texts. In addition, the RRA Group demonstrated ways in which countercultural rhetoric and imperial rhetoric display, interpret, and reflect in images as well as in words the materiality of both lived and imagined experience. In 2013, the RRA Group devoted an entire session at the annual meeting of the Society of Biblical Literature in Baltimore to the significance of SRI and material culture as a foundation for understanding the language of early Christian texts and how the language of the texts and about the texts itself shapes the past in interpreting material culture.

The Doxastic Nature of SRI

In setting forth the outlines of a critical rhetoric, McKerrow aptly notes two opposing kinds of rhetoric, one that is not characteristic of a critical rhetoric and one that is. On the one hand, there is a rhetoric that is epistemic, focusing on what can be known and more significantly what should be known. This epistemic rhetoric is characterized by fixed genres and classical terminology. In contrast and characteristic of a critical rhetoric, there is rhetoric that is doxastic. Doxastic rhetoric deals not with knowledge, but with beliefs and opinions that are critically tried out and navigated locally, usually in the give-and-take of face-to-face discussions rather than in the presentation of dogmatic assertion.

Much of the work done from the late 1960s through the 1980s on the rhetorical analysis of New Testament texts, including my own work on Philippians, is clearly epistemic in this definition.[23] It seeks the fixed structures of the Greco-Roman authors and handbooks, be it in the form of the landmark figures such as Isocrates, Cicero, and Quintillian and what is considered to have been their definitive shaping of all ancient rhetoric, or in the popular form of epistles and the epistolary handbooks, or in the Progymnasmata.[24] This epistemic rhetoric, or at least the attempt to analyze texts on the basis of it,

---

23. Compare especially the work of Hans Dieter Betz, *Galatians: A Commentary on Paul's Letter to the Churches in Galatia* (Hermeneia; Philadelphia: Fortress, 1979), and his use of the German original of Heinrich Lausberg, *Handbook of Literary Rhetoric: A Foundation for Literary Study*, trans. David E. Orton and R. Dean Anderson (Leiden: Brill, 1998; German orig. Munich: Hueber, 1960 [2 vols.]). For my work, see L. Gregory Bloomquist, *The Function of Suffering in Philippians* (JSNTSup 78; Sheffield: Sheffield Academic, 1993).

24. This epistemic approach is often associated with the use of Lausberg's *Handbook of Literary Rhetoric* for the rhetorical analysis of New Testament texts. On the epistles, see John L. White, *Light from Ancient Letters* (FF; Philadelphia: Fortress, 1986). On the progymnasmata, see the PhD thesis and working text of James R. Butts, *The Progymnasmata of Theon: A New Text with Translation and Commentary*, PhD diss., (Claremont Graduate School, 1986); George A. Kennedy, trans., *Progymnasmata: Greek Textbooks of Prose Composition and Rhetoric* (WGRW 10; Atlanta: SBL, 2003); and Craig A. Gibson, *Libanius's Progymnasmata: Model Exercises in Greek Prose Composition and Rhetoric* (WGRW 27; Atlanta: SBL, 2008).

functions well in the service of a guild that is itself theologically oriented to fixed certainties and language.

As rhetorical and linguistic studies assert again and again, and as the cultural identity of the NT guild has changed, however, certainties and fixed language including communication and the reflection of communication in writing are seen to be unlikely as the stuff of flesh-and-blood living. This shift is especially true in areas of rhetorical and linguistic study that also draw on reflections from cognitive science.[25] SRI has moved with those studies and with that shift in a strongly doxastic direction, a direction that attempts to get at the stuff of flesh-and-blood living as evidenced in and through texts.[26]

As such and true to doxastic form, SRI is both exciting and maddening. A hunch, a belief, an opinion, something that may or may not be evidenced in the text is not only the kind of thing that SRI gets at in its analysis of ancient texts but also the very kind of thing that characterizes SRI itself. A hunch, a belief, an opinion, or a recent reading by Robbins or someone invited to the table will lead Robbins or other SRI commentators to present discussants with a new trail through the forest of interpretation without knowing exactly where the trail leads, even though accompanied by critical analysis and self-critical awareness.

The doxastic-fueled hunt for new rhetorical data in SRI has also led Robbins, along the way, to map this new territory, territory for which there is as yet neither map nor even coordinates. He has done so in part by inventing new terms to identify the coordinates and the points on the map. For this reason, SRI is peppered with neologisms.

---

25. For example, see the work of Steven Pinker, *The Stuff of Thought: Language as a Window into Human Nature* (New York: Viking, 2007).

26. The "stuff" in this sense is exactly what pragmatics seeks to access. According to Robin Lakoff, pragmatics is about "the interesting stuff about language." See Robin Lakoff, "Lewis Carroll: Subversive Pragmaticist," *Pragmatics* 3, no. 4 (1993): 367. The citation is from Dawn Archer, Karin Aijmer, and Anne Wichmann, *Pragmatics: An Advanced Resource Book for Students* (Routledge Applied Linguistics; New York: Routledge, 2012), 3.

For example, a "rhetorolect" becomes a rhetorical dialect by which local users speak of *topoi* that are well-known but do so in a new, local way.[27] "Rhetology" becomes the technical term for enthymematic style argumentation within a rhetorolect, and "rhetography" becomes the technical term for the use of a rhetorolect to picture *topoi* in particular local ways and to use those *topoi* for the purposes of rhetorical argumentation.[28]

Another key to the doxastic nature of SRI is the preeminent place given precisely to *topoi*.[29] The *topos* is a locally constructed subset drawn from admittedly larger but vaguer constellations of familiarity, constellations that carry no more weight of scientific certainty than do the celestial constellations, but that, like those constellations, are strangely familiar. This characteristic of *topoi* is true whether we are speaking of the *topos* of "family" or of "the divine" or of "justice." Robbins's uniquely critical rhetorical contribution to such an approach is to provide clues for how to navigate among *topoi* that function within both ancient and contemporary local networks of interpretation. A major challenge for Robbins and SRI will be to continue to resist the temptation to identify the *topoi* and their networks epistemically.[30]

27. Vernon K. Robbins, "The Dialectical Nature of Early Christian Discourse," *Scriptura* 59 (1996): 353–62, http://www.religion.emory.edu/faculty/robbins/SRS/vkr/dialect.cfm (accessed 17 August 2014).

28. Robbins, *Invention*, 16–17. See, too, his redefinitions of such words as *topology* and *topography* in Robbins, *Invention*, 16. It is easy to see how *rhetology* and *rhetography* are drawn from the Aristotelian distinction between enthymematic and qualitative argumentation, but they are also different. Rhetology and rhetography underscore the use of particular forms of argumentation and particular images in language with a view to a transformative effect on particular bodies and groups of bodies.

29. See my discussion of *topos* in L. Gregory Bloomquist, "Paul's Inclusive Language: The Ideological Texture of Romans 1," in *Fabrics of Discourse: Essays in Honor of Vernon K. Robbins*, ed. David B. Gowler, L. Gregory Bloomquist, and Duane F. Watson (Harrisburg: Trinity, 2003), 165–93.

30. The challenge is all the greater given that Robbins considers *topoi* to be the basic critical elements in SRI even though rhetoricians agree that the *topos* is one of the most elusive elements, if not *the* most elusive element, in all of rhetoric. An excellent example of someone

SRI's Focus on Local Rhetoric

Allied with the notion of a critical rhetoric as a doxastic rhetoric is the notion that a critical rhetoric not only avoids universalizing ideological stances or the universalizing countercultural opposition to such stances by focusing on plausible *or doxastic* namings, but also does so, as I have already suggested, in local contexts. SRI identifies rhetorolects that can broadly be identified as forms of Mediterranean discourse, and it thus identifies rhetorolects as local to that extent. Robbins, however, insists that "rhetorolects" need also to be understood in terms of even more local rhetorical expressions of larger rhetorical discourse patterns.[31] The only question at present

who realizes this difficulty is found in a brief article by Thomas Conley, one of the *doyens* of rhetorical scholarship in America and one of Robbins's colleagues and mentors at the University of Illinois. See Thomas Conley, "What Counts as a Topos in Contemporary Research?" in *Topik und Rhetorik ein Interdisziplinäres Symposium*, ed. Thomas Schirren and Gert Ueding (Rhetorik-Forschungen; Tübingen: Niemeyer, 2000), 578–85.

31. By insisting on rhetorolects, Robbins has sought to combat the universalizing closure presented by those who use only the classical genres of rhetoric to classify all rhetorical practice within these genres. Against those who would reduce the rich, creative, and chaotic material opposition that is early Christian discourse to a simple expression of Hellenistic moral philosophy, for example, Robbins asserts, as Wuellner did, that "early Christian discourse is not Hellenistic moral discourse, even though it uses *topoi* important to the Hellenistic moralists." See Vernon K. Robbins, "Where is Wuellner's Anti-Hermeneutical Hermeneutic Taking Us? From Schleiermacher to Thistleton and Beyond," in Hester and Hester, *Rhetorics and Hermeneutics*, 123, http://www.religion.emory.edu/faculty/robbins/Pdfs/WuellnerRhetHerm.pdf (accessed 17 August 2014). According to Robbins, early Christian discourse is, to use Steven Mailloux's expression, "transcultural," that is, early Christian discourse engaged both Jewish culture and Greco-Roman culture as "conversational topics and interpretive objects." See ibid., 124. Robbins is quoting Stephen Mailloux, "Articulation and Understanding: The Pragmatic Intimacy between Rhetoric and Hermeneutics," in *Rhetoric and Hermeneutics in Our Time: A Reader*, ed. Walter Jost and Michael J. Hyde (New Haven: Yale University Press, 1997), 388. Thus, Robbins has recently attempted to make it clearer why he sees emerging Christianity as a "religious" movement rather than as a divinely energized and sanctioned "moral philosophy." Toward this end, his recent work has sought to develop more completely the notion of "rhetorolects" as transcultural transformative material means by which marginal groups, such as early Christians, seek to adopt and adapt dominant rhetorical languages for their local use. The case of the appropriation of dominant Greco-Roman and subcultural Hellenistic Jewish rhetorical languages in the New Testament is one such example. According to Robbins, "six rhetorolects functioned as prototypical modes of discourse that assisted early Christians in their energetic work of creating dynamic, adaptable, and persuasive modes of discourse within Mediterranean society and culture." See Robbins, *Invention*, 7.

is what to call both the broader, less local rhetorical dialects and the more narrowly local rhetorical dialects so as to ensure a differentiation.

Emphasis on the local nature of rhetorical discourses evidences Robbins's indebtedness, and therefore that of SRI as well, to the field of cultural anthropology, specifically the works of Clifford Geertz and of Robbins's own Emory University colleague Bradd Shore. Like Shore, Robbins argues for an understanding of meaning "as an ongoing process, an active construction by people, with the help of cultural resources" in local contexts.[32] Robbins successfully combines these cultural anthropological insights with the recent developments in cognitive science noted earlier. For "brain-culture" interactions reveal not only "the general cognitive processes of information" but also "the culturally diverse manifestations of those processes in action".[33]

This refinement brings SRI well beyond the form critical search for known and consistent (epistemic) forms across the early Christian world. It also pushes SRI well beyond the classical rhetorical New Testament search (also epistemic) for ways in which New Testament discourse could be viewed according to, say, the Aristotelian categories of forensic, deliberative, and epideictic rhetoric. By focusing on identifiable, local rhetorical practices, Robbins both helps to refine our knowledge of what is communicated in the text and also helps bring us closer to the actual voices in the text or to voices that could have been in the text. These voices bring us to the final characteristic of a critical rhetoric, namely, justice for absent voices.

---

32. Bradd Shore, *Culture in Mind: Cognition, Culture, and the Problem of Meaning* (Oxford: Oxford University Press, 1996), 7. In his own way, Robbins has appropriated Shore's attempt to overcome the "psychic unity muddle," that is, the notion that meaning is "given to us ready-made, simply immanent either in cultural forms or in the mind."

33. See ibid., 40.

SRI and Absent Voices

According to McKerrow, a critical rhetoric is not just about what is present but also about what is absent. This characteristic is especially true for voices that might otherwise have been really present in the world of the text but that are absent from the text. For example, it seems quite clear that among the absent voices from New Testament texts are likely to be the voices of women (both unmarried and married), slaves, children, and all those who were understood not to have a voice of their own. However, other voices are also likely absent, such as those of beggars, widows, lepers, and all the voices of those who once might have had a voice or a semblance of a voice but who no longer do. Robbins is of course not the first to emphasize these absent voices. Many other critical scholars have devoted their lives to the task of bringing these voices to the fore.[34]

Other critical scholars have helpfully found ways to give voice to absent voices in the text, and these have been hailed as well by Robbins.[35] For Robbins, however, the question of absent voices is allied to another question about absent *topoi*. Thus, Robbins asks not only what voices are missing from texts but also what *topoi* are and are not present in texts, and why, and according to whom.

Unfortunately, if, as noted above, *topoi* are themselves difficult to grasp, how much more difficult to grasp are *topoi* that are absent! True, there are rhetorical ways for engaging the difficulty, for example, by attempting to justify the first premise in an argument from silence.[36] This attempt can be valuable but there are other

---

34. One thinks here especially of the work of Schüssler Fiorenza, *In Memory of Her*, passim.

35. See Robbins's encomia of Schüssler Fiorenza's work at various points including but certainly not limited to Robbins, *Tapestry*, 194.

36. That premise would presumably be "a counterfactual conditional statement, the justification of which, ideally, would be the result of showing that its consequent follows *logically* from its antecedent and a set of relevant condition statements in virtue of one or more law statements." See John Lange, "The Argument from Silence," *H&T* 5, no. 3 (1966): 298–99.

ways as well. For example, while there are many absent *topoi* as well as voices in early Christian Gospels, we might be advised to look for absences that may be easily acknowledged as surprising for their absence.[37] Still, there will be many absences that are not easily identified.[38] This difficulty suggests that one of the key tasks for SRI in the future will be the identification of ways of finding and welcoming both absent voices and absent rhetorical *topoi* that are not present in the text.

I believe that this task will begin to happen in SRI now that rhetography, the use of visual texture in and for rhetorical argumentation, has been placed at the forefront for rhetorical investigation. Inviting biblical interpreters to picture the various elements in the rhetorical presentation encourages us to see elements in the text and their "topographical" role that would be otherwise unseen were we to be looking at the text in a primarily "topological" way, a way that has characterized rhetorical analysis of New Testament texts to the present. Thus, the ability to see in a text like the Gospel of John the recurrent *topos* of the Temple even where the Temple is not lexically identified enables us to identify an unseen but crucial *topos* and to see its argumentative function.[39]

---

37. For example, given the presence of a legal rhetorolect in Mark, it may be striking that discussion of circumcision is absent in the legal exchanges in Mark's Gospel. This omission is all the more surprising given that this Gospel may be later than Paul's letters, where the discussion is very present, and given that this Gospel may be written at a time, even in a place, in which the community of followers of Jesus includes Gentiles as is also the case in Paul's letters. Finally, this omission is also surprising given that one might at least consider it plausible that such a legal question could arise in a male-dominated Jewish or mixed community. A critical rhetoric might also ask why this absence is not voiced in the critical discussion of this Gospel.

38. For example, why are Galilean women-followers of Jesus not mentioned during Jesus' Galilean ministry, but only in the final episode of the story just outside the walls of Jerusalem? There have been some interesting but ultimately unsatisfying attempts to explain their presence at the end. See Schüssler Fiorenza, *In Memory of Her*, 319–23.

39. I presented this feature of my forthcoming Rhetoric of Religious Antiquity (RRA) commentary on the Gospel of John to the RRA Group of the SBL at the annual SBL meetings in Chicago in 2013.

SRI as Transformative Performance and Vernon Robbins as Critical Rhetorician

I believe it is clear that SRI is an example of a "critical rhetoric" as set forth by McKerrow. However, I also believe that SRI is a critical rhetoric because first of all Robbins is himself a critical rhetorician. In what follows, I want to substantiate my belief and to show why I have taken the approach that I have to Robbins and his work by envisioning this essay as a reflection on the "genealogy of rhetorical criticism" as I have.

As I noted at the outset, I could have carried out the task assigned to me by creating a kind of biblical genealogy of the kind with which scholars are familiar as, for example, Joachim Jeremias begat Norman Perrin, and Norman Perrin begat Vernon Robbins. Alternatively, I could have carried out the same task in a disciplinary fashion such that historical-critical study begat form criticism and form criticism begat SRI. In fact, some scholars have asserted that SRI is really only a child of form criticism.[40] While I have pointed to some influences on Robbins, I have chosen *not* to major on a genetic or causal genealogical approach to him or his work. I believe that to have done so would have missed the point of the contribution of SRI and Robbins.

The route that I have taken in exploring SRI as a critical rhetoric and in assessing Robbins and his contribution to rhetorical studies follows the map set out by Michel Foucault for a truly "genealogical" critique. For I believe that what Timothy Wilson writes about Foucault's "genealogical" critique could also be said of SRI understood as a critical rhetoric and Robbins understood as a critical rhetorician. Wilson writes that Foucault "does not allow the past to

---

40. See the criticism by R. Alan Culpepper, "Mapping the Textures of New Testament Criticism: A Response to Socio-Rhetorical Criticism," *JSNT* 70 (1998): 71–77.

present itself as it is in itself; rather, the past is endlessly re-presented on the basis of the schemata of the present."[41] In his landmark address, "L'ordre du discours," Foucault provides a key differentiation between mere criticism or analysis and "genealogy." Criticism, he says, "analyses the processes of rarefaction, consolidation, and unification in discourse" while "genealogy" "studies their formation, at once scattered, discontinuous and regular."[42] To explore this genealogy, Foucault, like critical rhetoricians such as McKerrow and Robbins, proposes some methodological guidelines, although not a method *per se*, that include reversal, discontinuity, specificity, and exteriority.[43] Each of these guidelines in and of themselves reads in Foucault's handling of them like a guidebook to McKerrow's critical principles and to the critical rhetorical dynamics found in SRI.

Similar to Foucault's genealogical analytic, Robbins's "interpretive analytic" attempts to provide a "disciplined diagnosis" of what is going on *and* what has gone wrong "in the social body."[44] Like Foucault, Robbins's goal is not merely criticism or analysis of the past, though it is that in part in the same sense as "archaeology" is an initial impetus and aspect of Foucault's "genealogy." Neither is Robbins's goal a re-presentation of the past, but rather a transformative analysis of the past, present, and future. Robbins asks how this text saw the world in which it arose differently from how other texts saw the world. He also asks: How did it end up changing the world in which it arose by presenting a reconfiguration of that world? How have readers, for better or worse, reconfigured and changed the text and subsequently their own worlds? How can a new or different reading of this text change us?

---

41. Timothy H. Wilson, "Foucault, Genealogy, History," *PT* 39, no. 2 (1995): 168.
42. Michel Foucault, *The Archaeology of Knowledge and the Discourse on Language*, trans. A. M. Sheridan Smith (New York: Harper & Row, 1972), 233.
43. Foucault, *The Archaeology of Knowledge and the Discourse on Language*, 229.
44. See note 12.

Is it surprising that Robbins's work, like Foucault's, troubles people? While all readers of Robbins's work regularly find new insights derived from critical analysis of the New Testament, astute readers also sense that within these insights there lies latent a veritable liberation from many of the imposed disciplinary constraints of a traditional critical analysis of the New Testament. These constraints are not today the same ones that the early Reformers or Enlightenment readers sought to throw off from dogmatic theology. They are, nonetheless, dogmatic assertions established by the heirs of the Reformers and the Enlightenment, for the most part mainline Protestants and their Roman Catholic adherents. The disciplinary guild that today shapes the principal hierarchies within Protestantism also establishes these dogmatic assertions and constraints from which Robbins and SRI seek liberation. These new heirs are found on both sides of the divide of conservative and liberal, to use easily identifiable categories. Both find Robbins and his work troubling. Why?

"Conservative" believers in the New Testament and "conservative" critics of the NT are both troubled that SRI is not more epistemic and that it emphasizes transformative readings. If only SRI, they say, were just a series of more fully refined methodological tools for historical-critical study, then we, too, could easily call ourselves sociorhetorical interpreters. They are troubled, in other words, not by the historical-critical facets of SRI but by its underlying, and essential, critical stance of being a transformative approach that gives us insight as to how original readers read the New Testament rhetorical presentations but that also jars contemporary critics from comfortable guild-authorized postures.

In some cases, conservative readers seek to co-opt elements of Robbins's phrasing, including the term *sociorhetorical*, which is the central identification of his work.[45] Even though some conservative readers see value in aspects of Robbins's work or at least in the name "sociorhetorical," they nevertheless undermine the critical rhetoric that lies at the very heart of SRI by making it into just another analytical tool for understanding others and their texts.[46] To his credit, Robbins is not swayed by them but continues to follow the lead of feminist theologians such as Elisabeth Schüssler Fiorenza and Rebecca Chopp. He remains convinced that SRI is an attempt at "a prolegomenon to a constructive theology guided by discourses of emancipatory transformation."[47]

The discomfort with Robbins's approach, however, is not limited to "conservative" readers, for even liberal readers who are sympathetic to its emancipatory goals and even some of those already involved in the RRA project itself are often discomfited by Robbins's approach. Again, this discomfort is due to the fact that SRI is transformative not just of the object of criticism but also of the critic her or himself, even the liberationist critic. Thus, for example, in response to Schüssler Fiorenza's criticism that his work is not sufficiently transformative, Robbins asserts that Schüssler Fiorenza has opted for an "oppositional" rhetoric that is significantly less than the liberating rhetoric she actually has sought and that actually has increased the guild's power to "dominate."[48] Robbins explains:

---

45. Ben Witherington seeks to make a "sociorhetorical" approach to New Testament texts one that is associated exclusively with his own name. See the array of volumes coming forth from him that begin with Ben Witherington III, *The Gospel of Mark: A Socio-Rhetorical Commentary* (Grand Rapids: Eerdmans, 2001). It is unclear why Witherington has settled his attention on the term *socio-rhetorical*, since his commentaries are more "theologico-historical" than anything else.

46. See the response to Witherington's work by Roy R. Jeal, "Review of Ben Witherington III, *New Testament Rhetoric: An Introductory Guide to the Art of Persuasion in and of the New Testament.* Eugene: Cascade Books, 2009" (paper presented at the Christian Scholars Conference, Pepperdine University, Malibu, CA, June 16, 2011).

47. Robbins, *Tapestry*, 11. Robbins is quoting Chopp, *Power to Speak*, 102–3.

48. Elisabeth Schüssler Fiorenza, "Challenging the Rhetorical Half-Turn: Feminist and Rhetorical Biblical Criticism," in *Rhetoric, Scripture and Theology: Essays from the 1994 Pretoria Conference*, ed. Stanley E. Porter and Thomas H. Olbricht (JSNTSup 131; Sheffield: Sheffield Academic, 1996), 28–53. For Robbins's response, see Robbins, "Rhetorical Full-Turn," 58.

If our rhetorical analyses reenact only one or two rhetorical modes within this literature, then we are making only a quarter- or half-turn within its rich discursive texture. To make our task complete, we must engage in political rhetoric and we must do it not only by joining voices and actions with women's voices and marginalized people in wide regions of our global village. We must engage in dialogical interpretation that includes disenfranchised voices, marginalized voices, recently liberated voices, and powerfully-located voices . . . so that we enable free and open discussion and controversy in an environment where we keep our colleagues on an equal playing field and keep the issues in an arena of specificity rather than staging them as typical actions to be attacked.[49]

Those of us who have known Robbins for any length of time know that this commitment to a truly and fully transformative dimension to criticism is an essential part of SRI precisely because it is an essential part of who Robbins is.

Not only does Robbins seek to identify in early Christian texts those rhetorics that attempt to engage and respond to "social practices that are ultimately harmful to the community," but he also seeks to do the same in his own life as a critic and in the other local worlds in which he finds himself.[50] His rhetoric engages the worlds of contemporary American political debates, of ecclesiological shifts in modern Christianity, of his circle of friends, of his intimate family gatherings, and of his own personal life.

In a truly critical rhetoric, one should expect this very thing, namely, that critical praxis and performance occur in the critic's life, not just in the fully bracketed, so-called analytical moments. Robbins is a remarkable example of that praxis of self-criticism that liberationist ideologies often proclaim but that liberationist ideologues often deny by their actions. For self-criticism is the crucial

---

49. Ibid., 58.
50. McKerrow, "Critical Rhetoric," 108. McKerrow is citing M. C. McGee, "Another Philippic: Notes on the Ideological Turn in Criticism," *Central States Speech Journal* 35 (1984): 43–50.

element in keeping critical analysis itself from becoming captive to ideology. A great challenge for SRI *after* Robbins will be for Robbins's heirs to find ways to *re*-incarnate Robbins's own rigorous practice of self-criticism.

From where will these true inheritors of Robbins's approach come? They will probably come from the margins rather than from the mainstream. It is not surprising to find currently that Robbins's approach has been adopted not so much by mainstream commentators but by scholars working on the margins that are in dialogue with the dominant culture. Basing himself on the work of Rebecca Chopp, Robbins years ago described the goal of SRI:

> [SRI attempts] to weave a discourse of judgment and transformation that shows 'the relation of language, politics, and subjectivity in the dominant social-symbolic order and, standing on the margins and in the breaks of that order, to glimpse and whisper possibilities of transformation.' One of the goals of socio-rhetorical criticism is to bring the margins and boundaries into view, to invite the interpreter into the discourses that dwell in those marginal spaces, to criticize the dominating interpretive practices that exclude these marginal discourses and to seek discourses of emancipation for marginalized, embodied voices and actions in the text.[51]

The same transcultural drive behind Robbins's critical rhetoric enables him both to draw on and to become a co-worker with those of us working on the margins by nurturing and helping us not simply to analyze texts in terms of the voices found in them but also to find our own voices within a variety of dominant, sub-cultural, counter-cultural, and liminal contexts.[52]

---

51. Robbins, *Tapestry*, 11. Robbins is quoting Chopp, *Power to Speak*, 102–3.
52. The language is that of K. A. Roberts, "Toward a Generic Concept of Counter-Culture," *SF* 11 (1978): 111–26. This language is found throughout Robbins's work. For example, see Vernon K. Robbins, *Exploring the Texture of Texts: A Guide to Socio-Rhetorical Interpretation* (Valley Forge: Trinity, 1996), 86–88.

He regularly remarks to me how thrilled he is to find SRI being used by people working at the margins of dominant cultural European and American biblical scholarship or at the margins of dominant Protestant and Catholic exegetical positions. It is not surprising, therefore, that his own work draws *on* and draws *in* scholars from South Africa, sub-Saharan Africa, Scandinavia, Hong Kong, and Canada, all marginal countries to the dominant powers of the current *Realpolitik*. His work also attracts those whose voices are only now beginning to be heard in the mainline, Protestant-dominated guild culture of biblical studies, from men and women, Pentecostals and Wesleyans, as well as a new generation of Jewish New Testament scholars and Christian scholars engaged in critical study of the Qur'an.[53]

By doing rhetorical analysis with us at the margins where early Christian discourse likely arose, Robbins has helped us see how rhetorical analysis of biblical texts can be done critically and thus genealogically at the margins today. This critical rhetoric, which is transformative at its core, will be Robbins's longstanding contribution and his true genealogy.

---

53. For the last example, see the work of Gordon D. Newby, "Folded Time: A Socio-Rhetorical Analysis of Qur'anic and Early Islamic Apocalyptic Discourse," in Gowler, Bloomquist, and Watson, *Fabrics of Discourse*, 333–54.

10

Response to L. Gregory Bloomquist: From the Social Sciences to Rhetography

Vernon K. Robbins

I want to thank Gregory Bloomquist for his highly perceptive presentation of the nature of socio-rhetorical interpretation (SRI) in the Rhetoric of Religious Antiquity (RRA) mode I have been pursuing and formulating since the early 1970s. I would like to present my overall response by discussing four developments I consider new in the study of the New Testament since 1970 and explain how SRI in an RRA mode has developed rhetorical exegetical practices that bring these new developments into rhetorical criticism. These developments result from experiences that begin at the University of Illinois at Urbana-Champaign during the 1970s, are influenced by a remarkable series of international Rhetorical

Conferences organized by Thomas Olbricht,[1] and are deepened through special experiences in South Africa beginning in 1996.[2]

Anthropology and Social-Scientific Criticism

The first development is what happened before and during the 1970s. Prior to the 1970s, as the social sciences invade New Testament studies and the study of early Christian society and culture, sociology is the dominant approach and the most easily used of all the social sciences.[3] While sociology may be the most natural social science ally of literary-historical studies, anthropology is the key ally of rhetorical studies, and the appearance of this approach in biblical studies is concurrent with the reintroduction of rhetoric to the study of the Bible.

Anthropology displays a dramatic presence in Hebrew Bible studies as early as the publication of Johannes Pedersen's *Israel: Its Life and Culture* in English in 1926.[4] Then, Amos N. Wilder features cultural anthropology in his presidential address to the Society of Biblical Literature in 1955.[5] Nevertheless, anthropology does not show a dramatic presence in New Testament studies until the 1970s. The journal *Semeia* begins publication in 1974 with a volume that champions a structural linguistic approach to the parables with a

---

1. Vernon K. Robbins, "From Heidelberg to Heidelberg: Rhetorical Interpretation of the Bible at the Seven 'Pepperdine' Conferences from 1992–2002," in *Rhetoric, Ethics, and Moral Persuasion in Biblical Discourse*, ed. Thomas H. Olbricht and Anders Eriksson (ESEC 11; New York: T&T Clark, 2005), 335–77.

2. Vernon K. Robbins, "Why Participate in African Biblical Interpretation?," in *Interpreting the New Testament in Africa*, ed. Mary N. Getui, Tinyiko S. Maluleke, and Justin Ukpong (Nairobi: Acton, 2001), 275–91.

3. Gerd Theissen, "Theoretische Probleme religionssoziologischer Forschung und die Analyse des Urchristentums," *Neue Zeitschrift für Systematische Theologie* 16 (1974): 35–56; idem, *Sociology of Early Palestinian Christianity* (Minneapolis: Fortress, 1978); idem, *The Social Setting of Pauline Christianity: Essays on Corinth* (Philadelphia: Fortress, 1982).

4. Johannes Pedersen, *Israel: Its Life and Culture* (Atlanta: Scholars, 1991).

5. Amos N. Wilder, "Scholars, Theologians, and Ancient Rhetoric," *JBL* 75 (1956): 1–11.

heritage in Claude Lévi-Strauss' *Structural Anthropology*.[6] Then, a cultural anthropology approach dramatically appears in 1981 with the publication of Bruce J. Malina's *The New Testament World: Insights from Cultural Anthropology*.[7] It is no coincidence that Wilhelm H. Wuellner and Hans Dieter Betz begin to reintroduce rhetorical analysis and interpretation to New Testament writings during the 1970s and 80s, when the focus in biblical studies shifts from sociology to anthropology.[8]

In contrast to sociologists, anthropologists love unusual cultures and try to understand them while sociologists tend to separate themselves from unusual cultures to find out what major culture is doing. Sociologists create questionnaires and statistical tables that create a distance between the analyst and the people who live in the area. Anthropologists, in contrast, like to live among the people, learn their language, and find out not only what the people themselves are doing but also how they understand what they are doing.

Cultural studies come into view during the 1970s in a context where some people assert that it is not possible to distinguish between society and culture. Some others rigorously focus on culture instead of focusing entirely or primarily on society, and the majority of these people are substantively interested in rhetoric. In my experience, an interpreter who is not able to distinguish between society and culture is not likely interested in books such as Clifford Geertz's *Interpretation of Cultures* and *Local Knowledge*, which lead to interpretation of local cultures, subcultures, countercultures of various kinds, contracultures, and marginal cultures.[9]

---

6. Robert W. Funk, ed., *A Structuralist Approach to the Parables* (Semeia 1; Missoula: Scholars, 1974).

7. Bruce J. Malina, *The New Testament World: Insights from Cultural Anthropology* (rev. ed.; Louisville: Westminster/John Knox, 1993).

8. James D. Hester and J. David Hester, eds., *Rhetorics and Hermeneutics: Wilhelm Wuellner and His Influence* (ESEC 9; New York: T&T Clark, 2004).

Within this intellectual milieu, in 1984 I launched Socio-Rhetorical Interpretation in *Jesus the Teacher: A Socio-Rhetorical Interpretation of Mark.*[10] I blended insights from Clifford Geertz's *Interpretation of Cultures* with Kenneth Burke's presentation of progressive form, repetitive form, conventional form, and minor form in his book entitled *Counterstatement.*[11] A major goal was to move beyond form-critical analysis and beyond interpretation of form and redaction-critical analysis of genre into a culturally driven analysis of rhetorical forms of communication in Mediterranean antiquity during the first century CE. A major result of this cultural-rhetorical approach was a merger of biblical-Jewish modes of calling, instructing, and sending forth of prophets with Greco-Roman modes of calling, instructing, and sending forth of student disciples in the Gospel of Mark.[12] A key challenge was to discover ways to merge

9. Clifford Geertz, *Interpretation of Cultures: Selected Essays* (New York: Basic, 1973); idem, *Local Knowledge: Further Essays in Interpretive Anthropology* (New York: Basic, 1983). See Vernon K. Robbins, *The Tapestry of Early Christian Discourse: Rhetoric, Society and Ideology* (London: Routledge, 1996), 167–74; idem, *Exploring the Texture of Texts: A Guide to Socio-Rhetorical Interpretation* (Harrisburg, PA: Trinity Press International; repr. New York: Bloomsbury Academic, 2012), 86–89; idem, "Rhetoric and Culture: Mark 4–11 as a Test Case," in *Sea Voyages and Beyond: Emerging Strategies in Socio-Rhetorical Interpretation*, ed. Vernon K. Robbins and David B. Gowler (ESEC 14; Blandford Forum: Deo, 2010), 145–81; idem, "Oral, Rhetorical, and Literary Cultures: A Response," in *Orality and Textuality is Early Christian Literature*, ed. Joanna Dewey (Semeia 65; Atlanta: Scholars, 1994): 75–91.

10. Vernon K. Robbins, *Jesus the Teacher: A Socio-Rhetorical Interpretation of Mark* (Minneapolis: Fortress Press, © 1984; 2009).

11. Kenneth Burke, *Counter-Statement* (Berkeley: University of California Press, 1968); Vernon K. Robbins, "Socio-rhetorical Criticism," in *Interpreting the Bible: A Handbook of Terms and Methods*, ed. W. Randolph Tate (Peabody: Hendrickson, 2006), 342–46; idem, "Socio-Rhetorical Interpretation," in *The Blackwell Companion to the New Testament*, ed. David E. Aune (Oxford: Wiley-Blackwell, 2010), 192–219; idem, "Socio-Rhetorical Criticism," in the *The Oxford Encyclopedia of Biblical Interpretation*, vol. 2 (New York: Oxford University Press, 2013), 311-18.

12. Vernon K. Robbins, "Mark I.14-20: An Interpretation at the Intersection of Jewish and Graeco-Roman Traditions," *NTS* 28 (1982): 220–36, repr. in *New Boundaries in Old Territory: Forms and Social Rhetoric in Mark*, ed. David B. Gowler (New York: Peter Lang, 1994), 137–54; idem, "Summons and Outline in Mark: The Three-Step Progression," *NovT* 23 (1981): 97–114, repr. in *The Composition of Mark's Gospel: Selected Studies from Novum Testamentum*, ed. D. E. Orton (RBS 3; Leiden: Brill, 1999), 103–20, and in Gowler, *New Boundaries in Old Territory*, 119–35.

social-scientific criticism with the newly emerging modes of literary criticism during the 1980s and 1990s.[13]

An anthropological approach naturally merges biblical-Jewish and Greco-Roman cultural modes, because they are all part of the mix of Mediterranean culture. It also naturally nurtures an interest in *topoi* and taxonomies. By 1990, it becomes obvious that the most promising cultural approaches to early Christianity are developing taxonomies on the basis of social-cultural topics that are rhetorically understood as *topoi* in the Mediterranean world in which early Christianity found its garden of growth.[14]

At this time, the SBL Context Group champions a taxonomy of social-cultural *topoi* that has become second-hand knowledge to more and more New Testament interpreters. In the research environment of this Group, there are five major social-cultural *topoi*: honor-shame, dyadic personality, limited good, kinship, and purity.[15] From a rhetorical standpoint, the challenge is to analyze and interpret how early Christians negotiated honor-shame, dyadic personality contracts, limited good perspective, kinship language, and purity practices in their discourse. Perhaps most of all, the social-scientific approach of the Context Group gives us glimpses of how to do rhetorical ethnography in our New Testament writings.

First and foremost, rhetorical interpreters need to find the social-cultural-ideological *topoi* early Christians were using in their discourse and argumentation and learn how to develop taxonomies

---

13. Vernon K. Robbins, "Social-Scientific Criticism and Literary Studies: Prospects for Cooperation in Biblical Interpretation," in *Modelling Early Christianity: Social-Scientific Studies of the New Testament in Its Context,* ed. Philip F. Esler (London: Routledge, 1995), 274–89, repr. in idem, *Sea Voyages,* 182–200.

14. Idem, *The Invention of Christian Discourse, Volume 1* (Blandford Forum: Deo, 2009), 81–84; Johan C. Thom, "'The Mind is Its Own Place': Defining the Topos," in *Early Christianity and Classical Culture: Comparative Studies in Honor of Abraham J. Malherbe,* ed. J. T. Fitzgerald, T. H. Olbricht, and L. M. White (NovTSup 110; Leiden: Brill, 2003), 555–73.

15. Malina, *The New Testament World* 28–183 (1981 ed. 25–152); Robbins, *Exploring the Texture of Texts,* 75–86.

that move beyond the rhetorical taxonomy of judicial, deliberative, and epideictic discourse of the Greek city-state. The overall challenge for a cultural-rhetorical taxonomy of early Christian discourse is to discern the *topoi* in biblical-Jewish and Greco-Roman cultural heritages that early Christians used to create their own rhetorical discourse and argumentation in the Mediterranean world.[16]

The *topos*-location taxonomy that has emerged in SRI in an RRA mode features six networks of *topoi*: wisdom as household rhetoric; prophetic as kingdom rhetoric; apocalyptic and precreation as empire rhetorics; miracle as rhetoric of the body; and priestly as temple rhetoric.[17] Most recently, Alexandra Gruca-Macaulay completed a full-scale study of the Lydia unit in Acts that is guided by SRI as a topos-oriented approach.[18] A fascinating variety of other applications of SRI has also appeared.[19]

---

16. L. Gregory Bloomquist, "Paul's Inclusive Language: The Ideological Texture of Romans 1," in *Fabrics of Discourse: Essays in Honor of Vernon K. Robbins*, ed. David B. Gowler, L. Gregory Bloomquist, and Duane F. Watson (New York: Trinity, 2003), 174–93; Carolyn R. Miller, "The Aristotelean *Topos*: Hunting for Novelty," in *Rereading Aristotle's Rhetoric*, ed. Alan G. Gross and Arthur E. Walzer (Carbondale: Southern Illinois University Press, 2000), 130–46; Barbara Warnick, "Two Systems of Invention: The Topics in *Rhetoric* and *The New Rhetoric*," in Gross and Walzer, *Rereading Aristotle's Rhetoric*, 107–29.

17. Robbins, *Invention*, xix–xxx; idem, "Conceptual Blending and Early Christian Imagination," in *Explaining Christian Origins and Early Judaism: Contributions from Cognitive and Social Science*, ed. Petri Luomanen, Ilkka Pyysiäinen, and Risto Uro (BIS 89; Leiden: Brill, 2007), 161–95; idem, "Socio-Rhetorical Interpretation," in Aune, *Blackwell Companion*, 199–203.

18. Alexandra Gruca-Macaulay, "The Role and Function of Lydia as a Rhetorical Construct in Acts: Sociorhetorical and Theological Interpretation," PhD diss. (St. Paul University, Ottawa, 2013).

19. Santosh V. Varghese, "Woe-Oracles in Habakkuk 2:6–20: A Socio-Rhetorical Reading," MTh thesis (Faith Theological Seminary, Manakala, Kerala, India, 2009); Keir Hammer, "Disambiguating Rebirth: A Socio-Rhetorical Exploration of Rebirth Language in 1 Peter," PhD diss. (University of Toronto, 2011); Kayle B. de Waal, *A Socio-Rhetorical Interpretation of the Seven Trumpets of Revelation: The Apocalyptic Challenge to Earthly Empire* (Lewiston: Mellen, 2012); Riku P. Tuppurainen, "The Contribution of Socio-Rhetorical Criticism to Spirit-Sensitive Hermeneutics: A Contextual Example—Luke 11:13," *JBPR* 4 (2012): 38–66; Ingeborg Mongstad-Kvammen, *Toward a Postcolonial Reading of the Epistle of James: James 2:1–13 in its Roman Imperial Context* (BIS 119; Leiden: Brill, 2013); David H. Wenkel, *Joy in Luke-Acts: The Intersection of Rhetoric, Narrative, and Emotion* (Paternoster Biblical Monographs; Carlisle, Cumbria: Paternoster, forthcoming).

This kind of multiple understanding of culture led to the invitation for me to come to South Africa in 1996.[20] This invitation put me in a context of eleven official languages with their respective cultures, and I really began to understand what it means to negotiate the cultures of emerging Christianity in the Mediterranean world.[21] This invitation also put me in the context where Elisabeth Schüssler Fiorenza had challenged my "scientistic, malestream" approach to rhetoric by using only classical Hellenistic-Roman rhetoric, to which I subsequently responded at conferences in Florence and Berlin.[22] This leads to the second development.

Blending Judaism and Hellenism with Help from the *Progymnasmata*

Prior to the years I visited South Africa and taught as an Extraordinary Professor there (1996–2004), I taught in the Department of Classics at the University of Illinois at Urbana-Champaign for fifteen years (1968–1983), and then brought this experience from the classics to Emory University for twelve years (1984–1996) after a Fulbright year at the University of Trondheim, Norway (1983–1984). In the context of the University of Illinois, I made major moves into Mediterranean society and culture with

20. Vernon K. Robbins, "Why Participate in African Biblical Interpretation?," in *Interpreting the New Testament in Africa*, ed. Mary N. Getui, Tinyiko S. Maluleke, and Justin Ukpong (Nairobi: Acton, 2001), 275–91.
21. Idem, "The Dialectical Nature of Early Christian Discourse," *Scriptura* 59 (1996): 353–62.
22. Elisabeth Schüssler Fiorenza, "Challenging the Rhetorical Half-Turn: Feminist and Rhetorical Biblical Criticism," in *Rhetoric, Scripture and Theology: Essays from the 1994 Pretoria Conference*, ed. Stanley E. Porter and Thomas H. Olbricht (JSNTSup 131; Sheffield: Sheffield Academic, 1996), 28–53; Vernon K. Robbins, "The Rhetorical Full-Turn in Biblical Interpretation: Reconfiguring Rhetorical-Political Analysis," in *Rhetorical Criticism and the Bible: Essays from the 1998 Florence Conference*, ed. Stanley E. Porter and Thomas H. Olbricht (JSNTSup 195; Sheffield: Sheffield Academic, 2002), 48–60; idem, "The Rhetorical Full-Turn in Biblical Interpretation and Its Relevance for Feminist Hermeneutics," in *Her Master's Tools? Feminist and Postcolonial Engagements of Historical-critical Discourse,* ed. Caroline Vander Stichele and Todd C. Penner (GPBS 9; Atlanta: SBL and Leiden: Brill, 2005), 109–27.

the help of Martin Hengel's two-volume *Judaism and Hellenism*, published in 1973 in German and 1974 in English.[23] Instead of Jewish society versus Greek society, he introduced us to Jews, Greeks, Romans, and all kinds of other people as participants in Mediterranean society and culture. Thus, it was possible to start a journey of trying to study the rhetoric of people in all different kinds of local cultures who were participating in an agglomeration of subcultures in Mediterranean culture.[24]

During this time, the model for rhetorical analysis and interpretation of the New Testament is classical Greco-Roman rhetoric under the influence of Hans Dieter Betz and George A. Kennedy. How, however, is one going to study the mix of Mediterranean cultures in earliest Christianity with a model of only three kinds of rhetoric that come from the Greek city-state? In the tradition of Greco-Roman rhetoric, the locations of the rhetoric are the courtroom, the political assembly, and the civil ceremony to honor some person or some special edifice such as a building, temple, or ship. These locations are too limited to analyze all of the locations in emerging Christianity. Would it be possible to find an indigenous mode of rhetoric in the Mediterranean world that could help us move beyond the horizons of the courtroom, political assembly, and civil ceremony?

A cultural breakthrough in Mediterranean rhetorical analysis and interpretation of New Testament writings begins with the discovery, translation, and interpretation of those "low grade" rhetorical textbooks called the *Progymnasmata*, the *Preliminary Exercise* manuals written by rhetoricians for grammarians to use when they were

---

23. Martin Hengel, *Judaism and Hellenism: Studies in Their Encounter in Palestine during the Early Hellenistic Period* (2 vols.; Philadelphia: Fortress, 1974).

24. Vernon K. Robbins, "Luke-Acts: A Mixed Population Seeks a Home in the Roman Empire," in *Images of Empire*, ed. Loveday Alexander (Sheffield: JSOT, 1991), 202–21; idem, "Oral, Rhetorical, and Literary Cultures."

preparing students at the end of their grammatical training for the rhetorical training that would follow.[25] Aelius Theon of Alexandria writes his *Progymnasmata* about the same time as the Gospels and Quintilian, with antecedents in the *Rhetorica ad Herrenium* written in the 80s BCE. Especially through the study of Theon's *Progymnasmata*, it becomes obvious that New Testament interpreters needed to move beyond the oratorical rhetoric of the Greek city-state into the progymnastic modes rhetoricians used to elaborate sayings, short stories, fable-like parables, and other literary and oral genres.[26]

This development occurred again as a result of location. In the Spring of 1982, I was granted an SBL Fellowship to work at the Institute for Antiquity and Christianity at Claremont. Just prior to that time, Thomas M. Conley moved from Berkeley to the University of Illinois at Urbana-Champaign, and I studied ancient, Byzantine, Medieval, and modern rhetoric in the Department of Speech Communication under him with the support of a faculty Fellowship for Study in a Second Discipline in the University.[27] When I went to the Institute for Antiquity and Christianity during spring 1982, I was ready and eager to work with the Rhetoric Group there.

At the beginning of the 1980s, some people at the Institute for Antiquity and Christianity at Claremont fortunately begin to realize the importance of *Progymnasmata,* those textbooks written by rhetoricians for grammarians to use in the Mediterranean context of *paideia* with the goal of attaining the highest level of instruction in

---

25. George A. Kennedy, trans., *Progymnasmata: Greek Textbooks of Prose Composition and Rhetoric* (WGRW 10; Atlanta: SBL, 2003).

26. Vernon K. Robbins, "Progymnastic Rhetorical Composition and Pre-Gospel Traditions: A New Approach," in *The Synoptic Gospels: Source Criticism and the New Literary Criticism*, ed. Camille Focant (BETL 110; Leuven: Leuven University Press, 1993), 111–47; Ronald F. Hock and Edward N. O'Neil, eds., *The Chreia and Ancient Rhetoric: Classroom Exercises* (WGRW 2; Atlanta: SBL, 2002).

27. Thomas M. Conley, *Rhetoric in the European Tradition* (White Plains: Longman, 1990).

the writing and delivery of oratorical rhetorical speeches. Toward the end of the grammatical training, the grammarian takes the student through all kinds of "preliminary" exercises (*progymnasmata*) that blend grammatical-syntactical training with "free composition" of brief narratives containing speech and action of well-known people in Greek and Roman history, society, and culture.[28] This blend of grammar, syntax, and "middle-school" rhetorical training is instructive for the social, cultural, and intellectual environment of earliest Christianity. In the early 1980s, scholars at the Institute for Antiquity and Christianity begin to translate into English the earliest *Progymnasmata*, namely the one written by Aelius Theon of Alexandria during the last part of the first century CE. This work, written in Greek, had never before been translated into English, and thus it was not readily accessible to English language students of the New Testament.

When I arrived at the Institute for Antiquity and Christianity at Claremont, Burton L. Mack, Ronald F. Hock, Edward N. O'Neill, and James M. Butts were meeting every other week to work through translations of Theon's *Progymnasmata* from Greek into English.[29] I joined them. When I saw the examples of abbreviated and expanded chreiai and the additions students were to make to them, I knew I was in the grammatical-syntactical-rhetorical environment of the Gospel writers and the writers of the majority of letters we encounter in the New Testament.[30]

---

28. Hock and O'Neil, *The Chreia and Ancient Rhetoric*, passim.
29. Ronald F. Hock and Edward N. O'Neil, eds., *The Chreia in Ancient Rhetoric, Volume I: The Progymnasmata* (SBLTT 27, Graeco-Roman Religion Series 9; Atlanta: Scholars, 1986); James R. Butts, "The 'Progymnasmata' of Theon: A New Text with Translation and Commentary," PhD diss. (Claremont Graduate School, 1986).
30. Hock and O'Neil, *The Chreia and Ancient Rhetoric: Classroom Exercises*, passim; George A. Kennedy, *Invention and Method: Two Rhetorical Treatises from the Hermogenic Corpus* (WGRW 15; Atlanta: SBL, 2005), passim.

The "low-grade" rhetoric exhibited in Theon's *Progymnasmata* is not going to help us argue the case that earliest Christianity was a prestigious, philosophically-reasoning culture. When we see the writing, rewriting, and reconfiguring of essays and stories in the *Progymnasmata*, however, things begin to click concerning the kind of culture in which speakers, writers, and scribes nurtured emerging Christianity. We begin to realize that the high oratorical rhetoric of Quintilian and others is a different cultural rhetoric at another level of Mediterranean society than the progymnastic rhetorical level we need to analyze.

The progymnastic rhetoric nurtures the elaborations, expansions, revisions, and summaries being produced in first-century Christianity. In the midst of translating Theon's *Progymnasmata,* I saw how Theon illustrates how a person is to expand, abbreviate, add to, speak against, speak for, and develop brief sayings into essays. I then began to realize that these were the rhetorical techniques of emerging Christians during the first century CE. They learned how to talk about something like righteousness and expand that *topos* through various kinds of chreiai, parables, and forms of argumentation for and against. They did not expand their topoi simply or primarily through the oratorical speech of the assembly, courtroom, or special occasion.[31]

In other words, a major problem for rhetorical interpretation of New Testament writings is their cultural level. For early Christians, the courtroom does not work very well, and neither does the political assembly that was praising some Roman emperor, nor civil ceremonies that were glorifying the initiation of a new temple to Zeus, Apollo, Athena, Artemis, or some other god or goddess.

---

31. Robbins, "Progymnastic Rhetorical Composition and Pre-Gospel Traditions;" idem, "Argumentative Textures in Socio-Rhetorical Interpretation," in *Rhetorical Argumentation in Biblical Texts: Essays from the Lund 2000 Conference*, ed. Anders Eriksson, Thomas H. Olbricht, and Walter Übelacker (ESEC 8; Harrisburg: Trinity, 2002), 27–65.

Instead, early Christians use Hellenistic-Roman rhetoric at a progymnastic rather than oratorical level.

Soon after my sabbatical time at the Institute for Antiquity and Christianity, I joined Burton L. Mack for an initial SRI application to the Synoptic Gospels of insights from the *Progymnasmata* and co-authored with him *Patterns of Persuasion in the Gospels*.[32] By 1995, I began to envision the reconfiguration of rhetorical analysis, interpretation, and commentary into an interpretive analytics that could move us forward into a new era of rhetorical interpretation of biblical and extrabiblical literature.[33] The publication in 1996 of *The Tapestry of Early Christian Discourse* and *Exploring the Texture of Texts* created the "textural" environment for moving us ahead.[34] By 2003, a number of scholars were contributing substantively to the project, and ideological texture was attracting special interest among some of them as an interpretive analytical environment for moving the project into new arenas of interpretation.[35]

Real and Imagined Locations for Emerging Progymnastic Christian Rhetoric: Merging Social Science with Cognitive Science to Interpret Rhetorolects

When it becomes clear that the earliest Christians are not creating their discourse in the environment of city-state courtrooms, political assemblies, and civil ceremonies, the question is where the locations

---

32. Burton L. Mack and Vernon K. Robbins, *Patterns of Persuasion in the Gospels* (FFLF; Sonoma: Polebridge, 1989; repr. Eugene: Wipf & Stock, 2008).

33. Vernon K. Robbins, "The Present and Future of Rhetorical Analysis," in *The Rhetorical Analysis of Scripture: Essays from the 1995 London Conference*, ed. Stanley E. Porter and Thomas H. Olbricht (JSNTSup 146; Sheffield: Sheffield Academic, 1997), 24–52; idem, *The Tapestry of Early Christian Discourse*, 1–43.

34. Robbins, *The Tapestry of Early Christian Discourse*; idem, *Exploring the Texture of Texts*; idem, "Socio-Rhetorical Criticism," 342–46.

35. Gowler, Bloomquist, and Watson, *Fabrics of Discourse*, 34–35, 64–125, 165–221, 242–80, 317–32.

of reasoning were for the early Christians for the development of their rhetoric. Focusing on "locations of reasoning" leads an interpreter beyond the social sciences into the cognitive sciences.

It becomes obvious that the rhetorical culture of emerging first-century Christianity is primarily progymnastic. So, I had to make a decision. Should I move forward in time to second- through fourth-century Christianity when oratorical rhetorical culture becomes prominent, as Averil Cameron shows as early as her Sather lectures in 1985–86 and Margaret M. Mitchell has so beautifully followed?[36] Or, should I stay with the progymnastic rhetoric of first-century emerging Christianity in the New Testament and figure out how to develop progymnastic forms of analysis and interpretation of this discourse? I decided to try to work out the progymnastic rhetoric of first-century CE emerging Christian writing and work from there into the succeeding centuries.

The first stream of influence comes from the social location of the implied author, cognitive geography theory, and critical spatiality theory. The initial step is the concept of the social location of the "implied author," since this location leads to the conceptual location of the "rhetoric" in the writing.[37] The next step is reading the insights from the Constructs of the Social and Cultural Worlds of Antiquity Group to understand conceptual location with special help from Jon L. Berquist and Claudia V. Camp in particular.[38] From the broader

36. Averil Cameron, *Christianity and the Rhetoric of Empire* (SCL 55; Berkeley: University of California Press, 1991); Margaret M. Mitchell, *The Heavenly Trumpet: John Chrysostom and the Art of Pauline Interpretation* (HUT 40; Tübingen: Mohr Siebeck, 2000).

37. Vernon K. Robbins, "The Social Location of the Implied Author of Luke-Acts," in *The Social World of Luke-Acts: Models for Interpretation*, ed. Jerome H. Neyrey (Peabody: Hendrickson, 1991), 305–32; Jerome H. Neyrey, "The Social Location of Paul: Education as the Key," in Gowler, Bloomquist, and Watson, *Fabrics of Discourse*, 126–64.

38. Jon L. Berquist, "Critical Spatiality and the Construction of the Ancient World," in *'Imagining' Biblical Worlds: Studies in Spatial, Social and Historical Constructs in Honor of James W. Flanagan*, ed. David M. Gunn and Paula M. McNutt (JSOTSup 359; Sheffield: Sheffield Academic, 2002), 14–29; Claudia V. Camp, "Storied Space, or, Ben Sira 'Tells' a Temple," in Gunn and

scholarly environment come applications of "cognitive geography" and "spatial location" to specific New Testament writings to help us develop strategies of analysis and interpretation.[39] Then, specific incorporation of insights from critical spatiality and cognitive geography comes into SRI.[40]

The second stream of influence comes from conceptual metaphor and conceptual blending/integration theory. The publication in 2002 of *The Way We Think* by Gilles Fauconnier and Mark Turner serves as a milestone for the Rhetoric of Religious Antiquity Research Group to begin the task of explicitly incorporating the cognitive sciences into SRI.[41] The integration of conceptual metaphor theory into rhetorical analysis and interpretation provides a bridge for further developments.[42] After this comes the initial definition of rhetorolects with the aid of critical spatiality and conceptual/blending theory.[43] Since then, Robert von Thaden, Jr., has produced a series of specific SRI applications of conceptual integration/blending theory to New

McNutt, *'Imagining' Biblical Worlds*, 64–80; Robbins, "Conceptual Blending and Early Christian Imagination," 163–64; idem, *Invention*, 14–16, 88–90; idem, "Socio-Rhetorical Interpretation," 199–200.

39. Robbins, "Luke-Acts," 202–21; idem, *Sea Voyages*, 109–113; Loveday Alexander, "Narrative Maps: Reflections on the Toponomy of Acts," in *The Bible in Human Society: Essays in Honour of John Rogerson*, ed. M. D. Carroll et al. (JSOTSup 200; Sheffield: Sheffield Academic, 1995), 15–57; idem, "Mapping Early Christianity: Acts and the Shape of Early Church History," *Int* 57 (2001): 163–73.

40. Robbins, "Bodies and Politics in Luke 1–2 and Sirach 44–50: Men, Women, and Boys," *Scriptura* 90 (2005): 724–838; idem, *Invention*, 88–90; Bart B. Bruehler, "From This Place: A Theoretical Framework for the Social-Spatial Analysis of Luke," in idem, *A Public and Political Christ: The Social-Spatial Characteristics of Luke 18:35-19:43 and the Gospel as a Whole in Its Ancient Context* (PTMS; Eugene: Pickwick, 2011), 31–54.

41. Gilles Fauconnier and Mark Turner, *The Way We Think: Conceptual Blending and the Mind's Hidden Complexities* (New York: Basic, 2002).

42. Lynn R. Huber, "KNOWING IS SEEING: Ancient, Medieval, and Modern Theories of Metaphor," in idem, *Like a Bride Adorned: Reading Metaphor in John's Apocalypse* (ESEC 10; New York: T&T Clark, 2007), 45–88.

43. Robbins, "Conceptual Blending and Early Christian Imagination," 161–95; Robert von Thaden, Jr., "A Cognitive Turn: Conceptual Blending within a Socio-Rhetorical Framework," in idem, *Sex, Christ, and Embodied Cognition: Paul's Wisdom for Corinth* (ESEC 16; Blandford Forum: Deo, 2012), 37–75.

Testament texts.[44] Also, supportive work is emerging from interpreters of the Hebrew Bible.[45]

A result of the use of insights from the social location of implied authors, cultural geography, critical spatiality theory, conceptual metaphor theory, and conceptual integration/blending theory is the emergence of robust socio-rhetorical analysis and interpretation of six first-century Christian rhetorolects that include wisdom, prophetic, apocalyptic, precreation, miracle, and priestly.[46] In other words, interpretation of rhetorolects from their introduction in 1996 and their further definition at the Lund conference in 2000 begin to take full form in 2005 in the context of critical spatiality theory and conceptual integration/blending theory.[47] This development leads to a distinction between rhetography and rhetology as well the development of a form of commentary that emphasizes the rhetography and rhetorical force of a text.

44. Von Thaden, *Sex, Christ, and Embodied Cognition*, 159–301; idem, "Pauline Rhetorical Invention: Seeing 1 Corinthians 6:12–7:7 through Conceptual Integration Theory," in *Cognitive Linguistic Explorations in Biblical Studies*, ed. Bonnie G. Howe and Joel B. Green (Cognitive Studies of Sacred Texts; Berlin: de Gruyter, 2014), 101–21; idem, "Bad Children, Children as Bad: Problematic Children from Proverbs to *Acts of Thomas* and Beyond," *Proceedings: Eastern Great Lakes and Midwestern Biblical Societies* 28 (2008): 67–75; idem, "Guiding Socio-Rhetorical Commentary with Conceptual Integration Theory (Blending Theory)," *Conversations with the Biblical World: Proceedings of the Eastern Great Lakes Biblical Society and Midwest Region Society of Biblical Literature* 31 (2011): 184–203; idem, "The Power of Pictures: Sex and Embodied Temples," *Conversations with the Biblical World: Proceedings of the Eastern Great Lakes Biblical Society & Midwest Region Society of Biblical Literature* 32 (2012), 109–26.

45. P. van Hecke, "Conceptual Blending: A Recent Approach to Metaphor Illustrated with the Pastoral Metaphor in Hos 4,16," in *Metaphor in the Hebrew Bible*, ed. idem (BETL 187; Leuven: University and Dudley: Peeters, 2005), 215–32.

46. Greg Carey and L. Gregory Bloomquist, eds., *Vision and Persuasion: Rhetorical Dimensions of Apocalyptic Discourse* (St. Louis: Chalice, 1999); Duane F. Watson, ed., *The Intertexture of Apocalyptic Discourse in the New Testament* (SBLSS 14; Atlanta: SBL, 2002); *R&T* 18 nos. 3–4 (2011): passim; Duane F. Watson, ed., *Miracle Discourse in the New Testament* (Atlanta: SBL, 2012); Robbins, *Invention*, 121–482; von Thaden, *Sex, Christ, and Embodied Cognition*, 76–292.

47. For the introduction of rhetorolects, see Robbins, "The Dialectical Nature of Early Christian Discourse," 353–62. For their further definition, see idem, "Argumentative Textures in Socio-Rhetorical Interpretation," 27–65. For their full form, see idem, "Conceptual Blending and Early Christian Imagination," 161–95.

Commentary Informed by Rhetography and Rhetorical Force

The road from my earliest formulation of rhetorolects to the beginnings of their robust analysis and interpretation was first informed by a study of enthymemes.[48] I had been encouraged to pursue analysis and interpretation of enthymemes by George A. Kennedy's discussion of them in his *New Testament Interpretation through Rhetorical Criticism*, which I have used regularly in my PhD seminars at Emory University.[49] By the time of the Lund Rhetoric Conference in 2000, my exploration of enthymemes had led to an initial display and interpretation of texts to describe six rhetorolects, which I named wisdom, miracle, prophetic, suffering-death, apocalyptic, and pre-creation.[50] After a brief period of time following the conference, the suffering-death rhetorolect became priestly rhetorolect.[51] Alongside this activity, I was developing analysis and interpretation of enthymemes in the Coptic Gospel of Thomas in the context of the SBL Thomasine Group as early as 1998.[52] In this context, I became aware that "picturing in the mind" is a very important phenomenon in interpretation of the enthymemes in Thomas.[53] By 2006, this insight develops into a full-scale thesis about a distinction between rhetology, namely rhetoric that produces

---

48. Idem, "From Enthymeme to Theology in Luke 11:1–13," in *Literary Studies in Luke-Acts: A Collection of Essays in Honor of Joseph B. Tyson*, ed. Richard P. Thompson and Thomas E. Phillips (Macon: Mercer University Press, 1998), 191–214; repr. in idem, *Sea Voyages*, 349–71.

49. George A. Kennedy, *New Testament Interpretation through Rhetorical Criticism* (Chapel Hill: University of North Carolina Press, 1984), 16–17, 48–61, and passim.

50. Robbins, "Argumentative Textures in Socio-Rhetorical Interpretation," 27–65.

51. For priestly rhetorolect, see Vernon K. Robbins and Jonathan M. Potter, eds., *Jesus and Mary Reimagined in Early Christian Literature* (WGRWSupp 6; Atlanta: SBL Press, 2014).

52. Idem, "Enthymemic Texture in the Gospel of Thomas," in *Society of Biblical Literature 1998 Seminar Papers* 37 (1998): 343–66.

53. Idem, "Enthymeme and Picture in the Gospel of Thomas," in *Thomasine Traditions in Antiquity: The Social and Cultural World of the Gospel of Thomas*, ed. Jon Ma. Asgeirsson, April D. DeConick, and Risto Uro (NHMS 59; Leiden: Brill, 2006), 175–207.

argumentation, and rhetography, namely rhetoric that evokes graphic images and pictures in the mind.[54]

Following my introduction of the terminology of rhetography, some members of the SBL Rhetoric of Religious Antiquity Group begin to produce essays using the approach. Roy R. Jeal led the way with a series of essays featuring analysis and interpretation of rhetography in texts.[55] David A. deSilva, Robert L. Webb, and Terrance Callan published initial essays featuring analysis and interpretation of rhetography in texts.[56] A wonderful contribution to analysis and interpretation of rhetography in New Testament texts appeared in books by Brigitte Kahl and Davina Lopez,[57] and stunning

---

54. Idem, "Rhetography: A New Way of Seeing the Familiar Text," in *Words Well Spoken: George Kennedy's Rhetoric of the New Testament*, ed. C. Clifton Black and Duane F. Watson (SRR 8; Waco: Baylor University Press, 2008), 81–106. This essay elaborates the concepts of rhetography and rhetorolect on the basis of the concept of "radical Christian rhetoric" in Kennedy, *New Testament Interpretation through Rhetorical Criticism*, 7, 93, 96, 104–6, 113, 159.

55. Roy R. Jeal, "Melody, Imagery and Memory in the Moral Persuasion of Paul," in *Rhetoric, Ethic and Moral Persuasion in Biblical Discourse*, ed. Anders Eriksson and Thomas H. Olbricht (New York: T&T Clark, 2005), 160–78; idem, "Clothes Make the (Wo)Man" *Scriptura* 90 (2005): 685–99; idem, "Seeing Images in Visible Words: Rhetography in Colossians" (paper presented to the Rhetoric of Religious Antiquity Seminar, Society of Biblical Literature Annual Meeting, Washington, 2006), http://www.boothuc.ca/sites/default/files/seeingimagesinvisible wordsnov2006.pdf (accessed 17 August 2014); idem, "Blending Two Arts: Rhetorical Words, Rhetorical Pictures and Social Formation in the Letter to Philemon," *Sino-Christian Studies* 5 (2008): 9–38; idem, "Visions of Marriage in Ephesians 5," in *Human Sexuality and the Nuptial Mystery*, ed. Roy R. Jeal (Eugene: Cascade, 2010), 116–30; idem, "Emerging Christian Discourse: The *Acts of Pilate* as the Rhetorical Development of Devotion," *Apocrypha* 21 (2010): 151–67.

56. David A. deSilva, "Seeing Things John's Way: Rhetography and Conceptual Blending in Revelation 14:6–13," *BBR* 18 no. 2 (2008): 271–98; Robert L. Webb, "The Rhetorical Function of Visual Imagery in Jude: A Socio-Rhetorical Experiment in Rhetography," in *Reading Jude with New Eyes: Methodological Reassessments of the Letter of Jude*, ed. Robert L. Webb and Peter H. Davids (London: T&T Clark, 2008), 109–35; Terrance Callan, "Rhetography and Rhetology of Apocalyptic Discourse in Second Peter," in *Reading Second Peter with New Eyes: Methodological Reassessments of the Second Letter of Peter*, ed. Robert L. Webb and Duane F. Watson (LNTS 382; London: T&T Clark, 2008), 59–90.

57. Brigitte Kahl, *Galatians Re-Imagined: Reading with the Eyes of the Vanquished* (Paul in Critical Contexts; Minneapolis: Fortress, 2010), passim; see the review by Vernon K. Robbins, http://www.bookreviews.org/bookdetail.asp?TitleId=7438 (accessed 17 August 2014); Davina Lopez, *Apostle to the Conquered: Reimagining Paul's Mission* (Minneapolis: Fortress, 2010), passim.

contributions are being made by Harry O. Maier and Rosemary Canavan.[58] In addition, there is growing literature on pictorial interpretation in both the New Testament and the Hebrew Bible.[59] The Mellon Sawyer Seminars at Emory University during academic year 2013-14[60] created a context for joining forces with Walter S. Melion, who has been producing works on Visual Exegesis of biblical texts through Christian art for a number of decades.[61] In the context of this ongoing research and publication, members of the Rhetoric

58. Harry O. Maier, "A Sly Civility: Colossians and Empire," *JSNT* 27 (2005): 323–40; idem, "Barbarians, Scythians and Imperial Iconography in the Epistle to the Colossians," in *Picturing the New Testament: Studies in Ancient Visual Images*, ed. Annette Weissenrieder, Friedericke Wendt, and Petra von Gemünden (WUNT 2.193; Tübingen: Mohr Siebeck, 2005), 385–406; idem, "Reading Colossians in the Ruins," in *Colossae in Space and Time: Linking to an Ancient City*, ed. Alan H. Cadwallader and Michael Trainor; (NTOA 94; Göttingen: Vandenhoeck & Ruprecht, 2011), 212–31; idem, *Picturing Paul in Empire: Imperial Image, Text and Persuasion in Colossians, Ephesians and the Pastoral Epistles* (London: T&T Clark/Bloomsbury, 2013); Rosemary Canavan, *Clothing the Body of Christ at Colossae: A Visual Construction of Identity* (WUNT 2.334; Tübingen: Mohr Siebeck, 2012), passim.

59. John Dominic Crossan and Jonathan L. Reed, *In Search of Paul: How Jesus' Apostle Opposed Rome's Empire with God's Kingdom* (San Francisco: HarperOne, 2004), passim; Neil Elliott and Mark Reasoner, *Documents and Images for the Study of Paul* (Minneapolis: Fortress, 2011), passim; Izaak J. de Hulster, *Iconographic Exegesis and Third Isaiah* (FAT 2.26; Tübingen: Mohr Siebeck, 2009), passim; Annang Asumang, "The Presence of the Shepherd: A Rhetgraphic Exegesis of Psalm 23," *Conspectus* 9 (2010): 1–23; Joel M. LeMon, *Yahweh's Winged Form in the Psalms: Exploring Congruent Iconography and Texts* (OBO; Göttingen: Vandenhoeck & Ruprecht, 2010), passim; Izaak J. de Hulster and Joel M. LeMon, *Image, Text, Exegesis: Iconographic Interpretation and the Hebrew Bible* (LHB/OTS; London: T&T Clark/Bloomsbury, 2014); Ryan Bonfiglio, "Archer Imagery in Zechariah 9:11–17 in Light of Achaemenid Iconography," *JBL* 131 (2012): 507–27.

60. "Mellon Foundation Sawyer Seminar Program: Visual Exegesis: Images as Instruments of Scriptural Interpretation and Hermeneutics," http://arthistory.emory.edu/home/assets/documents/lectures/sawyer_seminar/sawyer_ broadsheet_4-23-14.pdf (accessed 17 August 2014).

61. Jerome Nadal, *Annotations and Meditations on the Gospels*, ed. and trans. Frederick A. Homann (3 vols.; Philadelphia: Saint Joseph's University Press, 2003–2005), passim; Walter S. Melion, "Introductory Study," in Nadal, *Annotations and Meditations on the Gospels, Volume III: The Resurrection Narratives*, 1–32; idem, "Exegesis," in James Clifton and Walter S. Melion, *Scripture for the Eyes: Bible Illustration in Netherlandish Prints of the Sixteenth Century* (New York: Museum of Biblical Art, 2009), 124–41; Karl A. E. Enenkel and Walter Melion, eds., *Meditatio—Refashioning the Self: Theory and Practice in Late Medieval and Early Modern Intellectual Culture* (Intersections 17; Leiden: Brill, 2011), passim; James Clifton, Walter S. Melion, and Walter Weemans, eds., *Imago Exegetica: Visual Images as Exegetical Instruments, 1400-1700* (Leiden: Brill, 2014), passim.

of Religious Antiquity Group are producing full-scale commentaries with a sequential interpretive analytical format of Rhetography, Textural Interpretation (inner texture, intertexture, social-cultural texture, ideological texture, sacred texture), and Rhetorical Force as Emergent Discourse.[62]

Conclusion

When I introduced socio-rhetorical interpretation to the field of New Testament studies in 1984, I had no idea it would move beyond use of the social sciences into various branches of the cognitive sciences for analysis and interpretation of texts. For at least a decade, I championed the three forms of classical rhetoric in New Testament writings and argued along with George Kennedy that judicial, deliberative, and epideictic rhetoric were universal rhetorical categories that could apply to any text in any human society.

During the 1980s and 90s, I was guided by the *Progymnasmata* and gradually began to see that the dominant locations for first-century Christian rhetoric were not the courtroom, political assembly, and civil ceremony. Rather, Christian rhetoric emerged from real and imagined locations in households, market-places, synagogues and temple, contexts of healing, imperial displays of apocalyptic pronouncement, and prophetic confrontation in their concept of a kingdom they considered to be allied with God's power. The challenge of developing an understanding of first-century emerging Christian rhetoric was huge, and still is. Nevertheless, many fellow scholars have been contributing in one way or another to the challenge.

The problem, of course, is that the most natural inclination of scholars is to follow literary-historical modes of analysis and

---

62. Robbins, "Socio-Rhetorical Interpretation," 203–7.

interpretation that developed robustly during the nineteenth and twentieth centuries and still are vibrantly flourishing. The challenge now is to develop environments of research, analysis, and interpretation that merge the remarkable insights that have been, and still are, being gained by literary-historical methods with socio-rhetorical strategies of analysis and interpretation. This merger can lead us courageously forward with new insights about how texts participate in historical, social, cultural, ideological, and visual material culture. These cultures may be both religious and extra-religious from our perspective, but all of these cultures contribute to the meanings and meaning effects in our texts. Fortunately, we have many new "sciences" to help us as well as a new appreciation of visual material culture and ever-evolving strategies and techniques for bringing these new resources into environments of textual interpretation.

11

Of Mappings and Men (and Women): Reflections on Rhetorical Genealogies

Todd Penner and Davina C. Lopez

"What a useful thing a pocket-map is!" I remarked.

"That's another thing we've learned from your Nation," said Mein Herr, "map-making. But we've carried it much further than *you*. What do you consider the *largest* map that would be really useful?"

"About six inches to the mile."

"Only *six inches*!" exclaimed Mein Herr. "We very soon got to six *yards* to the mile. Then we tried a *hundred* yards to the mile. And then came the grandest idea of all! We actually made a map of the country, on the scale of *a mile to the mile!*"

"Have you used it much?" I enquired.

"It has never been spread out, yet," said Mein Herr: "The farmers object: they said it would cover the whole country, and shut out the sunlight! So we now use the country itself, as its own map, and I assure you it does nearly as well."

– Lewis Carroll, *Sylvie and Bruno Concluded*

Maps and mapmaking have always been with us.[1] Whether one draws the maps out on paper or gazes at the stars to determine direction or, for that matter, whether one deploys a genealogy to delineate the contours of the past, the need for a guide—a marking tool—has been essential to human experience. Guides are key elements not only in human survival but also in expressing the human imagination of what lies beyond the current location—the wonders, the territories, the empty black holes, and also the pasts of which we still desire to be a part. Every aspect of human knowledge and cultural production, in one sense or another, relies on mapping terrains of one sort or another. While the opening citation from Lewis Carroll pokes fun at the German character "Mein Herr" for his country's obsession with one-to-one correspondence in representation, we note that, in many ways, human mapmaking endeavors have generally sought to represent as accurately, or at least as fully as possible the terrain being mapped, some more successfully than others, of course. We may find the implied jabs at "Mein Herr" amusing, and certainly there is a point regarding the achievable limitation of representation. However, we should also recognize the value in the very desire to reach the unattainable—to reach for the stars, so to speak.

As we consider the essays in the present volume, we note that one way to frame the encounter with the differing titans, even stars, in the study of rhetorical criticism of New Testament and early Christian literatures and discourses is as an engagement with quintessential mapmakers. Hans Dieter Betz, George Kennedy, Wilhelm Wuellner, Elisabeth Schüssler Fiorenza, and Vernon K. Robbins, along with

---

1. The authors would like to express their immense gratitude to Troy W. Martin for his thoughtful and engaging feedback on this essay as well as his keen attention to detail. Moreover, his patience throughout the editing process has been enormously appreciated. Special thanks also are due to Neil Elliott, with whom we have had much critical and jovial conversation about rhetorical criticism of the New Testament that underlie many of the observations we make here.

their representatives and interlocutors, offer a rich and varied series of representations of rhetorical form, practice, and performance as applied to ancient texts and, in some cases, also to the modern reception and deployment of the same. While it might be stretching the metaphor to suggest that all of the main contributors in this volume are mapmakers in the same way and to the same degree, we can say that all of them are invested in providing a guiding framework on how to think about rhetoric in and of the Bible. Students of the New Testament and early Christian literature are in deep debt to these scholars, in large and small ways, sometimes knowingly and at other times unwittingly.

We also add, further, that taken together as a series of interactions, the essays and responses in this volume speak to a rich and exciting history of scholarly engagement and offer a map, of sorts, to the vast terrain shaped by the rhetorical approaches that have gained traction over nearly half a century of New Testament scholarship. In other words, the volume itself offers something of a guide to a fairly diverse rhetorical terrain. For certain, the editor of this collection, Troy W. Martin, to whom we owe a great debt for imagining this project and then organizing it, is no "Mein Herr." It is clear that this book is not intended to be a complete and total representation of the rhetorical landscape. Rather, this collection focuses on key topographical highlights that have, at a minimum, provided the contours to the broader lay of the land. Thus, we have, in some sense, a mapmaking project on rhetoric that involves the mapmakers themselves, and a grand idea and achievement that is. Better yet, the overarching metaphor for the mapmaking enterprise in this volume is "genealogy," a map to be sure, but definitely one of a different kind.

Genealogies pull us into our past and show us where we have come from and how things and people are connected, whether real, fictional, or a combination of both. They also function to point us toward a future. We are interested in where we have come from largely because we want to know where we are in our present and where we might go in our future. Indeed, genealogies as represented here help readers and interpreters find their way through what can, at times, seem like a bewildering maze of claims, methods, and exegetical strategies, all termed "rhetorical criticism." In this respect, beyond cataloging the individually rich and collectively substantial contributions of these particular interpreters (and, to some extent, their progeny), this volume makes an exceptional contribution to the intellectual history of an important complex of methods and approaches in New Testament studies, as well as biblical scholarship more broadly conceived.

At the present moment, it might seem as though rhetoric is a "natural" method to engage in the study of the New Testament and early Christian literature. For most of the field's modern history, however, this "natural" link between the study of the arts of persuasion and the literature of early Christianity has not been the case. The spirit of this volume lies in its effort to fill in the intellectual history of a robust area of inquiry. By examining the genealogies of rhetorical criticism in this volume, we can, and should, learn much about where we come from and where and how we fit within this scholarly method. In this respect, the scholars herein expound both individual mappings of particular rhetorical approaches and trajectories and, collectively, a larger map of rhetorical criticism of the New Testament as a whole. It is evident from reading these essays that rhetorical criticism is not something univocal, but rather is quite complex. In other words, the genealogies described herein do not produce a tightly woven, integrated system. Rather, the essay points us to the intricacies of our rhetorical pasts, presents, and futures.

Pushing further, we can ask what this genealogical map offers us not only in terms of how we assess and value rhetorical analysis and practice in the present but also in terms of how we might use these essays to think about alternative future rhetorical prospects and possibilities. It is this latter point that we seek to explore in the remaining part of this essay. The essays in this volume offer us compelling places from which to think and materials with which to engage. These contributions seek to explain the specifics of particular approaches to and frameworks of rhetorical analysis of the New Testament. In our view, these essays also offer a number of live and lively, unsettled and unsettling issues in the study of the New Testament and early Christian literature. They describe the various strands and threads comprising the complex of analytical and exegetical approaches called "rhetorical criticism," but also prompt us to consider how we aim to conduct New Testament studies and perhaps indeed all of biblical scholarship more generally. Such a discussion may prove useful for how we conceptualize mapmaking and genealogical formations in future discussions of the field. In our view, these discussions should include, at least in part, a criticism of the rhetorics of New Testament studies, including rhetorical criticism itself.

Genealogies of Rhetoric and Rhetorics of Genealogy

In terms of thinking about rhetorical criticism more broadly and with respect to the field as a whole, one obvious place to begin regarding these essays is the concept of genealogy as a descriptor and guiding principle. Despite the immediate benefits of this manner of mapping rhetorical criticism as method, there is also a clear and present challenge with respect to deploying *genealogy* as a classificatory rubric under which these various fathers and mother and their progeny might be located and sorted. To be sure, some practitioners of rhetorical-critical approaches may eschew the tidiness and connotations of linear progression of the very concept of "family ties" or "bloodlines" and note that a formidable strength and potential of rhetoric lies in its messiness, its pervasiveness, its native diversity of origins and forms and effects, and its capacity to disrupt so-called dominant modes of doing biblical scholarship.[2] However, we submit that genealogy, as a chosen organizing principle and strategy for this volume, may be, in this case, a rhetorically apt, if multivalent, descriptor for several reasons highlighted below.

It may be tempting for some readers and interpreters to take at face value the articulation of a genealogy of rhetorical criticism of the New Testament as a neatly arranged series of ancestors and *begets,* with a clear beginning and trajectory and boundaries that reify a sense of linearity and certainty as to "the way we got here." This approach is not the point of the current volume, of course. Nevertheless, we understand that genealogy as narrative, as family tree, and/or as statement of origins is attractive. Its very utterance offers a detectable air of knowing, of authority, of hierarchy, of finality, and of truth.[3] In being given an orderly account of the way things happened that names and places the various actors, one senses that in such an account we are receiving the whole story or at least all that there is to say on the issue at hand—even if authors such as the ones represented in this volume do not intend to communicate such a program. We might even say that genealogies tend to be accepted as documentarian in nature, singular in content, and developmental in outlook. They organize relationships between how things began,

---

2. For example, see J. David Hester (Amador), "The Wuellnerian Sublime: Rhetorics, Power, and the Ethics of Commun(icat)ion," in *Rhetorics and Hermeneutics: Wilhelm Wuellner and His Influence,* ed. James D. Hester and J. David Hester (Amador) (ESEC 9; New York: T&T Clark, 2004), 5. See also the contribution of James D. Hester and J. David Hester to the present volume.

3. For a reflection on the powerful pull of "genealogy" and its concomitant linear focus in the field of New Testament studies and in text criticism in particular, see Todd Penner, "'In the Beginning': Post-Critical Reflections on Early Christian Textual Transmission and Modern Textual Transgression," *PRSt* 33 (2006): 415–34.

how they are, and how they might be. Thus, genealogies serve as an important means of mapping the past and indeed, as we noted earlier, serve as charts in and of themselves.

We take it, then, that genealogies of rhetorical criticism of the New Testament, as represented in this volume, could signify for some readers a coherent and comprehensive map of or guide to this particular methodological orientation in the field. This volume attempts to self-consciously represent a series of genealogies and not a single, overarching interpretive schema. Nevertheless, rhetorical criticism is more complex and multivocal than this volume can capture, and we submit that one possible rhetorical effect of the particular classificatory designation "genealogy" already determines to some extent how this material, the representative and seminal figures, and the whole project of rhetorical criticism could be understood.

We can imagine, for example, an emergent scholar picking up this essay collection and hoping, based solely on what the title could be thought to promise—genealogies as family trees, as documentation of lineages, as explanation of origins and logic—that she or he will find a logically presented, cogent, and obvious map to the discipline, not to mention, perhaps, a "how-to" guide should one wish to identify as one of the offspring (even if grafted on) of these various family trees. We understand and empathize with this desire. Genealogies make such identification more expedient. Such discourse is not a new development of course. Scholars of an earlier era may have felt a similar need to declare allegiance with certain methods and practices, although then there were different types. For better or for worse, part of the guilding process in our current era involves the adoption of particular mimetic performances that aim to communicate how one becomes part of the various families or "tribes" that make up the larger "tent" housing our academic discipline.[4] In thinking ahead to the future of rhetorical practice and performance, therefore, we offer some words of caution.

Becoming a biblical scholar involves putting on the clothes, so to speak, of a group with which one desires to feel at "home." This principle is true whether the "clothes" are designated by identity politics or social location, "traditional" or "postmodern" methods, theological proclivities or church affiliation, or even the purported absence of the "theological" in favor of "religious studies." "Home" in this case can signify approximations of sameness, familiarity, and comfort. In the intellectual and physical spaces wherein one feels a sense of familial likeness and belonging, the rules of the house apply. Parents might bestow or revoke various forms of approval, including the so-called "birthright." Siblings might instigate and perpetuate rivalries. Other families and houses might bestow longstanding collaborations and conflicts onto their sons and daughters and heirs. When one becomes part of the family, one inherits the prestige, as well as the baggage. We make sense of the guild and our place in it through participating in mapping projects such as these. What is at stake in such inclinations toward "homeliness" as methodological orientation is rarely discussed, much less interrogated.[5] This volume offers us the chance to think more broadly about these larger issues.

When we are hailed into being through genealogical questions such as those articulated above, we tend to respond with language that reflects a family story of some kind, that helps to map this story, and that in the process locates us within the boundaries established by that map. If these essays are read structurally as representing the

---

4. On "tribes" as an organizational principle in the formation of biblical scholars(hip), see Vincent L. Wimbush, "Interpreters: Enslaving/Enslaved/Runagate," *JBL* 130, no. 1 (2011): 5–24.

5. For an exploration of homeliness and homelessness as metaphor for methodological identification in New Testament studies, see Todd Penner and Davina C. Lopez, "Homelessness as a Way Home? A Methodological Reflection and Proposal," in *Holy Land as Homeland? Models for Constructing the Historic Landscapes of Jesus*, ed. K. Whitelam (SWBA 2nd ser. 7; Sheffield: Sheffield Phoenix Academic, 2011), 180–203.

only options and trajectories available for rhetorical criticism rather than as contributing to a much larger conversation across time and disciplinary orientations, then this volume becomes a rather rigid and turgid map, which very much goes against the intention of this collection. To identify with a particular method—be it called rhetorical criticism, feminist or postcolonial criticism, historical or cultural criticism, Marxist or ideological criticism—and the list goes on, for the contemporary landscape is vast—is at once to identify with a present *and* a past. Given the professional habitat or *habitus* in which we find ourselves, it is easy to appreciate how genealogy, as ordering principle and structuring logic, might reflect and generate much resonance with scholars. Aside from providing an easy linear guide to familial history, articulations of genealogy also invite us in the present to imagine and insert ourselves into grand historical narratives and to find, as it were, our illustrious forefathers and foremothers, to "remember" a distinctive past of which we assume we are heirs.

Genealogy, then, has a tendency to function as a stabilizing and even *domesticating* strategy in biblical scholarship by rendering its practitioners as part of the *domus,* the "home." Presumably this tendency is the case in rhetorical criticism as well, although we note again that the present volume hopes to avoid precisely this strategy. Rather than make visible the enormous complexity and diversity and even randomness inherent in the approaches we adopt in studying our material, choosing to use genealogy as a way to organize our scholarly selves and work *might* serve the purpose of convincing us that disparate elements actually have a familial relationship with one another, designate an origin point, and narrate development and hierarchy across time and space.

A maxim of the study of rhetoric, as the study of language, is that words do not necessarily reflect reality as such, but are used to create, categorize, classify, order, and reify reality through their utterances and representations. Genealogies as discursive forms are similarly used. As rhetorical devices, genealogies can be used to impose an "order of things" that can, in turn, serve as a means to create a particular reality.[6] As discourse, then, genealogies can be used to instill a sense of order that is always and already thought to be present. The hidden yet ever-present nature of order provides the coherence and stability that is so critical for New Testament scholarship today. Despite recent shifts occasioned in no small part by the dissemination of critical perspectives concerning "order," this scholarship remains largely invested in the supposed inherent logic and meaning of early Christian literature. If this concern is generally true of New Testament scholarship, it is also the case with rhetorical-critical practices. The lure of *method*, especially one endowed with a prestigious *lineage*, can beguile the interpreter into using those practices in ways that stabilize and reify that order rather than raising questions about it and provoking further reflection and innovation that might lead to imagining differing rhetorical projects in the future. It is the latter purpose that this volume stimulates for us. This purpose is where our particular interests lie in these questions and innovations, which will concern us for the remainder of this essay.

Genealogy as Rhetoric

Given what we have been outlining above in terms of the rhetorical contours of genealogy, this project has encouraged us to consider how it could be the case that writing and mapping genealogies of

---

6. In this respect, Michel Foucault designates that order "is at one and the same time, that which is given in things as their inner law, the hidden network that determines the way they confront one another, and also that which has no existence except in the grid created by a glance, an examination, a language; and it is only in the blank spaces of this grid that order manifests itself in depth as though already there, waiting in silence for the moment of its expression." It is this hidden, and not-so-hidden, nature of order and ordering that concerns us here. See Foucault, *The Order of Things: An Archaeology of the Human Sciences* (New York: Vintage, 1970), xx.

rhetorical criticism are themselves a rhetorical enterprise. Almost all, if not all, of the contributors to this volume might attest that the category of genealogy, as with all rhetoric, has significant ideological dimensions worth exploring. Herein, we have the opportunity to use rhetorical-critical approaches to reflect critically on the rhetorical and ideological dimensions of rhetorical criticism itself. Some (socio-)rhetorical critics are ready and willing to develop new vocabularies and discourses to help invent, describe, and map the discourses we might ascribe to early Christians, their "world," their influences, and their legacies. These critics direct much less attention at *the rhetorics of rhetorical criticism*, however, not to mention what is actually at stake in circumscribing a complex of approaches to biblical scholarship under the single rubric *rhetorical criticism,* or how "rhetorical criticism" is located in space and time, or to what ends it might be deployed, for whom and what purpose such analysis is done, and what difference it makes to write ourselves into genealogical relationships such as these.[7] More importantly, we believe it is also necessary in this moment to reflect on the domesticating potential of rhetorical criticism and to exercise caution in what is at times our all-too-ready appropriation and application of differing rhetorical-critical analytical systems.

Far from being final, whole, transparent, and universal, genealogy as a classificatory mode is not, if it ever were, plainly and unquestionably about the *linearity* of lineage or the image of a stable family in a totalizing fashion. Rhetorically, there are other possibilities. Michel Foucault observes the tension between genealogy as a means to construct a naturalized, totalizing, and

---

7. As a counter-example, see the Bible and Culture Collective, *The Postmodern Bible* (New Haven: Yale University Press, 1995), passim; and J. David Hester Amador, *Academic Constraints in Rhetorical Criticism of the New Testament: An Introduction to a Rhetorics of Power* (Library of New Testament Studies 174; New York: T&T Clark, 1999), passim.

universalizing narrative and genealogy as a conscious, particular rhetorical creation. According to Foucault, who is heavily influenced by Friedrich Nietzsche, genealogy must always be partial and incomplete *and consciously so*.[8] For his part, Nietzsche critiques the use of genealogy as a means of domesticating the past to justify and serve the present. His counter-proposal involves developing a means to use historical inquiry to interrogate the naturalness, givenness, and seeming inevitability of current common understandings, and, in his specific case, modern morality.[9] Where historians of his day find "truth," Nietzsche finds individual investments, biases, and storytelling *couched as* "truth." Therein, it is possible to question what is taken for granted in the present by attempting to account for what, historically, may have contributed to the emergence of certain ideologies.

Extending Nietzsche's approach, Foucault suggests that genealogy itself could serve not solely as a means to create a totalizing narrative, but also as an analytical category in its own right. In other words, for Foucault, genealogy can function as a lens through which one might see beyond the appearance of truthfulness and totality of dominant ideologies toward the various power relationships inherent in the conditions that render such ideologies possible. Herein, a "genealogical criticism" contributes to a counter-narrative of knowledge, of history, and of the subject itself. It can be a powerful tool to historicize those ideas, discourses, and truths that are thought

---

8. Michel Foucault, "Nietzsche, Genealogy, History," in *Language, Counter-memory, Practice: Selected Essays and Interviews*, ed. Donald F. Bouchard (Ithaca: Cornell University Press, 1977), 139–64. We note at the outset of this discussion that *Foucault's* categorical claims about "genealogy" is not the way in which the contributors to this volume would understand their particular systems. Foucault is focusing on the totalizing nature of genealogical formulations. That said, we find aspects of his framework quite helpful for structuring this larger conversation.

9. See especially Friedrich Nietzsche, *On the Genealogy of Morals*, trans. W. Kaufmann (New York: Vintage, 1989), passim.

to be without or beyond history, especially when historians have effectively written the historical dimensions out of historical narratives.

Important for the present project, Foucault's reading and deployment of genealogy makes use of that concept to destabilize the universalizing tendencies of dominant ideological formations. He writes:

> The purpose of history, guided by genealogy, is not to discover the roots of our identity but to commit itself to its dissipation. It does not seek to define our unique threshold of emergence, the homeland to which metaphysicians promise a return; it seeks to make visible all of those discontinuities that cross us . . . if genealogy in its own right gives rise to questions concerning our native land, native language, or the laws that govern us, its intention is to reveal the heterogeneous systems which, masked by the self, inhibit the formation of any form of identity.[10]

Foucault proposes a movement away from genealogy as a reifying and/or domesticating strategy to genealogy as a mode of critique. Moreover, Foucault understands Nietzsche to be using history as a means to reveal the stories, identities, and discourses that are thought to be real, truthful, and universal as in fact nothing more than "masks." Genealogy, then, emerges as a guiding principle that challenges idealist and idealizing versions of history. It opposes the tendency to produce nostalgic reminiscences for a singular past, problematizes the idea that identity emerges from a continuous unbroken line of tradition with traceable origins, and challenges the notion that history, as written, constitutes a totalizing form of knowledge.

Genealogy also helps us position history as a human production in time and space, by noting that all historical narratives are written and produced by specific humans living in and shaped by specific

10. Foucault, "Nietzsche, Genealogy, History," 162.

historical circumstances and power relations. Of course, as Foucault notes elsewhere, such an approach results in a heterotopia, an unstable space where difference and otherness are affirmed, authoritarianism is challenged, and repression is escaped. Heterotopias are spaces that provide great contrast with the "consolation" and comfort of a utopia, which for Foucault represents the idealized space where society and its attendant hierarchies are reified. Heterotopias offer us the "disturbing" promise of disjunction and the impossibility to "name this *and* that," in this case narratives and counter-narratives, at the same time. Rather than producing fables and fantasies, a heterotopia offers us the cold comfort of "desiccated" speech.[11]

For Foucault, therefore, genealogy ultimately *ought to* function as a heuristic tool. It allows us to reveal "monumental history" as a mode of creating and stabilizing a singular past, composed of the "high points" and attendant actors to be venerated, and as a prevention of our actually seeing the messiness of human existence. This sort of history is "parodic," Foucault observes, because it beckons its subjects to adopt a costume in a grand masquerade.[12] Genealogy, as Foucault proposes its practice, should reveal that such re-dressing is but a means of choosing the past we desire out of multiple options and reifying this constructed past as natural, inevitable, and universal. Understood in this way, genealogy suggests that dominant forms of historical narratives offer a means of dressing plurality in the mask of singularity, of hiding the carnival of disparate and despairing masks under the rubric of family, of building a shelter to call home, and, perhaps most critically, of stabilizing ground that is anything but firm. Thus, "genealogies of rhetorical criticism," as we might encounter them through Foucault's conceptualization, can be seen as an effort to reveal that the history of New Testament studies

11. Foucault, *Order of Things*, xviii. Cf. Foucault, "Nietzsche, Genealogy, History," 378, 380–81.
12. Foucault, "Nietzsche, Genealogy, History," 161.

has *not* proceeded in a natural, universal, totalizing manner. The (re-)inscription of rhetorical criticism in all of its diversity into the history of the field as a whole can be a means of unmasking the field. When we use genealogy as a way to scratch the surface of our own genealogical offerings, therefore, we see that our dominant narratives about our own field (including the dominant narratives about "dominant scholarship" adopted by biblical scholars of all manner of social location) hide as much as they reveal.

We would thus warn against using the "genealogies" presented in this volume as a complete and universal map, corresponding (as did Mein Herr's map in our epigram) to the totality of options in rhetorical criticism today. Relying on Foucault's understanding of "genealogy" as an analytical method, we prefer to shift from thinking about "the way it was, is, and will be" to thinking about incomplete and partial ways of doing our own history, of understanding the past and the present of our discipline and its methods, of thinking with each other, and of thinking about the guild and the world.

The present volume, in our view, contributes greatly to this task. Such a move embedded therein involves us in alternative archaeologies of knowledge wherein we are seeking not the monuments under which we might seek shelter or the old costumes in which we might wrap ourselves but rather the projects in which we undo those comfortable ties. In so doing, we shift the focus from the writing of history and, in this volume, the history of rhetorical criticism, even as we recognize the value of that project within its own limits.

The sort of "rhetorical criticism" we have in mind incorporates critical engagement with the rhetoric of our field. Thus, we propose a further shift from the making of maps to asking questions about what it is we as biblical scholars think we are doing, what is at stake, and what difference it makes.[13] We better recognize that when we attempt to write history or to write ourselves into and onto it, we are always only writing the present. A more deliberate stance might seek not to excavate the original, pure, ideal past as an object of longing—ultimately a futile task, one holding potential for self-deception—but to respect the indeterminacy and complexity of the past and to accept our own responsibility for the ways we attempt to utilize it in the present.

Rhetorical Criticism: Imagining Selves and Others

In his public lecture series delivered in the early 1980s, Foucault articulates an important contrast between *parrhēsia* (often translated as "bold speech") and rhetoric. Based on his reading of ancient rhetorical theorists such as Quintilian and Cicero over against Greco-Roman moralists such as Seneca and Philodemus, Foucault defines *rhetoric* as that which focuses on the "game of the subject matter," and as that which organizes and structures the whole discursive form. In contrast, *parrhēsia* is not defined by the subject matter but is rather a "particular practice of true discourse defined by rules of prudence, skill, and the conditions that require one to say the truth at this moment, in this form, under these conditions, and to this individual inasmuch, and only as he is capable of receiving it, and receiving it best, at this moment in time."[14]

Now, to be clear, we are using Foucault here as a way of thinking about the larger issues outlined in this book rather than seeking to align particular schools and projects of rhetoric in this volume

---

13. For a provocative application of the archaeology of knowledge to the study of the New Testament and early Christianity and to scriptures and the process of scripturalizing more generally, see Vincent L. Wimbush, "Introduction: TEXTureS, Gestures, Power: Orientation to Radical Excavation," in *Signifying on Scriptures: New Orientations to a Cultural Phenomenon*, ed. idem (Signifying [on] Scriptures 1; New Brunswick: Rutgers University Press, 2008), 1–22.

14. Michel Foucault, *The Hermeneutics of the Subject: Lectures at the Collège de France 1981-1982*, ed. F. Gros, trans. G. Burchell (New York: Picador, 2005), 384. For the full discussion, see 381–91.

with one category or the other, *parrhēsia* or "rhetoric." Foucault is somewhat idiosyncratic in his deployment of the term "rhetoric" in this discussion, but his overall point is to address the power dynamics at play in all forms of rhetorical configurations. In this respect, *parrhēsia* represents "good rhetoric" over its other, which he designates simply as "rhetoric." The basic distinction is that "good rhetoric" or *parrhēsia* is moral formation and "simple" rhetoric is essentially *technē*.

For Foucault, then, one of the basic differences between the two is that "rhetoric" acts on others and represents the power of the self and has, in his estimation, a negative function,while *parrhēsia* presents the self as acting for and on behalf of others and represents a positive force for good. Rhetoric, then, seeks to persuade others to bend to the subject of the discourse and is an act of force, while *parrhēsia* seeks to encourage others to "build up a relationship of sovereignty to themselves" for the purpose of attaining a wise, happy, and virtuous state and is obviously an ideal.[15] In terms of thinking about the broader framework of this volume, *parrhēsia* is that which concerns ethics and eschatology, or the future of how things might look and how we might be, individually and communally.

Following Foucault, we think an appropriate and helpful task for rhetorical criticism of the New Testament, as we move forward, would be to attend more closely and persistently to the dynamics between self and other and the power relationships that are always negotiated through rhetoric, and even to attend to the rhetorical contours of the field itself. To this end, we might envision rhetorical criticism as being about exposing the relatedness, connectedness, and power-ladenness of authors, texts, and audiences in the past and in the present. It is here, and not solely in the vocabulary, the genres,

15. Foucault, *Hermeneutics of the Subject*, 385.

and/or the literary resonances themselves, where persuasiveness takes on a form that is more akin to the way in which the Greeks and Romans understood rhetoric, since for them the power relationships were paramount.

In this respect, it is important to reflect on some of the others who are neither represented in the present volume nor included as part of this discussion, but who nevertheless are important figures in genealogies of rhetorical criticism and add a great deal to thinking about and beyond the issues raised in this collection. Since every system of rhetoric and its logics and logistics is boundaried and, indeed, defined by the borders of other ideas and systems and scholars, it is worth asking how we might see our own rhetorical projects differently if we were to think about some of these "others." As Foucault notes, "there is no statement that does not presuppose others, there is no statement that is not surrounded by a field of coexistences, effects of series and succession, a distribution of functions and roles."[16] Mapping the terrain of rhetorical criticism and the genealogical traditions out of which such maps arise, and in which the cartographers make sense and acquire meaning, is thus an important way by which we may see how such dependence is constructed, articulated, negotiated, affirmed, and/or denied.[17]

One thinks, for instance, of James Muilenburg, whom we might consider one of the founders of rhetorical criticism, and of one of his premiere students, Phyllis Trible, who appreciates the promise of rhetoric as an extension of historical criticism. Though Muilenburg

16. Michel Foucault, *The Archaeology of Knowledge and the Discourse on Language*, trans. A. M. Sheridan Smith (New York: Pantheon, 1972), 99.

17. We note here that each of the scholars represented in this volume have certainly left significant, often indelible, marks on the field as a whole through their many contributions, not the least of which are to be located in relation to rhetorical criticism. Moreover, several have made important advances in helping us to understand what interpretive acts might lie at the intersections of ideology, identity, and power relationships in biblical scholarship. The following comments are thus intended to expand on the work that is presented in this volume.

wrote his dissertation on early Christian literature,[18] he did expend much scholarly effort on methodological questions for the field as a whole, as well as the study of the Hebrew Bible. Thus, even as he is not thought to be of immediate relevance to the project conceived here, Muilenburg's interest in the dynamics of prophetic rhetoric in its confrontation and engagement with institutional power informed a generation of Hebrew Bible scholars and caught the imaginations of New Testament scholars as well. Muilenburg's 1969 Society of Biblical Literature presidential address may seem rather tame and perhaps even innocuous now, when rhetorical criticism is no longer regarded as a new move in interpretation, but for its time it offered a radical challenge to move beyond the discipline's preoccupied grappling with the questionable and disturbing legacy of German biblical scholarship.[19] In this volume, however, Muilenburg's nascent methodological concerns about rhetoric do not figure prominently in the discussion, and thus he is not included in the genealogical delineations. That said, it is worth noting that Trible takes up Muilenburg's program, pushes it in a decisively feminist direction, and thereby demonstrates that Muilenburg's framework harbors great potential for radical ethical work in interpretation.[20] It is important to bear this rhetorical imprint from the past in mind as one engages the essays in this volume.

One could make a similar observation with respect to Norman Perrin, who, through his work with Amos Wilder and Paul Ricoeur along with his own hermeneutical turn to language and symbolism, similarly makes significant strides in shaping the foundation upon

18. Muilenburg submitted his dissertation on Barnabas and the Didache to Yale in 1926, and it was published as *The Literary Relations of the Epistle of Barnabas and the Teaching of the Twelve Apostles* (Marburg, 1929).

19. James Muilenburg, "Form Criticism and Beyond," *JBL* 88, no. 1 (1969): 1–18.

20. See especially Phyllis Trible, *Rhetorical Criticism: Context, Method, and the Book of Jonah* (GBS.OT; Minneapolis: Fortress, 1994), passim.

which many in this volume rely.[21] The scholarship of his student Mary Ann Tolbert offers a decisive strand of the interpretative system that Perrin proposed, and her work represents a rich tradition of rhetorically aware interpretation that pays close attention to how context, background, and social location interrelate with language and symbolism.[22] One might also note here the critical importance of Antoinette Clark Wire, whose highly influential work on the rhetoric of Paul in his response to the "Corinthian women prophets" relies on *The New Rhetoric* by Chaim Perelman and Lucie Olbrechts-Tyteca. Wire exposes the sometimes deceptively powerful role that rhetoric has in shaping audience perceptions, as well as the role of rhetoric in locating voices that are missing or lost.[23] Finally, Burton L. Mack also comes to mind with his groundbreaking work on mythmaking and early Christian ideological constructions, and Elizabeth Castelli, an heir to Mack's sophisticated rhetorical-ideological approach, offers a complex and multivalent elaboration on it through her use of critical theory as a part of discourse analysis.[24]

Through this brief exercise, we learn that some of the trajectories in rhetorical criticism of the New Testament that are missing from the present volume may in fact offer differently challenging questions and perhaps even ways forward out of our present situation of "talking amongst ourselves." Yet, these systems and their progenitors are, at the moment, seemingly left "off the map" and written out

21. Norman Perrin, *Jesus and the Language of the Kingdom: Symbol and Metaphor in New Testament Interpretation* (Philadelphia: Fortress, 1976). For discussion of Perrin's contributions to what is now known as rhetorical criticism, see Werner H. Kelber, "The Work of Norman Perrin: An Intellectual Pilgrimage," *Journal of Religion* 64, no. 4 (1984): 452–67.

22. For example, Mary Ann Tolbert, *Sowing the Gospel: Mark's World in Literary-historical Perspective* (Minneapolis: Fortress, 1989), passim. It should be noted that Vernon K. Robbins also is a Perrin student, and that his system of socio-rhetorical interpretation, particularly in its earlier formulations and incarnations, could be seen to bear a distinct resonance of the Perrin-imprint.

23. Antoinette Clark Wire, *The Corinthian Women Prophets: A Reconstruction through Paul's Rhetoric* (Minneapolis: Fortress, 1990), passim.

24. Elizabeth Castelli, *Imitating Paul: A Discourse of Power* (LCBI; Louisville: Westminster John Knox, 1991), passim.

of the genealogy. We should be clear that these scholars and perspectives were not purposefully excluded from this project, which had to have limits. We only note that their voices, as well as the voices of others we have not mentioned here, are largely missing from the discussions in the volume. Nevertheless, such figures are still present as coexistents, regardless of whether they are acknowledged or not, and all of them are coordinates in conversations about rhetorical criticism even when they are unrecognized as such. These scholars who have been left off the grid tend to understand in broad and critical ways the role of ideology and power in rhetorical criticism of the New Testament. Such figures signal not merely a slight adjustment to the backgrounds or the parallels that various trajectories suggest or even a codification of their own work into a universally applicable "method" or "house," but rather a significant challenge to methods in particular times and places.

The work of Burton L. Mack serves as a particularly arresting example of such methodological challenges. In some sense, his evolving approach has insisted on highlighting the rhetoric of myth-making (our "mapmaking") along with the deployment of such mythmaking rhetorics in ancient and modern contexts.[25] Mack's project explicitly asks us to rethink our means of constructing singular systems of rhetorical ontology, itself, as we noted earlier, an

---

25. In the last chapter of his *Myth of Innocence: Mark and Christian Origins* (FF; Minneapolis: Fortress, 1998), Burton L. Mack plants seeds concerning the shift from analysis of history as innocent to analysis of the human capacity for mythmaking in the ancient but especially modern worlds. These seeds bear much fruit in his *The Christian Myth: Origins, Logic, and Legacy* (London: Bloomsbury, 2003); *Myth and the Christian Nation: A Social Theory of Religion* (Religion in Culture; London: Equinox, 2008), and *Christian Mentality: The Entanglements of Power, Violence, and Fear* (Religion in Culture; London: Acumen, 2011). We note here that Mack is one of the few scholars of the New Testament and Christian origins to insist on linking the rhetoric of our field to the history of religion more broadly. For his earlier work on rhetoric, where he attempts to map rhetorical criticism's place as a method in modern New Testament scholarship, see Burton L. Mack, *Rhetoric and the New Testament* (GBS.NT; Minneapolis: Fortress, 1990), passim. See also Mack and Vernon K. Robbins, *Patterns of Persuasion in the Gospels* (Sonoma: Polebridge, 1989), passim.

illusion and a myth, although a critically important and potent one. Perhaps most strikingly, Mack, more so than any other scholar of rhetoric, challenges us to rethink the deeply religious and theological nature of our rhetorical commitments and orientations by noting that our conclusions and "portraits" of the ancient world cannot be dissociated from basic *a priori* assumptions about which we may not always be aware. For Mack, such portraits are to be located in the realm of mythmaking and storytelling, and it is not the *realia* but the rhetoric that matters and deserves critical scrutiny. In this respect, rhetorical-critical systems promote a system of interpretation, of knowledge, and of subjectivity that, as Foucault notes, "confirms our belief that the present rests upon profound intentions and immutable necessities."[26] In other words, if rhetoric is a thoroughly human creation and endeavor and a response to the world, then what are its worldly dimensions and implications, what difference does each pattern of persuasion make, about which realities are we persuaded, and to what ends?

We do need maps. On one level, we cannot find our way without them. Indeed, our disciplinary structures encourage and even demand the sorts of maps provided in this volume. We wish nevertheless to question whether a map also implicitly *dictates* our way. Maps serve particular purposes for specific times, places, audiences, and subject matter. At the same time, every map is also, in the very moment it is helpful in its revelations, problematic in its concealments. Whether we want them to be or not, maps are socially and temporally located. Indeed, we often need to rely on multiple maps, some of which appear to represent reality or the reality we desire better than others. Even in these cases, however, we must ask, "What reality are we using to judge the map in question?"[27]

---

26. Foucault, "Nietzsche, Genealogy, History," 155.

Thinking about maps in this way, we might use our rhetorical-critical narrative imagination to find ways in which we can cohabitate spaces where selves and others can be represented in all their differences without implying a hierarchical system as a cause or effect of those differences. We do not mean to imply here alignment with a (neo)liberal value system that seeks to accommodate and to accept and "appreciate" and "value" the other. Such projects predicated on the politics of identity are often short-sighted and only too accommodating to consumerist mentalities and material realities.[28] While sentiments about identities and representation are often persuasive in our global capitalist environment, they may serve little purpose for the rigorous work that must be done if one is truly to acknowledge otherness, diversity, and complexity.

In other words, to imagine future mapping projects such as this current one means that we cannot be concerned solely with which bodies are in the room, or in the book, and who is doing or not doing rhetorical-critical biblical scholarship. If we are indeed interested in "the world to come" and in moving beyond totalitarian régimes in both truth and politics, then in the process of realizing our interests,

---

27. Philip Kitcher, *Science Truth, and Democracy* (New York: Oxford University Press, 2001), passim. In an illuminating chapter in his book, Kitcher (55–62) notes, for instance, that the map to the London Underground does an excellent job of mapping the train routes and walkway connections but it works less well for those who would seek to bend its imaging to the actual spatial locations above ground. The function of the Underground map is quite particular and gives a specific kind of information. In an essay that the present authors have written elsewhere, we note something similar by comparing the rhetorical systems of Vernon K. Robbins and Elisabeth Schüssler Fiorenza. Based on function, one finds that they operate quite differently in terms of reading the text, but neither one is particularly "right" or "wrong" of necessity. It all depends on the other coordinates that are in play. See Todd Penner and Davina C. Lopez, "Rhetorical Approaches: Introducing the Art of Persuasion in Paul and Pauline Studies," in *Studying Paul's Letters: Contemporary Perspectives and Methods*, ed. J. Marchal (Minneapolis: Fortress, 2012), 33–52.

28. In a series of writings spanning nearly three decades, political theorist Nancy Fraser has called this issue the problem of "redistribution and recognition." For a recent appraisal of the serious and thoroughgoing drawbacks to social change projects derived solely from identity politics in late-capitalist culture, and with specific attention to feminist politics, see her "Feminism, Capitalism, and the Cunning of History," *New Left Review* 56 (2009); 97–117.

we will need to exercise self-reflexivity and work on our own limitations of recognizing otherness. The desire to bend the world to our will through our maps, our houses, and our family trees is perhaps as innate as the biological impulses that ground us in nature. As Reinhold Niebuhr so eloquently formulated in his Gifford Lectures, language allows us to transcend these base animal instincts.[29] It is the ability to imagine other worlds and to rise above the level of the inhuman(e) that makes us truly remarkable creatures.

Of course, we must first recognize our own humanity before we can begin to explore the vast otherness of others, and this is no easy task! Humanism, Edward Said poignantly argues,

> is the means, perhaps the consciousness we have for providing that kind of finally antinomian or oppositional analysis between the space of words and their various origins and deployments in physical and social place, from text to actualized site of either appropriation or resistance, to transmission, to reading and interpretation, from private to public, from silence to explication and utterance, and back again, as we encounter our own silence and mortality—all of it occurring in the world, on the ground of daily life and history and hopes, and the search for knowledge and justice, and then perhaps also for liberation.[30]

In our estimation, however, the first step towards this more expansive project for our work as critics of the New Testament, early Christianity, and biblical literature more broadly is in some sense to return to the ground, to the terrifying state of being entangled in a world that, despite our best efforts in the humanities, social sciences, and natural sciences, cannot be made into a unified whole with discernible purpose or an overarching universal ethic.

---

29. Reinhold Niebuhr, *The Nature and Destiny of Man* (Gifford Lectures; 2 vols.; New York: Scribner's, 1949), passim.
30. Edward W. Said, *Humanism and Democratic Criticism* (New York: Palgrave MacMillan, 2004), 83.

It is our ability to "order things" and to make meaning in and through language that brings all of this we feel and see into being. In so far as we have the capacity to imagine bigger and better worlds, we have every interest, in terms of our own survival, to do so. Working towards, for, and with others with *parrhēsia* in view is ultimately about emancipating ourselves from the rhetorical shackles we frequently place on our own mapping and meaning-making projects, and from the prisons we often create for (our)selves and others. Humanism and democracy and liberation are ongoing lifelong endeavors, but ones that can only take root when we move beyond our current rhetorical and situational limitations. Moving "beyond" has, in our view, long been precisely the promise and potential of rhetorical criticism. We thus eagerly anticipate all the future interventions and inheritances to come. In this respect, this volume and the mapmakers represented herein have offered us a rich and varied series of starting points. With these essays in hand, we look forward to drawing out our own guides on paper, or perhaps gazing upward, to determine the directions and spaces where our own mapping imagination might take us in the future.

Bibliography

Ahlstrom, Sidney. *A Religious History of the American People*. New Haven: Yale University Press, 1972.

Alcoff, Linda. "Cultural Feminism Versus Post-Structuralism: The Identity Crisis in Feminist Theory." *Signs* 13, no. 3 (1988): 405–36.

Aletti, Jean-Noël. "La Dispositio Rhétorique dans les Épitres Pauliniennes." *New Testament Studies* 38, no. 3 (1992): 385–401.

_____. "Review of H. D. Betz, *Galatians*," *Recherches de science religieuse* 69 (1981): 601–2.

_____. "Rhetoric of Romans 5–8." Pages 294–308 in *The Rhetorical Analysis of Scripture: Essays from the 1995 London Conference*. Edited by Stanley E. Porter and Thomas H. Olbricht. *Journal for the Study of the New Testament* Supplement Series 146. Sheffield: Sheffield Academic, 1997.

Alexander, Loveday. "Mapping Early Christianity: Acts and the Shape of Early Church History." *Interpretation* 57 (2001): 163–73.

_____. "Narrative Maps: Reflections on the Toponomy of Acts." Pages 15–57 in *The Bible in Human Society: Essays in Honour of John Rogerson*. Edited by M. D. Carroll et al. *Journal for the Study of the Old Testament* Supplement Series 200. Sheffield: Sheffield Academic, 1995.

Anderson, Janice Capel. "Mapping Feminist Biblical Criticism." *Critical Review of Books in Religion* 2 (1991): 21–44.

Anderson, R. Dean, Jr. *Ancient Rhetorical Theory and Paul.* Revised edition. Leuven: Peeters, 1999.

Anonymous, "Published Works of Elisabeth Schüssler Fiorenza." *Journal of Feminist Studies in Religion* 25, no. 1 (2009): 221–40.

Appiah, Kwame Anthony. *Cosmopolitanism: Ethics in a World of Strangers.* New York: Norton, 2006.

Archer, Dawn, Karin Aijmer, and Anne Wichmann. *Pragmatics: An Advanced Resource Book for Students.* Routledge Applied Linguistics. New York: Routledge, 2012.

Arendt, Hannah. *The Human Condition.* Chicago: University of Chicago Press, 1958.

Aristotle. *On Rhetoric: A Theory of Civic Discourse.* Translated by George A. Kennedy. New York: Oxford University Press, 1991.

Aronowitz, Stanley, and Henry Giroux. *Education Under Siege.* South Hadley: Bergin & Garvey, 1985.

Asumang, Annang. "The Presence of the Shepherd: A Rhetographic Exegesis of Psalm 23." *Conspectus: The Journal of the South African Theological Seminar* 9 (2010): 1–23.

Atkinson, Jane M. "'Wrapped Words': Poetry and Politics among the Wana of Central Sulawesi, Indonesia." Pages 34–68 in *Dangerous Words: Language and Politics in the Pacific.* Edited by Donald Brennis and Fred R. Meyers. Prospect Heights: Waveland, 1984.

Attridge, Harold W. "Argumentation in John 5." Pages 188–99 in *Rhetorical Argumentation in Biblical Texts: Essays from the Lund 2000 Conference.* Edited by Anders Eriksson, Thomas H. Olbricht, and Walter Übelacker. Emory Studies in Early Christianity 8. Harrisburg: Trinity, 2002.

Augustine. *Confessionum libri xiii.* Edited by L. Verheijen. Corpus Christianorum, Series Latina 27. Turnholti: Brepols, 1981.

Augustine. *De Doctrina Christiana.* Translated by R. P. H. Green. Oxford: Clarendon, 1995.

Aune, David E. *Greco-Roman Literature and the New Testament*. Society of Biblical Literature Sources for Biblical Studies 21. Atlanta: Scholars, 1988.

———. "Romans as a Logos Protreptikos in the Context of Ancient Religious and Philosophical Propaganda." Pages 91–121 in *Paulus und das antike Judentum: Tübingen-Durham-Symposium im Gedenken an den 50. Todestag Adolf Schlatters (†19.Mai 1938)*. Edited by Martin Hengel and Ulrich Heckel. Wissenschaftliche Untersuchungen zum Neuen Testament 58. Tübingen: Mohr Siebeck, 1991.

———. *The New Testament in Its Literary Environment*. Library of Early Christianity 8. Philadelphia: Westminster, 1987.

———. *The Westminster Dictionary of New Testament and Early Christian Literature and Rhetoric*. Louisville: Westminster John Knox, 2003.

Avalos, Hector. *The End of Biblical Studies*. Amherst, NY: Prometheus, 2007.

Barlas, Asma. *"Believing Women" in Islam: Unreading Patriarchal Interpretations of the Qur'an*. Austin: University of Texas Press, 2002.

Baron, Dennis. *Grammar and Gender*. New Haven: Yale University Press, 1986.

Barrett, Charles K. "Review of H. D. Betz, *Galatians*," *Interpretation* 34 (1980): 414–17.

Bass, Kenneth. "The Narrative and Rhetorical Use of Divine Necessity in Luke-Acts." *Journal of Biblical and Pneumatological Research* 1 (2009): 48–68.

Bayertz, Kurt. *Wissenschaft als historischer Prozess: Die antipositivistische Wende in der Wissenschaftstheorie*. Munich: Fink, 1980.

Bede, the Venerable. "Concerning Figures and Tropes." Pages 96–122 in *Readings in Medieval Rhetoric*. Edited by Joseph M. Miller, Michael H. Proser, and Thomas W. Benson. Bloomington: Indiana University Press, 1973.

Bender, John, and David E. Wellbery. "Rhetoricality: On the Modernist Return of Rhetoric." Pages 3–42 in idem and Wellbery, eds., *The Ends of Rhetoric*.

_____ and David E. Wellbery, eds. *The Ends of Rhetoric: History,Theory, Practice*. Stanford: Stanford University Press, 1990.

Benhabib, Seyla, ed. *Democracy and Difference: Contesting the Boundaries of the Political*. Princeton: Princeton University Press, 1996.

Berger, Klaus. "Hellenistische Gattungen im Neuen Testament." *Aufstieg und Niedergang der Römischen Welt* 25, no. 2 (1884): 1033–1431.

Bernstein, Richard. "What is the Difference that Makes a Difference? Gadamer, Habermas, and Rorty." Pages 343–76 in *Hermeneutics and Modern Philosophy*. Edited by Brice R. Wachterhauser. Albany: State University of New York Press, 1986.

Berquist, Jon L., and Claudia V. Camp, eds. *Constructions of Space I: Theory, Geography, and Narrative*. Library of Hebrew Bible/Old Testament Studies. New York: T&T Clark, 2007.

_____. "Critical Spatiality and the Construction of the Ancient World." Pages 14–29 in *'Imagining' Biblical Worlds: Studies in Spatial, Social and Historical Constructs in Honor of James W. Flanagan*. Edited by David M. Gunn and Paula M. McNutt. Journal for the Study of the Old Testament Supplement Series 359. Sheffield: Sheffield Academic, 2002.

Betz, Hans Dieter. "De laude ipsius (Plut. *Mor.* 539A-547F)." Pages 367–93 in *Plutarch's Ethical Writings and Early Christian Literature*. Edited by idem. Studia ad corpus hellenisticum Novi Testamenti 4. Leiden: E. J. Brill, 1978.

_____. *Der Apostel Paulus und die sokratische Trdition*. Beiträge zur historischen Theologie. Tübingen: Mohr Siebeck, 1972.

_____. *Galatians: A Commentary on Paul's Letter to the Churches in Galatia*. Hermeneia. Philadelphia: Fortress, 1979.

_____. "In Defense of the Spirit: Paul's Letter to the Galatians as a Document of Early Christian Apologetics." Pages 99–114 in *Aspects of Religious Propaganda in Judaism and Early Christianity*. Edited by Elisabeth Schüssler Fiorenza. Notre Dame: University of Notre Dame Press, 1976.

_____. "Review: George A. Kennedy, *New Testament Interpretation through Rhetorical Criticism* (Chapel Hill: University of North Carolina Press, 1984)." *Journal of Theological Studies* 37 (1986): 166–67.

_____. *Second Corinthians 8 and 9: A Commentary on Two Administrative Letters of the Apostle Paul*. Hermeneia. Philadelphia: Fortress, 1985.

_____. "The Literary Composition and Function of Paul's Letter to the Galatians." *New Testament Studies* 21, no. 3 (1975): 353–79. Reprinted as pages 3–28 in Nanos, ed., *The Galatians Debate*.

_____. *The "Mithras Liturgy:" Text, Translation and Commentary*. Studien und Texte zu Antike und Christentum 18. Tübingen: Mohr Siebeck, 2003.

_____. "The Problem of Rhetoric and Theology According to the Apostle Paul." Pages 16–23 in *L'apôtre Paul: Personnalité, style et conception du ministère*. Edited by A. Vanhoye. Bibliotheca ephemeridum theologicarum lovaniensium 73. Leuven: Leuven University, 1986.

_____. *The Sermon on the Mount: A Commentary on the Sermon on the Mount, including the Sermon on the Plain (Matthew 5:3-7:27 and Luke 6:20-49)*. Hermeneia. Minneapolis: Fortress, 1995.

Bird, Michael F. "Reassessing a Rhetorical Approach to Paul's Letters." *Expository Times* 119 (2008): 374–79.

Bitzer, Lloyd F. "Rhetoric and Public Knowledge." Pages 67–93 in *Rhetoric, Philosophy, and Literature*. Edited by D. Burks. Lafayette, IN: Purdue University Press, 1978.

_____. "The Rhetorical Situation." *Philosophy and Rhetoric* 1 (1968): 1–14.

Black, C. Clifton. "Kennedy and the Gospels: An Ambiguous Legacy, a Promising Bequest." Pages 63–80 in idem and Watson, eds., *Words Well Spoken*.

_____. *Mark: Images of an Apostolic Interpreter*. Studies on the Personalities of the New Testament. Minneapolis: Fortress and T&T Clark, 2001.

_____. *The Rhetoric of the Gospel: Theological Artistry in the Gospels and Acts*. Second edition. Louisville: Westminster John Knox, 2013.

_____ and Duane F. Watson, eds. *Words Well Spoken: George Kennedy's Rhetoric of the New Testament*. Studies in Rhetoric and Religion 8. Waco: Baylor University Press, 2008.

Blass, Friedrich Wilhelm, and Albert Debrunner. *A Greek Grammar of the New Testament*. Translated and Edited by Robert W. Funk. Chicago: University of Chicago Press, 1961. First German edition 1896.

Bloomquist, L. Gregory. "Paul's Inclusive Language: The Ideological Texture of Romans 1." Pages 165–93 in *Fabrics of Discourse: Essays in Honor of Vernon K. Robbins*. Edited by David B. Gowler, L. Gregory Bloomquist, and Duane F. Watson. Harrisburg: Trinity, 2003.

_____. *The Function of Suffering in Philippians*. Journal for the Study of the New Testament Supplement Series 78. Sheffield: Sheffield Academic, 1993.

Boers, Hendrikus. "The Form Critical Study of Paul's Letters: 1 Thessalonians as a Case Study." *New Testament Studies* 22, no. 2 (1974): 140–58.

Bonfiglio, Ryan. "Archer Imagery in Zechariah 9:11–17 in Light of Achaemenid Iconography." *Journal of Biblical Literature* 131 (2012): 507–27.

Bonnell, Victoria E., and Lynn Hunt, eds. *Beyond the Cultural Turn: New Directions in the Study of Society and Culture*. Berkeley: University of California Press, 1999.

Bonner, Stanley F. *Education in Ancient Rome: From the Elder Cato to the Younger Pliny*. Berkeley: University of California Press, 1977.

Booth, Wayne C. "Freedom of Interpretation: Bakhtin and the Challenge of Feminist Criticism." *Critical Inquiry* 9 (1982): 45–76.

Borg, Marcus, and John Dominic Crossan. *The First Paul: Reclaiming the Radical Visionary Behind the Church's Conservative Icon.* New York: HarperOne, 2009.

Bormann, Ernest. *The Force of Fantasy: Restoring the American Dream.* Carbondale: Southern Illinois University Press, 1985.

Brandt, William J. *The Rhetoric of Argumentation.* Indianapolis: Bobbs-Merrill, 1970.

Bräuninger, Bettina, Andreas Lange, and Kurt Lüscher. "Familienwissenschaftliche Rhetorik: Eine explorative Analyse ausgewählter Texte." Arbeitspapiere / Forschungsbereich Gesellschaft und Familie 20. 1996. Online: http://kops.ub.uni-konstanz.de/bitstream/handle/urn:nbn:de:bsz:352-opus-3853/385_1.pdf. Accessed 17 August 2014.

Brown, Richard H. *Society as Text: Essays on Rhetoric, Reason and Reality.* Chicago: University of Chicago Press, 1987.

Bruehler, Bart B. *A Public and Political Christ: The Social-Spatial Characteristics of Luke 18:35–19:43 and the Gospel as a Whole in Its Ancient Context.* Princeton Theological Monograph Series. Eugene: Pickwick, 2011.

Bultmann, Rudolf. *Der Stil der paulinischen Predigt und die kynisch-stoische Diatribe.* Forschungen zur Religion und Literatur des Alten und Neuen Testaments 13. Göttingen: Vandenhoeck & Ruprecht, 1910.

————. *History of the Synoptic Tradition.* Translated by John Marsh. New York: Harper & Row, 1963. Translation of *Die Geschichte der synoptischen Tradition.* Göttingen: Vandenhoeck, 1921.

Burke, Kenneth. *Counter-Statement.* Berkeley: University of California Press, 1968.

Butler, Judith. *Gender Trouble: Feminism and the Subversion of Identity.* New York: Routledge, 1990.

Butts, James R. *The Progymnasmata of Theon: A New Text with Translation and Commentary.* PhD dissertation, Claremont Graduate School, 1986.

Cadbury, Henry Joel. *The Style and Literary Method of Luke.* Vol. 1: *The Diction of Luke and Acts.* Cambridge, MA: Harvard University Press, 1920.

Callan, Terrance. "Rhetography and Rhetology of Apocalyptic Discourse in Second Peter." Pages 59–90 in *Reading Second Peter with New Eyes: Methodological Reassessments of the Second Letter of Peter.* Library of New Testament Studies 382. Edited by Robert L. Webb and Duane F. Watson. London: T&T Clark, 2008.

Cameron, Averil. *Christianity and the Rhetoric of Empire.* Sather Classical Lectures 55. Berkeley: University of California Press, 1991.

Camp, Claudia V. "Storied Space, or, Ben Sira 'Tells' a Temple." Pages 64–80 in *'Imagining' Biblical Worlds: Studies in Spatial, Social and Historical Constructs in Honor of James W. Flanagan.* Edited by David M. Gunn and Paula M. McNutt. *Journal for the Study of the Old Testament* Supplement Series 359. Sheffield: Sheffield Academic, 2002.

Canavan, Rosemary. *Clothing the Body of Christ at Colossae: A Visual Construction of Identity.* Wissenschaftliche Untersuchungen zum Neuen Testament 2.334. Tübingen: Mohr Siebeck, 2012.

Canty, Aaron. "Saint Paul in Augustine." Pages 115–42 in *A Companion to St. Paul in the Middle Ages.* Edited by Steven R. Cartwright. Leiden: Brill, 2013.

Carey, Greg. *Elusive Apocalypse: Reading Authority in the Revelation to John.* Studies in American Biblical Hermeneutics 15. Macon: Mercer University Press, 1999.

_____. "Moving an Audience: One Aspect of Pathos in the Book of Revelation." Pages 163–78 in Black and Watson, eds., *Words Well Spoken.*

_____ and L. Gregory Bloomquist, eds. *Vision and Persuasion: Rhetorical Dimensions of Apocalyptic Discourse.* St. Louis: Chalice, 1999.

Cassiodorus Senator. *An Introduction to Divine and Human Readings*. Translated by Leslie Webber Jones. New York: Norton, 1969.

Castelli, Elizabeth. "Heteroglossia, Hermeneutics and History: A Review Essay of Recent Feminist Studies of Early Christianity." *The Journal of Feminist Studies in Religion* 10, no. 2 (1994): 73–78.

_____. *Imitating Paul: A Discourse of Power*. Literary Currents in Biblical Interpretation. Louisville: Westminster John Knox, 1991.

Chatman, Seymour. *Story and Discourse: Narrative Structure in Fiction and Film*. Ithaca: Cornell University Press, 1980.

Chopp, Rebecca S. *The Power to Speak: Feminism, Language, God*. New York: Crossroad, 1989.

Chow, Rey. *Ethics after Idealism: Theory-Culture-Ethnicity-Reading*. Bloomington: Indiana University Press, 1998.

Church, F. Forrester. "Rhetorical Structure and Design in Paul's Letter to Philemon." *Harvard Theological Review* 71, nos. 1–2 (1978): 17–33.

Classen, Carl Joachim. "Kann die rhetorische Theorie helfen, das Neue Testament, vor allem die Briefe des Paulus, besser zu verstehen?" *Zeitschrift für die neutestamentliche Wissenschaft und die Kunde der älteren Kirche* 100 (2009): 145–72.

_____. "Paulus und die antike Rhetorik." *Zeitschrift für die neutestamentliche Wissenschaft und die Kunde der älteren Kirche* 82, no. 1 (1991): 1–32.

_____. *Rhetorical Criticism of the New Testament*. Wissenschaftliche Untersuchungen zum Neuen Testament 128. Tübingen: Mohr Siebeck, 2000.

_____. "St. Paul's Epistles and Ancient Greek and Roman Rhetoric." Pages 1–28 in idem, ed., *Rhetorical Criticism of the New Testament*.

_____. "St. Paul's Epistles and Ancient Greek and Roman Rhetoric." Pages 95–113 in Nanos, ed., *The Galatians Debate*.

————. "St. Paul's Epistles and Ancient Greek and Roman Rhetoric." Pages 265–91in *Rhetoric and the New Testament: Essays from the 1992 Heidelberg Conference.* Edited by Stanley E. Porter and Thomas H. Olbricht. *Journal for the Study of the New Testament* Supplement Series 90. Sheffield: Journal for the Study of the Old Testament, 1993.

————. "St. Paul's Epistles and Ancient Greek and Roman Rhetoric." *Rhetorica* 10, no. 4 (1992): 319–44.

Code, Lorraine. *Rhetorical Spaces: Essays on Gendered Locations.* New York: Continuum, 1995.

Collins, Raymond F. *First Corinthians.* Sacra Pagina Series 7. Collegeville: Liturgical, 1999.

Condit, Celeste Michelle. "Democracy and Civil Rights: The Universalizing Influence of Public Argumentation." *Communication Monographs* 54 (1987): 1–20.

Conley, Thomas M. *Rhetoric in the European Tradition.* White Plains: Longman, 1990.

————. "What Counts as a Topos in Contemporary Research?" Pages 578–85 in *Topik und Rhetorik ein Interdisziplinäres Symposium.* Edited by Thomas Schirren and Gert Ueding. Rhetorik-Forschungen. Tübingen: Niemeyer, 2000.

Connor, Robert W., ed. *Greek Orations, 4th Century B.C.: Lysias, Isocrates, Demosthenes, Aeschines, Hyperides, and Letter of Philip.* Prospect Heights: Waveland, 1987.

————. "Pygmies in the Cage." Pages 97–114 in *Literary Study, Measurement, and the Sublime: Disciplinary Assessment.* Edited by D. Heiland and L. J. Rosenthal. New York: Teagle Foundation, 2011.

Crossan, John Dominic, and Jonathan L. Reed. *In Search of Paul: How Jesus' Apostle Opposed Rome's Empire with God's Kingdom.* San Francisco: HarperOne, 2004.

Culpepper, R. Alan. *Anatomy of the Fourth Gospel: A Study in Literary Design.* Philadelphia: Fortress, 1983.

_____. "Mapping the Textures of New Testament Criticism: A Response to Socio-Rhetorical Criticism." *Journal for the Study of the New Testament* 70 (1998): 71–77.

Davies, W. D., and Dale C. Allison, Jr. *A Critical and Exegetical Commentary on the Gospel according to Saint Matthew.* International Critical Commentary. Edinburgh: T&T Clark, 1988.

_____, Paul W. Meyer, and David E. Aune. "Review of H. D. Betz, *Galatians: A Commentary on Paul's Letter to the Churches of Galatia.*" *Religious Studies Review* 7 (1981): 310–28.

De Hulster, Izaak J. *Iconographic Exegesis and Third Isaiah.* Forschungen zum Alten Testament 2.26. Tübingen: Mohr Siebeck, 2009.

_____ and Joel M. LeMon. *Image, Text, Exegesis: Iconographic Interpretation and the Hebrew Bible.* Library of Hebrew Bible/Old Testament. London: T&T Clark/Bloomsbury, 2014.

De Waal, Kayle B. *A Socio-rhetorical Interpretation of the Seven Trumpets of Revelation: The Apocalyptic Challenge to Earthly Empire.* Lewiston: Mellen, 2012.

DeConick, April D. *Network Criticism: An Embodied Historical Approach.* Online: http://aprildeconick.com/network-historicism/. Accessed 17 August 2014.

DeSilva, David A. "Meeting the Exigency of a Complex Rhetorical Situation: Paul's Strategy in 2 Corinthians 1 through 7." *Andrews University Seminary Studies* 34 (1996): 5–22.

_____. "Seeing Things John's Way: Rhetography and Conceptual Blending in Revelation 14:6-13." *Bulletin for Biblical Research* 18, no. 2 (2008): 271–98.

_____. *Seeing Things John's Way: The Rhetoric of the Book of Revelation.* Louisville: Westminster John Knox, 2009.

Dibelius, Martin. *From Tradition to Gospel.* Translated by Bertram Lee Woolf. New York: Scribner's, 1965. Translation of *Die Formgeschichte des Evangeliums.* Tübingen: Mohr, 1919.

————. *Studies in the Acts of the Apostles.* Translated by Heinrich Greeven. New York: Scribner's, 1956. Translation of *Aufsätze zur Apostelgeschichte.* Göttingen: Vandenhoeck & Ruprecht, 1951.

DiCicco, Mario M. *Paul's Use of Ethos, Pathos, and Logos in 2 Corinthians 10-13.* Mellen Biblical Press Series 31. Lewiston: Mellen, 1995.

Donawerth, Jane. *Rhetorical Theory by Women before 1900.* New York: Rowman & Littlefield, 2002.

Donfried, Karl Paul, and I. Howard Marshall. *The Theology of the Shorter Pauline Letters.* New Testament Theology. Cambridge: Cambridge University Press, 1993.

Doyle, Arthur Conan. *The New Annotated Sherlock Holmes.* Edited by Leslie S. Klinger. New York: Norton, 2005.

Dreyfus, Hubert L., and Paul Rabinow. *Michel Foucault: Beyond Structuralism and Hermeneutics.* Chicago: University of Chicago Press, 1983.

Edmondson, Ricca. *Rhetoric in Sociology.* London: Macmillan, 1984.

Elliott, John H. "Social-Scientific Criticism of the New Testament: More on Methods and Models." Pages 1–33 in *Social and Scientific Criticism of the New Testament and Its Social World.* Edited by idem. Semeia 35. Decatur: Scholars, 1986.

Elliott, Neil, and Mark Reasoner. *Documents and Images for the Study of Paul.* Minneapolis: Fortress, 2011.

————. *The Rhetoric of Romans. Journal for the Study of the New Testament* Supplement Series 45. Sheffield: Sheffield Academic, 1990.

Enenkel, Karl A. E., and Walter Melion, eds. *Meditatio—Refashioning the Self: Theory and Practice in Late Medieval and Early Modern Intellectual Culture.* Intersections: Interdisciplinary Studies in Early Modern Culture 17. Leiden: Brill, 2011.

Engberg-Pedersen, Troels. "The Concept of Paraenesis." Pages 47–72 in *Early Christian Paraenesis in Context*. Edited by James Starr and Troels Engberg-Pedersen. Beihefte zur *Zeitschrift für die neutestamentliche Wissenschaft* 125. Berlin: de Gruyter, 2005.

Eriksson, Anders. "Special Topics in 1 Corinthians 8-10." Pages 272–301 in *The Rhetorical Interpretation of Scripture: Essays from the 1996 Malibu Conference*. Edited by Stanley E. Porter and Dennis L. Stamps. *Journal for the Study of the New Testament* Supplement Series 180. Sheffield: Sheffield Academic, 1999.

————. *Traditions as Rhetorical Proof: Pauline Argumentation in 1 Corinthians*. Coniectanea biblica: New Testament Series 29. Stockholm: Almqvist & Wiksell, 1998.

Exler, Francis Xavier. *The Form of the Ancient Greek Letter: A Study in Greek Epistolography*. Washington: Catholic University of America, 1923.

Fairweather, Janet. "The Epistle to the Galatians and Classical Rhetoric." *Tyndale Bulletin* 45 (1994): 1–38, 213–43.

Fauconnier, Gilles, and Mark Turner. *The Way We Think: Conceptual Blending and the Mind's Hidden Complexities*. New York: Basic, 2003.

Felt, Ulrike, Helga Nowotny, and Klaus Taschwer. *Wissenschaftsforschung: Eine Einführung*. Frankfurt: Campus, 1995.

Ferguson, Frances. "A Commentary on Susan Guerlac's 'Longinus and the Subject of the Sublime.'" *New Literary History* 16, no. 2 (1985): 291–97.

Fewell, Danna Nolan, and Gary A. Philips, eds. *Bible and Ethics of Reading*. Semeia 77. Atlanta: Scholars, 1997.

Fish, Stanley. "Rhetoric." Pages 202–22 in *Critical Terms for Literary Study*. Edited by Frank Lentricchia and Thomas McLaughlin. Chicago: University of Chicago Press, 1990.

Fleck, Ludwik. *Entstehung und Entwicklung einer wissenschaftlichen Tatsache: Einführung in die Lehre vom Denkstil und Denkkollektiv*. Frankfurt: Suhrkamp, 1980.

Foucault, Michel. "Nietzsche, Genealogy, History." Pages 139–64 in *Language, Counter-memory, Practice: Selected Essays and Interviews.* Edited by Donald F. Bouchard. Ithaca: Cornell University Press, 1977.

————. *The Archaeology of Knowledge and the Discourse on Language.* Translated by A. M. Sheridan Smith. New York: Harper & Row, 1972.

————. *The Hermeneutics of the Subject: Lectures at the College de France 1981–1982.* Edited by F. Gros. Translated by G. Burchell. New York: Picador, 2005.

————. *The Order of Things: An Archaeology of the Human Sciences.* New York: Vintage Books, 1970.

Fraser, Nancy. "Feminism, Capitalism, and the Cunning of History." *New Left Review* 56 (2009): 97–117.

Frug, Mary. *Postmodern Legal Feminism.* New York: Routledge, 1992.

Fuchs, Esther. "Points of Resonance." Pages 1–20 in *On the Cutting Edge: The Study of Women in Biblical Worlds.* Edited by Jane Schaberg, Alice Bach, and Esther Fuchs. New York: Continuum, 2003.

Funk, Robert W., ed. *A Structuralist Approach to the Parables.* Semeia 1. Missoula: Scholars, 1974.

Geertz, Clifford. *Interpretation of Cultures: Selected Essays.* New York: Basic, 1973.

————. *Local Knowledge: Further Essays in Interpretive Anthropology.* New York: Basic, 1983.

Gibbs, Raymond W., Jr., and Gerard J. Steen, eds. *Metaphor in Cognitive Linguistics: Selected Papers from the Fifth International Cognitive Linguistics Conference, Amsterdam, July 1997.* Amsterdam Studies in the Theory and History of Linguistic Science: Series IV, Current Issues in Linguistic Theory 175. Amsterdam and Philadelphia: John Benjamins, 1999.

Glenn, Cheryl. *Rhetoric Retold: Regendering the Tradition from Antiquity through the Renaissance.* Carbondale: Southern Illinois University Press, 1997.

Gowler, David B. "The Development of Socio-Rhetorical Criticism." Pages 1–35 in *New Boundaries in Old Territory: Form and Social Rhetoric in Mark.* Edited by idem. Emory Studies in Early Christianity 3. New York: Lang, 1994.

———. "The End of the Beginning: The Continuing Maturation of Socio-Rhetorical Analysis." Pages 1–45 in Robbins, *Sea Voyages and Beyond.*

Grady, Joseph, Todd Oakley, and Seana Coulson. "Blending and Metaphor." Pages 101–24 in *Metaphor and Cognitive Science.* Edited by Gerard J. Steen and Raymond W. Gibbs, Jr. Amsterdam and Philadelphia: John Benjamins, 1999. Online: http://www.cogsci.ucsd.edu/~coulson/joe1.html. Accessed 17 August 2014.

Green, R. P. H. *Augustine:* De Doctrina Christiana. See Augustine, *De Doctrina Christiana.*

Greene, Gayle, and Coppélia Kahn, eds. *Making a Difference: Feminist Literary Criticism.* New York: Methuen, 1985.

Gruca-Macaulay, Alexandra. "The Role and Function of Lydia as a Rhetorical Construct in Acts: Sociorhetorical and Theological Interpretation." PhD dissertation, St. Paul University, Ottawa, 2013.

Guerlac, Suzanne. "Longinus and the Subject of the Sublime." *New Literary History* 16, no. 2 (1985): 275–89.

Habermas, Jürgen. "Ideology." in *Modern Interpretations of Marx.* Edited by Tom Bottomore. Oxford: Oxford University Press, 1981.

Hall, Robert G. "The Rhetorical Outline for Galatians: A Reconsideration." *Journal of Biblical Literature* 106, no. 2 (1987): 277-88. Reprinted as pages 29–38 in Nanos, ed., *The Galatians Debate.*

Hammer, Keir. "Disambiguating Rebirth: A Socio-Rhetorical Exploration of Rebirth Language in 1 Peter." PhD dissertation, University of Toronto, 2011.

Harding, Sandra. *Whose Science? Whose Knowledge? Thinking from Women's Lives*. Ithaca: Cornell University Press, 1991.

Harnisch, Wolfgang. "Einübung des neuen Seins: Paulinische Paränese am Beispiel des Galaterbriefs." *Zeitschrift für Theologie und Kirche* 84 (1987): 289–96.

Harris, Edward M. "Law and Oratory." Pages 130–40 in *Persuasion: Greek Rhetoric in Action*. Edited by Ian Worthington. London: Routledge, 1994.

Heiden-Sommer, Helga. "Soziologische Forschung und politische Interessen: Vorurteile und Frauen benachteiligende Begriffe in empirischen Studien zur Arbeitsteilung in den Familien." *Österreichische Zeitschrift für Soziologie* 19 (1994): 58–75.

Heintz, Bettina. "Wissenschaft im Kontext: Neuere Tendenzen der Wissenschaftssoziologie." *Koelner Zeitschrift für Soziologie und Sozialpsychologie* 45 (1993): 528–52.

Hellholm, David. "Amplificatio in the Macro-structure of Romans." Pages 123–51 in *Rhetoric and the New Testament: Essays from the 1992 Heidelberg Conference*. Edited by Stanley Porter and Thomas Olbricht. *Journal for the Study of the New Testament* Supplement Series 90. Sheffield: Journal for the Study of the Old Testament, 1993.

————. "Enthymemic Argumentation in Paul: The Case of Romans 6." Pages 119–79 in *Paul and His Hellenistic Context*. Edited by Troels Engberg-Pedersen. Minneapolis: Fortress, 1995.

Hengel, Martin. *Judaism and Hellenism: Studies in Their Encounter in Palestine during the Early Hellenistic Period*. 2 volumes. Philadelphia: Fortress, 1974.

Hermann, Anne C. and Abigail J. Stewart. *Theorizing Feminism: Parallel Trends in the Humanities and Social Sciences*. Second edition. Boulder: Westview, 2001.

Hermogenes. *On Types of Style*. Translated by Cecil W. Wooten. Chapel Hill: University of North Carolina Press, 1987.

Hernadi, Paul. "Literary Theory: A Compass for Critics." *Critical Inquiry* 3, no. 2 (1976): 369–86.

Hesford, Wendy S., and Eileen E. Schell. "Configurations of Transnationality: Locating Feminist Rhetorics." *College English* 70 (2008): 461–528.

Hester Amador, J. David. *Academic Constraints in Rhetorical Criticism of the New Testament: An Introduction to a Rhetoric of Power. Journal for the Study of the New Testament* Supplement Series 174. Sheffield: Sheffield Academic, 1999.

Hester (Amador), J. David. "The Wuellnerian Sublime: Rhetorics, Power, the Ethics of Commun(icat)ion." Pages 103–17 in *Rhetoric, Ethic, and Moral Persuasion in Biblical Discourse: Essays from the 2002 Heidelberg Conference.* Edited by Thomas H. Olbricht and Anders Eriksson. Emory Studies in Early Christianity 11. New York: T&T Clark, 2005.

Hester, J. David. "The Wuellnerian Sublime: Rhetorics, Power and the Ethics of Commun(icat)ion." Pages 3–22 in Hester and Hester (Amador), eds., *Rhetorics and Hermeneutics.*

Hester, James D. "Kennedy and the Reading of Paul: The Energy of Communication." Pages 139–61 in Black and Watson, eds., *Words Well Spoken.*

————. "Rhetoric in and for the New Millennium." Pages 6–12 in *Rhetorics in the New Millennium.* Edited by James D. Hester and J. David Hester. Studies in Antiquity and Christianity. New York: T&T Clark, 2010.

———— and J. David Hester (Amador), eds. *Rhetorics and Hermeneutics: Wilhelm Wuellner and His Influence.* Emory Studies in Early Christianity 9. New York: T&T Clark, 2004.

Hock, Ronald F. "Paul and Greco-Roman Education." Pages 198–227 in *Paul in the Greco-Roman World: A Handbook.* Edited by J. Paul Sampley. Harrisburg: Trinity, 2003.

_____ and Edward N. O'Neil, eds. *The Chreia and Ancient Rhetoric: Classroom Exercises.* Writings from the Greco-Roman World 2. Atlanta: Society of Biblical Literature, 2002.

_____ and Edward N. O'Neil, eds. *The Chreia in Ancient Rhetoric, Volume I: The Progymnasmata.* Society of Biblical Literature Texts and Translations 27, Graeco-Roman Religion Series 9. Atlanta: Scholars, 1986.

Huber, Lynn R. *Like a Bride Adorned: Reading Metaphor in John's Apocalypse.* Emory Studies in Early Christianity 10. New York: T&T Clark, 2007.

Hübner, Hans. "Der Galaterbrief und das Verhältnis von antiker Rhetorik und Epistolographie." *Theologische Literaturzeitung* 109 (1984): 241–50.

_____. "Review of H. D. Betz, *Galatians.*" *Theologische Literaturzeitung* 109 (1984): 341–50.

Hughes, Frank W. "George Kennedy's Contribution to Rhetorical Criticism of the Pauline Letters." Pages 125–37 in Black and Watson, eds., *Words Well Spoken.*

_____. "Rhetoric of 1 Thessalonians." Pages 94–116 in *The Thessalonian Correspondence.* Edited by Raymond F. Collins. Bibliotheca ephemeridum theologicarum lovaniensium 87. Leuven: Leuven University Press, 1990.

_____. "The Rhetoric of Letters." Pages 194–240 in *The Thessalonians Debate: Methodological Discord or Methodological Synthesis?* Edited by Karl P. Donfried and Johannes Beutler. Grand Rapids: Eerdmans, 2000.

Hyman, Naomi M. *Biblical Wo/men in the Midrash: A Sourcebook.* Northvale: Aronson, 1997.

J. David Sapir and J. C. Crocker, eds. *The Social Use of Metaphor: Essays on the Anthropology of Rhetoric.* Philadelphia: University of Pennsylvania Press, 1977.

Jameson, Fredric R. "The Symbolic Inference." Pages 68–91 in *Representing Kenneth Burke.* Edited by Hayden White and Margaret Brose. Baltimore: Johns Hopkins University Press, 1982.

Janssen-Jurreit, Marielouise. *Sexism: The Male Monopoly on History and Thought.* Translated by Verne Moberg. New York: Farrar Strauss & Giroux, 1982. Translation of *Sexismus: Über die Abtreibung der Frauenfrage.* Munich: Hanser, 1976.

Jarratt, Susan C. *Rereading the Sophists: Classical Rhetoric Refigured.* Carbondale: Southern Illinois University Press, 1991.

_____ and Nedra Reynolds. "The Splitting Image: Contemporary Feminisms and the Ethics of *ethos.*" Pages 37–64 in *Ethos: New Essays in Rhetorical and Critical Theory.* Edited by James S. Baumlin and Tita French Baumlin. Dallas: Southern Methodist University Press, 1994.

Jeal, Roy R. "Blending Two Arts: Rhetorical Words, Rhetorical Pictures and Social Formation in the Letter to Philemon." *Sino-Christian Studies* 5 (2008): 9–38.

_____. "Clothes Make the (Wo)Man." *Scriptura* 90 (2005): 685–99.

_____. "Emerging Christian Discourse: The *Acts of Pilate* as the Rhetorical Development of Devotion." *Apocrypha* 21 (2010): 151–67.

_____. "Melody, Imagery and Memory in the Moral Persuasion of Paul." Pages 160–78 in *Rhetoric, Ethic, and Moral Persuasion in Biblical Discourse.* Edited by Anders Eriksson and Thomas H. Olbricht. Emory Studies in Early Christianity 11. New York: T&T Clark, 2005.

_____. "Review of Ben Witherington III, *New Testament Rhetoric: An Introductory Guide to the Art of Persuasion in and of the New Testament.* Eugene: Cascade Books, 2009." Paper presented at the Christian Scholars Conference, Pepperdine University, Malibu, CA, 16 June 2011.

_____. "Seeing Images in Visible Words: Rhetography in Colossians." Paper presented at the Rhetoric of Religious Antiquity Seminar, Society of Biblical Literature Annual Meeting, Washington, 2006. Online: http://www.boothuc.ca/sites/default/files/seeingimagesinvisiblewordsnov 2006.pdf. Accessed 17 August 2014.

_____. "Visions of Marriage in Ephesians 5." Pages 116–30 in *Human Sexuality and the Nuptial Mystery*. Edited by idem. Eugene: Cascade Books, 2010.

Jewett, Robert. *Romans: A Commentary*. Hermeneia. Minneapolis: Fortress, 2007.

_____. *The Thessalonian Correspondence: Pauline Rhetoric and Millenarian Piety*. Philadelphia: Fortress, 1986.

Jobling, Jannine. *Feminist Biblical Interpretation in Theological Context: Restless Readings*. Burlington: Ashgate, 2002.

Jones, Leslie Webber. *Cassiodorus Senator:* An Introduction to Divine and Human Readings. See Cassiodorus Senator, *An Introduction to Divine and Human Readings*.

Kahl, Brigitte. *Galatians Re-Imagined: Reading with the Eyes of the Vanquished*. Paul in Critical Contexts. Minneapolis: Fortress, 2010.

Käsemann, Ernst. "Das Problem des historischen Jesus." *Zeitschrift für Theologie und Kirche* 51, no. 1 (1954): 125–53.

_____. *Essays on New Testament Themes*. Studies in Biblical Theology 41. London: SCM, 1964.

Kelber, Werner H. "The Work of Norman Perrin: An Intellectual Pilgrimage." *Journal of Religion* 64, no. 4 (1984): 452–67.

Kennedy, George A. "A Hoot in the Dark: The Evolution of General Rhetoric." *Philosophy and Rhetoric* 25, no. 1 (1992): 1–21.

_____. *A New History of Classical Rhetoric*. Princeton: Princeton University Press, 1994.

_____. *Aristotle:* On Rhetoric. See Aristotle, *On Rhetoric*

_____. "Classical and Christian Source Criticism." Pages 122–55 in *The Relationship among the Gospels: An Interdisciplinary Dialogue*. Edited by William O. Walker Jr. Trinity University Monograph Series in Religion 5. San Antonio: Trinity University Press, 1978.

_____. *Classical Rhetoric and Its Christian and Secular Tradition from Ancient to Modern Times.* Second edition. Chapel Hill: University of North Carolina Press, 1998.

_____. *Comparative Rhetoric: An Historical and Cross-Cultural Introduction.* New York: Oxford University Press, 1998.

_____. *Greek Rhetoric under Christian Emperors.* Princeton: Princeton University Press, 1983.

_____. *Invention and Method: Two Rhetorical Treatises from the Hermogenic Corpus.* Writings from the Greco-Roman World 15. Atlanta: Society of Biblical Literature, 2005.

_____. *New Testament Interpretation through Rhetorical Criticism.* Chapel Hill: University of North Carolina Press, 1984.

_____, trans. *Progymnasmata: Greek Textbooks of Prose Composition and Rhetoric.* Writings from the Greco-Roman World 10. Atlanta: Society of Biblical Literature, 2003.

_____. *Quintilian.* Twayne's World Authors Series 66. New York: Twayne, 1969.

_____. *The Art of Persuasion in Greece.* Princeton: Princeton University Press, 1963.

_____. *The Art of Rhetoric in the Roman World 300 B.C.–A.D. 300.* Princeton: Princeton University Press, 1972.

Kern, Kathi. *Mrs. Stanton's Bible.* Ithaca: Cornell University Press, 2001.

Kern, Philip H. *Rhetoric and Galatians: Assessing an Approach to Paul's Epistle.* Society for New Testament Studies Monograph Series 101. Cambridge: Cambridge University Press, 1998.

_____. "Rhetoric, Scholarship and Galatians: Assessing an Approach to Paul's Epistle." *Tyndale Bulletin* 46, no. 1 (1995): 201–3.

Kim, Nami, and Deborah Whitehead. "Editors' Introduction." *Journal of Feminist Studies in Religion* 25, no. 1 (2009): 1–18.

Kitcher, Philip. *Science, Truth, and Democracy*. New York: Oxford University Press, 2001.

Klauck, Hans-Josef. *Ancient Letters and the New Testament: A Guide to Context and Exegesis*. Waco: Baylor University Press, 2006.

Klein, Julie Thompson. "Text/Context: The Rhetoric of the Social Sciences." Pages 9–27 in *Writing the Social Text: Poetics and Politics in Social Science Discourse*. Edited by Richard H. Brown. New York: de Gruyter, 1992.

Kopperschmidt, Josef, ed. *Rhetorik als Texttheorie*. Darmstadt: Wissenschaftliche Buchgesellschaft, 1990.

Koskenniemi, Heikki. *Studien zur Idee und Phraseologie des griechischen Briefes bis 400 n. Chr.* Helsinki: Akateeminen Kirjakauppa, 1956.

Kövecses, Zoltán. *Metaphor in Culture: Universality and Variation*. Cambridge: Cambridge University Press, 2005.

Kreissl, Reinhard. *Text und Kontext: Die soziale Konstruktion wissenschaftlicher Texte*. Munich: Profil, 1985.

Kretzenbacher, Heinz L. "Wie durchsichtig ist die Sprache der Wissenschaft?" Pages 15–40 in *Linguistik der Wissenschaftssprache*. Edited by idem and Harald Weinrich. Akademie der Wissenschaften zu Berlin: Forschungsberichte. Berlin: de Gruyter, 1994.

Kruse, Volker. *"Geschichts- und Sozialphilosophie" oder "Wirklichkeitswissenschaft"? Die deutsche historische Soziologie und die logischen Kategorien René Königs und Max Webers*. Frankfurt: Suhrkamp, 1999.

Kuhn, Thomas. *The Structure of Scientific Revolutions*. Chicago: University of Chicago Press, 1962.

Lakoff, George, and Mark. Johnson. *Metaphors We Live By*. Chicago: University of Chicago Press, 1981.

Lakoff, Robin. "Lewis Carroll: Subversive Pragmaticist." *Pragmatics* 3, no. 4 (1993): 367–85.

Lampe, Peter. "Affects and Emotions in the Rhetoric of Paul's Letter to Philemon: A Rhetorical-Psychological Interpretation." Pages 61–77 in

Philemon in Perspective: Interpreting a Pauline Letter. Edited by D. François Tolmie. Berlin: de Gruyter, 2005.

_____. "Rhetorical Analysis of Pauline Texts—Quo Vadit?" Pages 3–21 in *Paul and Rhetoric.* Edited by J. Paul Sampley and Peter Lampe. New York: T&T Clark, 2010.

Lange, John. "The Argument from Silence." *History and Theory* 5, no. 3 (1966): 288–301.

Lau, Christoph, and Ulrich Beck. *Definitionsmacht und Grenzen angewandter Sozialwissenschaften: Eine Untersuchung am Beispiel der Bildungs- und Arbeitsmarktforschung.* Opladen: Westdeutscher, 1989.

Lauri Thurén. "Motivation as the Core of Paraenesis—Remarks on Peter and Paul as Persuaders." Pages 353–72 in *Early Christian Paraenesis in Context.* Edited by James Starr and Troels Engberg-Pedersen. Beihefte zur *Zeitschrift für die neutestamentliche Wissenschaft* 125. Berlin: de Gruyter, 2005.

Lausberg, Heinrich. *Elemente der Literarischen Rhetorik.* Munich: Hueber, 1963.

_____. *Handbook of Literary Rhetoric: A Foundation for Literary Study.* Edited and translated by David E. Orton and R. Dean Anderson. Leiden: Brill, 1998. Translation of *Handbuch der Literarischen Rhetorik.* 2 volumes. Munich: Hueber, 1960.

LeMon, Joel M. *Yahweh's Winged Form in the Psalms: Exploring Congruent Iconography and Texts.* Orbis Biblicus et Orientalis. Göttingen: Vandenhoeck & Ruprecht, 2010.

Lentricchia, Frank. *Criticism and Social Change.* Chicago: University of Chicago Press, 1983.

Leon, Judah Messer. *The Book of the Honeycomb's Flow.* Ithaca: Cornell University Press, 1982.

Lincoln, Andrew. *Truth on Trial: The Lawsuit Motif in the Fourth Gospel.* Peabody: Hendrickson, 2000.

Long, Fredrick J. *Ancient Rhetoric and Paul's Apology: The Compositional Unity of 2 Corinthians.* Society for New Testament Studies Monograph Series 131. Cambridge: Cambridge University Press, 2004.

Longinus. *On the Sublime.* Loeb Classical Library 199. Translated by W. Hamilton Fyfe. Cambridge, MA: Harvard University Press, 1982.

Lopez, Davina. *Apostle to the Conquered: Reimagining Paul's Mission.* Minneapolis: Fortress, 2010.

Lucaites, John Louis, Celeste Michelle Condit, and Sally Caudill, eds. *Contemporary Rhetorical Theory: A Reader.* New York: Guilford, 1999.

Lüdemann, Gerd. *Paul Apostle to the Gentiles: Studies in Chronology.* Philadelphia: Fortress, 1984.

Lyne, John. "Rhetorics of Inquiry." *Quarterly Journal of Speech* 71, no. 1 (1985): 65–73.

Lyons, George. *Pauline Autobiography: Toward a New Understanding.* Society of Biblical Literature Dissertation Series 73. Atlanta: Scholars, 1985.

Lyons, John. *Language, Meaning and Context.* Bungay: Suffolk-Chaucer, 1981.

Mack, Burton L. *Christian Mentality: The Entanglements of Power, Violence, and Fear.* Religion in Culture. London: Acumen, 2011.

————. *Myth and the Christian Nation: A Social Theory of Religion.* Religion in Culture. London: Equinox, 2008.

————. *Myth of Innocence: Mark and Christian Origins.* Foundations and Facets. Minneapolis: Fortress, 1998.

————. *Rhetoric and the New Testament.* Guides to Biblical Scholarship New Testament Series. Minneapolis: Fortress, 1990.

————. *The Christian Myth: Origins, Logic, and Legacy.* London: Bloomsbury, 2003.

———— and Vernon K. Robbins. *Patterns of Persuasion in the Gospels.* Foundations and Facets: Literary Facets. Sonoma: Polebridge, 1989. Reprinted, Eugene: Wipf & Stock, 2008.

Maier, Harry O. "A Sly Civility: Colossians and Empire." *Journal for the Study of the New Testament* 27 (2005): 323–40.

_____. "Barbarians, Scythians and Imperial Iconography in the Epistle to the Colossians." Pages 385–406 in *Picturing the New Testament: Studies in Ancient Visual Images*. Edited by Annette Weissenrieder, Friedericke Wendt, and Petra von Gemünden. Wissenschaftliche Untersuchungen zum Neuen Testament 2.193. Tübingen: Mohr Siebeck, 2005.

_____. *Picturing Paul in Empire: Imperial Image, Text and Persuasion in Colossians, Ephesians and the Pastoral Epistles*. London: T&T Clark/ Bloomsbury, 2013.

_____. "Reading Colossians in the Ruins." Pages 212–31 in *Colossae in Space and Time: Linking to an Ancient City*. Edited by Alan H. Cadwallader and Michael Trainor. Novum Testamentum et Orbis Antiquus 94. Göttingen: Vandenhoeck & Ruprecht, 2011.

Mailloux, Stephen. "Articulation and Understanding: The Pragmatic Intimacy between Rhetoric and Hermeneutics." Pages 378–94 in *Rhetoric and Hermeneutics in Our Time: A Reader*. Edited by Walter Jost and Michael J. Hyde. New Haven: Yale University Press, 1997.

Malherbe, Abraham J. "Ancient Epistolary Theorists." *Ohio Journal of Religious Studies* 5 (1977): 3–77. Reprinted as *Ancient Epistolary Theorists*. Society of Biblical Literature Sources for Biblical Study 19. Atlanta: Scholars, 1988.

Malina, Bruce J. "Rhetorical Criticism and Social-Scientific Criticism: Why Won't Romanticism Leave Us Alone?" Pages 72–96 in *Rhetoric, Scripture and Theology: Essays from the 1994 Pretoria Conference*. Edited by Stanley E. Porter and Thomas H. Olbricht. *Journal for the Study of the New Testament* Supplement Series 131. Sheffield: Sheffield Academic, 1996.

_____. *The New Testament World: Insights from Cultural Anthropology*. Third revised and expanded edition. Louisville: Westminster John Knox,

2001. Markus, H., R. Shweder, and M. Minow, eds. *The Free Exercise of Culture*. New York: Russell Sage Foundation, 2001.

Marshall, Gloria A. "Racial Classifications: Popular and Scientific." Pages 116–27 in *The "Racial" Economy of Science*. Edited by Sandra Harding. Bloomington: Indiana University Press, 1993.

Marshall, John W. "Paul's Ethical Appeal in Philippians." Pages 357–74 in *Rhetoric and the New Testament: Essays from the 1992 Heidelberg Conference*. Edited by Stanley Porter and Thomas Olbricht. *Journal for the Study of the New Testament* Supplement Series 90. Sheffield: Journal for the Study of the Old Testament, 1993.

Martin, Troy W. "Apostasy to Paganism: The Rhetorical Stasis of the Galatian Controversy." *Journal of Biblical Literature* 114, no. 3 (1995): 437–61. Reprinted as pages 73–94 in Nanos, ed., *The Galatians Debate*.

_____. "Invention and Arrangement in Recent Pauline Rhetorical Studies: A Survey of the Practices and the Problems." Pages 48–118 in *Paul and Rhetoric*. Edited by J. Paul Sampley and Peter Lampe. New York: T&T Clark, 2010.

_____. "Investigating the Pauline Letter Body: Issues, Methods, and Approaches." Pages 197–212 in *Paul and the Ancient Letter Form*. Edited by Stanley E. Porter and Sean A. Adams. Pauline Studies 6. Leiden: Brill, 2010.

_____. *Metaphor and Composition in First Peter*. Society of Biblical Literature Dissertation Series 131. Atlanta: Scholars, 1992.

_____. "The Voice of Emotion: Paul's Pathetic Persuasion (Gal 4:12–20)." Pages 189–201 in *Paul and Pathos*. Edited by Thomas H. Olbricht and Jerry L. Sumney. Society of Biblical Literature Symposium Series 16. Atlanta: Society of Biblical Literature, 2001.

_____. "Veiled Exhortations Regarding the Veil: Ethos as the Controlling Proof in Moral Persuasion (1 Cor 11:2–16)." Pages 255–73 in *Rhetoric, Ethic, and Moral Persuasion in Biblical Discourse: Essays from the 2002*

Heidelberg Conference. Edited by Thomas H. Olbricht and Anders Eriksson. Emory Studies in Early Christianity 11. New York: T&T Clark, 2005.

Martyn, J. Louis. *History and Theology in the Fourth Gospel.* Third edition. New Testament Library. Louisville: Westminster John Knox, 2003.

Marxsen, Willi. *Mark The Evangelist: Studies on the Redaction History of the Gospel.* Translated by James Boyce et al. New York: Abingdon, 1969. Translation of *Der Evangelist Markus: Studien zur Redaktionsgeschichte des Evangeliums.*Göttingen: Vandenhoeck & Ruprecht, 1956.

McCloskey, Deirdre N. *Crossing: A Memoir.* Chicago: University of Chicago Press, 2000.

_____. *The Rhetoric of Economics.* Second edition. Madison: University of Wisconsin Press, 1998.

McGee, M. C. "Another Philippic: Notes on the Ideological Turn in Criticism." *Central States Speech Journal* 35 (1984): 43–50.

McGowan, John. *Hannah Arendt: An Introduction.* Minneapolis: University of Minnesota Press, 1998.

McKerrow, Rayme E. "Critical Rhetoric: Theory and Praxis." *Communication Monographs* 56 (1989): 91–111.

_____. "Critical Rhetoric: Theory and Practice." Pages 441–63 in Lucaites et al., eds., *Contemporary Rhetorical Theory.*

Meeks, Wayne A. "*Hypomnēmata* from an Untamed Sceptic: A Response to George Kennedy." Pages 152–72 in *The Relationship among the Gospels: An Interdisciplinary Dialogue.* Edited by William O. Walker Jr. Trinity University Monograph Series in Religion 5.San Antonio: Trinity University Press, 1978.

_____. "Review of H. D. Betz, *Galatians.*" *Journal of Biblical Literature* 100, no. 2 (1981): 304–7.

Meese, Elizabeth A. *Crossing the Double-Cross: The Practice of Feminist Criticism.* Chapel Hill: University of North Carolina Press, 1986.

Melion, Walter S. "Exegesis." Pages 124–41 in *Scripture for the Eyes: Bible Illustration in Netherlandish Prints of the Sixteenth Century*. Edited by James Clifton and Walter S. Melion. New York: Museum of Biblical Art, 2009.

————. "Introductory Study." Pages 1–32 in Nadal, *Annotations and Meditations on the Gospels, Volume III: The Resurrection Narratives*.

Merton, Robert K. *The Sociology of Science: Theoretical and Empirical Investigations*. Chicago: University of Chicago Press, 1973.

Miller, Carolyn R. "The Aristotelean *Topos*: Hunting for Novelty." Pages 130–46 in *Rereading Aristotle's Rhetoric*. Edited by Alan G. Gross and Arthur E. Walzer. Carbondale: Southern Illinois University Press, 2000.

Miller, Casey, and Kate Swift. *Words and Women: New Language in New Times*. Garden City: Doubleday, 1977.

Minow, Martha. *Equality and the Bill of Rights*. Ithaca: Cornell University Press, 1992.

————. *Identities*. New Haven: Yale University Press, 1991.

Mitchell, Margaret M. *Paul and the Rhetoric of Reconciliation*. Louisville: Westminster John Knox, 1991. Reprinted as *Paul and the Rhetoric of Reconciliation: An Exegetical Investigation of the Language and Composition of 1 Corinthians*. Louisville: Westminister John Knox, 1993.

————. *The Heavenly Trumpet: John Chrysostom and the Art of Pauline Interpretation*. Hermeneutische Untersuchungen zur Theologie 40. Tübingen: Mohr Siebeck, 2000.

Mohanti, Chandra Talpade. "Introduction: Cartographies of Struggle." Pages 1–47 in *Third World Women and the Politics of Feminism*. Edited by idem, Ann Russo, and Lourdes Torres. Bloomington: Indiana University Press, 1991.

Mongstad-Kvammen, Ingeborg. *Toward a Postcolonial Reading of the Epistle of James: James 2:1–13 in its Roman Imperial Context*. Biblical Interpretation Series 119. Leiden: Brill, 2013.

Morrow, Raymond A. and David D. Baron. *Critical Theory and Methodology.* Thousand Oaks: Sage, 1994.

Mosco, V. "Critical Research and the Role of Labor." *Journal of Communication* 33 (1983): 237–48.

Mouffe, Chantal, ed. *Dimensions of Radical Democracy.* London: Verso, 1992.

Mountford, Roxanne. *The Gendered Pulpit.* Studies in Rhetorics and Feminisms. Carbondale: Southern Illinois University Press, 2003.

Muilenberg, James. "Form Criticism and Beyond." *Journal of Biblical Literature* 88, no. 1 (1969): 1–18.

_____. "The Book of Isaiah, Chapters 40–66: Introduction and Exegesis." Pages 381–773 in *The Interpreters Bible, Volume 5: Ecclesiastes, Song of Songs, Isaiah, Jeremiah.* Edited by George A. Buttrick. Nashville: Abingdon, 1956.

_____. *The Literary Relations of the Epistle of Barnabas and the Teaching of the Twelve Apostles.* PhD dissertation, Yale University, 1926. Marburg, 1929.

Mulkay, Michael. *Science and the Sociology of Knowledge.* London: Allen & Unwin, 1979.

Mumby, D. K. "The Political Function of Narrative in Organizations." *Communication Monographs* 54 (1987): 113–27.

Murphy-O'Connor, Jerome. *Paul the Letter-Writer: His World, His Options, His Skills.* Collegeville: Liturgical, 1995.

Nadal, Jerome. *Annotations and Meditations on the Gospels.* Edited and translated by Frederick A. Homann. 3 volumes. Philadelphia: Saint Joseph's University Press, 2003–2005.

Nadeau, Raymond E. "*On Stases*: A Translation with an Introduction and Notes." *Speech Monographs* 31 (1964): 361–424.

Nanos, Mark D., ed. *The Galatians Debate: Contemporary Issues in Rhetorical and Historical Interpretation.* Peabody: Hendrickson, 2002.

Nelson, John S. "Political Theory as Political Rhetoric." Pages 169–240 in *What Should Political Theory Be Now?* Edited by idem. Albany: State University of New York Press, 1983.

————— and Allan Megill. "Rhetoric of Inquiry: Projects and Prospects." *Quarterly Journal of Speech* 72, no. 1 (1986): 20-37.

—————, Allan Megill, and Donald N. McCloskey. "Rhetoric of Inquiry." Pages 3–18 in idem, eds., *The Rhetoric of the Human Sciences.*

—————, Allan Megill, and Donald McCloskey, eds. *The Rhetoric of the Human Sciences: Language and Argument in Scholarship and Public Affairs.* Madison: University of Wisconsin Press, 1987.

Newton, Judith, and Deborah Rosenfelt, eds. *Feminist Criticism and Social Change.* New York: Methuen, 1985.

Neyrey, Jerome H. "Encomium versus Vituperation: Contrasting Portraits of Jesus in the Fourth Gospel." *Journal of Biblical Literature* 126, no. 4 (2007): 529-52.

—————. "The Social Location of Paul: Education as the Key." Pages 126–64 in *Fabrics of Discourse: Essays in Honor of Vernon K. Robbins.* Edited by David B. Gowler, L. Gregory Bloomquist, and Duane Watson. Harrisburg: Trinity, 2003.

Niebuhr, Reinhold. *The Nature and Destiny of Man.* Gifford Lectures. 2 volumes. New York: Scribner's, 1949.

Nietzsche, Friedrich. *On the Genealogy of Morals.* Translated by W. Kaufmann. New York: Vintage Books, 1989.

Niederhauser, Jürg. "Metaphern in der Wissenschaftssprache als Thema der Linguistik." Pages 290–98 in *Metapher und Innovation: Die Rolle der Metapher im Wandel von Sprache und Wissenschaft.* Edited by Lutz Danneberg, Andreas Graeser, and Klaus Petrus. Berner Reihe philosophischer Studien 16. Bern: Haupt, 1995.

Norden, Eduard. *Agnostos Theos: Untersuchungen zur Formgeschichte religiöser Rede.* Leipzig: Teubner, 1913.

_____. *Die antike Kunstprosa vom VI. Jahrhunderts vor Christus in die Zeit der Renaissance*. Leipzig: Teubner, 1909.

O'Mahony, Kieran J. *Pauline Persuasion: A Sounding in 2 Corinthians 8–9*. Journal for the Study of the New Testament Supplement Series 199. Sheffield: Sheffield Academic, 2000.

Olbricht, Thomas H. "An Aristotelian Rhetorical Analysis of 1 Thessalonians." Pages 216–36 in *Greeks, Romans, and Christians: Essays in Honor of Abraham J. Malherbe*. Edited by David L. Balch, Everett Ferguson, and Wayne A. Meeks. Minneapolis: Fortress, 1990.

_____. "Introduction." Pages 1–4 in *Paul and Pathos*. Edited by idem and Jerry L. Sumney. Society of Biblical Literature Symposium Series 16. Atlanta: Society of Biblical Literature, 2001.

_____. "The Flowering of Rhetorical Criticism in America." Pages 79–102 in *The Rhetorical Analysis of Scripture: Essays from the 1995 London Conference*. Edited by Stanley E. Porter and Thomas H. Olbricht. *Journal for the Study of the New Testament* Supplement Series 146. Sheffield: Sheffield Academic Press, 1997.

_____. "Wilhelm Wuellner and the Promise of Rhetoric." Pages 78–104 in Hester and Hester (Amador), eds., *Rhetorics and Hermeneutics*.

Ong, Walter. *Orality and Literacy: The Technologizing of the Word*. New York: Methuen, 1982.

Parsenios, George L. *Rhetoric and Drama in the Johannine Lawsuit Motif*. Wissenschaftliche Untersuchungen zum Neuen Testament 258. Tübingen: Mohr Siebeck, 2010.

Patrick, Dale, and Allen Scult. *Rhetoric and Biblical Interpretation*. Sheffield: Almond, 1990.

Pedersen, Johannes. *Israel: Its Life and Culture*. Atlanta: Scholars, 1991.

Pelikan, Jaroslav. *Divine Rhetoric: The Sermon on the Mount as Message and as Model in Augustine, Chrysostom, and Luther*. Crestwood: St. Vladimir's Seminary Press, 2001.

Penner, Todd. "'In the Beginning': Post-Critical Reflections on Early Christian Textual Transmission and Modern Textual Transgression." *Perspectives in Religious Studies* 33 (2006): 415–34.

_____. "Reconfiguring the Rhetorical Study of Acts: Reflections on the Method in and Learning of a Progymnastic Poetics." *Perspectives in Religious Studies* 30 (2003): 425–39.

_____ and Caroline Vander Stichele. *Contextualizing Acts: Lukan Narrative and Greco-Roman Discourse.* Society of Biblical Literature Symposium Series 20. Atlanta: Society of Biblical Literature, 2003.

_____ and Davina C. Lopez. "Homelessness as a Way Home? A Methodological Reflection and Proposal." Pages 180–203 in *Holy Land as Homeland? Models for Constructing the Historic Landscapes of Jesus.* Edited by K. Whitelam. Social World of Biblical Antiquity, Second Series, 7. Sheffield: Sheffield Phoenix Academic, 2011.

_____ and Davina C. Lopez. "Rhetorical Approaches: Introducing the Art of Persuasion in Paul and Pauline Studies." Pages 33–52 in *Studying Paul's Letters: Contemporary Perspectives and Methods.* Edited by J. Marchal. Minneapolis: Fortress, 2012.

Perelman, Chaim. *Realm of Rhetoric.* Translated by William Kluback. London: University of Notre Dame Press, 1982.

_____ and Lucie Olbrechts-Tyteca. *The New Rhetoric: A Treatise on Argumentation.* Translated by John Wilkinson and Purcell Weaver. Notre Dame: University of Notre Dame Press, 1969.

Perrin, Norman. *Jesus and the Language of the Kingdom: Symbol and Metaphor in New Testament Interpretation.* Philadelphia: Fortress, 1976.

Peter, Hermann. *Der Brief in der römischen Literatur: Literargeschichtliche Untersuchungen und Zusammenfassungen.* Abhandlungen der Königlichen Sächsischen Gesellschaft der Wissenschaften, philologisch-historische Klasse 20.3. Leipzig: Teubner, 1901. Reprinted, Hildesheim: Georg Olms, 1965

Pickering, Andrew. "From Science as Knowledge to Science as Practice." Pages 1–26 in *Science as Practice and Culture*. Edited by idem. Chicago: University of Chicago Press, 1992.

Pinker, Steven. *The Stuff of Thought: Language as a Window into Human Nature*. New York: Viking, 2007.

Popkes, Wiard. "Paraenesis in the New Testament: An Exercise in Conceptuality." Pages 13–46 in *Early Christian Paraenesis in Context*. Edited by James Starr and Troels Engberg-Pedersen. Beihefte zur *Zeitschrift für die neutestamentliche Wissenschaft* 125. Berlin: de Gruyter, 2005.

Porter, Stanley E. "Paul as Epistolographer and Rhetorician?" Pages 98–125 in *The Rhetorical Interpretation of Scripture: Essays from the 1996 Malibu Conference*. Edited by idem and Dennis L. Stamps. *Journal for the Study of the New Testament* Supplement Series 180. Sheffield: Sheffield Academic, 1999.

_____. "Paul of Tarsus and His Letters." Pages 541–67 in *Handbook of Classical Rhetoric in the Hellenistic Period: 330 BC–AD 400*. Edited by idem. Leiden: E. J. Brill, 1997.

_____. "The Theoretical Justification for Application of Rhetorical Categories to Pauline Epistolary Literature." Pages 100–22 in *Rhetoric and the New Testament: Essays from the 1992 Heidelberg Conference*. Edited by idem and Thomas H. Olbricht. *Journal for the Study of the New Testament* Supplement Series 90. Sheffield: Journal for the Study of the Old Testament, 1993.

Poster, Carol. "Words and Works: Philosophical Protreptic and the Epistle of James." Pages 235–53 in *Rhetorics in the New Millennium: Promise and Fulfillment*. Edited by James D. Hester and J. David Hester. Studies in Antiquity and Christianity. New York: T&T Clark, 2010.

Prelli, Lawrence J. "The Rhetorical Construction of Scientific Ethos." Pages 48–68 in *Rhetoric in the Human Sciences*. Edited by Herbert W. Simons. Inquiries in Social Construction Series. London: Sage, 1989.

Probst, Hermann. *Paulus und der Brief: Die Rhetorik des antiken Briefes als Form der paulinischen Korintherkorrespondenz (1 Kor 8–10)*. Wissenschaftliche Untersuchungen zum Neuen Testament 2.45. Tübingen: Mohr Siebeck, 1991.

Pusch, Luise F. *Das Deutsche als Männersprache*. Frankfurt: Suhrkamp, 1984.

Rabinowitz, Nancy Sorkin, and Amy Richlin, eds. *Feminist Theory and the Classics*. New York: Routledge, 1993.

Ratcliffe, Krista. *Anglo-American Feminist Challenges to the Rhetorical Traditions*. Carbondale: Southern Illinois University Press, 1996.

Rebenich, Stefan. "Historical Prose." Pages 265–337 in *Handbook of Classical Rhetoric in the Hellenistic Period: 330 B.C.–A.D. 400*. Edited by Stanley E. Porter. Leiden: Brill, 2001.

Reed, Jeffrey T. "Using Ancient Rhetorical Categories to Interpret Paul's Letters: A Question of Genre." Pages 293–324 in *Rhetoric and the New Testament: Essays from the 1992 Heidelberg Conference*. Edited by Stanley Porter and Thomas Olbricht. Journal for the Study of the New Testament Supplement Series 90. Sheffield: Journal for the Study of the Old Testament, 1993.

Richards, Jennifer. *Rhetoric: The New Critical Idiom*. New York: Routledge, 2008.

Riley, Denise. *"Am I That Name?" Feminism and the Category of Women in History*. Minneapolis: University of Minnesota Press, 1988.

Robbins, Vernon K. "Argumentative Textures in Socio-Rhetorical Interpretation." Pages 27–65 in *Rhetorical Argumentation in Biblical Texts: Essays from the Lund 2000 Conference*. Edited by Anders Eriksson, Thomas H. Olbricht, and Walter Übelacker. Emory Studies in Early Christianity 8. Harrisburg: Trinity, 2002.

_____. "Bodies and Politics in Luke 1-2 and Sirach 44-50: Men, Women, and Boys." *Scriptura* 90 (2005): 724–838.

_____. "Conceptual Blending and Early Christian Imagination." Pages 161–95 in *Explaining Christian Origins and Early Judaism: Contributions from Cognitive and Social Science.* Edited by Petri Luomanen, Ilkka Pyysiäinen, and Risto Uro. Biblical Interpretation Series 89. Leiden: Brill, 2007.

_____. "Enthymeme and Picture in the Gospel of Thomas." Pages 175–207 in *Thomasine Traditions in Antiquity: The Social and Cultural World of the Gospel of Thomas.* Edited by Jon Ma. Asgeirsson, April D. DeConick, and Risto Uro. Nag Hammadi and Manichaean Studies 59. Leiden: Brill, 2006.

_____. *Exploring the Texture of Texts: A Guide to Socio-Rhetorical Interpretation.* Valley Forge: Trinity, 1996.

_____. "From Enthymeme to Theology in Luke 11:1–13." Pages 191–214 in *Literary Studies in Luke-Acts: A Collection of Essays in Honor of Joseph B. Tyson.* Edited by Richard P. Thompson and Thomas E. Phillips. Macon: Mercer University Press, 1998.

_____. "From Heidelberg to Heidelberg: Rhetorical Interpretation of the Bible at the Seven 'Pepperdine' Conferences from 1992 to 2002." Pages 335–77 in *Rhetoric, Ethic, and Moral Persuasion in Biblical Discourse.* Edited by Thomas H. Olbricht and Anders Eriksson. Emory Studies in Early Christianity 11. New York: T&T Clark, 2005.

_____. *Jesus the Teacher: A Socio-Rhetorical Interpretation of Mark.* Minneapolis: Fortress, 2009.

_____. "Luke-Acts: A Mixed Population Seeks a Home in the Roman Empire." Pages 202–21 in *Images of Empire.* Edited by Loveday Alexander. Sheffield: Journal for the Study of the Old Testament, 1991.

_____. "Mark I.14–20: An Interpretation at the Intersection of Jewish and Graeco-Roman Traditions." *New Testament Studies* 28, no. 2 (1982): 220–36. Reprinted as pages 137–154 in *New Boundaries in Old Territory:*

Forms and Social Rhetoric in Mark. Edited by David B. Gowler. New York: Peter Lang, 1994.

————. "Oral, Rhetorical, and Literary Cultures: A Response." Pages 75–91 in *Orality and Textuality in Early Christian Literature*. Edited by Joanna Dewey. Semeia 65. Atlanta: Scholars, 1994.

————. "Progymnastic Rhetorical Composition and Pre-Gospel Traditions: A New Approach." Pages 111–47 in *The Synoptic Gospels: Source Criticism and the New Literary Criticism*. Edited by Camille Focant. Bibliotheca ephemeridum theologicarum Lovaniensium 110. Leuven: Leuven University Press, 1993.

————. "Rhetography: A New Way of Seeing the Familiar Text." Pages 81–106 in Black and Watson, eds., *Words Well Spoken*.

————. "Rhetoric and Culture: Mark 4-11 as a Test Case." Pages 145–81 in idem, *Sea Voyages and Beyond*.

————. *Sea Voyages and Beyond: Emerging Strategies in Socio-Rhetorical Interpretation*. Emory Studies in Early Christianity 14. Blandford Forum: Deo, 2010.

————. "Social-Scientific Criticism and Literary Studies: Prospects for Cooperation in Biblical Interpretation." Pages 274–89 in *Modelling Early Christianity: Social-Scientific Studies of the New Testament in Its Context*. Edited by Philip F. Esler. London: Routledge, 1995. Reprinted as pages 182–200 in idem, *Sea Voyages and Beyond*.

————. "Socio-rhetorical Criticism." Pages 342–46 in *Interpreting the Bible: A Handbook of Terms and Methods*. Edited by W. Randolph Tate. Peabody: Hendrickson, 2006.

————. "Socio-Rhetorical Interpretation." Pages 199–203 in *The Blackwell Companion to the New Testament*. Edited by David E. Aune. Oxford: Wiley-Blackwell, 2010.

————. "Summons and Outline in Mark: The Three-Step Progression." *Novum Testamentum* 23, no. 1 (1981): 97–114. Reprinted as pages 103–20 in *The Composition of Mark's Gospel: Selected Studies from Novum Testamentum.* Edited by D. E. Orton. Brill's Readers in Biblical Studies 3. Leiden: Brill, 1999. Reprinted as pages 119–35 in *New Boundaries in Old Territory: Forms and Social Rhetoric in Mark.* Edited by David B. Gowler. New York: Peter Lang, 1994.

_____. "The Dialectical Nature of Early Christian Discourse." *Scriptura* 59 (1996): 353–62. Online: http://www.religion.emory.edu/faculty/robbins/ SRS/vkr/dialect.cfm. Accessed 17 August 2014.

_____. *The Invention of Christian Discourse, Volume 1.* Rhetoric of Religious Antiquity 1. Blandford Forum: Deo, 2009.

_____. "The Present and Future of Rhetorical Analysis." Pages 24–52 in *The Rhetorical Analysis of Scripture: Essays from the 1995 London Conference.* Edited by Stanley E. Porter and Thomas H. Olbricht. *Journal for the Study of the New Testament* Supplement Series 146. Sheffield: Sheffield Academic, 1997.

_____, ed. *The Rhetoric of Pronouncement.* Semeia 64. Atlanta: Scholars, 1994.

_____. "The Rhetorical Full-Turn in Biblical Interpretation: Reconfiguring Rhetorical-Political Analysis." Pages 48–60 in *Rhetorical Criticism and the Bible: Essays from the 1998 Florence Conference.* Edited by Stanley E. Porter and Thomas H. Olbricht. *Journal for the Study of the New Testament* Supplement Series 195. Sheffield: Sheffield Academic, 2002. Online: http://www.emory.edu/COLLEGE/RELIGION/faculty/ robbins/Pdfs/FullTurnFlorPubPgs.pdf (accessed 17 August 2014).

_____. "The Rhetorical Full-Turn in Biblical Interpretation and Its Relevance for Feminist Hermeneutics." Pages 109–27 in *Her Master's Tools? Feminist and Postcolonial Engagements of Historical-critical Discourse.* Edited by Caroline Vander Stichele and Todd C. Penner. Global Perspectives on Biblical Scholarship 9. Atlanta: Society of Biblical Literature and Leiden: Brill, 2005.

_____. "The Social Location of the Implied Author of Luke-Acts." Pages 305–32 in *The Social World of Luke-Acts: Models for Interpretation*. Edited by Jerome H. Neyrey. Peabody: Hendrickson, 1991.

_____. *The Tapestry of Early Christian Discourse: Rhetoric, Society and Ideology*. London: Routledge, 1996.

_____. "Where is Wuellner's Anti-Hermeneutical Hermeneutic Taking Us? From Schleiermacher to Thistleton and Beyond." Pages 105–25 in Hester and Hester (Amador), eds., *Rhetorics and Hermeneutics*. Online: http://www.religion.emory.edu/faculty/robbins/Pdfs/WuellnerRhet Herm.pdf (accessed 17 August 2014).

_____. "Why Participate in African Biblical Interpretation?" Pages 275–91 in *Interpreting the New Testament in Africa*. Edited by Mary N. Getui, Tinyiko S. Maluleke, and Justin Ukpong. Nairobi: Acton, 2001.

Roberts, Jennifer Tolbert. *Athens on Trial: The Antidemocratic Tradition in Western Thought*. Princeton: Princeton University Press, 1994.

Roberts, R. H., and J. M. M. Good, eds. *The Recovery of Rhetoric: Persuasive Discourse and Disciplinarity in the Human Sciences*. Bristol: Bristol Classical; Charlottesville: University Press of Virginia, 1993.

Robins, Robert H. *A Short History of Linguistics*. London: Longman, 1979.

Rohrbaugh, Richard L., ed. *The Social Sciences and New Testament Interpretation*. Peabody: Hendrickson, 1996.

Rorty, Amélie Oksenberg, ed. *Essays on Aristotle's Rhetoric*. Berkeley: University of California Press, 1996.

Rose, Hilary. "Rhetoric, Feminism and Scientific Knowledge: Or From Either/Or to Both/And." Pages 203–23 in Roberts and Good, eds., *The Recovery of Rhetoric*.

Royster, Jacqueline Jones. *Traces of a Stream: Literary and Social Change Among African American Women*. Pittsburgh: University of Pittsburgh Press, 2000.

_____ and Gesa E. Kirsch. *Feminist Rhetorical Practices: New Horizons for Rhetoric, Composition and Literacy Studies*. Carbondale: Southern Illinois University Press, 2012.

Said, Edward W. *Humanism and Democratic Criticism*. New York: Palgrave MacMillan, 2004.

Samuels, Warren J. *Economics as Discourse: An Analysis of the Language of Economists*. Boston: Kluwer Academic, 1990.

Sänger, Dieter. "'Vergeblich bemüht' (Gal 4.11)?: Zur paulinischen Argumentationsstrategie im Galaterbrief." *New Testament Studies* 48, no. 3 (2002): 377–99.

Saunders, Ernest W. *Searching the Scriptures: A History of the Society of Biblical Literature, 1880–1980*. Chico: Scholars, 1982.

Schell, Eileen E., and K. J. Rawson, eds. *Rhetorica in Motion: Feminist Rhetorical Methods and Methodologies*. Pittsburgh Series in Composition, Literacy, and Culture. Pittsburgh: University of Pittsburgh Press, 2010.

Schneiders, Sandra. *The Revelatory Text: Interpreting the New Testament as Sacred Scripture*. New York: HarperSanFrancisco, 1991.

Schröder, Hannelore. "Feministische Gesellschaftstheorie," Pages 449–76 in *Feminismus, Inspektion der Herrenkultur: Ein Handbuch*. Edited by Luise F. Pusch. Frankfurt: Suhrkamp, 1983.

Schröder, Hartmut, ed. *Fachtextpragmatik*. Tübingen: Narr, 1993.

Schüssler Fiorenza, Elisabeth. *But She Said: Feminist Practices of Biblical Interpretation*. Boston: Beacon, 1992.

_____. "Challenging the Rhetorical Half-Turn: Feminist and Rhetorical Biblical Criticism." Pages 28–53 in *Rhetoric, Scripture and Theology: Essays from the 1994 Pretoria Conference*. Edited by Stanley E. Porter and Thomas H. Olbricht. *Journal for the Study of the New Testament* Supplement Series 131. Sheffield: Sheffield Academic, 1996.

_____. *Changing Horizons: Explorations in Feminist Interpretation*. Minneapolis: Fortress, 2013.

_____. *Democratizing Biblical Studies: Toward an Emancipatory Educational Space.* Louisville: Westminster John Knox, 2009.

_____. "Disciplinary Matters: A Critical Rhetoric and Ethic of Inquiry." Pages 9–32 in *Rhetoric, Ethic, and Moral Persuasion in Biblical Discourse.* Edited by Thomas H. Olbricht and Anders Eriksson. Emory Studies in Early Christianity 11. New York: T&T Clark, 2005.

_____. *Grenzen überschreiten: Der theoretische Anspruch feministischer Theologie.* Münster: Lit, 2004.

_____. *In Memory of Her: A Feminist Theological Reconstruction of Christian Origins.* 10th Anniversary Edition. New York: Crossroad, 1994.

_____. *Jesus and the Politics of Interpretation.* New York: Continuum, 2000.

_____. *Jesus: Miriam's Child, Sophia's Prophet.* New York: Continuum, 1995.

_____. "Method in Wo/men's Studies in Religion: A Critical Feminist Hermeneutics." Pages 207–41 in *Methodology in Religious Studies: The Interface with Women's Studies.* Edited by Arvind Sharma. Albany: State University of New York Press, 2002.

_____. "Re-Visioning Christian Origins: *In Memory of Her* Revisited." Pages 225–50 in *Christian Beginnings: Worship, Belief and Society.* Edited by Kieran O'Mahony. London: Continuum, 2003.

_____. *Rhetoric and Ethic: The Politics of Biblical Studies.* Minneapolis: Fortress, 1999.

_____. *Sharing Her Word: Feminist Biblical Interpretation in Context.* Boston: Beacon, 1998.

_____. "The Ethics of Biblical Interpretation: Decentering Biblical Scholarship." *Journal of Biblical Literature* 107, no. 1 (1988): 3–17.

_____. "The Rhetoric of Inquiry." Pages 23–48 in *Rhetorics in the New Millennium: Promise and Fulfillment.* Edited by James D. Hester and J. David Hester. Studies in Antiquity and Christianity. New York: T&T Clark, 2010.

_____. *The Power of the Word: Scripture and the Rhetoric of Empire.* Minneapolis: Fortress, 2007.

_____. *Transforming Vision: Explorations in Feminist The*logy.* Minneapolis: Fortress, 2011.

_____. *Wisdom Ways: Introducing Feminist Biblical Interpretation.* Maryknoll: Orbis, 2001.

Segovia, Fernando F. "Looking Back, Looking Around, Looking Ahead: An Interview with Elisabeth Schüssler Fiorenza." Pages 1–30 in *Toward a New Heaven and a New Earth.* Edited by idem. Maryknoll: Orbis, 2003.

Shapiro, Susan. "Rhetoric as Ideology Critique: The Gadamer-Habermas Debate Reinvented." *Journal of the American Academy of Religion* 62, no. 1 (1994): 123–50.

Shiner, Whitney. *Proclaiming the Gospel: First Century Performance of Mark.* Harrisburg: Trinity, 2003.

Shipp, Blake. "George Kennedy's Influence on Rhetorical Interpretation of the Acts of the Apostles." Pages 107–23 in Black and Watson, eds., *Words Well Spoken*).

_____. *Paul the Reluctant Witness: Power and Weakness in Luke's Portrayal.* Eugene: Cascade, 2005.

Shore, Bradd. *Culture in Mind: Cognition, Culture, and the Problem of Meaning.* Oxford: Oxford University Press, 1996.

Simons, Herbert W. *The Rhetorical Turn: Invention and Persuasion in the Conduct of Inquiry.* Chicago: University of Chicago Press, 1990.

Slingerland, Edward. *What Science Offers the Humanities: Integrating Body and Culture.* Cambridge: Cambridge University Press, 2008.

Sloan, Thomas O. "Rhetoric: Rhetoric in Literature." Pages 758–62 in vol. 26 of *The New Encyclopædia Britannica.* Edited by Philip W. Goetz, Robert McHenry, and Dale Hoiberg. Fifteenth edition. 32 volumes. Chicago: Encyclopædia Brittanica, 1985–2010.

Smit, Joop. "Redactie in de brief aan de Galaten: Retorische analyze van Gal. 4,12–6,18." *Tijdschrift voor theologie* 26 (1986): 113–114.

———. "The Letter of Paul to the Galatians: A Deliberative Speech." *New Testament Studies* 35, no. 1 (1989): 1–26. Reprinted in Nanos, ed., *The Galatians Debate*.

Smith, Bonnie G. "Gender, Objectivity, and the Rise of Scientific History." Pages 51–66 in *Objectivity and Its Other*. Edited by W. Natter et al. Multidisciplinary Studies in Social Theory. New York: Guilford, 1995.

Smith, Daniel Lynwood. *The Rhetoric of Interruption: Speech-Making, Turn-Taking, and Rule-Breaking in Luke-Acts and Ancient Greek Narrative.* Beihefte zur *Zeitschrift für die neutestamentliche Wissenschaft* 193. Berlin: de Gruyter, 2012.

Starr, James. "Was Paraenesis for Beginners?" Pages 73–111 in *Early Christian Paraenesis in Context*. Edited by James Starr and Troels Engberg-Pedersen. Beihefte zur *Zeitschrift für die neutestamentliche Wissenschaft* 125. Berlin: de Gruyter, 2005.

Stegemann, Ekkehard W., and Wolfgang Stegemann. *The Jesus Movement: A Social History of its First Century*. Translated by O. C. Dean, Jr. Minneapolis: Fortress, 1999. Translation of *Urchristliche Sozialgeschichte: Die Anfänge im Judentum und die Christusgemeinden in der mediterranen Welt*. Stuttgart: Kohlhammer, 1995.

Stepan, Nancy L., and Sander L. Gilman. "Appropriating the Idioms of Science: The Rejection of Scientific Racism." Pages 170–93 in *The "Racial" Economy of Science: Toward a Democratic Future*. Edited by Sandra Harding. Bloomington: Indiana University Press, 1993.

Stowasser, Barbara F. *Women in the Qur'an: Traditions and Interpretations*. New York: Oxford University Press, 1994.

Stowers, Stanley K. *Letter Writing in Greco-Roman Antiquity*. Library of Early Christianity 5. Philadelphia: Westminster, 1986.

Strecker, Georg. *Literaturgeschichte des Neuen Testaments.* Göttingen: Vandenhoeck & Ruprecht, 1992.

Stube, John Carlson. *A Graeco–Roman Rhetorical Reading of the Farewell Discourse.* Library of New Testament Studies 309. London: T&T Clark, 2006.

Sutton, Jane. "The Death of Rhetoric and Its Rebirth in Philosophy." *Rhetorica* 4 (1986): 203–26.

————. "The Taming of Polos/Polis: Rhetoric as an Achievement without Women." Pages 101–27 in Lucaites et al., eds., *Contemporary Rhetorical Theory.*

Thatcher, Tom. "John's Memory Theater: The Fourth Gospel and Ancient Mnemo-Rhetoric." *Catholic Biblical Quarterly* 69, no. 3 (2007): 487–505.

Theissen, Gerd. "Methodenkonkurrenz und hermeneutischer Konflikt: Pluralismus in Exegese und Lektüre der Bibel." Pages 127-40 in *Pluralismus und Identität.* Edited by Joachim Mehlhausen. Gütersloh: Kaiser, 1995.

————. "Theoretische Probleme religionssoziologischer Forschung und die Analyse des Urchristentums." *Neue Zeitschrift für Systematische Theologie* 16 (1974): 35–56.

————. *Sociology of Early Palestinian Christianity.* Minneapolis: Fortress, 1978.

————. *The Social Setting of Pauline Christianity: Essays on Corinth.* Philadelphia: Fortress, 1982.

Thibeaux, Evelyn R. "'Known to Be a Sinner': The Narrative Rhetoric of Luke 7:36–50." *Biblical Theology Bulletin* 23 (1993): 151–60.

Thiselton, C. *The First Epistle to the Corinthians: A Commentary on the Greek Text.* New International Greek Text Commentary Series. Grand Rapids: Eerdmans, 2000.

Thom, Johan C. "'The Mind is Its Own Place': Defining the Topos." Pages 555–73 in *Early Christianity and Classical Culture: Comparative Studies in*

Honor of Abraham J. Malherbe. Edited by J. T. Fitzgerald, T. H. Olbricht, and L. M. White. Novum Testamentum Supplements 110. Leiden: Brill, 2003.

Thompson, John B. *Studies in the Theory of Ideology.* Cambridge: Cambridge University Press, 1984.

Tilley, Christopher. *Metaphor and Material Culture.* Social Archaeology Series. Oxford: Blackwell, 1999.

Tobin, Thomas. *Paul's Rhetoric in Its Contexts: The Arguments of Romans.* Peabody: Hendrickson, 2004.

Tolbert, Mary Ann. *Sowing the Gospel: Mark's World in Literary-historical Perspective.* Minneapolis: Fortress, 1989.

Toohey, Peter. "Epic and Rhetoric." Pages 153–73 in *Persuasion: Greek Rhetoric in Action.* Edited by Ian Worthington. London: Routledge, 1994.

Treibel, Annett. "Die Sprache der Soziologie: Eine ganz normale Wissenschaftssprache?" *Österreichische Zeitschrift für Soziologie* 20 (1995): 20–45.

Trible, Phyllis. *Rhetorical Criticism: Context, Method, and the Book of Jonah.* Guides to Biblical Scholarship: Old Testament Series. Minneapolis: Fortress, 1994.

Tuppurainen, Riku P. "The Contribution of Socio-Rhetorical Criticism to Spirit-Sensitive Hermeneutics: A Contextual Example—Luke 11:13." *Journal of Biblical and Pneumatological Research* 4 (2012): 38–66.

Van Hecke, P. "Conceptual Blending: A Recent Approach to Metaphor Illustrated with the Pastoral Metaphor in Hos 4,16." Pages 215–32 in *Metaphor in the Hebrew Bible.* Bibliotheca ephemeridum theologicarum Lovaniensium 187. Edited by idem. Leuven: University and Dudley: Peeters, 2005.

Varghese, Santosh V. "Woe-Oracles in Habakkuk 2:6-20: A Socio-Rhetorical Reading." MTh thesis, Faith Theological Seminary, Manakala, Kerala, India, 2009.

Verheijen, L., ed. *Augustine:* Confessionum libri xiii. See Augustine, *Confessionum libri xiii.*

Vetterling-Braggin, Mary. *Sexist Language: A Modern Philosophical Analysis.* Totowa: Rowman and Littlefield, 1981.

Von Thaden, Robert, Jr. "Bad Children, Children as Bad: Problematic Children from Proverbs to *Acts of Thomas* and Beyond." *Proceedings: Eastern Great Lakes and Midwestern Biblical Societies* 28 (2008): 67–75.

————. "Guiding Socio-Rhetorical Commentary with Conceptual Integration Theory (Blending Theory)." *Conversations with the Biblical World: Proceedings of the Eastern Great Lakes Biblical Society and Midwest Region Society of Biblical Literature* 31 (2011): 184–203.

————. "Pauline Rhetorical Invention: Seeing 1 Corinthians 6:12–7:7 through Conceptual Integration Theory." In *Cognitive Linguistic Explorations in Biblical Studies.* Edited by Bonnie G. Howe and Joel B. Green. Cognitive Studies of Sacred Texts. Berlin: de Gruyter, forthcoming.

————. *Sex, Christ, and Embodied Cognition: Paul's Wisdom for Corinth.* Emory Studies in Early Christianity 16. Blandford Forum: Deo, 2012.

————. "The Power of Pictures: Sex and Embodied Temples." *Conversations with the Biblical World: Proceedings of the Eastern Great Lakes Biblical Society and Midwest Region Society of Biblical Literature* 32 (2012): 109–26.

Vos, Johan S. "Das Rätsel von 1 Kor 12:1–3." *Novum Testamentum* 35, no. 3 (1993): 251–69.

————. "Paul and Sophistic Rhetoric: A Perspective on His Argumentation in the Letter to the Galatians." Pages 29–52 in *Exploring New Rhetorical Approaches to Galatians: Papers Presented at an International Conference.* Edited by D. François Tolmie. *Acta Theologica* Supplement 9. Bloemfontein: University of the Free State, 2007.

Vouga, François. "Zur rhetorischen Gattung des Galaterbriefes." *Zeitschrift für die neutestamentliche Wissenschaft und die Kunde der älteren Kirche* 79, no. 4 (1988): 291–92.

Wadud, Amina. *Qur'an and Woman: Rereading the Sacred Text from a Woman's Perspective.* Oxford: Oxford University Press, 1999.

Wagner, Peter, Björn Wittrock, and Richard Whitley, eds. *Discourses on Society: The Shaping of the Social Science Disciplines.* Dordrecht: Kluwer Academic, 1990.

_____. *Soziologie der Moderne: Freiheit und Disziplin.* Frankfurt: Campus, 1995.

Wanamaker, Charles A. *Commentary on 1 & 2 Thessalonians.* New International Greek Text Commentary Series. Grand Rapids: Eerdmans, 1990.

Warnick, Barbara. "Two Systems of Invention: The Topics in *Rhetoric* and *The New Rhetoric*." Pages 107–29 in *Rereading Aristotle's Rhetoric.* Edited by Alan G. Gross and Arthur E. Walzer. Carbondale: Southern Illinois University Press, 2000.

Watson, Duane F. *Invention, Arrangement, and Style: Rhetorical Criticism of Jude and 2 Peter.* Society of Biblical Literature Dissertation Series 104. Atlanta: Scholars, 1988.

_____. "James 2 in Light of Greco-Roman Schemes of Argumentation." *New Testament Studies* 39, no. 1 (1993): 94–121.

_____, ed. *Miracle Discourse in the New Testament.* Atlanta: Society of Biblical Literature, 2012.

_____. "Paul and Boasting." Pages 77–100 in *Paul in the Greco-Roman World.* Edited by J. Paul Sampley. Harrisburg: Trinity, 2003.

_____. "Paul's Boasting in 2 Corinthians 10–13 as Defense of His Honor: A Socio-Rhetorical Analysis." Pages 260–75 in *Rhetorical Argumentation in Biblical Texts: Essays from the Lund 2000 Conference.* Edited by Anders

Eriksson, Thomas H. Olbricht, and Walter Überlacker. Emory Studies in Early Christianity 8. Harrisburg: Trinity, 2002.

_____. "Paul's Speech to the Ephesian Elders (Acts 20.17–38): Epideictic Rhetoric of Farewell." Pages 184–208 in *Persuasive Artistry: Studies in New Testament Rhetoric in Honor of George A. Kennedy.* Edited by Duane F. Watson. *Journal for the Study of the New Testament* Supplement Series 50. Sheffield: Journal for the Study of the Old Testament, 1991.

_____. "Rhetorical Criticism of the Pauline Epistles since 1975." *Currents in Research: Biblical Studies* 3 (1995): 219–48.

_____, ed. *The Intertexture of Apocalyptic Discourse in the New Testament.* Society of Biblical Literature Symposium Series 14. Atlanta: Society of Biblical Literature, 2002.

_____. *The Rhetoric of the New Testament: A Bibliographic Survey.* Tools for Biblical Study 8. Blandford Forum: Deo, 2006.

_____. "The Three Species of Rhetoric and the Study of the Pauline Epistles." Pages 25–47 in *Paul and Rhetoric.* Edited by J. Paul Sampley and Peter Lampe. New York: T&T Clark, 2010.

_____ and Alan J. Hauser. *Rhetorical Criticism of the Bible: A Comprehensive Bibliography with Notes on History and Method.* Biblical Interpretation Series 4. Leiden: E. J. Brill, 1994.

Webb, Robert L. "The Rhetorical Function of Visual Imagery in Jude: A Socio-Rhetorical Experiment in Rhetography." Pages 109–35 in *Reading Jude with New Eyes: Methodological Reassessments of the Letter of Jude.* Edited by idem and Peter H. Davids. London: T&T Clark, 2008.

Welch, Kathleen E. "Compositionality, Rhetoricity, and Electricity: A Partial History of Some Composition and Rhetoric Studies." *Enculturation* 5, no. 1 (2003). Online: http://www.enculturation.net/5_1/welch.html.

_____. *The Contemporary Reception of Classical Rhetoric: Appropriations of Ancient Discourse.* Hillsdale: Erlbaum, 1990.

Wenkel, David H. *Joy in Luke-Acts: The Intersection of Rhetoric, Narrative, and Emotion.* Paternoster Monographs. Carlisle, Cumbria: Paternoster, forthcoming.

Whitaker, Robyn. "Rhetoric of Fear: Ekphrasis, Emotion, and Persuasion in Revelation 1:9–20." Paper presented at the New Testament Colloquium, Princeton Theological Seminary, Princeton, NJ, 21 October 2011.

White, Hayden. *Tropics of Discourse: Essays in Cultural Criticism.* Baltimore: Johns Hopkins University Press, 1978.

White, John L. "Epistolary Formulas and Cliches in Greek Papyrus Letters." *Society of Biblical Literature 1978 Seminar Papers* 2 (1978): 289–319.

———. "Introductory Formulae in the Body of the Pauline Letter." *Journal of Biblical Literature* 90, no. 1 (1971): 91–97.

———. *Light from Ancient Letters.* Foundations and Facets. Philadelphia: Fortress, 1986.

———. *The Form and Function of the Body of the Greek Letter: A Study of the Letter-Body in Non-Literary Papyri and in Paul the Apostle.* Society of Biblical Literature Dissertation Series 2. Missoula: Society of Biblical Literature, 1972.

Wilder, Amos N. *Early Christian Rhetoric: The Language of the Gospel.* Cambridge, MA: Harvard University Press, 1971.

———. "Scholars, Theologians, and Ancient Rhetoric." *Journal of Biblical Literature* 75, no. 1 (1956): 1–11.

Wilke, C. G. *Die neutestamentliche Rhetorik: ein Seitenstück zur Grammatik des neutestamentlichen Sprachidioms.* Dresden: Arnold, 1843.

Wilson, Timothy H. "Foucault, Genealogy, History." *Philosophy Today* 39, no. 2 (1995): 157–70.

Wimbush, Vincent L. "Interpreters: Enslaving/Enslaved/Runagate." *Journal of Biblical Literature* 130, no. 1 (2011): 5–24.

———. "Introduction: TEXTureS, Gestures, Power: Orientation to Radical Excavation." Pages 1–22 in *Signifying on Scriptures: New*

Orientations to a Cultural Phenomenon. Edited by Vincent L. Wimbush. Signifying [on] Scriptures 1. New Brunswick, NJ: Rutgers University Press, 2008.

Wire, Antoinette Clark. *The Corinthian Women Prophets: A Reconstruction through Paul's Rhetoric.* Minneapolis: Fortress, 1990.

Witherington, Ben, III. *The Gospel of Mark: A Socio-Rhetorical Commentary.* Grand Rapids: Eerdmans, 2001.

Woolf, Virginia. *Three Guineas.* New York: Harcourt Brace Jovanovich, 1966.

Wooten, Cecil W. *Hermogenes' On Types of Style.* See Hermogenes, *On Types of Style.*

Wuellner, Wilhelm. "Biblical Exegesis in the Light of History and Historicity of Rhetoric and the Nature of the Rhetoric of Religion." Pages 492–513 in *Rhetoric and the New Testament: Essays from the 1992 Heidelberg Conference.* Edited by Stanley Porter and Thomas Olbricht. *Journal for the Study of the New Testament* Supplement Series 90. Sheffield: Journal for the Study of the Old Testament, 1993.

————. "Death and Rebirth of Rhetoric in Late Twentieth Century Biblical Exegesis." Pages 917–30 in *Texts and Contexts: Biblical Texts in Their Textual and Situational Contexts: Essays in Honour of Lars Hartman.* Edited byDavid Hellholm and Tord Fonberg. Oslo: Scandanivian University Press, 1995.

————. "Haggadic Homily Genre in 1 Cor. 1–3." *Journal of Biblical Literature* 89, no. 2 (1970): 199–204.

————. "Hermeneutics and Rhetorics: From 'Truth and Method' to 'Truth and Power.'" *Scriptura* Special Issue S3 (1989): 1–54.

————. "Paul as Pastor: The Function of Rhetorical Questions in First Corinthians." Pages 49–77 in *L'Apôtre Paul: Personalité, Style et Conception du Ministère.* Edited by A. Vanhoye. Bibliotheca ephemeridum theologicarum lovaniensium 73. Leuven: Leuven University Press, 1986.

_____. "Paul's Rhetoric of Argumentation in Romans: An Alternative to the Donfried-Karris Debate Over Romans." *Catholic Biblical Quarterly* 38, no. 2 (1976): 330–51. Reprinted as pages 128–46 in *The Romans Debate: Revised and Expanded Edition.* Edited byKarl Donfried. Peabody: Hendrikson, 1995.

_____. "Putting Life Back into the Lazarus Story and Its Reading: The Narrative Rhetoric of John 11 as the Narration of Faith." Pages 113–32 in *Poststructuralism as Exegesis.* Edited by David Jobling and Stephen D. Moore. Semeia 54. Atlanta: Scholars, 1991.

_____. "Reading Romans in Context." Pages 106–139 in *Celebrating Romans: Template for Pauline Theology.* Edited by Sheila McGinn. Grand Rapids: Eerdmans, 2004.

_____. "Reconceiving a Rhetoric of Religion: A Rhetorics of Power and the Power of the Sublime." Pages 23–77 in Hester and Hester (Amador), eds., *Rhetorics and Hermeneutics.*

_____. "Rhetorical Criticism." Pages 149–86 in *The Postmodern Bible: The Bible and Culture Collective.* Edited by Elizabeth A. Castelli et al. New Haven: Yale University Press, 1995.

_____. "Rhetorical Criticism and Its Theory in Cultural Critical Perspective: The Narrative Rhetoric of John 11." Pages 167–81 in *Text and Interpretation: New Approaches in the Criticism of the New Testament.* Edited by P. J. Hartin and J. H. Petzer. New Testament Tools and Studies 15. Leiden: E. J. Brill, 1991.

_____. "The Argumentative Structure of 1 Thessalonians as Paradoxical Encomium." Pages 117–36 in *The Thessalonian Correspondence.* Edited by Raymond F. Collins. Bibliotheca ephemeridum theologicarum lovaniensium 87. Leuven: Leuven University Press, 1990.

_____. "The Rhetorical Structure of Luke 12 in Its Wider Context." *Neotestamentica* 22 (1989): 283–310.

_____. "Toposforschung und Torahinterpretation bei Paulus und Jesus." *New Testament Studies* 24, no. 4 (1978): 463–83.

_____. "Where is Rhetorical Criticism Taking Us?" *Catholic Biblical Quarterly* 49, no. 3 (1987): 448–463.

Ziemann, Ferdinandus. *De epistularum Graecarum formulis sollemnibus quaestiones selectae.* Berlin: Haas, 1912.

Zulick, Margaret D. "The Recollection of Rhetoric: A Brief History." Pages 7–19 in Black and Watson, eds., *Words Well Spoken.*

Index

Adams, Sean A., 86–87

Ahlstrom, Sidney, 121

Aijmer, Karin, 211

Alcoff, Linda, 153

Aletti, Jean-Noël, 18, 35–36

Alexander, Loveday, 238

Allison, Dale C., Jr., 53

Anderson, Janice Capel, 167

Anderson, R. Dean, Jr., 61, 88, 99, 210

Appiah, Kwame Anthony, 193

Archer, Dawn, 211

Arendt, Hannah, 154, 193–94

Aronowitz, Stanley, 159

Asgeirsson, Jon Ma, 240

Asumang, Annang, 242

Atkinson, Jane M., 74–75

Attridge, Harold W., 65

Aune, David E., 17–19, 22, 36–37, 40–41, 81, 88–89, 228

Avalos, Hector, 160

Bach, Alice, 167, 171

Baker, Cynthia, 167

Bakhtin, Mikhail, 98

Balch, David L., 124

Barlas, Asma, 167

Baron, David D., 195

Baron, Dennis, 172

Barrett, Charles K., 18

Bass, Dorothy C., 168

Bass, Kenneth, 62–63

Baumlin, James S., 153

Baumlin, Tita French, 153

Bayertz, Kurt, 177

Beck, Ulrich, 178

Bender, John, 165, 182

Benhabib, Seyla, 192

Benson, Thomas W., 53

Berger, Klaus, 22

Bergmann, Gustav, 142

Bernstein, Richard, 186

Berquist, Jon L., 209, 237

Betz, Hans Dieter, vii–viii, 2–4, 13–21, 23–43, 45, 49, 53, 59–60, 86, 100, 128, 210, 227, 232, 247

Beutler, Johannes, 30

Bird, Michael F., 61

Bitzer, Lloyd F., 101

Black, C. Clifton, viii, 2, 4–5, 51, 53–54, 60, 63, 69, 73, 79–80, 83, 85–86, 103, 241

Blackwell, Antoinette, 168

Blass, Friedrich Wilhelm, 56

Bloom, Harold   , 98

Bloomquist, L. Gregory, viii, 2, 8–9, 201, 210, 212, 223, 225, 230, 236–37, 239

Boers, Hendrikus, 21

Bonfiglio, Ryan, 242

Bonnell, Victoria E., 186

Bonner, Stanley F., 54

Booth, Wayne C., 98, 175

Borg, Marcus, 124

Borgen, Peder, 109

Bormann, Ernest, 98–99, 119

Bottomore, Tom, 195

Bouchard, Donald F., 256

Bovon, François, 47

Brandt, William J., 98, 128

Bräuninger, Bettina, 179

Brose, Margaret, 175

Brown, Richard H., 178, 182

Bruehler, Bart B., 238

Bultmann, Rudolf, 46, 56, 67

Burchell, G., 260

Burke, Kenneth, 104, 122, 175, 228

Burks, D., 101

Burrick, George A., 53

Butler, Judith, 167

Butts, James R., 210, 234

Cadbury, Henry Joel, 64

Cadwallader, Alan H., 242

Callan, Terrance, 241

Cameron, Averil, 237

Camp, Claudia V., 209, 237

Canavan, Rosemary, 241–42

Canty, Aaron, 17

Carey, Greg, 63, 239

Carroll, Lewis, 246

Carroll, M. D., 238

Cartwright, Steven R., 17

Castelli, Elizabeth A., 97, 108–9, 167, 171, 191, 264

Caudill, Sally, 183, 194–95

Chatman, Seymour, 68–69

Chopp, Rebecca S., 205, 220, 222

Chow, Rey, 189

Church, F. Forrester, 34, 61

Classen, Carl Joachim, 5–17, 29–30, 32, 45, 60–61, 65, 88, 90

Clifton, James, 242
Code, Lorraine, 177, 182
Collins, Raymond F., 30, 36, 130
Condit, Celeste Michelle, 183,
    189, 194–95
Conley, Thomas M., 128, 213,
    233
Connor, Robert W., 57, 118
Coulson, Seana, 209
Crocker, J. C., 209
Crossan, John Dominic, 124, 242
Culler, Jonathan, 98
Culpepper, R. Alan, 66–69, 217

Danneberg, Lutz, 178
Davids, Peter H., 241
Davies, W. D., 18, 53
de Hulster, Izaak J., 242
de Waal, Kayle B., 230
Dean, O. C., Jr., 173
Debrunner, Albert, 56
DeConick, April D., 208, 240
Derrida, Jacques, 68
deSilva, David A., 34, 90, 241
Dewey, Joanna, 228
Dewey, John, 146
Dibelius, Martin, 62, 67
DiCicco, Mario M., 41
Donawerth, Jane, 171, 179
Donfried, Karl Paul, 16, 26, 30,
    108

Doyle, Arthur Conan, 66
Dreyfus, Hubert L., 206

Eagleton, Terry, 98
Edmondson, Ricca, 178
Elliott, John H., 206
Elliott, Neil, ix, 36–37, 242, 246
Enenkel, Karl A. E., 242
Engberg-Pedersen, Troels, 37
Eriksson, Anders, 38, 41, 65, 87,
    120, 125, 128, 148, 235, 241
Esler, Philip F., 229
Exler, Francis Xavier, 20, 22

Fairweather, Janet, 16, 61–62
Fauconnier, Gilles, 209, 238
Felt, Ulrike, 177
Ferguson, Everett, 124
Ferguson, Frances, 119
Fewell, Danna Nolan, 188
Fish, Stanley, 128, 175
Fitzgerald, John T., 229
Flanagan, James W., 237
Fleck, Ludwik, 177
Fonberg, Tord, 97
Foucault, Michel, 204, 217–19,
    254, 256–62, 266
Fraser, Nancy, 267
Frug, Mary, 192
Fuchs, Esther, 167, 171
Funk, Robert W., 56, 227

Fyfe, W. Hamilton, 108

Gadamer, Hans-Georg, 98
Geertz, Clifford, 146, 214, 227–28
Getui, Mary N., 226, 231
Gibbs, Raymond W., Jr., 209
Gibson, Craig A., 210
Gilman, Sander L., 154
Giroux, Henry, 159
Glenn, Cheryl, 182
Goetz, Philip W., 104
Good, James M. M., 170, 177, 179
Gowler, David B., 201–2, 212,
    223, 228, 230, 236–37
Grady, Joseph, 209
Graeser, Andreas, 178
Green, Joel B., 239
Green, R. P. H., 55
Greene, Gayle, 175
Greeven, Heinrich, 62
Gros, F., 260
Gross, Alan G., 230
Gruca-Macaulay, Alexandra, 230
Guerlac, Suzanne, 119
Gunn, David M., 237

Habermas, Jürgen, 195, 205
Hall, Robert G., 26–27
Hammer, Keir, 230
Harding, Sandra, 154, 172, 177
Harnisch, Wolfgang, 36

Harris, Edward M., 54
Hartin, P. J., 100
Hauser, Alan J., 29, 33, 65, 81
Heckel, Ulrich, 37
Heiden-Sommer, Helga, 178
Heiland, D., 118
Heinrici, Georg, 46
Heintz, Bettina, 177
Hellholm, David, 37, 39, 97
Hengel, Martin, 37, 232
Hermann, Anne C., 166
Hernadi, Paul, 174
Hesford, Wendy S., 199
Hester (Amador), J. David, viii, 2,
    5–6, 62, 66, 93–94, 96, 104–7,
    116, 120, 122, 125, 127–28,
    130, 137, 208, 213, 227, 250,
    255
Hester, James D., viii, 2, 5–6, 60,
    62, 66, 93–94, 96, 103, 107,
    127–28, 130, 208, 213, 227,
    250
Hock, Ronald F., 67, 90, 233–34
Hoiberg, Dale, 104
Homann, Frederick A., 242
Howe, Bonnie G., 239
Huber, Lynn R., 238
Hübner, Hans, 18, 29, 35
Hueber, Max, 99
Hughes, Frank W., 30, 33, 36, 60,
    86

Hunt, Lynn, 186
Hyde, Michael J., 213
Hyman, Naomi M., 171

Ilan, Tal, 167

Jameson, Fredric R., 175
Janssen-Jurreit, Marielouise, 173
Jarratt, Susan C., 153–54, 185
Jaspers, David, 98
Jeal, Roy R., 220, 241
Jeremias, Joachim, 217
Jewett, Robert, 30, 34
Jobling, David, 97
Jobling, Jannine, 171
Johnson, Mark, 209
Jones, Leslie Webber, 55
Jost, Walter, 213

Kahl, Brigitte, 241
Kahn, Coppélia, 175
Karris, Robert, 16, 108, 114
Käsemann, Ernst, 46
Kaufmann, W., 256
Kelber, Werner H., 264
Kennedy, George A., vii–viii, 2,
    4–5, 24, 39, 51–53, 56–60,
    62–77, 79–86, 88–91, 98, 103,
    105, 107–8, 111, 115–16, 121,
    123, 138–39, 210, 232–34,
    240–41, 243, 247

Kern, Kathi, 168
Kern, Philip H., 30, 61
Kim, Nami, 133–35
Kirsch, Gesa E., 199
Kitcher, Philip, 267
Klauck, Hans-Josef, 38
Klein, Julie Thompson, 178
Klinger, Leslie S., 66
Kluback, William, 110
Kopperschmidt, Josef, 177
Koskenniemi, Heikki, 20
Kövecses, Zoltán, 209
Kreissl, Reinhard, 178
Kretzenbacher, Heinz L., 178
Kruse, Volker, 186–87
Kuhn, Thomas, 142, 177
Kustas, George, 128

Lakoff, George, 209
Lakoff, Robin, 211
Lampe, Peter, 14, 16, 19, 21, 26,
    60–61, 86
Lanci, John R., viii, 2, 6–7, 133,
    165–66
Lange, Andreas, 179
Lange, John, 215
Larsen, Lillian I., viii, 1
Lau, Christoph, 178
Lausberg, Heinrich, 99, 108, 210
LeMon, Joel M., 242
Lentricchia, Frank, 175, 189

Levine, Amy-Jill, 167
Lévi-Strauss, Claude, 227
Lincoln, Andrew, 68
Long, Fredrick J., 30
Lopez, Davina C., viii, 2, 241, 245, 252, 267
Lucaites, John Louis, 183, 195
Lüdemann, Gerd, 30
Luomanen, Petri, 209, 230
Lüscher, Kurt, 179
Lyne, John, 142
Lyons, George, 41
Lyons, John, 104–5

Mack, Burton L., 82–83, 234, 236, 264–66
Maier, Harry O., 242
Mailloux, Stephen, 98, 213
Malherbe, Abraham J., 21–22, 88, 124, 229
Malina, Bruce J., 188, 206, 227, 229
Maluleke, Tinyiko S., 226, 231
Marchal, J., 267
Markus, H., 192
Marshall, Gloria A., 172
Marshall, I. Howard, 26
Marshall, John W., 40
Martin, Troy W., ix, 2–3, 13, 16, 21–22, 31, 38–39, 41, 45, 60, 86–87, 246–47

Martyn, J. Louis, 68
Marxsen, Willi, 71
McCloskey, Donald, 142, 144, 146–47, 177, 182
McGee, M. C., 221
McGinn, Sheila, 96, 108
McGowan, John, 154
McHenry, Robert, 104
McKerrow, Rayme E., 195, 202–6, 208, 215, 217–18, 221
McLaughlin, Thomas, 175
McNutt, Paula M., 237–38
Meeks, Wayne A., 18, 53, 58–59, 124
Meese, Elizabeth A., 176
Megill, Allan, 142–47, 177
Mehlhausen, Joachim, 181
Melion, Walter S., 242
Merton, Robert K., 194
Meyer, Paul W., 18
Meyers, Fred R., 75
Miller, Carolyn R., 230
Miller, Casey, 172
Miller, J. Hillis, 98
Miller, Joseph M., 53
Minow, Martha, 192
Mitchell, Margaret M. , 39, 55, 138, 237
Moberg, Verne, 173
Mohanti, Chandra Talpade, 194

Mongstad-Kvammen, Ingeborg, 230

Moore, Stephen, 97

Morrison-Atkins, Kelsi, 165

Morrow, Raymond A., 195

Mosco, V., 203

Mouffe, Chantal, 192

Mountford, Roxanne, 171, 179

Muilenberg, James, 17, 53, 93, 263

Mulkay, Michael, 194

Mumby, D. K., 208

Murphy-O'Connor, Jerome, 29

Nadal, Jerome, 242

Nadeau, Raymond E., 57

Nanos, Mark D., 15, 26, 35, 39, 86

Natter, W., 154

Nelson, John S., 142–47, 177

Newby, Gordon D., 223

Newsom, Carol, 169

Newton, Judith, 176

Neyrey, Jerome H., 72, 237

Niebuhr, Reinhold, 268

Niederhauser, Jürg, 178

Nietzsche, Friedrich, 143, 256–57, 266

Norden, Eduard, 53, 61

Nowotny, Helga, 177

Oakley, Todd, 209

Olbrechts-Tyteca, Lucie, 82, 102, 144, 264

Olbricht, Thomas H., viii, 2, 6, 16, 29, 36, 40–41, 61, 65, 87, 96–98, 104, 120, 124–25, 127–28, 130, 148, 188, 207, 220, 226, 229, 231, 235–36, 241

O'Mahony, Kieran J., 31–32, 198

O'Neil, Edward N., 67, 233–34

Ong, Walter, 98, 103

Orton, David E., 99, 210, 228

Ostriker, Alicia Suskin, 167

Pardes, Ilana, 167

Parsenios, George L., 68

Patrick, Dale, 180

Pedersen, Johannes, 226

Pelikan, Jaroslav, 55

Penner, Todd, viii, 2, 63, 85, 231, 245, 250, 252, 267

Perelman, Chaim, 82, 98, 102, 106–7, 110, 113, 115, 144, 205, 264

Perrin, Norman, 217, 264

Peter, Hermann, 89

Petrus, Klaus, 178

Petzer, J. H., 100

Philips, Gary A., 188

Phillips, Thomas E., 240

Phillips, William B., 128–29

Pickering, Andrew, 178
Pinker, Steven, 211
Popkes, Wiard, 37
Porter, Stanley E., 16, 29–31, 36,
    38, 40, 61, 84, 86–87, 97, 104,
    128, 188, 207, 220, 231, 236
Poster, Carol, 61–62
Prelli, Lawrence J., 194
Probst, Hermann, 33
Proser, Michael H., 53
Pusch, Luise F., 173–74
Pyysiäinen, Ilkka, 209, 230

Rabinow, Paul, 206
Rabinowitz, Nancy Sorkin, 172
Ratcliffe, Krista, 171, 179
Rawson, K. J., 171, 179, 199
Reasoner, Mark, 242
Rebenich, Stefan, 84–85
Reed, Jeffrey T., 30, 61
Reed, Jonathan L., 242
Reinhartz, Adele, 167
Reynolds, Nedra, 153–54
Rhoads, Anna Ely, 168
Richards, Jennifer, 171, 179
Richlin, Amy, 172
Ricoeur, Paul, 128, 264
Riley, Denise, 167
Ringe, Sharon, 169
Robbins, Vernon K., vii–viii, 2,
    8–10, 40, 66, 83, 96, 103, 105,

128, 141, 201–2, 204–9,
    211–15, 217–23, 225–26,
    228–32, 235–41, 243, 247, 264,
    266–67
Roberts, Jennifer Tolbert, 194
Roberts, K. A., 222
Roberts, Richard H., 170, 177, 179
Robins, Robert H., 172
Rogerson, John, 238
Rohrbaugh, Richard L., 206
Rorty, Amélie Oksenberg, 54
Rorty, Richard, 142, 186
Rose, Hilary, 179
Rosenfelt, Deborah, 176
Rosenthal, L. J., 118
Royster, Jaqueline Jones, 179, 199
Russo, Ann, 194

Said, Edward, 268
Sampley, J. Paul, 14, 16, 26, 60
    86–87, 90
Samuels, Warren J., 178
Sänger, Dieter, 38
Sapir, J. David, 209
Saunders, Ernest W., 168
Schaberg, Jane , 167, 171
Schell, Eileen E., 171, 179, 199
Schlatter, Adolf, 37
Schneiders, Sandra, 196
Schröder, Hannelore, 174
Schröder, Hartmut, 177

Schüssler Fiorenza, Elisabeth, vii–viii, 2, 6–8, 25, 133–42, 147–62, 165–66, 168, 170, 172, 184, 196, 198, 204, 215–16, 220, 231, 247, 267
Scult, Allen, 180
Searle, John, 98, 128
Segovia, Fernando F., 158, 162
Shapiro, Susan, 181
Sharma, Arvind, 170
Shiner, Whitney, 103
Shipp, Blake, 62, 85
Shore, Bradd, 214
Shweder, R., 192
Simons, Herbert W., 141, 143, 145, 194
Slingerland, Edward, 208
Sloan, Thomas O., 104
Smit, Joop, 27, 35–36
Smith, Bonnie G., 154
Smith, Daniel Lynwood, 63
Stamps, Dennis L., 30, 38
Stanton, Elizabeth Cady, 168–69
Starr, James, 37
Steen, Gerard J., 209
Stegemann, Ekkehard W., 173
Stegemann, Wolfgang, 173
Stepan, Nancy L., 154
Stewart, Abigail J., 166
Stewart, Anna Maria, 168
Stowasser, Barbara F., 167

Stowers, Stanley K., 22, 88
Strecker, Georg, 88
Stube, John Carlson, 72
Sumney, Jerry L., 41
Sutton, Jane, 194
Swift, Kate, 172

Taschwer, Klaus, 177
Tate, W. Randolph, 228
Thatcher, Tom, 71–72
Theissen, Gerd, 181, 226
Thibeaux, Evelyn R., 65
Thiselton, C., 38
Thom, Johan C., 229
Thompson, John B., 187
Thompson, Richard P., 240
Thurén, Lauri, 37
Tilley, Christopher, 209
Tobin, Thomas, 61
Tolbert, Mary Ann, 264
Tolmie, D. François, 61–62
Toohey, Peter, 54
Torres, Lourdes, 194
Toulmin, Stephen, 205
Trainor, Michael, 242
Treibel, Annett, 178
Trible, Phyllis, 263
Truth, Sojourner, 168
Tuppurainen, Riku P., 230
Turner, Mark, 209, 238
Tyson, Joseph B., 240

Übelacker, Walter, 87, 235

Ukpong, Justin, 226, 235

Uro, Risto, 209, 230, 240

Van Hecke, P., 239

Vander Stichele, Caroline, 85, 231

Vanhoye, Albert, 16, 108

Varghese, Santosh V., 230

Verheijen, L., 17

Vetterling-Braggin, Mary, 172

Von Gemünden, Petra, 242

Von Thaden, Robert, Jr., 238–39

Vos, Johan S., 33–34, 62

Vouga, François, 35

Wachterhauser Brice R., 186

Wadud, Amina, 167

Wagner, Peter, 178

Walker, William O., Jr., 52

Walzer, Arthur E., 230

Wanamaker, Charles A., 30

Warnick, Barbara, 230

Watson, Duane F., viii, 2, 4–5, 26–27, 29, 33, 39–40, 51, 60, 63, 65, 73, 79–81, 83–87, 90, 103, 212, 223, 230, 236–37, 239, 241

Weaver, Purcell, 82, 102

Webb, Robert L., 241

Weber, Max, 186–87

Weinrich, Harald, 178

Weissenrieder, Annette, 242

Welch, Kathleen E., 138, 140, 178

Wellbery, David E., 165, 182

Wendt, Friedericke, 242

Wenkel, David H., 230

Whitaker, Robyn, 63

White, Hayden, 175, 182

White, John L., 21, 210

White, L. Michael, 229

Whitehead, Deborah, 133–35

Whitelam, K., 252

Whitley, Richard, 178

Wichmann, Anne, 211

Wilder, Amos N., 24, 53, 64, 93, 127, 180, 226, 264

Wilke, C. G., 68

Wilkinson, John, 82, 102

Wilson, Timothy H., 217–18

Wimbush, Vincent L., 252, 260

Wire, Antoinette Clark, 112, 140, 264

Witherington, Ben, III, 220

Wittgenstein, Ludwig, 143, 146

Wittrock, Björn, 178

Woolf, Virginia, 167–68

Wooten, Cecil W., 56

Wuellner, Wilhelm, vii–viii, 2, 5–6, 16, 24, 41–42, 60, 66, 81, 93–118, 120–31, 207–8, 213, 227, 250

Zulick, Margaret D., 72, 73

Ziemann, Ferdinandus, 20

Zumstein, Jean, 47